This remarkable book offers a perspective on the Buddha's Noble Eightfold Path that is at once solidly rooted in the canonical texts of early Buddhism, yet astutely attuned to the needs of contemporary readers seeking to navigate our frantic, directionless culture.

Kramer's treatment of each path factor is immensely insightful, marked by an abundance of detail and enriched by personal insights . . . drawn from decades of study and practice. While he bases his explanations squarely on the Buddha's discourses, he does not merely regurgitate old formulas, but provides an expanded view of the Path that extends its relevance beyond the domain of individual, private practice. . . .

*A Whole-Life Path* should prove to be a major source for understanding and practicing the Buddha's Eightfold Path in its many different dimensions of relevance, including dimensions generally overlooked by traditional Buddhism.

**BHIKKHU BODHI**  Buddhist scholar and translator

The gift of Gregory Kramer's new book is its peerless translation of the Buddha's original teachings into wisdom for more skillfully engaging *every aspect* of our everyday, lived experiences—including the roughest edges of our ordinary lives. In the voice of a gentle and trusted guide, Kramer offers a map for doing what we do with clear intention, and, with increasing attention to how we do it, unfolding in these pages a whole-life path marked by the potential of liberation within the inner work of each instant. It just may be the perfect companion for deepening the practices we call mindfulness in these unprecedented times.

**RHONDA V. MAGEE**  Author of *The Inner Work of Racial Justice: Healing Ourselves and Transforming Our Communities Through Mindfulness*

*A Whole-Life Path* offers a vital and timely validation that "our entire life is our field of practice." . . . This insightful offering endorses a lay practitioner lifestyle with the same value as a monastic vocation, confirming that both lifestyles offer equal opportunity for realizing and embodying the considerable fruits of being guided by the timeless truths of the Dharma. This is a masterful contribution for all seeking an integrated approach, which, rather than prescriptive, invites direct personal inquiry, leading to an authentic, insightful, heart-full, and meaningful life.

**THANISSARA**   Buddhist teacher; author of *Time to Stand Up : A Buddhist Manifesto for Our Earth*

Reading this book gave me a deeper appreciation for the teachings of the Buddha. As I read, my heart welled up with enthusiasm for the opportunity to take a more thorough look at these eight areas of my life. It was wonderful how Gregory would connect these precious teachings to the challenges we are experiencing in this day and age—individual and social injustices, unconscious biases, and a need for greater compassion, including for the earth itself.

As a woman, mother, grandmother, and biracial person of color, the concerns I have for humanity were given respect. Even for those who have been "on the path" for what seems a long time, I found this book offers an opportunity to up-level one's practice in new ways.

**KAMALA MASTERS**   Cofounder, Maui Dharma Sanctuary (USA); guiding teacher, Insight Meditation Society (USA)

[A] compelling and insightful book. . . . *A Whole-Life Path* is a wholly creative, wholly noble, wholly serious effort to re-present the ancient wisdom of the Buddha for a new time, a new place, and a new generation.

Kramer brings a sophisticated understanding of our contemporary world. . . . [He] addresses the issues of individual and social actions and results again and again in a way that seeks a creative middle way between the self-seclusion of a hermit-practitioner and the self-responsibility of a compassionate, nondelusional, lay Buddhist practitioner.

May the wisdom-practice it offers transform the lives of one and all.

**MU SOENG**   Scholar emeritus, Barre Center for Buddhist Studies (USA)

Kramer masterfully translates the Buddha's core teachings on enlightened living for use in our day and age. This is a book I wish I had when starting out on the Buddhist path, one that presents the Dharma as imminently related to every moment of my life. To read this book is to encounter the truth that you already have what you need to awaken. It will not only enrich your practice of meditation. It may very well change your life.

**LAMA WILLA MILLER**  Founding teacher and spiritual director, Natural Dharma Fellowship (USA)

A clear and inspiring book for living a liberating life, written by a wonderfully creative, dedicated, and engaging Buddhist teacher.

Buddhism is for our whole life, and this book brings our whole life into Buddhism. Kramer has written a clear and inspiring guide to a wholehearted engagement with the path of liberation.

*A Whole-Life Path* is a compelling, practical, and inspiring guide for how lay Buddhists can fully engage in the Buddhist Path. I recommend it for everyone.     **GIL FRONSDAL**  Teacher, Insight Meditation Center and Insight Retreat Center (USA)

*A Whole-Life Path* is a thoughtful and thorough exploration of how Dhamma practice can infuse every aspect of our lives. Gregory's unique perspective, born from years of practice and study, combines an impressive breadth of application to our lives in the world with a profound understanding of practices leading to the highest peace. This work is worthy of careful study as we investigate the causes of suffering and the possibilities of freedom.

**JOSEPH GOLDSTEIN**  Author of *Mindfulness: A Practical Guide to Awakening*

[*A Whole-Life Path*] helps to bring the approach to practice as a full steeping of oneself in the refuges of Buddha, Dhamma, and Sangha, not excluding any of the traditional aspects of the teachings of the Buddha, but reconsidering [them] in ways that are appropriate for a modern society. This book is . . . a valuable contribution to the many seekers of the path in the present time. I liked it and feel it is a good book that will be useful for people.

Anumodana! **PASANNO BHIKKHU** Guiding elder and former abbot, Abhayagiri Buddhist Monastery (USA)

I love this book! We haven't really had a guide to integration that is so specific, practical, and complete before, even after forty-five years of teachers teaching. Whether beginning or after years of immersion, you can learn practical new ways [of] meditative awareness, combined with relational practice. . . .

Gregory's use of language is creative, precise, and moving; his understanding of Dharma often brings tears of recognition and appreciation to my eyes. Anyone who has Dharma sonar can feel that the writing is born of intense meditative practice experience combined with hard-won relational know-how that is integrated with his granular knowledge of early Buddhist psychology. He translates the classic teachings into innovative exercises and explanations that are both powerful and congruent with daily life.

**TRUDY GOODMAN, PHD** Founding teacher, InsightLA (USA)

Gregory Kramer has written a comprehensive guide that not only elucidates the Buddhist Eightfold Path but makes it come alive. *A Whole-Life Path* is both down-to-earth and practical. But even more, it is "practiceable," giving the reader an in-depth invitation to live the teachings in an embodied way, both on and off the cushion. A truly wonderful contribution. *Sadhu, sadhu, sadhu!* Well done!

**JAMES BARAZ** Cofounding teacher, Spirit Rock Meditation Center (USA); coauthor, *Awakening Joy: 10 Steps to Happiness*

Ehipassiko! Come and see!

Here is a healing elixir, distilled from over forty years of deep immersion in Dhamma practice, contemplative study and Dhamma teaching, a compelling invitation to drink deep for all who yearn for truth, happiness, peace—for self, for others, for our world.

Here is the medicine—essential teachings on every aspect of the Buddha's Noble Eightfold Path, eloquently and insightfully explored, offering innovative ways to deepen our enquiry, elucidating the way to fully integrate everyday life and spiritual path.

Here is the cure. This profound handbook for liberation, practical manual for daily use, detailed contemporary map of the timeless terrain, leaves no stone unturned. Every facet of life, alone and in relationship, is an opportunity for practice, is Path, leading onward toward boundless goodness, wisdom, love, and freedom.

Kramer's work is a light and a blessing in my life. I will be reading *A Whole-Life Path* again and again.

Ehipassiko!　　　　　**AJAHN BRAHMAVARA**　Buddhist nun

Wise, innovative, clear, and rich, Gregory Kramer's *A Whole-Life Path* brings the traditional Noble Eightfold Path to modern-day life, offering practical and essential methods for how to live our happiest, most wholesome lives right here in the spin of things. Drawing from a lifetime of practice and deep meditative insight, as well as experience in bringing these practices home, Kramer goes right to the heart of the matter. . . . Especially in our time of uncertainty and groundlessness, this book is a must-read for all who are looking for a clear path toward happiness, wellbeing, and sanity—no matter what.

**DEVON HASE**　Coauthor of *How Not to Be a Hot Mess: A Survival Guide for Modern Life*

If you want to understand the Buddhist Eightfold Path, illuminated in wise, clear, practical ways and a modern perspective, *A Whole-Life Path* will serve you well. Working with real problems, ranging from climate change to intimate relationship, Gregory Kramer shows how the core teachings can be a guide to wisdom and wellbeing in every part of life.　　**JACK KORNFIELD**　Author of *A Path With Heart: A Guide Through the Perils and Promises of Spiritual Life*

In *A Whole-Life Path*, Gregory Kramer offers laypeople a brilliant and practical guide for bringing Buddhist wisdom alive in our relationships, work, and through each moment of the day. Reading this book will help you realign with what matters most to your heart.

**TARA BRACH**  Author of *Radical Compassion : Learning to Love Yourself and Your World with the Practice of RAIN*

In this book, Gregory Kramer offers us the fruits of his forty years of deep inquiry into how we can live the Buddhist path of liberation in all aspects of our life. . . . [H]e unfolds, with clarity and passion . . . how each of the eight stages of the Noble Path is so much more than an individual practice, but relational and communal as well. I think that any committed student of liberation can benefit a lot from the many practical suggestions Gregory offers to expand our understanding of the all-inclusive nature of the path and to strengthen our joy in and trust of our potential to live it.

**CAROL WILSON**  Guiding teacher, Insight Meditation Society (USA)

Gregory Kramer makes the wisdom of the Buddhist path relevant for our times. He brings to the forefront the insights that arise in "the dynamic circumstances of interpersonal contact." His invitation to engage directly in the relational nature of practice provides a foundation for shifting the social systems in which we live to be more aligned with sīla, dāna, and the Eightfold Path. This book is timely and practical for the world we are confronted with in this day and age.

**BRIAN LESAGE**  Guiding teacher, Flagstaff Insight Meditation Community (USA)

Gregory Kramer guides you in transforming an ordinary journey of life into a journey of awakening. Based on decades of practice and teaching, and a deep confidence in the potential of the Noble Eightfold Path, he invites you to bring the whole of your life to the practice and to bring the practice to the whole of your life.

**BHIKKHUNI ANANDABODHI**  Cofounder, Aloka Vihara Forest Monastery (USA)

[A] wonderful resource for anyone who sincerely aspires to live a life that is dedicated to the path to awakening. . . . Kramer urges us to apply the teachings to all aspects of our modern life and examine not only our inner world, but also our relationships, our community, our society, and the planet in the light of the Dhamma.

His presentation of the teachings—insightful and filled with compassion—also includes many practice suggestions that make it an invaluable and trustworthy practice guide on the path. Personally, I was inspired by the holistic vision that this book offers and touched by the humanness and devotion to the Dhamma that come through.

**YUKA NAKAMURA**   Teacher, Meditation Center Beatenberg (Switzerland), Insight Meditation Center (USA), and Bodhi College (UK)

*A Whole-Life Path* is a welcome invitation to wake up in life, to life, for life. It makes accessible what Gregory has dedicated himself to revealing—that the Buddha's profound teachings are to be seen as precious practices. . . .

Gregory's warm and accessible voice runs through this book like a refreshing stream. He explains this human condition in human terms, and encourages us out beyond limitations in ways that call the heart with kindness. This is a must read for all who wish to bring the practice into wider, deeper, and broader areas of life.

**NATHAN GLYDE**   Dharma teacher, Gaia House (UK); cofounder, SanghaSeva (UK)

This book is an invaluable resource of inspiration and practical support for everyone aspiring to live and manifest the Dhamma in all aspects of their lives. It shows Gregory's unremitted dedication to the Buddhist path and relational awakening based on a whole life of practice and teaching. His words, "This whole life is the Path" echoes the invitation of the fully awakened Buddhist nun Rohini 2,600 years ago: "The Path isn't a line on a map, it's a great shining world; enter wherever you like."

**VENERABLE ANOPAMA**   Buddhist nun

This is a grand, beautiful, and exceptionally thorough vision and guide to living this precious human life. . . . The book brings immediacy, momentum, depth, and breadth to the practice of illuminating the living Dhamma of each moment. . . .

Kramer has unique brilliance in pointing toward the potential power of relationship in the Dhamma, of spiritual friendship, to enhance and enlarge our realization of each path factor and the interarising of all the factors working together. The power of relational practice and its contribution to social transformation lights up every page. He beautifully points to the individual, interpersonal, and social dimensions of the path working together.

I imagine that this book can be read, digested, and contemplated again and again, and at many stages and moments of our lives. It is a huge, comprehensive reference to be reread and referenced as a guide to practice, for beginners and those well instructed on the Path. This is an enormous contribution for accessing, channeling, and realizing the liberative power of the Path.

**JANET SURREY**  Insight Dialogue teacher; coauthor of *The Buddha's Wife: The Path of Awakening Together*

How about living a life not infatuated by cravings and fears, not pushing away the hard bits of reality, but turning everything into a path to deep wellbeing, care, and harmony, making every event an opportunity to add less harm and more heart in the world? *A Whole-Life Path* will be your excellent companion in that noble endeavor, a beautiful tool to help you further reflect on the path you have chosen to tread on. It will show you the richness, depth, breadth, meaning, implications, and applications of the Dhamma in your messy and precious life, assisting you in creating the world you want to share with others and leave behind.

It's a joy to read; we can feel how truly engaged Gregory Kramer is on his path to harmlessness, connection, and inner freedom, and how he wants us to make our whole life a path too.

**PASCAL AUCLAIR**  Core teacher, Insight Meditation Society (USA); cofounder, True North Insight Meditation Centre (Canada)

This book is the fruit of these years of inquiry, and it offers a unique and powerful perspective on how to infuse every aspect of life with the transformative wisdom of the Buddha.

Using the classical framework of the Noble Eightfold Path, Gregory Kramer . . . invites us to inquire deeply into every aspect of modern life, including technology and media, the arts, psychotherapy, social injustice, and climate change.

Within each chapter, carefully considered questions invite individuals and groups to explore how the path factors are operating in their own lives, and through that process of inquiry, to create a life oriented toward compassion and clarity, in service of the deepest freedom of heart and mind.

**JILL SHEPHERD** Insight meditation and Insight Dialogue teacher; guiding teacher, Auckland Insight Meditation (New Zealand)

With this clear and inviting roadmap, Gregory demystifies the Eightfold Path and offers a treasure trove of guidance for reflection and practice, both personal and interpersonal. If you want support and encouragement to make the Dharma truly "onward-leading" in your life, this book is for you. It's so full of good practice suggestions that I think lots of us will be drawing on it for a long time to come. **JAYA RUDGARD** Teacher, Insight Meditation Society (USA) and Gaia House (UK)

Gregory Kramer has taken traditional spiritual teachings and expanded them into areas that are often neglected. With deep grounding in the early Buddhist discourses, he manages to bridge the depths of practice with the stuff of our lives, forming an integrated vision of the Buddhist path. This book serves as a valuable blueprint for practicing the Buddha's Eightfold Path in all areas of life. **LEIGH BRASINGTON** Author of *Right Concentration : A Practical Guide to the Jhanas*

Somewhere along the way we . . . decided we could neatly parcel the Dhamma up and pack it away into a retreat or a method or a tradition. Those of us who look for inspiration and wisdom to the Buddha's teachings are by no means immune to such a response; we too easily imagine that we can solve the problem just by quoting a sutta. Which is where this book steps in.

Gregory Kramer is not one to settle for easy answers or to shy away from the complexities of the real world application of the theory. When reading his words, I found myself wanting to talk with him, to engage in his ideas. The spiritual path is strange, and even after all this time, largely unknowable. But if we take a good book like this one with us, the journey becomes a little less lonely.

**SUJATO** Cofounder, SuttaCentral

*A Whole-Life Path* is an invitation to practice the depth of the Dharma in a way that is refreshingly personal, as well as precise. Gregory Kramer . . . points directly to the truth of our relatedness, which is just the medicine needed for our beautiful and troubled world.

This treasured book points to a way of life that is holistic, just as awareness and the Path are holistic. What touches me most about this timely offering is that when I soak up the pages, it is experiential. I feel the mystery, power, and truth of what it means to be human—not just the idea of relationship, but an experience of the field through which we awaken.

*A Whole-Life Path* is a friend for the journey, pointing to the freedom our hearts seek, guiding us to touch this right here in the middle of it all. Read it slowly, read it with friends if you can, and savor each wise page.

**ERIN TREAT** Guiding teacher, Vallecitos Mountain Retreat Center (USA); teacher council member, Spirit Rock Meditation Center (USA)

Gregory Kramer has written a must-read, comprehensive book that gives the reader the historical framework for one of the most fundamental teachings in Buddhism, the Eightfold Path, as well as showing us the relevance of these ancient teachings in the incredibly tenuous social, racial, political, and global climate of this decade.

I deeply appreciate the flow, meditation, and reflective exercises, as well as Kramer's depth of lived and studied experience. I will gladly add this book to my repertoire of recommendations for both the beginner and experienced practitioner alike.

**JOANNA HARDY**  Dharma teacher

[A] unique and much needed approach to Dharma practice, . . . a profound and accessible set of illuminating teachings, and a wake-up call to the whole of life, this book . . . answers a need of modern-day practitioners. It weaves together the personal, relational, societal, and global aspects of the Path.

Gregory's message is as clearly expressed as it is radical in content . . . teaching us how we can embrace the complexity and diversity of our lives and include them on the Path in ways that deepen and enrich the Path itself. I feel it is urgent that we listen, for our own happiness and for the wellbeing of our planet and the beings that share it. So I wholeheartedly recommend this book to all. It is truly a Dharma sharing for, and of, our times.

**ZOHAR LAVIE**  Dharma teacher, Gaia House
(UK); cofounder, SanghaSeva (UK)

*A Whole-Life Path* is refreshing and bold. What is unique about this book is that it succeeds in addressing the widely shared experience that it is difficult to sustain the feeling of inner peace and wisdom gained in formal practice of meditation after a retreat. Instead, the principles and practices bring the Buddhist teachings alive in the moment for the reader in daily practice. By following the principles and investigation practices it offers, I noticed significant changes in my feelings, thoughts, and actions. I highly recommend this book to meditators who want to grow and explore proven practices for a wiser response to life.

**NOLITHA TSENGIWE**  Guiding teacher, Dharmagiri
(South Africa); psychologist, executive coach,
and consultant in leadership development

# a
# WHOLE-
# LIFE
# PATH

*a*

# WHOLE-
# LIFE
# PATH

A Lay Buddhist's
Guide to Crafting a
Dhamma-Infused Life

GREGORY KRAMER

Insight Dialogue
Community

Insight Dialogue Community
P.O. Box 99172
Seattle, WA 98139
InsightDialogue.org

Published 2020
First edition

Cover and interior design by Karen Polaski

Printed in the United States of America

Library of Congress Control Number: 2020916409

Print book ISBN 978-0-9666727-1-8

Ebook ISBN 978-0-9666727-2-5

This book is dedicated to the global
community committed to following the
thread of spiritual friendship to its fruition
in a whole-life path of kindness, social
responsibility, and liberating wisdom.

# CONTENTS

~

# AUTHOR'S NOTE

## Source of Citations

Except where specifically noted, all of the sutta references and quotations are drawn from Bhikkhu Bodhi's translations published by Wisdom Publications. These include:

> *The Middle Length Discourses of the Buddha: A Translation of the Majjhima Nikāya* (1995; with Bhikkhu Ñāṇamoli). Abbreviation in citations: MN.

> *The Connected Discourses of the Buddha: A Translation of the Samyutta Nikāya* (2000). Abbreviation in citations: SN.

> *The Numerical Discourses of the Buddha: A Translation of the Anguttara Nikāya* (2012). Abbreviation in citations: AN.

> *The Suttanipāta: An Ancient Collection of the Buddha's Discourses Together with Its Commentaries* (2017). Abbreviation in citations: Sn.

## Translations of Four Key Words

Within sutta quotations, I have replaced the translator's chosen English term for three key Pali words—*mettā, āsava, saṅkhāra*—with three new terms to more clearly convey the meanings I believe are intended by the early texts. Also, I have left the Pali term *samādhi* untranslated instead of using the common translation of "concentration." I offer these retranslations as a practitioner and teacher, not as a scholar. Nevertheless, I believe their etymology fully supports the choices.

**Mettā:** This term is most often translated as *lovingkindness,* a construction devised by the first British translators of the Pali Canon. I have decided to render *mettā* as "true friendship" or to retain the Pali term. The word *love* is too easily construed as something emotional or, worse, distant, elevated from everyday access, not easily experienced, or less natural. *Friendship,* on the other hand, is a natural outcome of undefended availability to another and implies the essential quality of goodwill. However, where *lovingkindness* may be formalizing or distant, *friendship* alone errs on side of too mundane. Spiritual friendship, or *kalyāṇa-mittatā,* is closer to the mark but too easily leaves out the universal, unlimited nature of *mettā.* So I have added *true* to *friendship* to convey this sense of thoroughness or depth of friendship, goodwill, and, yes, universal love. *Mettā* is drawn from the root *mid,* which can imply softness or fatness, as well as love or friendliness. Rendering *mettā* as "true friendship" keeps the term close to *mitta, mitra,* and the Vedic *maitri.*

**Āsava:** The first English translations of the Pali Canon rendered *āsava* as "taints," and this rendering has carried through all of Bhikkhu Bodhi's influential and excellent translations. However, "taints" fails to capture the way this trio of ignorance, sensuality, and becoming overwhelm the mind. It also lacks some important etymological connections. I have chosen to render *āsava* as "intoxicants," following on of the Pali Text Society's indications: "spirit, the intoxicating extract or secretion of a tree or flower."[1] A similar rendering is "floods," a translation preferred by some contemporary teachers. Other teachers use "effluents" and "outflows," and both accord with the root etymology. The construal of "intoxicants" as both inebriating and poisonous is intended, as it implies the temporary insanity of drunkenness. Fortuitously, this translation also opens up the introduction of the opposites of the *āsava* to be classified as agents of detoxification: wisdom for ignorance, relinquishment for sensuality, and effacement for becoming.

*Saṅkhāra:* Bhikkhu Bodhi and others translate *saṅkhāra* as "formations," meaning both mental formations (when employed in the context of the aggregates) and volitional formations (in the context of dependent origination). Bodhi has explained his choice of this rendering in his introduction to the *The Middle Length Discourses of the Buddha.*[2] I respect his choices and explanations, but find that rendering *saṅkhāra* as "constructions" remains closer to the etymological root of "making together" while linking the contemporary mind to the use of constructions as they are found in modern and post-modern philosophy and hence in common usage (e.g., "how we construct the world"). Other translations capture this understanding with words such as *fabrications* and *concoctions.*

*Samādhi:* The most common translation of *samādhi* is "concentration." In our contemporary understanding, concentration usually has a rigid quality; the mind's attention is forcefully held on an object. This understanding is very different from how samādhi is described in the early Buddhist texts, where it is characterized by a mind both serene and gathered. Further, samādhi emerges out of rapture and happiness and generates further happiness and refreshment.

There is really no single English term that adequately captures the combination of power and stillness conveyed by *samādhi.* So after much reflection, I decided to leave the word *samādhi* largely untranslated.

Yet retaining the word *samādhi* presents its own set of problems. The English-Pali combination of "right samādhi" is accurate but awkward. Also, the Pali language allows for expressions of *samādhi* as, for example, a noun (*concentration*), a gerund (*concentrating*), and an adjective (*concentrated*). I have mostly substituted workable English words, and in one sutta quotation I coined the term *samādhied* to capture the adjectival expression of *samādhi.*

## On Dhamma and Dharma

In my teaching and throughout this book, I use the word *Dhamma* to refer to the Buddha's teachings and to the natural law that these teachings describe. *Dhamma* is the Pali equivalent of the Sanskrit *Dharma*. Pali derives from the languages commonly used in Northern India in the Buddha's time. The Buddha taught in the popular tongue, so he could speak to even the simplest people. Sanskrit was a language of the elite, used in literature and in Hindu sacred texts. Eventually Buddhist texts also were composed and preserved in Sanskrit, and these two languages are present throughout Buddhist history. Pali was associated with the southern Buddhist lineages, mostly in Southeast Asia, while Sanskrit was the language of the northern lineages. Most Sanskrit Buddhist texts were translated into Chinese and Tibetan, and they have carried through to Chinese, Korean, Japanese, and Tibetan forms of Buddhism, though each of these cultures also generated a considerable textual tradition in their own languages.

All of my Buddhist training has been with Theravada monastics from Southeast Asia. *Dhamma* rather than *Dharma*, like *kamma/karma*, *nibbāna/nirvāṇa*, and *sutta/sutra*, was the language in which I received the teachings. Naturally, I use this language today. Also, the word *Dharma* is burdened with a wide variety of additional meanings due to Sanskrit also being the language of much Hindu scripture. These meanings are often not in alignment with the Buddha's apparent usages of the word *Dhamma*. Using *Dhamma* has the benefit of identifying the referred teachings with early Buddhist texts, which I turn to as root sources.

~

# CHAPTER 1

# THE NEED FOR A WHOLE-LIFE PATH

The Buddha's Noble Eightfold Path provides a wiser way through life than any offered by our conditioning. It's an intentional path through life's tangle. And intention is necessary. Any change for the good must face the momentum that made things as they are now. Old habits run deep within us; we complicate, palliate, protect, and meander. Norms are sustained in relationships. Patterns are perpetuated by family and social precedents. Organizational structures are built around ignorance, greed, and aversion. When we feel threatened or enticed, personal and social responses like aggression or lust often overpower reflection or compassion. Things big and small call for our attention, and mindfulness and self-awareness are not givens.

Although the Eightfold Path is an intentional path, designed specifically to counteract the ways in which our lives are compacted, we usually miss out on the full extent of the freedom the Path offers. Why? Because we apply the Buddha's teachings to our lives in only a semi-intentional way. If we truly aspire to ending our personal ignorance and craving, supporting relationships rooted in mettā and compassion, and contributing to human flourishing and to a just and humane society, then we need a fully immersive, always-on engagement with the Noble Eightfold Path. We need to engage the Buddha's Path as a *whole-life* path.

## THE HUMAN PREDICAMENT

You and I are so sensitive. Virtual clouds of nerves wrapped in skin, we are drawn to or repelled by every touch. The slightest changes of light trigger responses in the eyes; the slightest changes of air pressure alert the ears to the unexpected. Molecules from afar touch the nose; those nearby touch the tongue. Electrochemical changes in the brain register as thoughts that touch the mind. And when what contacts our senses is perceived as another person, neural and hormonal processes that evolved with the brain itself activate. All of these things are happening right now, as you read these words. Your sensitivities and mine are meeting right here.

This is how we meet the whole world. Placed in an environment in constant change, we organisms seek air, food, safety, and the comfort of others. Affection and loneliness, competition and fear, anger and isolation join the sharp and soft touches of the material world. But that world is out of our control. Hungers drive us, but we can't have what we want. The fragility of the body assures a constant flow of pleasure and pain, injury and illness, aging and loss. We feel belonging and isolation, protected and traumatized. This sensitive life culminates in our own death and the death of those we love.

The body-mind's sensitivity is the seedbed of longings and their occasional gratification. The entire organism tenses against the world's sensory and social onslaught, hungering in vain for stability and settling instead for temporary pleasant stimulation. We interweave with others to satisfy cravings and enhance protection; relationships and groups also become loci of action. Pings of pleasure cause a reflexive grasping as we struggle, individually and collectively, to hold on to what we like and avoid what we don't like. This tension forms into a core sense of self, an "I" or a "we" that would be protected and satisfied. The self's appetite keeps us off balance as it clings to one thing (or person or group) and then another. Gripped by its project of satisfaction and becoming, the body-mind is blind to the fact that its suffering is self-inflicted.

There are no moments, no events, no interactions, no relationships that do not affect the body-mind. Every thought and action, here and now, combines with all we have done and said to determine the direction and tenor of our individual lives and society as a whole. Learning, memory, and family and cultural conditioning collude to form how we perceive the world. There is no moment when we, as individuals and as a society, are not navigating the body-mind's responses to the world, because every moment conditions the next.

The question is, *how* are we navigating these responses? If we choose to let wisdom guide us, our responses are intentional, and our movement through this life is conscious. If we choose to ignore our power to learn, our responses are habitual, and our movement through life is unconscious. Depending upon which choice we make, there is suffering or there is peace; there is cruelty or harmlessness.

## THE PROMISE OF THE NOBLE EIGHTFOLD PATH

The Buddha recognized the suffering born of the body-mind's endless appetite, and despite the enormous challenges presented by his own untrained mind, he found his way clear to setting down the burden.

He described the human predicament in the Four Noble Truths. The first noble truth is the suffering (*dukkha*), at once blunt and subtle, of the driven life. His second noble truth recognized that suffering is born of the sensitive body-mind's endless appetite. The organism's longing for pleasure and stability is the urgent energy, the hunger (*taṇhā*), that drives suffering. His third noble truth, that cessation of this hunger will free us from the self-inflicted pain of dukkha, provides a wholly new vision of human and social possibility: we need not be prisoners of our own ignorance and craving; a profoundly better life is possible for ourselves and for all. The fourth noble truth names the Noble Eightfold Path as the wisdom that, when applied intentionally, leads to a diminishing and even cessation of the ignorance and hunger that has been so painful for ourselves, so limiting to our relationships, and so harmful for society. The wisdom inherent in the Buddha's path allows us to navigate the body-mind's responses with greater dignity, choice, kindness, and the joy and equanimity intrinsic to awareness.

The Noble Eightfold Path, described by the early Buddhist texts and carried forward in multiple Buddhist religions, draws from the exceptional experience of an exceptional teacher. These teachings were offered as practical guidance for navigating the tangles at the intersection of the human organism and its changing environment, and the perspective is offered by someone who successfully traversed the path from bio-psycho-social reactivity to freedom of response within this very body and mind.[3] The Buddha's eight path factors—right view (*sammā diṭṭhi*), right intention (*sammā saṅkappa*), right speech (*sammā vācā*), right action (*sammā kammanta*), right livelihood (*sammā ājīva*), right effort (*sammā vāyāma*), right mindfulness (*sammā sati*), and right *samādhi* (*sammā samādhi*)—provide guidance for developing the mind and acting in the world. The teachings have been tested for millennia. They offer a wiser, more effective navigation system than whatever we might cobble together from our family, cultural, and formal education.

## A WHOLE-LIFE PATH: AN IMMERSIVE PATH FOR BUDDHIST LAYPEOPLE

How much of the Path's full promise we experience depends on how we engage it. When we dabble in the teachings, we can experience a fraction of its liberative power, but not enough to fully escape from the body-mind's relentless habits or offer our highest gifts to a suffering planet. To bring about the profound shifts we aspire to, both within ourselves and in our world, we must bring the teachings into every corner, every facet, every moment of our lives.

Historically, an immersive life has been available mostly to monastics, whose vow essentially stipulates a whole-life engagement with Buddhist principles and practices. But the Buddha's eight path factors can be applied to the totality of our lives as laypeople if we break down each path factor to its essences, then recast it with the assumption that each must encompass life as we actually live it today—with other people, sex, money, social injustice, technology, jobs, complex financial systems, and so on. A whole-life path is one in which the eight path factors are understood and intentionally applied in such a way that, taken together, no moment and no aspect of our individual or collective lives is left out.

The purpose of this book is to help you skillfully craft a whole-life path for yourself. It will point you to the breadth and depth, and the particulars, of the Dhamma's liberating possibilities and how they can be applied to every aspect of life—personal, relational, and social. You might think of it as a layperson's guide to a life inspired by monastic immersion, but that also values the challenges and opportunities of living in the cultured wilds of humanity.

Chapter 2 provides six tenets of a whole-life path. These tenets convey a sense of possibility and basic principles for applying the Dhamma in a whole-life way. They will help you absorb a sense of an always-on path and of how the riches of the early Buddhist teachings can come alive in your life.

Chapter 3 continues with a short look at "the path to the path." The Buddha taught that the practices of giving, morality, and true friendliness (mettā) come first, before the Dhamma of the Four Noble Truths. These are all relational practices, and none of them are optional. We then look at some basic frameworks for assessing the whole-life path to see whether we're on track. What does "right" mean in right view or right speech? What is wholesome and skillful? What is Dhamma, and what is not Dhamma? These frameworks will provide reference points throughout the remainder of the book.

Chapters 4 through 11 are dedicated to the eight factors of the Noble Eightfold Path. Each chapter includes a summary of the traditional understanding of the path factor. Then it extends this understanding to include the perspective of our contemporary lives, forged as they are in the cauldron of technology, presumed individualism, scientific viewpoints, the internet, and large social, economic, and national systems of support or oppression. For many in the West, life within these systems has been infiltrated by relative physical comfort and countless false urgencies. For many, this is a life short on the graces of loving relationship and community that should be our birthright.

The practices embedded in each chapter offer you the opportunity to not just understand how this factor can be lived within your whole-life path, but to check it out for yourself and help make the teachings experientially alive. I invite you to approach each practice in the spirit of *ehipassiko*, or "Let me try this and see what is true in my life."

## CRAFTING *YOUR* WHOLE-LIFE PATH

The Buddha suggested that each of us craft a path that is most fitting for us. He explicitly noted that we can determine our path by giving attention to what works. The following teaching applies this notion to an individual discerning for themselves which of the four foundations of mindfulness is most suitable for them.

> Suppose, Bhikkhus, a wise, competent, skillful cook were to present a king or a royal minister with various kinds of curries: sour, bitter, pungent, sweet, sharp, mild, salty, bland.
>
> That wise, competent skillful cook picks up the sign of his own master's preference: "Today this curry pleased my master . . . or he spoke in praise of this bland one."
>
> That wise, competent skillful cook gains clothing, wages, and bonuses . . . because that wise . . . cook picks up the sign of his own master's preference.

So too, Bhikkhus, here some wise, competent, skillful bhikkhu dwells contemplating the body in the body . . . his mind becomes concentrated, his corruptions are abandoned, he picks up that sign. He dwells contemplating feelings in feelings . . . mind in mind . . . phenomena in phenomena . . . While he dwells contemplating phenomena in phenomena, his mind becomes concentrated, his corruptions are abandoned, he picks up that sign.

That wise, competent, skillful bhikkhu gains pleasant dwelling in this very life and he gains mindfulness and clear comprehension. For what reason? Because, Bhikkhus, that wise . . . bhikkhu picks up the sign of his own mind.[4]

This teaching is empowering: *you* discern what works and put it into effect. Each person's path arises from each person's life. We can craft a path on our own, and we can turn to others for guidance, inspiration, support, and energy. In each case, we reflect and adjust as we go. What is working? What is not?

In every moment of our lives, there are countless options for engagement. That's the key message of this book: the whole-life path is everywhere, and our perpetually creative, skillful move is to recognize where the path is manifesting *right now*. Just the math should be encouraging. There are eight path factors, and each can be cultivated (1) individually in formal practice; (2) interpersonally in formal practice; (3) individually in informal practice that is embedded in our lives; and (4) interpersonally in informal practice. Eight factors times four domains of application—that alone makes for thirty-two entry points. When you see that each factor has multiple elements, the options are further multiplied. Life is vast and, by definition, a whole-life path is as vast as life. We enter anywhere. In any moment we just need to see how to enter and then do it. The eightfold path schema is just a construct to help us do that. What is workable? Where can you find support of others? Where do you feel called?

Start anywhere you feel inspired. For example, you might reflect on your life's overarching direction (right intention). Maybe you feel drawn to the challenge presented by the explicit practices to steady the mind (right concentration). You may choose to begin with an area in which you already feel some development, some success. For example, maybe you are already well established in speaking truthfully, and you'd like to leverage that to new practices of right speech and right expression. Or just observe your mind in this present moment and ask, "How clearly am I seeing the world right now?" Right mindfulness and view come together; it can be that simple. As you develop your version of the whole-life path, pay attention to what uplifts you, to what sustains your interest and brings a living sense of the path into everyday experience.

By definition, a whole-life path unfolds in the messiness and delicacy of life. Going against the stream of unkindness and injustice, against the tides of thirst for excitement and possessiveness, is a path of peace, but that does not mean it is all rosy. It is in this mix that the promise of liberation unfolds. Nibbāna is described as the pinnacle of equanimity, of contentment that is not dependent upon outer conditions. In a burning world, we need this. Acutely. In the midst of this equanimity, our whole-life path supports our aspiration to function from love. From here, any action can be wise action. And any wise action enables boundless change for the good.

⌒

# CHAPTER 2

# SIX TENETS FOR A WHOLE-LIFE PATH

From the beginning, my experience of the Buddhist path was inspired but fragmented. Formal meditation could be peaceful; daily life was agitated and crammed. Meditation retreats felt great, but I felt a split upon re-entry into everyday life. Elevated states gave way to the messy and confused "me" I was trying to improve. The beauty of giving and the power of morality, like the blissful states described in the discourses, felt a long way from my rumpled life. I longed for continuity, and I unconsciously believed it would manifest as a continuity of the mindfulness I experienced in sitting meditation practice. Yet how could that kind of continuity ever develop given my jumpy mind and busy life?

At the same time, it was painful to encounter my own unkindness. Experiences of pride, longing, and hardness made my mind hurt. The Dhamma sometimes felt far away. I had to consciously bring in questions that would reorient me: "Is this greed? What does it feel like?" "How am I fabricating a self right now around this conceit?" "Am I doing this nice thing out of kindness, hunger for praise, or both?" I didn't know it at the time, but I was beginning to regard the Dhamma as a reference point outside the system of my conditioned views and personal obsessions.

As I continued to study the Dhamma, the teachings continued to excite and inspire me. I assumed the teachings really applied to my life, but it wasn't clear how I could implement them. Any time I interpreted a teaching as merely a description of my mind and life, the spark of conceptual interest I'd felt quickly faded. When I received that same teaching as a practice, something to be tested in my messy life, it invariably sprang to life as an embodied, richly textured experience. Likewise, when I interpreted the teachings as guidance for a unitary, heroic individual, they felt narrow and far away. As I learned to implement the Dhamma interpersonally and socially, the teachings became freely available and compelling to me.

The tougher life got, the more I felt called to put the teachings to work. I learned to tap into Dhamma wisdom in the midst of illness, death, emotional defeat, and the falls from grace that came with my privileged callousness. The Dhamma rose up in the hospitals I was staying in; in my kitchen, bedroom, and studio; and in all my relationships. When I excluded teachings that were difficult to absorb or held certain teachings at a distance, my path would reflect my narrow personality more than the Buddha's uplifting wisdom. When I included my present experience of shame, regret, or loss in the light of the Dhamma, something always opened up beyond my fabricated worldview—always.

Gradually, a workable whole-life path emerged. As I reflected on how this emergence was happening, I saw a set of tenets naturally underpinning the path:

1  Ground in the Dhamma.
2  Engage all the teachings as practices.
3  Exclude no moment, experience, or teaching.
4  Find each teaching in the here and now.
5  Let all the teachings in fully.
6  Engage the teachings individually, in relationship, and socially.

These tenets have served me well as I've sought to apply the Dhamma to the whole of my life: to meditation, intimate relationships, work, and to my participation in the human family. They've applied, more intuitively than explicitly, in times of struggle, when my mind has been unruly and my actions unskillful. Rooted in my experience of the subtle beauty, piercing intensity, and aliveness of the teachings, these six tenets have provided the grounding I need to skillfully meet life's complexities.

These tenets aren't abstract principles or directions to be followed. They're principles of engagement—a means of engaging the Dhamma regardless of what we're experiencing or doing. Taken together, they support a working relationship between formal Buddhist teachings and our lived lives. From this relationship, our whole-life path—what we do and how we live—naturally emerges.

What is the basis and purpose of each tenet?

## TENET 1: GROUND IN THE DHAMMA

The earliest Buddhist teachings provide a sound, consistent basis for a modern whole-life path. They help us act skillfully with others, find peace even as the world rages, and turn towards joy and freedom even when our minds and lives feel tangled. All of the later Buddhist schools or contemporary approaches derived from Buddhism rest on this same foundation but don't focus explicitly on the early teachings. Zen teachings, for example, may emphasize lineage founders over early texts; mindfulness teachers have often chosen to assume a secular veneer and not refer to the root sources of their methods. However, by grounding in primary sources, we ensure that we don't lose our footing.

Because the Dhamma serves as the foundation of a whole-life path, unpacking each path factor from its original meaning can help ensure that it does not become oversimplified. Distortions can happen without realizing it when teachings move from person to person and culture to culture across two thousand years of pre-industrial, pre-technological history. Religious norms can drain immediacy and relevance from this vital life guidance. To reclaim the aliveness, each path factor can be reduced to its essential meaning, and this meaning must be unpacked in such a way that we can apply it to life as we actually live it today—within our global economy, scientific mindset, and modern sense of individuality, relationship, and society.

## TENET 2: ENGAGE ALL THE TEACHINGS AS PRACTICES

All of the earliest Buddhist teachings are practice guidance, not philosophy.[5]

On a whole-life path, we invite these teachings into our lives not as dogma, but as doorways to experience. Life is insistent, and the teachings are not abstract observations. The Buddha said many times that the grand philosophical questions were not important and not what he was teaching.[6] Suffering and the end of suffering are the kernels of the Buddhadhamma, and realizing these truths its central task.[7] This tenet calls us to take the teachings not as literature to interpret, but as practical guidance for our lives. To take the early discourses as descriptions of reality rather than guidance for how to live and learn is to immediately place them at a distance. ("This is a description of life" is very different from "These are practices for me to engage if I'm serious about untangling.")

Taking the path factor of right intention as an example, we examine present-moment experience with the framework "What aspect of experience right now is this thing called intention? What is my aim right now? What is the purpose of this action I'm engaged in? Which of my motivations are wholesome, and which are not?" As you'll see when we look in depth at right intention (see chapter 5), this investigation includes how we can cultivate specific, wholesome intentions as we mindfully engage in the world. There is mindfulness of present-moment experience, and this mindfulness is guided by wisdom that comes from outside the self-referential system. We are engaged in a practice that shifts our basic view of what it is to be living in the world. A changed view yields changed experience and behaviors. This is the Dhamma at work.

## TENET 3: EXCLUDE NO MOMENT, EXPERIENCE, OR TEACHING

The totality of the teachings applies to the totality of our lives as they actually are in this time and place.

Our entire life is our field of practice. It is in these everyday moments and encounters that we can so easily fall into mindless, even harmful, thoughts and behaviors. Because every moment and every experience matters, there is no moment, experience, thought, or action that is not part of the movement toward goodness or harm, happiness or suffering. Or put another way, what thought or action could possibly not be part of this movement, even if only to continue the psychological and neural-hormonal status quo? When we ask, "When is my path active?" the answer is, "Always."

The idea of an always-on, full-spectrum path might sound overwhelming. But really this tenet is just asking us to bring in this wisdom element as best we can. Yes, each of us will still be forgetful and tender. Our hearts will resist change to our cherished and painful patterns. But the Dhamma is here, in its patience and breadth, in each and every moment. When we recognize this availability, it can help us to more clearly discern wholesome perspectives and actions.

The Buddha helps us to understand that a pick-and-choose approach to the Dhamma will not yield the whole-life benefit. The guidance offered in the early Buddhist texts is vast, and much of what was offered has been either ignored by Western practitioners or watered down. Taking in the whole of the teachings strengthens their whole-life potency.

At the same time, by naming eight things to remember, the Buddha makes a life oriented toward unbinding simpler, more workable. That simple breakdown can cover all of this profoundly complex modern life because the essentials of the human body-mind remain mostly identical today to the what they were in the Buddha's time: eyes and ears; sights and sounds; unspeakably complex minds; language, urges, and fears more elemental than culture; and lives fully interwoven with each other. We have the same astonishing capacity for learning; we also have an astonishing capacity to fool ourselves. This capacity continuum has been a key feature of social, political, and cultural thought across time. That's why the Path outlined by the Buddha in roughly 400 BCE is equally relevant here and now.[8]

## TENET 4: FIND EACH TEACHING IN THE HERE AND NOW

Nearly all of the Buddha's teachings, even those on subtle aspects of body-mind and refined meditative states, can be directly experienced by just about everyone.

The Dhamma can illuminate present-moment experience as we're actually experiencing it. It is not distant or abstract. The Buddha taught as a fleshy human being to other fleshy human beings. His felt experience of sensations and emotions, of thoughts, and of worldly contacts was much the same as ours. The fact of the Buddha's humanity, no less than the fact of his release, are what make his life so inspiring. We think, "If he can do it, so can I." The Noble Eightfold Path is an explicitly human one. And it is explicitly available as *our* path, in these living moments.

Some teachings *are* subtle. For example, some teachings refer to exceptional depths of concentration, and fully understanding them is only possible when you have directly experienced the mind states or insights associated with those depths. But at least some aspect or trace of a teaching is usually available to us and can provide a valuable sense of direction. Most of us can experience most of the teachings here and now in their fullness. If we look, we often recognize the impermanence of feelings and thoughts, or the stress that often accompanies even pleasant experiences. Do not assume that any teaching is beyond you, too subtle for you, too tough for you to enact.

With this tenet, we come to see our lives as rich in possibilities for wholesome qualities and genuine insight. We contemplate the discourses as pointing to presently living capacities, asking not only, "What does this teaching mean?" but also, "How am I experiencing this teaching now?"

## TENET 5: LET ALL THE TEACHINGS IN FULLY

Arms-length Buddhism doesn't serve us. For an unbridled experience of the teachings, we need to let them in all the way. Some of the teachings will challenge us, and that's okay. If we know this going in, we can accept the challenges and widen our sense of what's possible.

Inevitably, growth in understanding involves times of pain. Meeting our suffering directly is a prerequisite for release. Allowing joy to manifest is an essential source of energy and refreshment. We will feel vulnerable as our lives and relationships change. Still, we are called to let the teachings into our hearts. A path held apart from the most intimate, the most normal, and the most humble moments of our lives, a path relegated exclusively to weekly groups, retreat centers, or nightstand reading, will lack the strength of impact needed to see through a lifetime of entanglement and encourage deep realization. The Noble Eightfold Path is meant to fully infuse the human experience.

As we approach the Buddha's discourses, our modern, individualistic minds may be baffled by descriptions of elevated mind states. Our scientism may be challenged by teachings on rebirth, and our religions or cultures that posit a self or soul may not immediately mesh with teachings on momentariness and relinquishment. But we must be willing to be confronted by those challenges and willing to not know the answers. We cannot separate out mindfulness or those Dhamma teachings that immediately speak to us from the vast map of the Buddhadhamma and still enjoy the full benefits afforded by a whole-life, always-on perspective. We must allow the core teachings to touch us, to impinge on our comforts, and disturb and inspire us to new ways of being. Vulnerable and humble, we invite the teachings to saturate us.

## TENET 6: ENGAGE THE TEACHINGS INDIVIDUALLY, IN RELATIONSHIP, AND SOCIALLY

We are intrinsically social animals, and much of our suffering arises in relationship to other people. It is in relationship that a sense of self is generated. It is in relationship that the language from which we construct a world emerges. And in relationship, our reactive patterns surface in ways they don't when we are alone. Because we are relational and social, a whole-life application of the Buddhist Path must be too. Humans meeting humans is a complex thing. Our relatedness is always operating, even when we're alone, and it's not optional. We need the Dhamma wisdom at the tender points of contact. To truly live all of the teachings as practices, we are called to enact them not only individually, but also in our casual and most intimate relationships and in our engagement with society.

Just as suffering arises during interactions with others, so can the cooling of the heart. With others we can see what we cannot see alone. We may notice hunger and clinging, letting go and compassion, as they arise in our interactions, though these direct experiences remain invisible to us in our individual practice. Patterns of grasping and ignorance that have formed relationally are often most readily recognized and released in relational practice. Opportunities to cultivate compassion, to practice giving and kindness, and to promote peace and reconciliation are most fully available when we are in active relationship with others. Also, challenging teachings, like the subtleties of dependent origination or the suffering that comes with clinging to identity, will benefit from interpersonal and group practices, in which mindfulness, energy, and investigation are amplified as they are supported by more than one mind.

Because a whole-life path can be challenging—scary, confusing, tiring, and just difficult to sustain—the Buddha made clear the importance of spiritual friends and community.[9] Intuitively, we might sense how much we need the warmth, modeling, energy, and guidance of our friends on the path. The kindness and care of others can give us courage to let in the teachings all the way. The support of others who are also committed to mindfulness and the Dhamma we value helps us remember those values.

Finally, this tenet reminds us that our practices and our understanding of a whole-life path reflect a breadth of purpose: individually cooling the hungry and intoxicated mind, relationally living with greater kindness and compassion, and establishing a just and humane society. A whole-life path puts us in touch with both the humanity of the Noble Eightfold Path and with our own humanity.

PRACTICE
## THE TENET SWEEP

The tenet sweep is an exploration of your foundational relationship with the Buddha's teachings. In sum, you are asking, "What is my relationship to the Dhamma right now?"

The following are some reflection questions for each tenet. As you become more familiar with the content and attitude of the tenets, each bare tenet will reveal its full wisdom tone. Soon you might well be able to mentally touch each tenet using hardly any words.

The tenet sweep is best undertaken with an attitude of kindness and patience. We are all ripening gradually in wisdom.

1 **Ground in the Dhamma.** What teachings can I apply to my life right now? Do I sense the working of natural laws: in my mind, in relationship, in the world? Can I name them, learn from them? As I study or reflect or engage in conversation,

am I considering what I am saying from the standpoint of the early Buddhist teachings? Other wisdom traditions?

2  **Engage all the teachings as practices.** Am I merely thinking about the Dhamma or actually practicing it right now? When I read or hear about a teaching, do I put it to work in my life? Which approaches to enacting the Dhamma fit best right now: close observation of my thoughts and behaviors, deep reflection on the teaching, concrete physical actions and social engagements?

3  **Exclude no moment, experience, or teaching.** Is this one moment, now, guided by wisdom? Am I excluding anything from the path: my intimate personal life, my professional life, my art or craft, my playtime? Am I avoiding teachings that are difficult to understand? Am I excluding teachings that challenge my belief systems?

4  **Find each teaching in the here and now.** Whatever teaching or practice I'm reflecting on or enacting, do I feel it is available for me to experience right now? How is this teaching manifesting in my thought processes, in my bodily experience? What is deeply true in this teaching, and how does it feel to touch that truth here and now?

5  **Let all the teachings in fully.** Which teachings are closest to my heart right now? Which am I guarded against or pushing away? Can I feel the possibility of an unintoxicated mind, balanced and clear? Can I sense in my body the energy, challenge, and possibility of the teachings? Am I moved and inspired by this Dhamma-rich path?

6  **Engage the teachings individually, in relationship, and socially.** Can I feel that the person I am with right now is a spiritual friend? How am I treating them—with

compassion, with generosity? How might we engage the path together, right now, in our conversation or in what we're doing? Could our togetherness be a doorway out of a heroic and lonely stance? How am I supported and morally challenged by society and humankind as a whole? How can I, alone and collaboratively, bring the wisdom of the Dhamma into these relational and social encounters?

~

Taken together, the six tenets are a way of charging our lives with wisdom. If the Buddha's teachings feel distant, or if the noises of a vacant culture dull our minds, we can invoke these six tenets one at a time or sweep through all of them. We can explicitly call them up to invigorate our relationship to the whole-life path, or we can sense their presence in the background of a busy but well-intended life. Guided like this, we can craft for ourselves a path that is relevant to a person living in contemporary society, replete with its tacit belief systems and technologies, its economic and social contingencies, and all the brokenness and beauty of its complexity. I know firsthand that such a path can make sense, draw you in emotionally, and fully allow the mystery of consciousness and our conjoined human hearts.

We must engage a whole-life path at an ever-shifting balance point between urgency and patience.[10] Death is near; unskillfulness and delusion are easy to get lost in, and we practice as if our hair were on fire.[11] This is our urgency. At the same time, we can feel a serene confidence in the path and our engagement with it. The Buddhist path has traditionally been conceived of as unfolding over multiple lifetimes.[12] Our modern cosmologies do not provide this same kind and patient framework, so we need to remember the deep roots of our hunger and confusion, let them build ardor in our hearts, and with patience, appreciate that a workable path is available to us here and now.

# CHAPTER 3

# PREPARING FOR
# AND ASSESSING
# A WHOLE-LIFE PATH

ow do you begin? How can you enter into a whole-life perspective on and practice of the Noble Eightfold Path? This chapter explores several starting points, each touching different parts of our lives.

The first, the path scan, is a pause, taken at any time, for a quick inner view of how each path factor is operating in your life in that moment. As a light touch on any or all of the path factors, it can be a good way to get started. This same path scan matures as your understanding of the path factors deepens.

You could also begin where the Buddha suggested: with the relational practices of giving, morality, and true friendliness. These relational practices are not only essential; they lead immediately to peace and harmony within and around you. Renunciation is another practice the Buddha named as preliminary to the Noble Eightfold Path. Ironically, renunciation also can be one of the most challenging and refined aspects of the Path, from beginning to end.

You might also begin by reflecting on what is Path and not Path using the Buddha's two key points of discernment, "right" and "wholesome," and his eight criteria of Dhamma. Beginning your whole-life path with these reflections is valuable, as these teachings are woven into each and every path factor.

As you get started, you may well ask, "What is the point of the Path? Why should I even be interested?" This question is directly and repeatedly addressed in the discourses. We are, the Buddha offers, in the thrall of intoxicants (āsava). Driven, deluded, causing harm to ourselves and others, we contribute to the pains and tangles of our society. Reflecting on this intoxication, and the possibility of detox, is another good place to begin.

Taken together, this chapter offers abundant possibilities for starting on your whole-life path. You may even choose to explore these starting points for a while before you dive into individual path factors.

## THE PATH SCAN

The path scan is an ever-present compass and rudder of a whole-life path. Done as you embark on your whole-life path, it can help you orient to the whole of the path, or decide which of the eight path factors you might want to explore first. As your whole-life path evolves, it helps you assess how the path is going and make on-the-spot changes to orient your actions towards skill and care.

In certain cases, you may choose to focus your scan on one particular path factor or survey just two or three rather than all eight. When you find wisdom already at work, the scan can boost your confidence. When you feel the need, the scan can point you towards specific guidance from the Buddha's teachings: what Path guidance can I bring into this moment? Creativity is also at work: how will I enact this guidance given what is happening, the people I'm with, and how I feel?

The directions that follow will help get you started with the path scan, but over time you'll find a way of engaging this fundamental practice that suits your mind and life—and matches your unique whole-life path.

# THE PATH SCAN

The path scan is a quick practice you can do any time. In essence, you pause from habitual thoughts to ask, "What path factors are operating right now?" You check your mind, your circumstances, and your actions, scanning through the eight path factors. As you do so, I recommend holding an attitude of curiosity and kindness rather than judgment. Inquire, "How is the path alive, now?"

What follows is a collection of guiding questions for each path factor. At first glance, asking all these questions could seem like a lot of mental activity, but they actually point to aspects of the Path that you can bring in close and feel in the energetic body or sense in the mind's activities. Over time, you will naturally remember the scope of each factor, and simply calling each to mind will be enough. You will feel, nonverbally, what each comprises and the opportunities it presents.

**Right View** (Sammā Diṭṭhi): How is my perspective affecting how I see things right now? Can I see how cause and effect are operating? Do I discern dissatisfaction or the hunger that drives it? Can I feel or imagine that release is possible right now? How is my relatedness manifesting: With care? In loneliness? In wise conversations? Where is there wisdom in what I am speaking, thinking, or reading?

**Right Intention** (Sammā Saṅkappa): What is the purpose of the action I'm doing, the words I'm saying, or the relationship I'm in? Can I sense the overarching direction of my life right now? Is it aimed towards shedding or accumulating? Towards kindness or securing the self? What vows, commitments, or goals are orienting me now? How am I engaging the power of shared intention with my current companions?

**Right Speech** (Sammā Vācā): Is what I am about to say (or withhold saying) true? Beneficial? Timely? Am I speaking (or not speaking) out of kindness? For whose harm or benefit am I writing this email, blog post, or creative expression? Am I engaging in gossip or divisive speech? Do my words carry compassion or expressions of joy? Am I listening well?

**Right Action** (Sammā Kammanta): Am I acting with care for others, creating safety and not harm? How might this action impact my own mind? How might it impact other people and my relationships with them? What might the social and environmental impact of this action be? Am I acting wisely with sexuality and intoxicants? Does what I am doing proactively contribute to the wellbeing and safety of others?

**Right Livelihood** (Sammā Ājīva): In this moment, how am I using the requisites of food, shelter, clothing, and medicine? How about transportation and communications? How am I affecting my ecological footprint in this moment? Do my current professional activities reflect my values? What is the moral provenance of this money I'm earning? What is the impact of how I'm spending money? Is the practice of giving present in what I am doing (saying, thinking) now?

**Right Effort** (Sammā Vāyāma): Am I bringing energy to the whole-life path? Where do I see laziness, and if it is present, can I rise up through it and apply myself to what is good? If things are difficult now, am I persevering? What is my effort in this moment to abandon the unwholesome, like greed or aversion? To cultivate the wholesome, like generosity or mettā? Is this an appropriate moment for an intentional practice of friendliness, generosity, patience, or tranquility?

**Right Mindfulness** (Sammā Sati): *Why* am I practicing awareness right now? *What* am I aware of: The body? Feelings?

Mind states? How Dhamma frameworks reveal and focus experience? Am I aware of awareness? *How* am I aware: Internally or externally? Noting the rising and vanishing of phenomena? *Where* am I practicing awareness: Here? In this body? Is there distance between mind and object? *When* am I practicing awareness? Can I sense the immediacy of now?

**Right Samādhi** (Sammā Samādhi): Is the mind tranquil? Is it gathered? To what extent does the mind rest easily where I place it, or to what extent does it jump around? How is this present action or this relationship contributing to stillness or agitation? Are faith, happiness, or contentment present now, and does the mind settle in them? Can I experience a pleasant abiding in how things are right now?

## A PATH TO THE PATH: GIVING, MORALITY, AND TRUE FRIENDLINESS

The Buddha did not teach the Noble Eightfold Path to people new to his dispensation; he knew there was work to do to prepare the heart for deep, wholesome change. So he named three beginning points for a life of awakening. The Path begins, he taught, with giving, morality, and true friendliness—all of which are relational acts.[13] A whole-life path is inherently relational, and you cannot skip over these foundational practices if you are going to be on one.

### Giving

The Buddha's first teaching was always on the importance of giving. It is an act that requires sensing other people's needs, which requires stepping out of self-centeredness. Giving, or *dāna*, also requires letting go, relinquishing ownership and control over something, however modest or large. Giving conditions the mind to relatedness, yields social harmony, softens the self, and conduces to release of clinging. It is concrete, practicable, and visible here and now.

Giving is to be practiced wherever and with whomever possible. From a practical standpoint, giving is also the basis on which the Buddha's teachings have been authentically shared. Monastics, living without recourse to money, are in continual relationship with laypeople who support them. Some contemporary lay meditation teachers continue this pattern, providing a field in which others can practice giving. Protected from the powerful distortions that nearly always follow mercantile inclinations, a river of freely offered teachings has been flowing for more than 2,500 years. Each of us receives these gifts. If support continues to flow, so will the teachings. If we forego the opportunity to practice giving and to support the Dhamma, the flow stops with us. We have received but not offered freely, and something fundamental breaks. In this way, giving is participatory intelligence. It is crucial to the tradition, just as it is crucial to freeing our hearts of self-concern and opening us to the joy of care for others.

PRACTICE

## THE FELT EXPERIENCE OF GIVING

Like all actions, a concrete act of giving is preceded by the action of the mind. So to develop giving, it helps to begin with recognizing the felt experience of the impetus to give.

Think about a recent act of giving that you did—perhaps offering a holiday or birthday gift, serving a meal at a food pantry, donating to a charity, offering support to a teacher, or simply giving a meal to your dog or cat. Sit quietly as you reflect on this act. Can you recall the first spark of intention—how it felt, the bodily sensations and images? Can you review the actual act of navigating the charity website, typing in an amount, and clicking "donate"? Can you sense how the body felt or the emotional experience of actually setting down the pet's bowl of food?

In giving, the mind opens towards the recipient, outside of self-concern. There is friendliness and care—enough to generate the cascade of thoughts that lead to action. When the path of giving is intimate, not arm's length, how does this feel?

As a next step, observe the mind during the act of giving. This step can be especially effective when you're practicing giving in a new way. If you don't usually give money to poor people on the street, try doing so; if you already do this, see how it feels to deeply see the recipient and increase the amount you give, at the same time wishing for his or her wellbeing. Or devote a week to giving money to every person on the street who asks for it. Don't deny any judgment or aversion that may arise, but give particular attention to feelings of care and joy. Then notice the *action:* reaching into your wallet for the money and opening the hand in giving. How does that feel?

It can be helpful to have a partner in this practice. Check in with them; talk about how it feels, how it's going. Is giving having the effect that Buddha proposed of beautifying the mind?[14]

## Morality

Following giving, the Buddha taught ethical conduct. Moral action takes birth in care for others, which takes us out of the shell of self-concern. The practice of morality, *sīla,* can be understood as internally cultivating the mind and externally giving safety. It is another form of giving: giving safety to others by preventing their harm. When you don't lie, others can relax into your trustworthiness. When you ensure your sexual activity is appropriate, others experience respect and safety in your presence. When you refrain from intoxicants, those around you are protected from your out-of-bounds actions. Wise comportment yields social harmony. More than this, moral behavior requires mindfulness, wise action, and putting others' wellbeing above your own urges. Control of mind and body are the basis for deep training in morality.

In our time, entering the Noble Eightfold Path rests on the foundation of the mental and moral development that comes with Western civilization and millennia of Judeo-Christian values. We may or may not be well practiced in giving, but the decency of nonharming, nonstealing, sexual appropriateness, and care with intoxicants are widely understood in our society, if imperfectly realized. Ethical conduct is not only a personal practice; it is also engaged at the level of whole societies by way of their legal systems and social norms. Development of wholesome qualities is impacted by these social systems, and the social systems are impacted, indeed formed, by aggregated individual behaviors and thoughts. By cultivating morality, no less than generosity and mindfulness, we are often swimming against the stream. It is worth it; it is essential.

PRACTICE
## INVESTIGATING MORALITY

To begin or refine your practice of sīla, consider the sīla by which you already live. Take a specific aspect, like not stealing, not taking what is not given. Rather than look for transgressions, look for where you manifest this virtue. What is it like to walk through a store where you could easily snag some wanted item, but you don't? Can you go beneath any assumptions of "of course I don't steal" to trace back the feeling of maintaining a stable relationship with this store, this society? Can you locate a root respect for not stealing as a norm that fosters trust and ease, internally and externally?

Extend this investigation to a more difficult arena. How might your social privileges or your investments, including any union or pension funds you benefit from, be based on institutional stealing—that is, on structural inequities in the dominant socio-economic system? Consider a mutual fund that invests in companies that extract resources in an exploitive way or that profits by hiring workers at below living wages. This kind of structural theft may be unseen when there is ignorance, but by seeing it and acting to change your behaviors or investments, your own mind is shifted towards the wholesome at the same time that you are mitigating harm to others and thinking about their wellbeing.

From mind states to obvious local actions to systemic assumptions and conduct, investigating and practicing moral behavior is a demanding, always-on task. If you have a practice partner, turn to them for support; talk about the challenges and joys. The more mindful and particular the conversation, the more effect it will have on freeing the heart.

## True Friendliness

The third preliminary to the Buddha's teachings on the Path is cultivating boundless relational availability, most notably true friendliness (mettā). *Mettā*, often translated as "lovingkindness," refers to this natural goodwill and core relatedness that arise from a spacious mind. Pali literature calls mettā and the other divine abidings that emerge from it—compassion, appreciative joy, and engaged equanimity—"illimitables," a reference to the unbounded relational breadth of mind that is developed.

When the Buddha speaks of beginning the Path by reflecting on the heavens, we may have difficulty understanding what this means if we don't believe in metaphysical realms.[15] But one thing is clear: this is a call to widen our sense of the world beyond the small, skin-encapsulated self. This reflection on "heavens" prepares the mind for the Eightfold Path by making it wide and soft, connected and caring. Formal practices of true friendliness and compassion are only part of the picture. A life saturated with goodwill, care, and human tenderness is good here and now; it opens the way for the continued process of releasing hunger and clinging and the process of caring social engagement.

## EXPANDING THE HEART IN DIVINE RELATEDNESS

Begin with a simple practice of getting in touch with the felt experience of friendliness. Imagine a friend you frankly like or deeply love. As you think of this person, give attention to whatever kindness, care, and warmth you feel towards them. Where do you feel it in the body? What mind states are present in moments when the friendliness surges forward? Is it pleasant or unpleasant? Expanded or contracted? Calm or agitated? Be as precise and particular as you can. Notice the virtual presence of this person in your body-mind.

You can also engage in this step with a friend who is physically present. With or without looking at them, again give priority to investigating the experience of warmth, care, and goodwill that you feel toward them. If it is comfortable for both of you, speak aloud what you are noticing.

A next step in this practice is to extend the range of warmth and care from your friend to encompass a wider field. This warm caring is nothing other than the care native to awareness that is not cloaked by selfishness. This is the connection between awareness and love. It is the awareness of this inherently relational being that is being extended. As you imagine the mind expanding outward, this kind awareness touches all in your area, beyond where you sit, to an envisioned wider field, and outward, boundlessly, beyond the ends of the universe.

Extending from a specific person and location to boundlessness may seem like a big jump at first, so take your time. You can expand slowly or all at once; you can be precise or vague. Practice however it works for you.

And let this expansion be unstable; it's natural for the mind to contract into thought, expand again, and so on. As the mind relaxes, as concentration naturally manifests, the boundless quality of true friendliness will become more accessible and stable. The heart becomes open, the mind malleable.

## RENUNCIATION

Each of the preliminary relational steps—giving, morality, and true friendliness—conditions the mind towards release. There is the release of belongings by acts of giving, the release of self-centered behavior by morality, and the release of an egocentric attitude by cultivating mettā. By naming renunciation as a specific next step, the Buddha was pointing us towards noninfatuation with our comforts and fears. If we live an infatuated life, we will never see things clearly, never dedicate ourselves to a path of freedom for ourselves or others. If we blindly follow sensory and social desires, the pressures and noises will keep the body-mind agitated, and all of our thoughts and actions will be aimed at satisfying the urges and avoiding the pains. And the results of relentlessly pushing to fulfill sensory desires will lead to social harm and the destruction of the natural environment.

While the Noble Eightfold Path itself points to liberation from this pressure, an initial turn of the heart is necessary to even begin this Path. Renunciation is that initial turn.

It is easy to see renunciation as its more ultimate form of monastic vows or otherwise as a foreswearing of pleasures we cherish. However, it can begin with contemplating where you have already set aside sensual and social stimulants simply because they no longer fit your evolving life.

PRACTICE

### TRACKING THE NATURAL TURN TOWARDS RENUNCIATION

I recommend undertaking this reflection throughout your days, perhaps for a week or two. Then get together with a small group of friends who have done the same and reflect on what you've learned.

You know better than anyone what your reflections should focus on. You might ask yourself, "What food, drink, or entertainment indulgences no longer attract me?" Be sure to also ask, "How has this decreased attraction changed the tenor of my life? How do I feel this in the body, and how is this reflected in my overall mood?"

Another question might be, "What social excitements have naturally faded, and how has their diminishment shifted my priorities?"

While reflecting, you may encounter sensory and social excitements that feel so essential that you are fixated on them and have no intention of releasing them. Without judgment, notice these, too, including how they register in the body and what mind states these fixations arouse. Then re-aim the mind towards where you see natural renunciation taking place.

Finally, you could explore whether there are any sensory or social passions or habits that you would care to intentionally release, where you might experiment with diminishing or doing without so you can experience how that feels.

## DISCERNING, ASSESSING, AND LIVING A WHOLE-LIFE PATH

When we are following an intentional path, it stands to reason that some ways of thinking and acting will serve our intentions and some will not. How do we know the difference? I offer some touch points by which you can assess how your whole-life path is unfolding.

The first is a rather blunt word used by the Buddha: *right*. Is this the right path, the right action, the right way of thinking? The next reference point is, is it *wholesome*? Then we will look at eight criteria the Buddha offered that can be used to evaluate whether our path is well aimed. In this book, these eight points will be applied to all the path factors—sometimes explicitly, sometimes implicitly. And finally, an entire whole-life path is reckoned according to the human goodness that the Buddha linked to a gradual erosion of self-obsession. Does this path wear away the hard edges of self that form the foundation of our suffering and of all interpersonal and social conflict?

These points are not abstract. On a life path where nothing is left out, they guide thought and action, alone and with others, on the path towards unbinding. These points will be woven throughout this book, reminding us of our overall direction and purpose.

## Right (Sammā)

Because our path is intended to head in a specific direction—away from the unnecessary pain born of ignorance and driven by endless thirst—each aspect of our path must foster this direction. If it does, it is right, or sammā. *Right* is a condensed way of referring to a group of qualities. Most often translated as "right" or "wise," *sammā* also suggests "skillful" or "harmonious." Right means that it fits the task at hand: it is right for ending suffering; it is skillful for ending suffering. Other nuances of *sammā* include "completion," "togetherness," and "coherence"; the word can also suggest the sense of "perfect" or "ideal," "the summit" (same Sanskrit root as *sammā*) of practice. One might speak about *right* livelihood or *complete* mindfulness or *wise* understanding; in all cases the aim is eradicating ignorance and craving, and the pointer in the Buddha's teachings is this word *sammā*.

## Wholesome (Kusala)

Just how sammā, or rightness, is determined brings us to a consideration of another key Pali term, *kusala,* usually translated as "wholesome." Kusala is primarily a moral evaluation. On the surface, the basis for the evaluation is simple: does this action lead to harm for others, for myself, or for both? If so, it is *akusala,* unwholesome. If not, it is kusala. If it is kusala, wholesome, it is right. This is a key benchmark for any thought, word, or action, and even just reflecting on wholesomeness—its presence, as well as its absence—is a powerfully beneficial practice.

## Eight Criteria for Dhamma

In these two simple principles of sammā and kusala—rightness and wholesomeness—we have the foundations for a workable way of evaluating our path in general and each action we might take. Will this thought or action lead to what is beneficial, good, harmonious, liberating? But this basic assessment just leads us to the next question: what are skillful parameters of a good or liberating path? How do we recognize the Dhamma? The Buddha answered this question after his stepmother, Mahāpajāpatī Gotamī, asked him to teach the Dhamma in brief:

> As for the qualities of which you may know, "These qualities lead:
>
> to dispassion, not to passion;
> to being unfettered, not to being fettered;
> to shedding, not to accumulating;
> to modesty, not to self-aggrandizement;
> to contentment, not to discontent;
> to seclusion, not to entanglement;
> to aroused persistence, not to laziness;
> to being unburdensome, not to being burdensome":
>
> You may categorically hold, "This is the Dhamma, this is the Vinaya, this is the Teacher's instruction." [16]

All of these eight assessments are powerful even at face value. In a culture built on sensual desire and consumption, an inquiry about shedding or accumulating carries an immediate punch. Our personal sense of importance can be kept in check by the assessment of modesty and self-aggrandizement. Our spiritual path, and the individual actions we take or do not take—to meditate, study, offer service—will benefit from the question about aroused persistence and laziness. At the same time, we can ask whether our friendships incline the heart towards contentment or discontent, towards being burdensome or unburdensome.

And just as these criteria can be used to evaluate given actions, they can be applied to our understanding of the eight factors on the Noble Eightfold Path. What view will lead to passion or dispassion, to the nonattachment of mental seclusion or to entanglement? Such a view will be "right" and "wholesome." What quality of effort or mindfulness, what attitude towards meditation, will lead to contentment, persistence, and the fading of self-aggrandizement? What livelihood will support shedding and not accumulating? Making these assessments still calls for experience, honesty, and intelligence, but at least we have a clear set of criteria as a starting point.

The Buddha's assessment criteria provide guidance for everyday values and, at the same time, tap deeply into the vast teachings of the Dhamma. When we ask what is meant by "fettered and unfettered," for example, we can accept this phrase as a general reference to bondage. So we might ask, "Does this home I live in tie me down with costs and upkeep, or does it free me to live with enough comfort and stability that I can remain healthy and focused on things that matter to me?" There will usually be no simple answers to such questions, but asking them with sincerity will help us clarify our whole-life path. If we go deeper into the discourses, we might recognize the word *fetter* as a technical reference to the Buddha's teaching on the five higher and five lower fetters. If we accept the challenge offered by this doctrinal use of the word, we are launched into considering our home choice in terms of sensual desire and conceit, identity view, and giving power to external authorities.[17] This is quite another layer of assessment!

Going back to the early teachings, we get a clear message that the Path is properly set in the direction of being a good person—in Yiddish, a *mensch*. In these eight criteria, and throughout the discourses, human goodness and meditative development were spoken of in one breath. Overcoming maliciousness, envy, gossip, laziness, anger and revenge, fraud and arrogance was placed alongside "knowledge and vision of release," the code language in the canon for full liberation. They are linked by a gradual erosion of the self-sense at the heart of our suffering and of all interpersonal conflict and social oppression.[18]

## A WHOLE-LIFE PATH OF RELEASE

We find a whole-life path at this intersection of social human good-ness and liberation. We can refer to this intersection as "goodness and freedom," but only if we have enough context to condense it with such simple words. Chan Buddhists recognized that goodness is what arises when freedom functions. The two are not separate. After all, as intrinsically relational beings, both goodness and free-dom apply simultaneously to the inner life of this mind, to each specific relationship as a manifestation of the human system beyond the skin's shell, to our groups and our society, and to all beings with whom we share this very moment. "Goodness and freedom" is a way of naming the direction of a whole-life path.

Goodness and freedom share of one taste: release. Understanding this null vision of the path—release—is essential. With a whole-life path, our primary orientation is not fixing or getting this self "right." Positive words like *freedom* are inspiring; we need them. But our intention is freedom *from* something, and that something is suffering and its causes of ignorance and craving—individually, interpersonally, and socially. This freedom is the ending of fash-ioning and grasping at what we've fashioned. What remains is the natural manifesting of freedom.

## THE INTOXICANTS AND ROOT AIMS OF A WHOLE-LIFE PATH

A whole-life path is one of discovering that the boundless mind is already here and allowing it to manifest. This understanding is only effective when it is coupled with the knowledge that the pro-cess of untangling and unbinding will sometimes lead us into the places of the tightest knots. Our accumulated biases and traumas, conjoined with the body-mind's urges for constructing and satisfy-ing a self, will challenge us. The path of wisdom will at times be difficult. Intention that is informed by wise understanding is neces-sary; good friendships, perseverance, and patience are also essential. This is why the Buddha offered teachings on release that included nonclinging, non–ill will, nongreed, and cessation of becoming, as well as the positive cultivation of mettā, giving, and other wholesome qualities.

Dhamma medicine in a whole-life path includes both positive engagement and the erosion of negative qualities. We understand that the mind is fundamentally luminous but obscured by the frantic tangles of its own making.[19] Our clever minds are capable of turning teachings of relinquishment and compassion into instruments of self-judgment. Questions like, "What is wrong with me?" and "Am I compassionate enough?" just bind the self tighter to a life of suffering.

The shorthand in the discourses for what overwhelms the mind and hides our deepest potential for peace is the intoxicants, the āsava. They are also referred to as *taints* or *floods*. The so-called defilements of greed, aversion, and delusion invade the mind moment by moment, but the āsava are the tripod of suffering that sustain our entanglement. The intoxicant of sensuality drives this body-mind to distraction and harm. The intoxicant of becoming flows out from the self that seeks its own pleasures; the never-ending project of self-protection and aggrandizement floods the body-mind. And the third intoxicant, ignorance, is not knowing that this whole process is happening, and so it just keeps going on: passion, fetters, accumulation, aggrandizement, discontent, entanglement, laziness, and being burdensome are the inevitable result.

The āsava offer another powerful way to assess our path by pointing to three root aims that directly oppose these intoxicants, leading to their release:

• Relinquishment is the untangling from sensual obsession.
• Effacement is the unbinding of self-becoming.
• Awakening is the evaporation of ignorance.

Together, these three aspects of development form a detox program. Freedom from the intoxicants, more than any other teaching, is synonymous with nibbāna, the utter cooling of stress. We will have "done what had to be done, laid down the burden." This is the promise of the Path.

Nibbāna is not nothingness: it is a life without tangling, without fashioning. Mettā is the natural response to others, and when others are suffering, compassion manifests as the natural response. In this heartfully awake response, natural action is wise action, and happiness that is not dependent upon outer conditions is the norm. Freedom is release, and release allows what is already here. "He turns his mind away from those states and directs it towards the deathless element thus: 'This is the peaceful, this is the sublime, that is, the stilling of all formations, the relinquishing of all attachments, the destruction of craving, dispassion, cessation, Nibbāna.'"[20] This freedom *functions*. The personal, interpersonal, and social results are nested within each other: personal unbinding, unfettered relational intimacy, and a just and humane society.

~

# CHAPTER 4

# RIGHT VIEW

## *Sammā Ditṭṭhi*

s you read these words, you are engaging in a practice of right view: you are contemplating a path to understand suffering and its ending. You would not even be reading these words without some degree of belief that enhanced understanding is possible and there are things you can do to bring it about.

Because all thoughts and actions—and all suffering and joy—emerge from our view, or perspective, it is no wonder that right view is the first factor of the Noble Eightfold Path. If you have some inkling, intellectually or intuitively, that this mind, this life, can be better, then you are already beginning to engage with this path factor.

Right view is understanding the world in such a way that we can recognize what increases suffering, now and in the future, and what reduces suffering or ends it. The practice of right view includes those mental activities that bring about this understanding. This path factor assumes that both the mind and its perspective are malleable. With the practice of right view, we put the power of the mind to work to free itself.

## HOW OUR VIEW FORMS AND
## HOW IT AFFECTS OUR LIVES

Every moment the mind is working to understand the world. Since infancy, when a million neuronal connections were being made every second, the senses are touched by the world, and the body-mind is asking, "What is this? Am I secure? Where is food? Where are pleasure and safety?" Perceptions of light and color, loudness and location, temperature and texture are being woven into the sense of having a body, of there being a world, and of that world behaving a certain way: Things fall down, not up. Certain things hurt, and others feel good. Certain people are threats, and others are a refuge.

A sense of self forms as a locus of reaction to these perceptions, and there evolves a thought world that parallels the physical world. This thought world says to the body-mind, "I am my hands, my voice, my thinking mind" and "Pleasant sensations are satisfying, comforting." Strategy, and what is sometimes called personality, evolves as we behave in certain ways based on how we see things. Regardless of whether or not we see things with a high level of fidelity, we believe that we are experiencing the world as it truly is. This view (diṭṭhi) is exactly the source of limitation—and release—addressed by the Buddha's teachings.

Our minds take in multiple views based on personal and cultural forces and then use them to impose order on the impermanent and subtle world of experience. Our views not only condition what we think but also serve as the lens through which we experience the world. In fact, the lens created by our views is the plan by which the mind constructs its experience of the world. When we perceive the world a certain way, we are inclined to value or devalue certain things or experiences. We believe the world is safe or unsafe. We like or dislike certain people, organizations, and rules. We think that friends should act a certain way. We think that people different from us are dangerous. We value or ignore natural and human resources. We think that land and objects can be owned and protected and that owning and protecting them will provide security. The list goes on to include the biggest frameworks of all:

What brings happiness? What is my highest purpose? What is the next compassionate response? Understood in this way, our conditioned view is total in its effect and as vast as our lives. It shapes the tenor of our entire lives and conditions all of our actions.

How we view things is largely invisible to us, so bringing about a fundamental change in our conditioned view is not a trivial matter. It is made even more difficult by the fact that our conditioned view has been forming since infancy and continues forming in each and every moment.

Fortunately, like all constructed things, our view is changeable. To bring about the changes we seek and for those changes to endure, we have to apply wisdom, and we have to apply it ubiquitously. How we do so is the practice of right view.

## THE DHAMMA UNDERSTANDING
## OF RIGHT VIEW

The views that the Buddha regarded as "right" or "wrong" were those with consequences leading towards or away from liberation. Only insofar as a view leads towards untangling is it sammā, or "right." The views he labeled micchā, or "wrong," were views leading away from liberation, into entanglement. The Buddha was simply not interested in the correctness or incorrectness of opinions or speculations about such things as how the world was formed; he often refused to engage in conversation about such matters. So we understand that right view is not about holding opinions that are correct, or accurate, or in harmony with the opinions of those around us.

### Wrong View

The wrong views mentioned in the suttas generally involve believing something harmful to be beneficial, assigning some permanence to the world or to the self, or denying causality. A mind polluted by wastefulness, cruelty, and killing is locked in selfish and limited views. A mind locked in hidden biases and greed-driven consumption ties up this self-sense and propels it towards harm.

Identification maintains ignorance. Stress upsets the body-mind. Wrong view is the natural flowering of identification, stress, attachment, and aversion.

Notice that such wrong view could be a reasoned position or an inarticulate orientation towards the world—or anything in between. You may or may not know you hold a particular view; that is how ignorance is sustained. Wrong view tends, in turn, to maintain the conditions of intoxication and to prevent the mind from settling into the tranquility, concentration, and equanimity necessary for seeing the interrelated, impermanent, and empty nature of the process we call body-mind. When people have wrong view, they tend to get all the path factors wrong: wrong intention, wrong speech, wrong action, and so on.

The *Bījasutta* compares the effect of wrong view to a plant growing from the seed of a bitter species: inevitably, the rainwater and soil only contribute to its bitterness. But when there is right view, the other right path factors arise as well. And, like plants of sugarcane, rice, or grapes growing from seeds, the deeds undertaken in line with that view "all lead to what is agreeable, pleasing, charming, profitable, and easeful."[21]

## Right View in Relation to the Other Path Factors

Right view logically comes first on the list of path factors because its activity is necessary for the discernment of the others, for distinguishing their right (or sammā) forms from false paths and counterfeits. Right view is also necessary for the sense of direction and purpose that underlies the development of and confidence in every other factor. Recognizing the "right" version of each path factor—the version that works with the other factors and leads toward untangling—is our right view. Because the mind is nearly always thinking, right or wrong perspectives are always in play. Right view is at work as each path factor ripens because intrinsic to that ripening are the processes of inquiry, reflection, study, conversation, moral choices, and deep meditation.

The discourses point particularly to the collective power of right view, right effort, and right mindfulness. The Buddha's wisest disciple, Sariputta, taught, "These three qualities—right view, right effort, and right mindfulness—run and circle around [each path factor]."[22] This is a pragmatic teaching. For example, the path factor of sati, or right mindfulness, may help us notice anger as it is arising, making it possible to recognize the fear behind that anger and the danger of letting it run unchecked. On the other hand, mindfulness could be used to hold in mind the emotional motivation to target another person with a gun; in most contexts, this is wrong mindfulness, or mindfulness that leads to suffering. The effort of abandoning the wrong factor and entering upon the right factor is right effort; remembering to do so is right mindfulness. Right view is what guides this entire process.

Right view is the most essential, most continuous practice the Buddha taught. Through the action of discernment, right view makes the Path itself possible. Rightly speaking, *vipassanā* and Insight Dialogue are practices of right view, and right view—together with ethics—is the substance and point of the entire Noble Eightfold Path. Right view as an understanding of the world is both the starting point and the destination of that Path.

We are practicing right view, the understanding of the Dhamma and its efficacy to our lives, when we recollect the importance of mindfulness, when we decide to do an ethical act, and when we breathe deeply and remember how much we treasure peacefulness. And we are practicing right view when we first learn and then put to work the Dhamma teachings on the workings of the mind—teachings like the sneaky urges of craving, the blindness of delusion, the power of love, and the ever-present operation of dependent origination. Right view, like right effort and right mindfulness, permeates the entire whole-life path.

## PRACTICES OF RIGHT VIEW

Right view, as an overarching practice, is the discernment of which views lead us away from suffering and towards compassion and peace, and which views lead to a here-and-now hell, for oneself and others. Any practices that cultivate this discernment constitute the path factor of right view.

## Sorting the Unwholesome from the Wholesome

In the *Dvedhāvitakkasutta*, the Buddha describes an experiment of sorting thoughts into those that give rise to suffering and those that lead to its cessation.[23] Sorting in this way is a practice of right view.

The disciple Sariputta also addressed this practice in his discourse on right view: "When, friends, a noble disciple understands the unwholesome and the root of the unwholesome, the wholesome and the root of the wholesome, in that way he is one of right view, whose view is made straight."[24]

As he went on to explain, "the wholesome" and "the unwholesome" refer to actions—physical, verbal, and also mental. "The root of the unwholesome" refers to the underlying thoughts and attitudes of greed, hatred, and delusion that set us up for unwholesome actions. "The root of the wholesome" refers to thoughts and attitudes of renunciation and generosity, kindness, and compassion, which set us up for wholesome actions. Right view is both the sense of things that can tell which is which and the practice of developing that discernment. We know, for example, that releasing a fixation on accumulating praise will bring peace, while grasping at praise will yield tension for ourselves and possibly harm for others.

However, this sorting operation is only the beginning of this right view practice. As our sorting activity continues, we come face to face with the basic perspectives that bring about self-oriented greed and hatred. What self is to be served by this greed, avenged by this hatred? Will actions stemming from this greed and hatred bring satisfaction? How does this mind concoct its view of the world such that the world appears this way right now? We come to see the mind at its previously dark work, and gradually the map of the world, and of what works in this world, is redrawn.

Sariputta said that a noble disciple who understands how the mind naturally constructs its self-oriented view will abandon the root of the unwholesome. Their mind, having fully integrated an un-self-centered perspective, understands that nothing is fit to be clung to. From this perspective, they abandon those same unwholesome thoughts the Buddha found problematic and abandoned: "In that way too a noble disciple is one of right view."[25]

So right view is the understanding that allows us to discern the unwholesome from the wholesome and to follow through to actually do the sorting. This multifaceted wisdom practice of right view is the foundation of ethical action (right speech, action, and livelihood).

PRACTICE
## SORTING THOUGHTS

Set aside a quiet time to reflect on your thoughts and priorities. If it helps you get some traction, consider thoughts associated with different facets of your life: thoughts related to work; thoughts about family, friends, and other close relationships; and thoughts related to your direction in life, like your spiritual practices or your sense of meaning and value. Questions you could ask yourself include what thoughts, feelings, images, and emotions arise when I think of this situation, or this person? What arises when I'm actually with this person or in this situation? What arises spontaneously as I sit here now?

It is possible a stream of thoughts will arise—not just one or two clear candidates for examination. For example, you might think, "He's got a lot of money and friends" or "She's kind and I feel good with her." Or, "The work I do at this job helps a lot of people." If you find yourself with multiple thoughts, you will need to choose which one to explore first. When a thought, recollected or presently arising, seems particularly strong, presents itself repeatedly, or somehow strikes you as salient in some way—different from the others, associated with stronger bodily reaction, or perhaps exceptionally clear and concise—take this one as the "truth" to be explored right now.

Inquire: Does this thought have roots in pulling and holding (greed), aversion, or delusion? Or in nongreed and generosity, nonhatred and kindness, or nondelusion and clear understanding? Might this thought lead to action that would harm myself, another, or both? How can this thought provide an avenue, right now, by which I can better understand the connections between greed or hatred and suffering? Does this lead to my seeing anything useful about the cessation of suffering?

This kind of inquiry will involve going back and forth between the word-based thought that's easy to catch and the more subtle "thoughts" of the belly, solar plexus, heart, or throat.

As you inquire, keep checking in to the full spectrum of mind-body activity. Take your time, pause often for the refreshment of silence, and be sure to close your session with a short reflection on mettā and gratitude for the opportunity to explore things that matter.

You can engage this practice on your own or with a trusted friend. It is probably best to set aside time for the practice, particularly when you first do it, but the same reflections can be embedded in your everyday life.

## Seeing for Yourself

The Buddha pointed his teachings in certain directions and always said, "See for yourself." For example, to test the axiom that generosity helps free the mind of grasping, we can give freely and see whether or not that generosity inclines the mind toward happiness and harmony for ourselves and others. We can even spend a day intentionally occupied with pettiness and gossip and see how we feel at the end of the day. We can engage in the practice of sorting the wholesome from the unwholesome over a period of time and notice whether or not it really does show us underlying thoughts and attitudes of greed, hatred, and delusion that set us up for unwholesome actions. Because these investigations are grounded in natural consequences, they can be tested personally by anyone who wishes. Like sorting, seeing for ourselves is a practice of right view.

## Thinking, Talking, and Insight

The Buddha clearly said that reflection, study, and conversation, as well as meditation, are important to the practice of right view. In the *Anuggahītasutta*, the Buddha said, "Bhikkhus, when right view is assisted by five factors, it has liberation of mind as its fruit . . . What five? Here, right view is assisted by virtuous behavior, learning, discussion, calm, and insight."[26]

Virtue (sīla) lifts the heart out of self-obsession and calms the mind, and its realization and refinement demands cultivating a high level of discernment. Learning, or study (*suta*), is a direct practice of maturing our understanding. Reflective study is a direct path to intellectual comprehension that establishes the conditions for the intuitive apprehension we call right view.

Discussion (*sākacchā*) is the vector for the movement of information among people, a form of mind-to-mind contact. Seminal learning opportunities take place in discussion, including learning from elders and teachers and learning from people of different backgrounds. The Buddha's dialogic inquiries with his disciples make up a substantial portion of the discourses. Discussions are more than active replacements for book knowledge. When we interact with people, explore questions, pursue lines of inquiry, and arouse energy and interest in meaningful topics, discussions can become forums for radical inquiry.

Calm (*samatha*) is the foundation of insight. Because it does not get caught up in and attached to everything that moves, the tranquil mind is able to perceive the essential characteristics of life. It is also able to remain stable in the face of the incomprehensible, which is often how new perspectives first appear to us. Insight (*vipassanā*) is, by definition, an experience of intuitive wisdom, and insight practices are practices of right view.

Taken together, these five activities offer a balanced and trustworthy approach to the practice of right view. Many meditators, however, have an uneasy relationship with thinking and talking. The path of spiritual development is often idealized as solely involved with silent practices and wordless, even unworldly, experiences. Understanding that all five of these individual practices are important will help heal any conceived split between the power of thought, the power of speech, and the power of meditative awareness. Intentional thinking, interpersonal discourse, and meditation all work together on the path to unbinding. They all can be practices of right view.

### Skillful Thinking

Clearly, the mind's capacity to think, reflect, inquire, memorize, construe, and test ideas was valued by the Buddha. Indeed, we see throughout the suttas the Buddha referring to his own thought processes at crucial junctures. They were part of his wisdom path.

Often, though, we view thoughts as intruders, as injecting noise into realms we would rather remain silent. We understand well the way thoughts proliferate, sustaining delusion and aggravating greed and hatred. As a result, we construe meditation solely as a practice of releasing, abandoning, or otherwise getting rid of thoughts. A wrestling match is set up that pits a controlling factor of meditative skill against a geyser of agitated tendencies that blow forth thoughts as no more than the random detritus of an agitated life. In this painful conflict, the wholesome power of thought is thrown out.

While it is true that unskillful thinking is both intrusive to meditation and unsupportive of mental development, intentional thinking is enormously powerful and was clearly part of the Buddha's teaching on liberative practices. Skillful thinking helps to guide and settle the mind, to intimately and skillfully examine present-moment experience and, at its best, to see the empty nature of the mind's constructive processes. Because the brain developed to constantly assess its natural and social environment, thinking is happening all the time; turning this forward energy in a wholesome direction is an essential part of the always-on path.

However, skillful thinking does not refer to mindless absorption of dogma; a wisdom component is essential. Fortunately, the practice of skillful thinking contains its own fail-safe: reasoning and reflection, alone and with others, contain the power to point beyond its own limitations. Included within the practice of right view is the understanding that clinging to any view, Buddhist or otherwise, will bring suffering.[27] Rigidity, self-centeredness around being right, and arguments about beliefs all carry the seeds of ignorance and suffering. Recognizing that all views are empty, contingent, is intrinsic to the cultivation of skillful thinking as a practice of right view.

## THE PRACTICE OF DIRECTED THINKING
A PERSONAL STORY

The meditation retreat began innocently enough. The teacher, Venerable Punnaji Mahathero, instructed us to sit quietly so the body could calm down a bit. But then we were given instructions to think about the Buddha—about his life, his mind. Who was this human being? What qualities allowed him to discover such a profound and beautiful path? Think on these questions, we were told, while sitting on our cushions, while walking, while eating, and during all the in-between times of our retreat. I found this instruction odd, but I trusted the teacher.

For at least two days I thought of nothing else. When my mind wandered, I would bring it back to this line of thinking and not, as I had previously done, to the breath or some other aspect of the body or feelings. I tapped into what I knew of the Buddha's life, pondered the stories of his awakening, and thought about the Dhamma while holding the question of what mind could bring such a stunning system of understanding into being.

At first, my practice was dutiful but not remarkable. Then I began to notice that my own mind was changing. I felt as though the luminosity, clear intelligence, and unfettered flow of experience that I imputed to the Buddha were manifesting in my own mind. I experienced a lightness of body, a steadiness of mental and physical energy, and joy. These very qualities were then available as I followed subsequent instructions to think only about the Dhamma and finally about the Sangha, particularly the monastic Sangha. This was a classical reflection on "the triple gem." Towards the end of the retreat, I realized the mind had become highly concentrated, easily keeping in mind the selected contemplations. The body had become calm, and I felt a steady equipoise.

I did not know it at the time, but I had just devoted an entire retreat to *directed thinking* as a practice of right view. This process would be advanced at a following retreat, when I would contemplate, among other things, the impermanence of all my possessions, relationships, and perceptions—that they were out of my control and so unsatisfactory, and that none of it could be claimed as I or mine. From the beginning, these practices of right view led spontaneously to the arising of the path factors of right intention, effort, and mindfulness. I would later come to see that these practices were drawn directly from the Buddha's discourses and that the factors of awakening, such as mindfulness, investigation, energy, and tranquility, made directed thinking an excellent complement to traditional vipassanā practice.

### Skillful Talking

Talking is how people think together. It is easy to overlook the fact that the suttas, our teachers' Dhamma talks, even the activity in our own minds by which we guide our meditation practices, all involve guidance via language. Wise conversations can help the teachings of the discourses become practices, and by way of practice, they gradually transform into wisdom.

As we will see when we consider the path factor of right speech, conversation is a form of mind-to-mind contact and a powerful factor in forming our life perspective. Like thinking generally, conversation can easily run to the unwholesome, so we are wise to approach it with care. But we'll see that harnessing our linguistic and intellectual capacities in service of wise understanding is an indispensable part of the whole-life path.

## The Important Role of Calm and Insight

There is a reason tranquility and insight practices hold a special place on the Buddhist path. There are some things that cannot be understood by the thinking mind. Language is too coarse to apprehend what lies beneath and before language. To get to the heart of impermanence, to experience the constructed and empty nature of self, the noise of habitual thinking must be calmed.

With a sufficient degree of stillness and the natural inquiry of mindfulness, the movement of thought is seen to be automatic and conditioned. Life's precious stories are seen as vaporous—impactful in our everyday experience, but inherently insubstantial. Such apprehensions can radically alter our understanding of the human experience. We may release self-images and habits of behavior that have been binding us and creating suffering for both others and ourselves.

Calming the mind for the purposes of insight places such tranquility practice within right view. However, it is also possible to practice calming the body-mind with the primary intention of bringing worldly ease. Understanding that both approaches to meditation are possible, and what the various results will be, is a discernment made possible by the practice of right view. One can study or learn from others about these differences, but the crucial next step is to directly experience different forms of tranquility practice and see for yourself. This is where the shift in understanding will occur. Right view includes knowing about and developing different practices of right view.

## CORE BUDDHIST TEACHINGS AS DOORWAYS OF INVESTIGATION

There are a few core understandings that constitute right view from a Buddhist standpoint: the Four Noble Truths, cause and effect, and the three characteristics of impermanence, suffering, and not-self. As we survey the connections between right view and these teachings, we will explore how we can develop this path factor in both individual and interpersonal practices and how, when we engage these practices formally and informally, they can become fully embedded into our lives. This breadth of application, together with the scope of the teachings on right view, show that wise, or appropriate, view is crucial to a viable, living whole-life path.

### Engaging the Four Noble Truths as a Practice of Right View

Right view is most frequently characterized as understanding and practicing the Four Noble Truths. Initially, these truths provide us with a sort of map of what is awry in life and how it may be made right. They follow the diagnostic grid of ancient Indian medicine: diagnosis, etiology, possibility of a cure, prescription to bring about the cure. We may feel skeptical while we are first beginning to apply it, but this system of understanding will prove to be a reliable guide for inquiry.

Suffering can motivate us to question how we see things. When we experience pain in our lives, especially strong or prolonged pain, we are shaken from our complacency.

> And what is the result of suffering? It's when someone who is overcome and overwhelmed by suffering sorrows and pines and cries, beating their breast and falling into confusion. Or else, overcome by that suffering, they begin an external search,

wondering: 'Who knows one or two phrases to stop this suffering?'
The result of suffering is either confusion or a search, I say.[28]

When we ask ourselves where our thoughts or actions lead, we open to insight, even if it is partial insight. We might feel broken inside, partial in our understanding, but it is the taste of suffering that sparks a conscious search for wise guidance beyond our current frameworks. Initial glimpses of the truth of suffering and its birth in the grasping mind lead to a little bit of release and relief and to more ethical behavior, which in turn leads to a calmer mind. That calmer mind is more able to see past the urgency of immediate pain or pleasure, to apprehend causes and effects more clearly. Release and relief also build confidence in our own innate wisdom. This is not confidence that we are right, but confidence that supports asking questions like, "What is going on right now?" and "What is this nurturing in me?" It is confidence that inclines us to continue the search. Also, each experience of calming down and awakening has its own impact and supports the deeper practices of stillness that can be refined sources of right view.

Gradually we realize that the first noble truth, dukkha, refers not only to blatant pain, fear, or loneliness, but also to the insecurity built into the mind's grasping at any perception or construct, the chafing of living life through an ego. We see the second truth, suffering's origin in the organism's constant thirst for what is arising, not only as the desire for comfort and validation but also the appetite for the next moment, the deep discontent of the clinging mind. The third truth does not just hint at a lesser suffering, but slowly reveals to the sensitive and discerning mind that the cessation of grief and ignorance is latent in each moment: hunger and ignorance can be radically unraveled and released, individually, relationally, and socially. Even a small taste of this freedom has real-world impact; we begin to reorganize our priorities, opinions, and activities.

When we understand that the Four Noble Truths describe the arising and cessation of suffering, we see that the fourth truth, the Noble Eightfold Path, refers to nothing less than how we live the totality of this very life. The Path offers an alternate approach to the suffering of the senses, of relationships, and of society. We cease to be dominated by thoughts and emotions that are driven by hunger and sustained by clinging, and we become disenchanted by the continual re-birthing into ignorance rooted in those habits of self. This view fosters strength and commitment on the Path, which leads gradually to a direct, unmediated sense of a life well lived. This too is right view—not the content of what is seen or known, much less the attempt to formulate it in words. The direct seeing is the practice of right view, along with the spontaneous rearrangement of our thinking processes that goes with it.

Thus, the Four Noble Truths are not just a map or teaching for beginners. These four truths are practices, and as they are apprehended more and more directly, they can be seen as the shape of liberation itself. The deepest transformations involve a collapse of self-concept and a temporary cessation of constructing self and other. Such experiences may be brief or enduring. Following them, the construction processes and social engagements may begin again by habit, but the resultant thoughts and emotions are not identified with and so not fed. We've seen behind the wizard's curtain and no longer believe the illusions the mind creates. We recognize the fabrications and the fabricating process of the heart-mind and the unjust social patterns born of ignorance. This recognition—not any proposition about it—is right view.

PRACTICE
## QUESTIONING THE FOUR NOBLE TRUTHS

Observing our experience and testing whether the Four Noble Truths are actually true is another form that the practice of right view can take. In the *Dhammacakkappavattanasutta*, considered to be a record of the first teaching given by Gautama Buddha after he attained enlightenment, the Buddha lists the Four Noble Truths.[29] You can engage this teaching as a practice of right view by pausing to question each assertion. Be sure to question with the bodily sense and nonverbal mind states, as well as with the thinking mind.

"Now this, bhikkhus, is the noble truth of suffering: birth is suffering, aging is suffering, illness is suffering, death is suffering; union with what is displeasing is suffering; separation from what is pleasing is suffering; not to get what one wants is suffering; in brief, the five aggregates subject to clinging are suffering."

Take a moment to consider whether this assertion rings true. Can you touch the suffering of death or of being separated from what or whom you love? Of oppression or of not getting what you want?

"Now this, bhikkhus, is the noble truth of the origin of suffering: it is this craving which leads to renewed existence, accompanied by delight and lust, seeking delight here and there; that is, craving for sensual pleasures, craving for existence, craving for extermination."

Does craving, a gnawing hunger for pleasure, or for the ending of pain, ring true to you as a condition for the arising of suffering? Or the body-mind's push for the next moment of becoming, the wish to be safe, to be seen and acknowledged by others? How does it feel in the body to want to escape this life, to get away from the pain or the onslaught of impressions and demands?

"Now this, bhikkhus, is the noble truth of the cessation of suffering: it is the remainderless fading away and cessation of that same craving, the giving up and relinquishing of it, freedom from it, nonreliance on it."

It might make logical sense that the ending of this craving would bring ease, but can you, right now, sense more deeply into this possibility? It can help to consider a longing you used to have but that has now faded. You could also contemplate where outer circumstances are painful and yet your reactions and ways of engagement are no longer driven by thirst and fear. Is there relief? Sometimes a patient, gentle, and deft regard is required to observe what has ceased.

"Now this, bhikkhus, is the noble truth of the way leading to the cessation of suffering: it is this Noble Eightfold Path; that is, right view, right intention, right speech, right action, right livelihood, right effort, right mindfulness, and right concentration."[30]

Does this path make sense? Does it inspire? Or might it inspire you after further study?

This individual, formal reflection can also be undertaken with spiritual friends. Also, you could select one of the truths as a contemplation you take into your daily life: a roving practice of right view.

## Engaging Cause and Effect as a Practice of Right View

Just as observing and reflecting on the Four Noble Truths is a practice of right view, so is investigating the causal connections that shape our lives: Why am I hurting? Why do people abuse each other? What can ease my pain? What brings happiness? Or we may ask: What caused the results I see in my life and in my culture? How might I act or think differently in order to bring about a different result? When I act with kindness, what happens? When I lie or gossip, how do I feel? When I ignore other people's suffering, what is the tone of my life? What about when I live and act with compassion? What are the effects of meditation? These questions parallel the second and third of the Noble Truths: the cause of suffering and the possibility of its cessation. The investigation is not about trying to make our lives fit some framework, Buddhist or otherwise.

Instead it involves referring to our own lives while we are asking, and seeking to answer, the same questions the Buddha asked: What is the source of suffering? How can this tangle be ended? With this kind of inquiry, and supported by sufficient prior understanding, considering any teaching can become a practice of right view.

Sometimes the relation of cause to effect is obvious; almost everyone except the person in question knows where certain actions will lead. A man begins selling cocaine to his office mates. This is not going to set anyone up for dispassion, being unfettered, contentment, and the rest; it is guaranteed to dig him deeper into suffering. Yet he does not see it that way. At other times the relationship is not so obvious: padding business deductions, or frequently playing violent video games, or talking behind someone's back, or remaining silent when you should speak up, or nurturing a grudge. And what about a subtle identification with your job, your house, your kids, your skill, your religion? Maybe you think these things have no effect on you, but have you really traced their potential effects carefully? Or do you just hope and want to believe these are innocuous actions? Our own wrong view is seldom obvious.

We need strong motivation to sustain a careful and completely honest examination of our thoughts and actions according to their results in our lives. It requires asking big, tough questions and examining the data of our lives carefully and accurately. Such inquiry is entirely practical: we are not likely to become more skillful until we recognize the causes of how we are doing now. This right view practice is necessary for ethical behavior and for the basic practice of untangling.

PRACTICE

**REFLECTING ON CAUSE AND EFFECT**

Select a time for reflection on cause and effect as you directly experience it. This can be a set aside time, more like a formal practice. Or you might integrate this reflection into your daily maintains the constructs of this life, this "me." We constantly tell ourselves stories and provide internal verbal commentary about the world. This storytelling forms and reforms our sense of purpose. Being mindful of intention opens us up to possibilities for escaping karmic patterns and fundamentally shifting the constructs we call personality or character.

Choose a domain of your life that is in flux right now. It might be your work, your community life, your art or other vocation, or an intimate relationship. Contemplate the stories you tell yourself: the running commentary on climate change, money, loneliness. Sense the whole tableau these stories create in the mind. Note your felt responses, the emotional tones that arise. How do these feelings orient the mind? What actions tend to flow from this stream of thought?

## MOMENTARY, EPISODIC, AND OVERARCHING INTENTIONS

To get a clear sense of the territory of intention to which the Buddha refers, it can help to see intention as manifesting on three different time scales: momentary, episodic, and overarching.

### Momentary Intentions

The direction of the mind changes from moment to moment as we come into contact with the world. Maybe we catch sight of someone we like, and a desire to be seen arises—or maybe what appears is lust or desire for material benefit. Maybe the next moment we encounter dog poop, and annoyance towards the dog's owner arises. So the mind goes: changing direction moment by moment. We can easily be swept along by the stream of these momentary and reactive intentions because they are conditioned and largely invisible to us. Translations of *saṅkappa* as "volition" or "thought" bring out this mercurial aspect. To discover this facet of saṅkappa we can ask, "What is the mind's direction in this moment?"

life by choosing to do it during a specific activity. Whichever you choose, establishing a clear beginning and ending will help the mind remember the practice and apply attention to it.

In can be supportive to begin with actions that have been satisfying, that appear wholesome or joyful. For example, you might contemplate a recent act of kindness you performed. Then inquire: What kinds of effects might this act have on my mind? How might my actions have affected the person I was interacting with? How might this act have affected others who were looking on?

In addition to a cognitive inquiry, drop into an awareness of your body and mind states and see if you can sense answers there.

You could continue by reflecting on an aspect of your life that is felt, here and now, as a knot, as a place of confusion or pain. If you have a difficult relationship or you feel stuck in your career, ask what brings suffering here: What hunger or fear is in play? How is my current situation flowing naturally from prior thoughts, words, and deeds? If I am the heir to my actions, what actions might be flowing out of this pain? Is this how I want to act, to live? Are there more wholesome, or skillful, responses to the same outer conditions?

If possible, engage this practice with a spiritual friend; interpersonal practice will help sustain your focus and, with your friend's participation, widen your view.

## Engaging the Three Characteristics as a Practice of Right View

Pursued honestly, an investigation of cause and effect will expose the way certain kinds of views set us up for suffering: the expectation that sense pleasures will last or will satisfy us; the expectation that certain circumstances or relationships in our life are permanent; the expectation that we ourselves will stay the same. We become intimate with these views not by way of clever thinking, but by direct experience of things as they actually are. In deep meditation we may experience the dissolution of the body or of each thought. Throughout life, we may notice both slow and abrupt changes in the body. With ever-changing experiences of gain and loss, pleasure and pain, we are given opportunities to confront the knot of grasping and experience its release. Such insights into impermanence, suffering, and not-self (dukkha, *anicca, anattā*) correspond to traditional definitions of right view—they are right view's namable, recognizable face, as it were. The process of uncovering these insights is another practice of right view.

## THE THREE CHARACTERISTICS

Here are three examples of right-view practices, one for each characteristic.

**Impermanence:** Sitting silently, observe the body-mind. Don't try to focus on anything in particular, such as the breath. Just notice whatever arises—sensations, thoughts, emotions. Let one question frame each and every experience: Is this stable? That is, does this particular experience last? Does this feeling in my leg stay one way, or does it change in shape or intensity? Does this thought stay still, even for a moment? It's important to present the question to the mind and then release the words entirely. Dwell with immediate experience. Even if you only do this practice for five minutes, what might be learned? If you are able to engage this practice with a co-meditator, you can include observation of the impermanence of the act of speaking, the flux of your partner as he moves or talks, and the changing experience of the relationship—intimate, distant, energized, calm, and so on.

**Suffering:** Abide with these two questions: when is the mind satisfied, and when is it dissatisfied? Some potential sub-inquiries:

Why do I get up to drink or use the toilet? How often do discomforts in the body motivate the beginning or ending of an action? What is the feeling in the body, and the motivation, for beginning or ending a conversation? What emotions arise when I consider the condition of politics, the environment, or society at large? Is the body-mind reaction pleasant or unpleasant? When it is pleasant, can I will it to continue that way? What do I experience when I see other people who are suffering? How often do I experience contentment? When I'm with someone, what motivates our mutual urge to speak or remain silent? This is a good embedded practice, one you can do as you go through your day at work or with friends or family.

**Not-self:** Set aside some time with a trusted friend or fellow practitioner. After taking some time to settle the mind, and with many pauses to enable mindfulness, share with each other what you are seeing, hearing, feeling, and thinking now. As you do so, with each pause, hold one guiding inquiry: Who is doing this speaking? Is what I am saying fresh, or is it just the reformulation of old ideas? Is the me who speaks about what I am seeing the same me who speaks about thinking? Is the me who speaks out one thought the same me who speaks out the next thought? Is there a stable me who is listening? If the words of the other are changing, is the self who is hearing them unchanging? Where are these questions coming from; is a self asking them right now? Is it stable, enduring?

## HOW OUR NATURAL HUMAN RELATEDNESS CAN SERVE OUR PRACTICE OF RIGHT VIEW

Ignorance regarding impermanence and the fluidity of the self are foundational to the view that the self is a separate, isolated unit, functioning independently in a world made up of other isolated individuals. This individuality view is another key aspect of wrong view. Conversely, understanding that humans are as intrinsically relational as they are individual is a key component of right view. Like the wise understanding of impermanence or cause and effect, understanding relatedness is veridical: it matches how things actually are. The self is empty and ever changing, and in each instant that it forms, it is a self-in-relation.

In the Buddha's time, people intuitively experienced belonging to certain nested communities: family, clan, village, kingdom. Their assumed view, in other words, was that the human experience was intrinsically relational. Later notions of individuality and utter self-determination would not take root for another two millennia. The sense of oneself as inter-dependent with other people and belonging to community was sustained by human neurobiology and hence by social structures associated with nurturance and survival. Intrinsic relational urges and capabilities were employed as key aspects of the Buddhist path in the concepts of Sangha, community gathered around mutual support for the Noble Eightfold Path, and kalyāṇa-mittatā, or spiritual friendship.

Intrinsic relatedness has been described in many ways by social psychologists, evolutionary theorists, philosophers, and others. Even so, modern people cling to their separateness despite the obvious gaps in human understanding that this view leaves, and despite the obvious personal suffering born of isolation and selfishness. The social impact of the individuality view has been enormous: economic injustice; amplification of divisions by race, class, and religion; and a culture of consumption as selves try to fill an unfillable hole. Religious and ethical teachings have been formulated to address the effects of self-centered view; practices that address the root cause of this unitary-self perspective are part of the practice of right view.

It is also worth exploring how companions are essential to cultivating right view, and so come to appreciate the deep value of spiritual friendship. With others, we learn new things and find inspiration, and when we hit our edges we are met with compassion.

Supported and nourished, we dare to let the teachings in fully. In community, we practice love; we grow in compassion. Compassion naturally flows from the understanding of intrinsic relatedness; that is, the *function* of relational right view is compassionate thought and interpersonal and social compassionate action.

## Wise Attention and the Voice of Another

We are astonishingly sensitive to the input of other humans. We are touched and swayed by the continual stream of influence coming from other people, both those present with us and those who affect us indirectly. The Buddha points out that our sensitivity to other people can either help or hinder the development of right view:

> Monks, there are these two conditions for the arising of wrong view. Which two? The voice of another and inappropriate attention. These are the two conditions for the arising of wrong view.
>
> Monks, there are these two conditions for the arising of right view. Which two? The voice of another and appropriate attention. These are the two conditions for the arising of right view.[31]

Wrong view and inappropriate attention are what we casually refer to as listening to bad influences. But when appropriate attention encounters unalloyed right view via the voice of another—teachings that are relevant, clear, worthy of confidence, and inviting verification—such contact is seminal and potent.

Appropriate, or wise, attention means exercising discernment. We need not accept everything as presented or as being on the same level. We attend to or imitate only what is excellent and leave the rest. Even faultless teachings need to be met with wise attention for right view to arise. Many people encountered the Buddha in his day and listened to his teaching, yet got little benefit.

The Pali phrase for appropriate attention is *yoniso manasikāra*. *Yoniso* means "down to the foundation." Venerable Ñanananda translates it as "radical," or to the root. So appropriate attention penetrates beneath the surface to discover the true nature of something. An additional sense of the word has to do with being thorough, complete, or even exhaustive. No angle of approach is left unconsidered. Yoniso manasikāra is not casual hearing, but a completeness of listening. It encompasses remembering, pondering, and testing. It involves a willingness to make use of the good that is found and to allow it to change our lives, perhaps radically. Only with careful attention can we let the teachings in fully.

There are many examples of the Buddha offering teaching on "the voice of another," or spiritual friendship, as a means of developing right view. One took place when the Buddha was living among his own people, the Sakya. At that time, he famously corrected his cousin and steward Ananda, saying that admirable friendship, companionship, and camaraderie were not half of the holy life, as Ananda had just said, but the whole of it.[32]

A person with admirable friends, he elaborated, can be expected to develop the Eightfold Path. These are friends with a high moral standard, as well as an abiding orientation towards clearly understanding what it means to live a wholesome life. They are "accomplished in faith, virtuous behavior, generosity, and wisdom," and the person who associates with them seeks to emulate them.[33]

The practice of right view here looks like associating with a mixed group of people who are role models and who will point you towards wisdom. Clearly, such influence is important for growth and progress.

Introspection and engaging with others are right-view practices that work together. If we encounter teachings that are consonant with what we have personally discovered, we will naturally have confidence in their validity. We are willing to give them a serious try. For example, we may come to see how self-doubt hinders energy and joy, and then encounter the Buddha's teachings on how the hindrances (nīvaraṇa) obstruct the factors of awakening. If the teaching continues to correspond to life as we know it, we will start to be confident about other parts of the teaching—even parts that seem puzzling or are beyond our present ability to verify. Such confidence leads us to further investigation, in which we are able to use others' experience to guide our questions and our practice.

Giving the teachings a try in experience is a dynamic aspect of appropriate attention. Attention that is thorough—yoniso—looks very carefully at the evidence uncovered in practice; it is more concerned with the actualities of this life than with confirming a cherished view.

With careful, persistent attention, another's partially correct view might help us attain right view. The Buddha worked deeply with other teachers—spiritual friends—before his enlightenment, and this brought him to the place where he could go the rest of the distance on his own. A partially correct teaching may help us move forward until we are able to do better. Myths of rewards and punishments in the afterlife may start us on the road to moral behavior; a psychology of self, skillfully applied, may be the first step in lifting the burden of self-obsession. Even an obviously wrong view might shock us into right view, if we are paying appropriate attention: maybe a grieving friend says of their lost beloved, "S/he should never have died!" and as the mind rejects this absurdity, the inevitability of death opens before us.

## SPEAKING AND LISTENING: INTERPERSONAL RIGHT VIEW

Very often, human contact is involved in catalyzing a new perspective. In one famous story, Kisa Gotami, a mother insane with grief, asks the Buddha for medicine to revive her child who had died days before. He agrees, but tells her he needs a mustard seed from a family where no one has died. As she knocks on doors asking for this seed, she hears, over and over again, that death has visited this house. She gets no mustard seed. Instead, she gets the truth that death is universal. The reality of her son's death finally sinks in—not because of some abstract teaching, but from hearing this basic human truth over and over again from a long series of others. Later, as a nun, Kisa Gotami declares she has "conquered the army of death, and dwell without defiling *intoxicants.*"[34] Her awakening began with the words of another, offered to assuage her grief.

As social beings, we are always, inevitably, interpreting our experience in ways influenced by other people. The language and imagery of our thinking, the questions we ask, all have come to us from others. Whatever our experiences are, they are surrounded by ideas and interpretations inherited from the human community. Interpersonal contacts and public media are continually influencing each individual's views. Collective greed, hatred, and delusion, as well as the binding forces of altruism and compassion, drive society forward, and the circulating of views—conceits, fears, alliances—are survival mechanisms of the social organism. In this way, societies define what is true, or valuable, or worthless. And in the absence of conscious effort, individuals are carried by this flood.

Wholesome communication with others is an essential antidote to this flood. The voice of another and wise attention can be broadly understood as speaking and listening. This is a teaching on the effects of dialogue, but dialogue of a specific kind: with clear mindedness and a guiding reference of wise understanding. Wise attention requires sensitivity to the challenges inherent in all communication. For the speaker, wise attention involves pausing to check the urge to speak, reflecting before speaking on the truth of our words, and finding a truth that emerges from the simplicity of present-moment apprehension. For the listener, wise attention involves pausing from the associations that are triggered when another's words meet our conditioned responses. Calming down in the very moment of human contact, we listen with sensitivity to language and to the layers of meaning embedded in intonation and metaphor. We meet and we are met.

Just putting our observations into words can crystallize what we did not know we knew. For me to tell you that fatigue is hurting my ability to pay attention to tasks and people, I must get clear enough about this connection to express it. Your listening draws forth my speech—and my clear thinking. At the same time, my speech provides you with access to my new understanding. If we are paying attention, both internally and externally, we can receive the wisdom that ripens between us. Wisdom does not just take the form of clear and simple Dhamma insights. Incrementally, small observations may be reflected in a shared investigation, leading where no single meditator would go.

Right view blooms not only as conceptual knowledge, but also as an internal, visceral experience of "Oh, I get it!" In this embodied format, there may be no words. The belly gets it, the mind states or emotions get it: there is some release. Perhaps the conceptual mind eventually "gets it" too, making sense of what the gut tells it only after the dialogue has ended. Perhaps we realize that pushing and grasping are painful; they scatter the mind and hurt the heart. This is the move from what the Buddha called heard knowledge (*sutamayā*), to reflective learning (*cintāmayā*), to direct experience and intuitive wisdom (*bhāvanāmayā*).[35] It is common in Insight Dialogue retreats, for example, for full understanding to blossom in the silent sitting or walking practice that follows a dialogue. Wisdom arises from within the mind. The mind suddenly apprehends that the release of self-pushing yields comfort and joy. What is heard corresponds to truth as we have experienced it, even as it extends or transcends what we consciously know.

PRACTICE
**LISTENING AND SPEAKING**

This is a formal interpersonal practice. Prepare a small segment of root wisdom texts, like a pithy excerpt from the Buddha's discourses, and sit down with a spiritual friend to explore the text together. For example, take these two short discourses:

"I don't envision a single thing that, when undeveloped, leads to such great harm as the mind. The mind, when undeveloped leads to great harm."

"I don't envision a single thing that, when developed, leads to such great benefit as the mind. The mind, when developed leads to great benefit."[36]

Maybe you can both read the text just before you speak, but then set it aside and hold the teaching in mind as a guide for your inquiry. You might ask, "Do these strike me as true? How do I experience this now, or how do I not experience it right now?"

As you inquire, do you notice that your spiritual friend is speaking from a different perspective from yours? Does their view contribute to the breadth of your view?[37] Ask, "Is inquiring with this person keeping me on track right now? What is the impact of having to form my thoughts into words I can speak?"

As you turn this contemplation over between you, does your understanding evolve? And importantly, do thoughts and feelings emerging from this practice shine into your life? Do they lead to dispassion, not to passion? To shedding, not accumulating?

---

## ～ REFLECTION

Right view is the beginning and foundation of the Noble Eightfold Path. To the extent that we are confused or misinformed about cause and effect, our actions will lack harmony and tend to create suffering. We may repeatedly make bad choices when we do not see causal connections. To the extent that we are confused about the causes of the mind's dissatisfactions and discontent, or don't understand the possibility of escaping the whirlpool of habit, we lose the ability to navigate this confusing human experience. Without some right view, we cannot see a path; there is no way forward for us.

The first glimmers of right view can launch us forward on the Path. Our view may correspond more or less to how the world works; to the extent that it conforms to how things are, and can point the way towards the mind's unbinding, it is wise, or right. This is useful for keeping us out of trouble. With some right view, the mind inclines towards happiness because it is in alignment with reality. The beginning of right view launches a process of increasing discernment. Our practice includes establishing the conditions that foster this virtuous cycle of wisdom. Can the mind be unfettered? Can we apprehend things as they actually are?

Right view is also the end of the Path and its goal, for the Noble Eightfold Path is circular. A wise understanding of this human experience—one that includes intellectual and somatic knowing while transcending them—manifests naturally when the Path is ripe. Right view has an effect. It yields a heart-mind that is outside selfishness. Our relationships and actions in the world are expressions of this disentangled perspective.

Right view also manifests relationally. Interactions with others contribute to and sustain ways of seeing the world. The small social systems of relationships not only reflect the views of the individuals involved, but they are also a milieu for collective views. Likewise, views take form and evolve in societies, and to the extent that kind and liberative understandings are part of the social fabric, right view does its good work here, too. Right view manifests socially as compassion, and its *practice* in society yields harmony and justice.

Compassion and clear seeing manifest as one and the same. Seeing directly the arising and cessation of phenomena is right view. So is seeing the harm of ill will and the emptiness of self-constructs. Such insight yields detachment and thus relinquishment. A perspective may not seem to have any material substance, but we see that it can make the difference between a life of imprisonment and a life of freedom. With the help of our wise companions in this holy life, we can untangle that tangle.

Right view is always part of our practice, whether intentionally or otherwise. The mind is plastic, forming and reforming a sense of how things are from one moment to the next. The Buddha prescribed countless practices of right view in the form of a vast array of Dhamma teachings. All teachings are practices. All can be experienced here and now. When we pick up these teachings and reflect on them, when we simply wake up to observe what is happening this moment, in and around us, we open this door to wise understanding. Nothing is left out.

~

# CHAPTER 5

# RIGHT INTENTION

## *Sammā Saṅkappa*

W hat is motivating you to read these words right now? From one moment to the next, something is moving you to put forth the energy to read, to reflect, and to attempt to understand. Something is aiming the mind such that it wants to know more about a whole-life application of the Noble Eightfold Path.

Behind every action, even every thought, there is an intention: no intention + no thought = no action. Right intention sits at the interface of mind and how we live. As the mental factor that propels and guides everything we think and do, it saturates every moment of our lives.

Intention is also the aim of the heart. It has to do with purpose and motivation, and it flows from an unspoken sense of direction that connects our life perspective with how we act. It is the emotional element that flows from right view and gives impetus to right speech, right action, and right livelihood.

Right intention (sammā saṅkappa) arises naturally from right view. If we have right view—when we really get how suffering works, how it is caused, and how its causes can be abandoned—it just makes sense, both emotionally and intellectually, to apply that knowledge. We want to. As a practice, right intention is implementing the understanding of right view to deliberately aim the mind. As a ripened quality, right intention is more intimate than wanting to apply some principle; it manifests as the spontaneous emotional blossoming of understanding in a way that bears action as its fruit.

We might think of right view as a map showing the route to a desired destination. Right intention is both the big choice to use that map and the many smaller choices—one at every intersection—to follow its guidance right here, right now. Sometimes the map is known and accessed by the thinking mind; usually the map is known intuitively and functioning naturally. Cognitively or intuitively, right intention registers as volition; it flows from prior urges and actions, and it conditions future ones. It also calls up the emotional energy or motivation to keep moving across the terrain; it is the urge to take a step in a certain direction before actually taking that step. Without the impetus of right intention, right view remains unconnected to action or to life—a map framed and hung on the wall as decoration.

## FACETS OF INTENTION

To work with intention, we need to first understand what is meant by the word *saṅkappa*. Common definitions include "thought," "intention," "purpose," and "plan." Because it flows from right view, intention that is sammā, "right," will be aimed towards attitudes and actions that support the cessation of hunger and ignorance.

In looking at right view, we saw how the Buddha divided thoughts into two groups according to their effects. Right view sees what leads to the arising of suffering, dukkha, and what leads to its cessation. The thoughts (*vitakka*) he was sorting, however, were described in the categories of saṅkappa, intention: thoughts of sensual desire or renunciation, thoughts of ill will or goodwill, thoughts of cruelty or compassion.[38] These three basic emotional inclinations are the Buddha's technical distillation of what he meant by intention. Renunciation is rooted in wisdom, non–ill will in mettā, and noncruelty in compassion.

One of my teachers, Venerable Punnaji, translated saṅkappa as "disposition" or "orientation." This understanding implies an inclination or tendency with some stability: right disposition, right orientation. The disposition towards renunciation, the disposition towards non–ill will, the disposition towards noncruelty. The orientation towards renunciation, the orientation towards non–ill will, the orientation towards noncruelty. This understanding brings out a sense of something extended in time and anchored in habit or character—the latent tendencies of the mind from which momentary impulses spring.

It can be useful to also consider other translations of saṅkappa, such as "resolve" or "directing the mind." The word direction, for instance, can help us see how the mind is heading somewhere, orienting in a certain way in the present. The future is also implied: "this is where I'm headed."

The idea of direction easily takes a passive sense: the mind is naturally directed by the views it holds. We are not always aware of why we're doing what we do. Some actions don't even seem to have any intention behind them; we just act without forethought. Even unreflected actions, however, are not wholly without intention. Each moment of thought has a volitional aspect (cetanā).[39] But to acquiesce to whatever latent tendencies emerge too often reinforces patterns of ignorance and selfishness, especially early in our training.

Contrast this passive sense with direction's active sense, involving will or volition: we can direct the mind actively, choosing how and where we offer our attention, and towards what goals. When the mind's strength is directed towards a goal to which one is fully committed, the power of intention can be astonishing. The work of great leaders like Mohandas Gandhi and Nelson Mandela was directed by clear intention, and their results speak to us still.

The set points of intention can shift towards the wholesome with practice and with good friendships. They can also easily drift towards the unwholesome by way of negative media and social influences. The mind is directed by intentions, yoked to our choices. This is why right intention is a practice worthy of the Eightfold Path towards unbinding.

PRACTICE
## WRONG INTENTION

Get together with a trusted friend to explore unwholesome intentions: what is present in your mind, what it feels like when they are operating. What is the felt sense of a mind oriented towards sensual satisfaction? Consider what occupies the mind: an image of the sexual other, a remembering and longing for that sweet dessert. And the body: is it relaxed in that moment of fixation on the possession or experience you lust after?

With the mind so occupied and the body stimulated, what is the relationship with the people and tasks in front of you here and now? Are you attuned to present-moment experiences, or are you consumed with those images and thoughts of what would be acquired? And what of the mind states? With the mind directed towards acquiring and holding to pleasant sensations, is there serenity? Is there peace? Get clear about the entire experience of a mind whose intentions direct it towards attachment and away from release.

PRACTICE
## NOTICING DIRECTION BY STORIES

In the *Mahācattārīsakasutta*, the Buddha includes verbal formation in a list of sub-categories of intention.[40] This highlights how images, concepts, language, and ultimately speech are involved in the forming and aiming of intention. Intention, especially as crystallized in language, spins and

The Buddha's teaching on contact and perception, *phassa* and *saññā*, provides a window into the moment-by-moment processes that constitute experience, including the role intention plays.

As a visible object, the eye, and consciousness make contact, the experience of seeing arises along with a feeling tone—pleasant, unpleasant, or neutral. At this same moment, perception—it is *this* object with *these* qualities—arises. Even such a basic aspect of experience as cognizing (i.e., consciousness, *viññāṇa*) is understood as arising based upon all prior conditioned, volitional moments (*saṅkhāra paccaya viññāṇa*).

Put in materialistic and psychological terms, each moment of experience arises conditioned by the sum of the neural and hormonal conditions. So upon contact, the ignorant body-mind reflexively grasps at experience to hold the moment near or push it away, and the resultant tension becomes the locus of "me" in that moment. Wrapped up in engagement with the object, "I am" the one seeing and feeling this now. "I am" the one wanting this lovely object or this person's kind words. Thus, the world arises one moment and vanishes the next.[41]

This freshly born "me," with its archive of tendencies, gives rise to impulses that lead to action of body, speech, and mind. With mindfulness, we can see momentary intentions as they arise with sensations and flow into actions. With practice and effort, they can be redirected. We can choose to reinforce responses that support our larger-scale intentions and to release those that do not. Lust becomes dispassion; anger becomes compassion. This constitutes an ongoing and embedded practice of sammā saṅkappa.

---

PRACTICE

**EXPERIENCING THE FIRST TOUCH
OF THE MIND'S INCLINATION**

Sit quietly, and after letting the body-mind calm down, call to mind a person or a task that feels relevant for you right now.

Notice how the thought—the words or image—touches the mind. What immediately follows that touch? Don't try to figure it out or give words to the experience. Just notice the touch and the felt response.

As you sit with this, do you notice any inclination of the mind—for example, towards friendliness or anger, towards dispassion, or towards wanting things to turn out a certain way? Don't try to manipulate the response; just being aware of it is enough right now, particularly if the mind is balanced while observing.

After you've sat with this observation for a while, how do you feel? Do you notice any change in relationship to the person or task?

## Episodic Intentions

At the next time scale of intention, an overall direction has been established for a specific task or social encounter—for one small episode of our lives. Episodic intention can carry within it thought moments that are contrary to the mind's overall direction. For example, we might be volunteering at a food pantry. One moment we feel compassion for someone who is poor or injured; the next moment we feel a wave of involuntary disgust for someone who smells bad or acts abrasively. But our service commitment for the duration of that hour sustains the overall direction of the mind towards kindness and compassion, even though less skillful moment-to-moment thoughts and emotions come and go.

Translations of *saṅkappa* as "intention" and "resolve" highlight its episodic manifestation. Episodic intention involves a situation with a clear beginning and end. To discover this facet of saṅkappa, we can ask, before and during, "Why am I doing this . . . (this job, this social event, this practice, this task)?"

Episodic intentions are perhaps most easily seen and most workable from the standpoint of practice: at this level, we have the best chance of effectively intervening. For example, you might resolve, "At this meeting with my brother, I'm going to focus on forgiveness no matter what he says and no matter what habitual emotions arise in me." Intention associated with specific tasks or events has some muscle in its directedness. It involves both the conscious direction of conceptual thought and the monitoring of emotion. Without such direction, episodic intentions can reinforce existing patterns that are reactive and predictable. But with mindfulness and effort, episodic intentions can be directed into new patterns—patterns that then continue to incline the mind, becoming wholesome habits.

PRACTICE
**FOR JUST THIS EPISODE**

Select one meeting, one encounter, during which you will resolutely practice unconditional kindness. Make certain this episode has a clear beginning and ending; this will help you maintain your energy and focus. Regardless of what the other(s) says, return to kindness; watch the mind carefully, and let all speech, even all thoughts, find their roots there. Afterwards, reflect on the experience. What did you notice? How did it feel? Do you want to try this practice again?

## Overarching Intentions

The third time scale of intention involves the overall direction of one's life. Perhaps your overarching intention is to be liberated from suffering by nonclinging or not doing harm; perhaps you have devoted your life, or aspire to devote it, to compassionate service; or maybe you are aiming at comfort, both now and in old age. Whatever the intention, there will be all kinds of variations along the way. Sights and sounds and thoughts will give rise to momentary intentions of anger or love, generosity, or selfishness. Tasks and relationships will evoke episodic commitments and orientations: an intention to be kind at a family reunion or an intention to be efficient at work, for example. But the overarching direction of our lives stands outside of time. Such intentions are a kind of beacon by which the navigation system of our lives stays oriented: towards grasping or release, compassion or selfishness.

Overarching intention is associated with long-term or life-long goals and values, and it is experienced as a broad image or felt sense of life. Translations such as "direction" and "orientation" reflect this aspect of saṅkappa. We can locate overarching intention by asking ourselves, "What is my life's direction?"

Overarching intentions are not always visible to us. Latent tendencies of the heart influence day-to-day perspectives and decisions, and we may just experience these tendencies as, "This is how things are." The Buddha spoke of them like this: "Dependent upon the ill will element [latent anger], the perception of ill will arises."[42] That is, we see the person in front of us through the lens of preexisting anger (or insecurity, or lust, or kindness, and so on). The intention or mental direction of anger is established, leading us through the growing urges of desire and passion. It is this urge, or pressure in the heart-mind, that blossoms as we speak words of anger or withdraw in aversion.

The overarching aspect of intention is the one most intimately tied to how we view the world. It constitutes the spiritual, existential tone of our lives and helps to shape momentary and episodic intentions. Overarching intentions manifest as character and are not easily shifted. When they do change, they have the power to pull our thoughts and actions along with them; that is why they are so heavily emphasized in religions and other thought systems. A vow is an overarching intention, and to take a vow is to formally commit to practicing that intention. In Buddhism, the mind is oriented towards clearly seeing present-moment experience and inclining the heart towards relinquishment and compassion. Having a Buddha-image at home to help you recollect this orientation is a practice of overarching right intention. In the Abrahamic religions we are implored to give our lives over to the mercy of Christ, to think always of Allah, to remember the Jewish Shema: "And you shall love the Lord your God with all your heart and with all your soul and with all your might." These are all practices for fostering a life according to a religion's values. Even without the strong overtones of faith in a divinity, however, overarching intentions can play a powerful role in our path.

PRACTICE

## DEVELOPING AND CHECKING
## OVERARCHING INTENTION

Set aside time to reflect on what values and aspirations pull you forward. Look carefully; sometimes our most deeply held values are invisible to us. Kindness to others may be lost to view; a wish for people who are suffering to find relief may seem like it's "only natural," not really a value. Look, too, for a mental direction that you may not condone. For example, most of us are continually looking for pleasurable sensations or mental entertainments. Do these congeal into an encompassing, if not always visible, life direction?

Once you have clarified some overarching intentions, inquire whether your life actions and decisions are aligned with them. If actions are aligned with the unwholesome or futile directions, by what gradual path might this alignment be altered? If your life is not yet strongly inclined towards wholesome intentions, what images, practices, stories, friendships, employment, study, and reflection might bring about a gradual, patient, and enduring shift in that direction? Are there vows or rituals, domestic or community supports, that will help maintain and increase these overarching intentions?

This practice can be done alone or with a trusted and respected friend.

## Nested Intentions

The three time scales of intention are overlapping and interwoven. The shorter scales are nested within the longer. What you think (momentary saṅkappa) and the plans and resolutions behind what you do (episodic saṅkappa) are important because they shape your life's trajectory and goals (overarching saṅkappa). Taking the question associated with each of the three time frames from the bottom up, we see that "What is the basis of thought in this moment?" is nested inside "Why am I doing this action?" and both are contained within the overarching question, "What is my life's direction?" This interweaving of long and short scales of intention can also be seen in the reverse direction, top to bottom: good overarching intentions condition good task-based intentions, and both together condition immediate, moment-to-moment intentions—kindness here and now. (See figure 1.)

These three aspects of intention became clear to me one morning when I was first exploring these ideas. I had been observing how these teachings were operating in my mind and working out my thoughts in writing since before dawn. Then it was time to wake my youngest son, Max, for school. Reflecting on my current mind state, I became aware that my overarching intention in relation to my son was towards love and compassion: to help him be comfortable and confident in the world. More broadly, my whole life was oriented in no small part towards kindness and the release that comes from service.

I was also aware of intentions limited to that specific, small time frame: the orientation of feelings and thoughts around the tasks of

*Figure 1*  Nested Intentions

| OVERARCHING What is my life's direction? |
| EPISODIC Why am I doing this action? |
| MOMENTARY What is the basis of thought right now? |

getting him ready for school, making the process comfortable for him, and getting his lunch ready. These task-oriented intentions were colored by love and compassion: wanting to prepare him for the pain of growing up and the pain of life, so he can minimize the pain and maximize the potential for awakening.

Momentary intentions motivated me to rise from my desk and walk up the stairs. As I did so, I noticed how the energy of each footstep was derived from and motivated by the overarching compassion and love, and those steps were oriented towards this specific task. I saw how acting mindfully reinforced the intentions: how each movement of the mind and the body, observed and approved, reinforced the direction from which it sprang.

On this occasion I was aware of the stream of momentary intentions, but I also knew that I sometimes "launch" an action like this and then coast on the episodic and overarching intention or direction. That is, I might walk mindlessly up the stairs. But I knew right then that moment-by-moment mindfulness can be strong one moment and weak the next. A thought of resistance could have arisen: for example, "I wish I could keep working." But right then, the mind was moving in the direction of compassion and care for my son. This direction was a deep part of my character; I could trust that. When I brought mindfulness to them, these wholesome intentions were strengthened across all time scales.

The basis of all of these intentions was right view. Even without thinking about it, I knew, I felt, that mental actions of love have wholesome consequences. I knew this was all contingent; giving my best in this situation was not covering up life's difficulties. It was clear in my bones that generosity has wholesome results—for me and for Max.

---

PRACTICE

**REVERSE ENGINEERING THE MOMENT**

Intentions can be observed in mental directions that are already established in your life. Select a couple of wholesome actions (an easier place to begin), and reflect on the good that is already present.

Here are a couple of examples of this practice:

- I'm washing the dishes—again. I pause and reflect inwardly: what wholesome intentions are operating? Cleaning the dishes, like cleaning the house, has about it a quality of relinquishment. When things are clean, they tend to be simple. In this thought, my mind settles. I notice I'm also washing my spouse's dishes and notice there is kindness, generosity in this. Even though she is not with me now, I feel her presence as I wash her fork, her plate. There is no wish to be washing dishes, but neither is there any aversion. The mind is aimed towards the middle way.

- Before I sit down to meditate, I walk over to an area with some objects of remembering. A needlepoint my mother made for me decades ago that, by virtue of all the work in it, recalls her care for me: gratitude and respect arise. A Buddha statue given me by one of my teachers: my mind aims towards his example of love and wisdom. I approach my cushion, and already the mind is inclining towards this path of release; it is inclining towards peace. I sit and close my eyes, and whether my mind is disturbed or cool, the very act of sitting points towards equanimity.

## PRACTICING WITH THE TIME SCALES OF INTENTION

Wholesome and unwholesome intentions are woven throughout our lives and can show up at any time scale. Very long episodes—like "as long as I'm employed at this job" may not be distinguishable from an overall life direction. Likewise, a very short episode, like "just while I take this one bite of dessert I'm going to practice nonclinging," may be indistinguishable from a momentary intention. The time scales are not wholly separate; they are just useful concepts for understanding and thinking more clearly about the movements of the mind and locating ourselves on the path.

Practicing with any one time scale of intention may not be the most effective approach. Intention is strongly influenced by habits and conditioned patterns, and we likely need to work with stronger patterns in a variety of ways. We might intend for an encounter with our manager to be compassionate, but that intention may be swamped by habitual reaction patterns during the meeting. Or it may fade after the meeting is over. Good momentary intentions without the context of episodic or overarching direction are not robust. On the spur of the moment, I may want to give up alcoholic beverages, but the next day, in the absence of the long-term commitment to such renunciation, I find myself out for a drink with a friend. The episodic "I'm not going to smoke cannabis today" needs the support of the longer-term vow "I am committed to cultivating clarity of mind." Likewise, good overarching intentions, such as, "I will simplify my life," will need the support of specific episodic intentions—"When I visit my family this weekend, I'm not going to try to solve everybody's problems"—in order to influence moment-to-moment thoughts and inclinations, such as, "I can love my child but won't leap in now to fix things." Taking all these together, we begin to see the outlines of skillful practices.

Overarching mental directions can conflict with each other—as when some are conscious but not yet conditioned into habit and character, while others are unconscious, conditioned, and automatic. For example, a conscious desire to be more peaceful may conflict with a personality that is habitually directed towards anger. Think of the lustful meditation teacher or the peace activist who is angry with her partner. When conflicts of mental direction arise, the emotional basis nearly always takes precedence. Practices like mettā meditation can shift the mind's overall direction. Diligence is the key.

## INTENTIONS AND KARMA

Intentions at all three time scales are expansive, invasive. Their emotional momentum impels us to action and actions have concrete results in our lives, for ourselves and others. Actions we take, even those that seem highly rational, are based upon emotions, gut feelings formed over years of prior thought and emotion. This is one way of describing karma: action and results of action.

Intentions lie at the heart of the Buddha's teaching on karma. Brahmanic concepts of reincarnation and karma saturated the culture of the Buddha's time. While he inherited and used the language of karma, the Buddha developed and expanded the concept of karma in ways that went far beyond anything known to his contemporaries. He did not accept the idea of a soul that migrated, intact, from life to life, and he cut through popular and Brahmanic ideas that karma is influenced by ritual actions such as sacrifice. Instead, he directly linked karma and intention. He insisted that the ethical character of action, and especially of the intentions behind action, is what creates the fruits of karma, or *kamma vipāka*.[43] He also explained in detail which types of karma lead to which spheres of rebirth. It was a psychologically sophisticated conception of the rebirth process, which he fully integrated into his teachings on morality and liberation.

When we are just coasting along on automatic, some of our actions are largely the result of causes and conditions outside of our present choosing. Many have to do with our previous actions, other people's choices, the norms of our society, or external circumstances. We may not be consciously thinking, "I'm going to try and diminish my fixation on recognition for my work," but we nevertheless are inclining in the direction of modesty. Or we may not be aware of the emotion behind following an internet link to a gossipy news site, but those emotional tendencies are nevertheless being reinforced. Yet even when we are barely conscious of choosing, the actions we perform with our bodies and minds affect us more profoundly than external events. Even on autopilot, emotions and actions contribute, drop by drop, to habit and character, reinforcing links between hormones and behaviors, forming and reinforcing neuronal pathways in the brain. This cause-and-effect relationship is at the heart of understanding karma.

When we are even a little bit mindful, we have a degree of choice about our actions and about the emotional constructs and motivations we choose. We have real, though not unlimited, freedom. With awareness, we can call our thoughts and impulses into question; we can test them against a standard, like the two components of right view: wholesome (leading away from suffering) or unwholesome (leading towards suffering)? When we consciously influence the emotional constructions that dominate our awareness and generate our actions, like by intentionally responding to someone with patience rather than agitation, their impact on us increases enormously.

When choices are made consciously, they become powerfully generative of karma. Consciously chosen behavior has a stronger sculpting effect on us than behavior born of habit. With choice, volition is strong, and new neural networks are being formed and reinforced. The cumulative nature of repeated choices is capable of reprogramming us—capable of weakening and eliminating old habits and tendencies, capable of forming new and different ones.

Years ago I began an ongoing effort to develop in myself the inclination to give—specifically, to give money. While I was growing up, nongenerosity was often modeled for me when it came to the small but frequent opportunities to give tips to people in service positions. I learned from this modeling and could be, in a word, miserly. Then as an adult, I observed how, whenever we'd check out of a hotel room, my wife would leave money on the counter for the people who cleaned the rooms. I was moved by this and inspired to develop that action—or more importantly, the understanding and urge behind it. I began doing so, always with the reflection on my own privilege and the likely lack of privilege of those who were invisibly serving me. Even when I was rushed, I made it a point to remember to give. Now, countless hotel stays later, it's an action that brings joy; there's even remorse on the occasions when I forget. Some wholesome reprogramming seems to have taken hold. I personally enjoy the results; the worldly fruits of this generosity are untrackable.

Conscious volitional action also has a social impact. In everyday settings, our posture and expression—perhaps even our thoughts and energetic field—announce something of our intentions; we are intentionally saying something to those around us, and they orient themselves accordingly. Nearly all of us know how to read an aggressive movement or a loving smile. The intentions behind our actions towards others extend all the way up to legal constructions such as "unpremeditated murder" and "malice aforethought." In many codes of law, an action is defined differently and assigned different penalties depending on the absence or presence of consciously chosen intention.

The path factor of sammā saṅkappa can point us towards skillful ways of working with karma, with cause and effect, in our lives. Thought by thought, tendencies of the mind are constructed. Neural associations are formed and strengthened. Thought formations give rise to actions and personality formations. In aggregate, these associations and networks, deeply interwoven and enmeshed, form a personality. Thus, momentary intentions compound to form lasting patterns in the mind. If we make wise and mindful choices—of friends, jobs, and activities—wholesome intentions will lead to wholesome life patterns. Good character is built, action by action, intention by intention.

---

PRACTICE

**ACTION AND CHARACTER**

Think about one of your wholesome character traits. Perhaps you are concerned with and active in racial or economic justice. Maybe you are respectful of elders or kind to animals or generous towards homeless people. Maybe you possess a native sense of fairness or dedication to honesty. A concern for global ecological balance would be associated with the intention of relinquishing or abandoning harmful habits of consumption. Caring about racial justice has roots in compassion and nonharming.

Fully tracing the origins of this wholesome quality will not be possible, but as you sit here now, can you locate any specific people, jobs, or social norms that nurtured it? It helps to be sensitive not just to fully formed memories but also to images or unnamed feelings in the body.

From there, can you remember any specific incidents that planted the seeds of this characteristic? And can you notice any thought processes or emotional tendencies that nourish and support it? Give particular attention to the sense that this characteristic comes from somewhere, that it is a spontaneous expression of a history.

This practice may be easier to sustain, and possibly more interesting, if you engage with another person, or even with a few people. You'll hear of their finer qualities and perhaps be inspired to cultivate those traits in yourself. You may also gain a sense of the wholesome impact you have on others.

## SHIFTING FROM AUTOMATIC RESPONSES TO CONSCIOUS DIRECTION: THE ROLE OF INTENTION

We've seen how intention functions emotionally. As an orientation of the mind, it is pre-cognitive. Thoughts and emotions mutually condition each other, ripening into action.

The Buddha traced the chain of conditioned events by which intentions shape our lives. The thoughts and impulses that lead to wholesome and unwholesome action arise from identifiable causes, and their development follows a predictable path. He analyzed these intentions one by one—sensuality, ill will, and cruelty, along with their opposites, renunciation, goodwill, and harmlessness—breaking each one down in the same way.

> In dependence on the sensuality element there arises sensual perception; in dependence on sensual perception there arises sensual intention (saṅkappa); in dependence on sensual intention there arises sensual desire; in dependence on sensual desire there arises sensual passion; in dependence on sensual passion there arises sensual quest. Engaged in sensual quest, the uninstructed worldling conducts himself wrongly in three ways—with body, speech, and mind.[44]

Wholesome and unwholesome roots follow the same path of arising: from an element or latent tendency to a perception that combines what we perceive with a meaning or possibility. The perception is of something actual—an object, event, or person—but we perceive it in terms of the latent emotional tendency. It is filtered or colored by our minds, but it seems true, that it is just as we perceive it. Then from that tinged perception, intention arises. Implicit racial bias is one example of a tinged perception. Maybe something we see triggers a compassionate element in us, and a compassionate perception arises—a perception in which an object and a desire to alleviate suffering are superimposed or merged. Then, from that compassionate perception, a compassionate intention arises: thoughts and feelings oriented towards doing something to alleviate another's pain begin to form. I step forward and offer help to someone ill with a virus. I vote or work for a principled politician.

Latent tendencies remain dormant in the mind until activated. Below the level of consciousness, our minds have many tendencies, some wholesome and others not. Conscious input can steer the mind's direction. For example, one can know of one's tendency towards unkind words and, with enough mindfulness, curtail some automatic reactions. Both consciously willed and automatic responses hurry us along to new choices and new actions. When intention arises, it gives rise to desire, passion, and the formation of a plan, a quest. How long does this process take? It can be very, very quick: "Suppose . . . a man would drop a blazing grass torch into a thicket of dry grass. If he does not quickly extinguish it with his hands and feet, the creatures living in the grass . . . will meet with calamity and disaster."[45] When the thoughts are those of renunciation, non–ill will, and harmlessness, however, such a one "conducts himself rightly in three ways—with body, speech, and mind."

Because our thoughts and actions bear fruit, our acquisitiveness and ill will set up suffering. But because intention is malleable, such a cycle can be broken by practice. The basic intoxicants (āsava) that cause us to remain mired in unconscious and reflexive cycles can be removed. Right saṅkappa—wholesome intention or mental direction—plays a pivotal role in this removal. With the aid of right mindfulness and right effort, unwholesome intentions can be interrupted and wholesome intentions cultivated.

PRACTICE

**TRACING THE ORIGINS AND BLOSSOMING OF ACTION**

Set aside a quiet time, perhaps while sitting in nature or while taking a walk. Call to mind someone towards whom you feel enmity. Perhaps they have caused you trouble or hurt you or someone you love. Notice the sensations in the body as you imagine this person. These feelings are traces of what the Buddha called the latent "ill will element" arising upon your mental contact with that person.

Now picture an opportunity to speak ill of that person. Perhaps you meet someone who might consider hiring that person or might introduce them to a friend for a possible romantic relationship. You could easily say something negative. It would be true—and so deserved. Feel what the heart-mind does. Be honest with yourself. Do you feel any pull towards ill will? Does the mind turn in that direction? If this situation were real, would the mind's inclination ripen into speech?

Now consider that same person's vulnerability, their hurts. They have a lot of pain, just as you do. They too seek happiness. Perhaps the knots in their hearts make it hard to find peace. Let your heart vibrate with their pain. Consider also that, if you speak ill of them, it will hurt not only them but yourself as well, leaving a toxic feeling in your heart.

Now sustain any feelings of compassion and concern that may arise, and picture again the opportunity to say something about this person that will have an influence. Does the heart soften? Does the mind incline towards non–ill will? How would you speak?

Close by reflecting on how mental direction is both automatic and, prior to action, malleable. Has working with this latent tendency been a good use of your time?

## THE EFFECTS OF INTERPERSONAL AND SOCIAL CONTACT

Cultivating the path factor of right intention with others may be the ideal way to intervene in this chain of conditioned reactions. Simply put, contact with others brings out our unwholesome "stuff." When personal reaction becomes interpersonal inter-reaction, interrupting this sequence early requires subtle observation and a nimble response. Shared intention, where all parties are aligned with values of relinquishment, powerfully supports our waking up to latent tendencies, but doing the work unilaterally is often our most available option. Later in the body-mind process, and when emotions have been aroused in relationship, strong effort is required to interrupt the momentum. As my teacher Venerable Punnaji used to say, whenever thought and emotion are in conflict about what to do, emotion will always win. Saṅkappa stands in the middle of this sequence, which turns out to be a surprisingly workable place.

As participants in a social system, we are constantly impacted by intentions, and we are constantly recirculating intentions. Seeing other people's facial expressions, we automatically respond as mirror neurons trigger similar emotions in us. At the same time, we see others through the lens of our latent tendencies, the root source of implicit bias. We believe we are seeing others objectively, "as they actually are," but our hopes and fears, admiration and judgments, are at work. Actions then follow from how we feel.

We also take in large amounts of emotionally triggering stimuli from the media and from advertising. Advertising is all about motivating others to act in a way favorable to someone else's financial concerns. It seeks to activate underlying tendencies and then stampede them toward action. Often it does this by activating and entraining sympathetic responses: we are shown images of a person's happiness or relief as a result of using a product; because we have evolved to mirror the emotions we see in others, these attitudes are rehearsed in our hormones, neurons, and emotions, whether we approve or not.

Working with all this conditioning presents a formidable challenge. Still, there's good news. First, knowing that our responses are constructed opens a new path forward. Conditioned patterns may be tenacious, but they are not immutable. Whatever has been constructed can be changed. Whatever is conditioned can be reconditioned or, with diligence, deconditioned. Neural networks can be defused and new ones configured, and we can have a hand in the direction this neural reconstruction takes. Wedding rings, religious art, and communal vows all attest to this fact.

Second, many of the problems caused by conditioning have societal and systemic aspects, but most of the remedies—short of a society-wide reform, which is a worthy aspiration—can initially be addressed at either personal or interpersonal scales. Because there is a relational component to the mechanism of intention, there is also the possibility that we can support one another's good intentions and help one another notice and deconstruct unwanted patterns of intention.

## THE POWER OF SHARED INTENTION

It's not hard to recognize the power of people working together with a common aim. It is the essential dynamic of hospitals and armies, aid groups and manufacturers, labor unions and social justice movements. To understand this power, and its role in this path factor, it can be helpful to look at shared intention unfolding with interpersonal contact at the level of corporate entities like churches and governments and at the level of one's culture. In all cases, overarching, episodic, and momentary mental directions are operating.

Perhaps we can better understand the potency of shared intention by looking at where there is alignment or nonalignment; whether the shared direction is explicit or implicit; and most crucially from an ethical perspective, whether the aim is wholesome or unwholesome. We'll begin with a look beneath the surface at what happens when two or more people work together, using the lens of Buddhist psychology, particularly becoming (*bhava*), or identification.

When people come together to do something, individual intention is already at work. Each participant is doing the action for a purpose, consciously or unconsciously. In taking up a task, the self identifies as the doer of that task. What helps the task helps me, what is antagonistic to the task is antagonistic to me, and the strength of this conflation directly tracks the strength of identification. In that moment, one feels "I am the task; the task is me."

When two or more people are engaged with each other, all of these aspects of intention are at play within each individual: the rolling forward of perception, desire, passion, and action. But the perceptions and desires are never a fixed thing; they rise and fall, like all mental and physical phenomena, and crucially, they are interacting with those of all of the other co-actors. So the "I" that would be established, protected, and satisfied by doing an action is now also a "we." Multiple individuals identifying with, for example, a work group or a sports team, are continually sending messages to each other, verbal and nonverbal, that not only coordinate action but also check on alignment of intention. The "we" is driven by the aggregate urges for pleasure and for the continued sense that we—our group, our family, our team—exist. This we is also blinded by collective ignorance regarding the impermanence and insubstantiality of its existence. In other words, the āsava, or intoxicants (also called the taints), are operating at scale. The couple, the family, the work group, the nation, "we white people," "we cisgendered men," function together unaware of the urges that may drive intentions of harm or harmlessness, accumulation or liberation.

The power of shared intention can incline towards the wholesome or the unwholesome. This means that collective practices of right intention are not only possible, but also essential if we are to skillfully redress the enormous harm done by actions born of wrong collective intentions: social, economic, and climate injustice, along with all the local harms born of group selfishness and cruelty. *How* we practice to positively shift overarching collective intentions is exactly what religions, national creeds, and other wholesome moral and social systems seek to address.

In addition to pointing power towards the good, practices of shared intention are a key to understanding how shared emotional motivation, perception, and action operate. During shared practices, mindfulness of wholesome intention will allow an accumulation of experiential data that reveals strengths and weaknesses and the details of cause and effect at the interpersonal and social scale. It will also inspire continued collective effort to abandon the unwholesome and cultivate the wholesome. Social movements rooted in mindfulness and wisdom are not easy to implement, but neither are they impossible. A whole-life path insists that we try—at whatever scale is available to us.

## Shared Intention and the Three Time Scales

This understanding of shared intention can be integrated into the three time scales. Overarching intentions for the larger collective entities are often referred to as values. There are stated values, like being a good world citizen, and tacit values, often associated with institutionalized greed, hatred, and delusion. Strategy and policy also relate to the overarching intention, or aim. Because overarching intentions that truly emerge from the collective take a while to form, they are not usually operating in the mercurial relationships of temporary smaller groups. Such groups function more from the tacit overlaps of shorter-term intentions.

Episodic intentions in a large entity are often called tactics or plans, and they are associated with projects, ventures, and programs. They are nested within the overarching intentions and cover a range of time scales, from single meetings to multiyear initiatives. The coherence of the "we" can vary greatly, but to some extent, each individual's sense of identity is joined with, and aimed by, the collective: an employee feels, "If Amazon does well, I do well."

Applying the notion of momentary intentions to that of shared intention is tricky. Can we say that even just two people doing something together are so tightly coupled that the instantaneous shifts of mind can be named as one tandem thing? And the question gets trickier as the groups get larger. A family, working team, or crowd at a rally may share common aims, but within the mind of each individual, to what extent is the uniting, or even merging, of thought reaching down to the level of rising and vanishing of consciousness? I don't know, but I think it will be helpful to recognize that mental activity is not monolithic; that is, a person in a crowd may at one moment have thoughts arising that are strongly linked with many others present, and in the very next moment they can be concerned about getting their very personal and private body to a toilet. A moment of collective hatred or love may be followed by a moment of individual desire (for comfort). From these complex layers, actions, group and personal, follow intentions, group and personal.

---

PRACTICE
**EXPLORING SHARED INTENTION**

Gather a group of people who work with you who are willing to engage in an honest exploration of collective motivation. Frankly acknowledge that the collective *self* of the organization is likely to resist the close scrutiny of this shared reflection.

Describe to your co-practitioners the classical wholesome and unwholesome intentions: sensual desire and relinquishment, which at the corporate level might be profit, and altruistic generosity; hatred and love, which might be framed as aggressive or defaming competition and professional goodwill; and harmfulness and harmlessness (sometimes named as cruelty and compassion), which might take collective form as callousness and proactive concern about causing harm (i.e., group conscience). Acknowledge that all of these inclinations are going to be present at different times and to varying degrees, whether your organization is a neighborhood food pantry or an accounting firm. Also keep in mind that this kind of reflection is, in and of itself, without further action, the beginning of an effective practice; action for change can come later, when there is sufficient motivation and clarity.

This reflection can be done in one or more formal group meetings, or participants could engage in an embedded reflection, taking notes throughout the workweek, then gathering to share and discuss what was found.

For closure, consider together how group and individual intentions are or are not in alignment, and ask what kinds of shifts in intention might positively impact the wellbeing of the group and its members. How might these shifts be brought about?

## ENGAGING THE POWER OF SHARED INTENTION: THREE GUIDING QUESTIONS

The dynamics of shared intention, in groups small and large, are complex, comprising both gross and subtle dynamics. But for the purposes of the whole-life path, they can be put simply: in the formation of this we, the power of each me is amplified. To ensure that we're engaging the power of shared intention with care, consider these three questions when approaching a shared intention.

**Is there alignment or nonalignment?** When the countless micro-messages—and identities—being exchanged during the process of shared work are in alignment, the energy for that work is amplified. At the simple level of the task, decisions about how to get something done are aiming the same direction and so contribute to that task. If you and I are forming a new business and your primary motivation is to contribute a needed service to a community, but my primary intention is to maximize profit, then our shared decisions, each representing these disparate intentions, will be hindered by that lack of alignment. On the other hand, if our minds are clearly focused in the same direction, we'll do our shared work with greater efficiency and happiness. The lining up of aim sharpens each individual's focus and the group's focus, increasing potency and reducing friction.

**Is the shared direction explicit or implicit?** One way of fostering alignment is to name the purpose clearly and for everyone in a group to agree on exactly why they're are doing what they're doing. Of course, such agreement is often not easily reached. The vagaries of language, differences of culture, and assumptions about context and best methods are among the countless factors that can throw us off.

Consider the case of two people meditating together in Insight Dialogue. Your intention is to see clearly how things actually are and so diminish suffering; my intention is to enjoy social contact. Your practice will incline towards inquiry and tranquility, while mine will incline towards identified storytelling and social stimulation. My lust for pleasure is unlikely to be satisfied by your mindful pauses; your inclination towards serenity is unlikely to be supported by my agitation. For both of us, useful practice is still possible, but the lack of alignment will dampen the focus and power of the practice. It is unlikely the practice will readily yield the insights and natural quality of compassion that emerge freely in co-meditation when intentions are aligned.

If a shared group direction is clearly named—by a meditation teacher or political leader—each participant in the group endeavor will be better able to ascertain when they are headed in different directions and so more likely to skillfully adjust their thoughts and behaviors. Explicit shared intention is thus more likely to be improved and refined. (Think of organizations developing ethics statements, sharing them with their constituents, developing those statements further, and implementing them transparently.) When intentions are implicitly shared, the felt sense of a common vision, a common direction, may be strong, but whether or not that vision is actually the same among participants is another matter. It is not so easy to craft something that is unnamed.

**Is the aim wholesome or unwholesome?** Given the power of shared intention, it matters whether or not what we are doing brings harm to oneself, others, or both. The Buddha pointed to the three unwholesome and three wholesome roots of all thoughts: greed, aversion, and delusion, and nongreed, nonaversion, and nondelusion.[46] When the intention is unwholesome, the dynamics that generate energy and focus are operating in service to thoughts and actions that bring harm to oneself and others. For example, the energy of shared intention is present for a few neighbors joined in an effort to prevent certain people from moving into their neighborhood. Aversion for the *other*, a greed-based desire to maintain property values, and delusion about the true causes and effects at work in that moment are all operating. Internally, each moment of mental contact builds on the next, sustained and amplified in the collective. And externally, bodily and mental harm take place as the growing mental energy generates wrong action.

Shared intention can have wholesome results if its roots are wholesome. Aid agencies work coherently to alleviate the suffering due to disaster, draught, or disease; environmental justice groups focus their minds on naming and alleviating the social impacts of climate change; two friends join together to study the Dhamma. Even with just two people talking, one's intention of nonharm and of the friendliness inherent in nonaversion helps the other to feel safe to speak the truth.[47] If you and I are gathered in both true friendliness and wisdom, the shared identity of the we may condition a moment of unbinding. The knot of the individual self can relax in the shared goodwill, and even the identity of a *we* may be released as mindfulness finds the stability and courage to remain with the selfless impermanence of all phenomena.

## INJECTING A WHOLESOME INTENTION
## INTO AN EXISTING TEAM PROCESS

An entire group's intention can be made explicit. You can experiment with this at work if the setting is conducive to such an exploration. The simple shared aspiration of a work group to do a good job—say, a software team's commitment to producing high-quality code—calls forth energy, concentration, perseverance, and dedication. Can this same commitment be infused with an ethical component, like honesty or kindness? Might your team be interested in finding out? If the shared quality commitment from the workplace can be melded with elements of service and compassion, you're all set with a practice of wholesome mental direction.

## Shared Intention as a Relational Factor of Awakening

We've seen that when two or more people get together to do something, and their minds are thoroughly aimed in the same direction, the results—wholesome or unwholesome—can be powerful. A synergy takes place whereby the strength and clarity of intent is mutually prompted and so continually sustained. Energy is evoked by the companionship of purpose. Joy is fostered by the vitality of that energy, as well as by the experience of alignment.

The power of shared intention on the path is so great that I offer it as one of the relational factors of awakening, along with the four brahmavihāras. It sets the conditions for the arising and amplification of compassion. At the same time, shared intention is a potent force for strengthening mindfulness, investigation, energy, and concentration—all of which set the conditions for liberating insight to arise. When the joy and energy are directed towards cultivating compassion and wise understanding, the results of the Eightfold Path can be experienced here and now. When we practice together, love yields love yields love. We support each other in the shared movement towards equanimity.

## THE FURTHERMOST REFINEMENT OF INTENTION

Intention as a practice of the Noble Eightfold Path is putting the strength and clarity of the mind towards release from entanglement. Right intention is part of the Path, not its exclusive goal. So we need to look at intention within the larger map of liberation. The breadth of the Dhamma, the breadth of the Buddha's mind, and the breadth of our potential includes a mode of living wherein even refined intentions no longer take hold.

In highly refined meditation practice, the Buddha pointed out, wrong intentions are excluded.[48] He also explained that wholesome intentions arise by the same mechanism as the unwholesome ones. Both kinds come from root tendencies and their associated perceptions. He then said that even wholesome intentions cease beginning in the second *jhāna*. The emotional energy is thoroughly, if temporarily, calmed.

This teaching points towards the more lasting cessation of karma-making that is associated with total unbinding. It can be helpful, even on our humble paths, to reflect on the qualities of a mind not bound and motivated by self-concept. The Buddha spoke of "nonfashioning" (*atammayatā*) with respect to rarified meditative attainments and associated such nonfashioning with integrity—with what he called "the true man," or true person. He said,

> By completely surmounting the base of neither-perception-nor-non-perception, a true (person) enters upon and abides in the cessation of perception and feeling. And their taints are destroyed

by their seeing with wisdom. This bhikkhu does not conceive anything, they do not conceive in regard to anything, they do not conceive in any way.[49]

That is to say, a person who has reached the goal not only does not concoct an identity or sense of superiority based on attainments, but they also do not concoct or construct anything, including intention. Such a person still acts in the world, but their actions emerge without reference to a self and so do not register in a self-centered archive of memory and personality. There is freedom *and* engagement.

The continued engagement with the world, as modeled by the Buddha, is an essential piece of a whole-life path. Just because one is beyond all self-making does not mean there is no wholesome action. On the contrary, actions born of mental activity that is devoid of the impulse to develop oneself, to be compassionate, or any other fashioning, become exceptionally clear and powerful. Such actions carry weight that words, even wise words of teachings, often lack. The Buddha exemplified this ultimate enactment of wisdom: compassion in action. The following story, drawn from the *Mahavaga*, provides an example of this.

Now at that time a certain monk was sick with dysentery. He lay fouled in his own urine & excrement. Then the Blessed One, on an inspection tour of the lodgings with Ven. Ananda as his attendant, went to that monk's dwelling and, on arrival, saw the monk lying fouled in his own urine & excrement. On seeing him, he went to the monk and said, "What is your sickness, monk?"

"I have dysentery, O Blessed One."

"But do you have an attendant?"

"No, O Blessed One."

"Then why don't the monks attend to you?"

"I don't do anything for the monks, lord, which is why they don't attend to me."

Then the Blessed One addressed Ven. Ananda: "Go fetch some water, Ananda. We will wash this monk."

"As you say, lord," Ven. Ananda replied, and he fetched some water. The Blessed One sprinkled water on the monk, and Ven. Ananda washed him off. Then—with the Blessed One taking the monk by the head, and Ven. Ananda taking him by the feet—they lifted him up and placed him on a bed.

Then the Blessed One, from this cause, because of this event, had the monks assembled and asked them: "Is there a sick monk in that dwelling over there?"

"Yes, O Blessed One, there is."

"And what is his sickness?"

"He has dysentery, O Blessed One."

"But does he have an attendant?"

"No, O Blessed One."

"Then why don't the monks attend to him?"

"He doesn't do anything for the monks, lord, which is why they don't attend to him."

"Monks, you have no mother, you have no father, who might tend to you. If you don't tend to one another, who then will tend to you? Whoever would tend to me, should tend to the sick."[50]

Reflecting on the Buddha's character, and on how a fully awakened person manifests in this hurting world, has been for many people, for more than two thousand years, a practice of right intention.

## ∼ REFLECTION

When we truly see how our personal experience of suffering is based upon the thirsting of the heart and mind, how such thirsts cannot ever be adequately and lastingly satisfied, and how happiness arises with the diminishing of such thirsts, our minds will naturally incline towards renunciation and kindness. When we see how selfishness brings pain and service to others arouses joy, the heart finds ease. Such seeing is right view, which naturally inclines the mind towards right intentions.

Clearly knowing our own, personal suffering inclines our hearts towards renunciation; letting go is the way out of suffering. And clearly understanding the truth of suffering in others' lives inclines our hearts towards noncruelty and harmlessness. Thus, the means of abandoning wrong intentions includes deeply discerning this shared human predicament. The path to cultivating wholesome intentions also includes discerning our shared human potential. Ever deeper love, ever clearer seeing, is possible.

This is the Buddha's root teaching on the role of wisdom, love, and compassion in our lives: wisdom is the force behind renunciation, love is the active manifestation of non–ill will and of fully receiving the world, and compassion is the active manifestation of noncruelty, the harmlessness born of unbounded relatedness. Notice that two of these three wise intentions are explicitly relational (as are their unwise counterparts). Ill will and cruelty, love and compassion, are cultivated towards other people, in the presence of other people, and often in cooperation with other people. A truly whole-life path is more than just an individual path.

As we work in personal and interpersonal practice, both formally and informally, we come to see more and more clearly how these things—cause and effect, thought and action, action and result—are related. This direct seeing of how things actually work—the origin of suffering and how it proliferates among us—and the inclinations that arise naturally from that direct seeing, are perhaps the ultimate practice of right intention. Such direct seeing is at once the culmination of practice and the fruit of practice. A heart well aimed yields a life well aimed. Nothing is left out.

~

# CHAPTER 6

# RIGHT SPEECH

## *Sammā Vācā*

You and I are in a karmic feedback loop. These words emerge from the tip of my conditioned moment. The archive of my life speaks. This mind indexes the conditioned source of every word and deed, trying to convey to you this thought about language and communication. In that it is wholesome and inclines towards wise understanding, it is right speech.

Through text, these words reach your eyes. From your eyes to your mind, the words form internally as you read. Language processing happens. The words become part of your life archive. And they're doing so right now, however it may feel. The words touch. From this moment and this archive arises the experience: "this is what he means." Contact. Mind-to-mind transmission has occurred, even if through the mysterious haze of our different backgrounds. Through writing, I am speaking to you; through reading, you are listening to me.

Because we are communicating across time and space via text, your feedback to me may be direct or indirect. You may choose to contact me by email, if I'm still alive. Or, more likely, your feedback comes to me through the social web we participate in together.

Regardless of the time and distance over which it forms, and the medium by which the words are exchanged, the communicative loop of listening and speaking forms a powerful karmic workshop. As we internally frame speech, and as we deliver it, we condition the mind. Speech is a tool of skillful understanding, but it is also part of the mechanism by which constructions and delusions are made. These things are created even while we are preparing our speech, deciding what to say. Then the choice to speak, the act of speaking, is an assent to and a reinforcement of the impulses and intentions that prompted it.

Once unleashed into the world, a communication act conditions the minds of others. It initiates cascading sequences of effects between speaker and listener(s) and may spread rapidly and broadly among other people. These effects can take a long time to work themselves out and can be as surprising as they are potent. Because what we speak influences our world—our relationships and the society we live in—the speech act returns to condition us yet again.

The karmic potency of the communicative act is present even if others are not present during the act of creation—as is the case with writing, painting, or video, for example. While the repercussions of asynchronous communication do not reverberate between sender and receiver(s) so powerfully as they do in a conversation or live encounter, those repercussions can keep cascading through society for a long time. The effects of some acts of communication, like the writing of religious texts, have reverberated for millennia and affected billions of human beings.

Given the potentially wide and lasting impact even a small, single act of communication can have, we can see why speech, one of many human actions, is important enough to merit its own path factor. We can also begin to see what makes right speech such a deep and subtle practice.

## RIGHT SPEECH AS A PATH FACTOR

With right speech, we come into the three path factors involving ethics (sīla): right speech, right action, and right livelihood. The sīla factors are the home territory of the interpersonal and social. Our words, actions, and means of livelihood are judged right or wrong, skillful or unskillful, wholesome or unwholesome, not only by how they affect us, but also by how they affect other people. To a considerable extent, their consequences for us can be estimated by how they affect others: if others are harmed by what we do, we will also suffer.

The suttas define right speech as the avoidance of wrong speech. Wrong speech is defined as speech that is false, divisive, abusive, or idle. Right speech is also defined positively as speech that is timely, true, gentle, beneficial, and spoken in true friendliness. These attributes apply to the full range of human communications, including live events such as public lectures or dramatic performances—communicative contexts known in the Buddha's time. The same attributes can be seen clearly in today's asynchronous communications and all forms of media. A letter, an email, a newspaper article, a novel, a website, a comment on a blog, or a book—each of these can be true or false, useful or idle, kind or abusive.

Nonverbal forms of communication can also convey truth or deception, be timely or intrusive, beneficial or damaging to those who receive them. And because communication involves both sending and receiving a message, considering the path factor of right speech must consider the acts of listening/receiving, in addition to the act of speaking. Therefore, in this book, the traditional designations for this path factor, *sammā vācā* or *right speech,* will frequently serve to name the whole, sometimes in alternation with *right communication* or *right expression.*

## THE KARMIC POWER OF SPEECH

To evaluate speech and other expressive acts in terms of their cause and their effect is to look at them through the lens of karma. The karmic significance of these actions and the weight of their fruits is due to volition (cetanā). Every volitional act—of mind, speech, or body—leaves a trace in us, one that is correlated with changes in our neural networks, cells, and hormones. In aggregate, these traces condition the body-mind going forward. Our present thoughts and actions condition how we will experience future life events. For example: does a speech act increase or decrease hatred? In this question, right speech and right effort come together: an increase of wholesome tendencies and a decrease of unwholesome ones is the work of right effort and essential to the whole Path.

The conditioning power of language operates internally and externally. Internal speech gives form and staying power to what might otherwise have been a passing emotion. Mental speech participates in an internal feedback loop: it stabilizes and shapes intention so that it can move outward into expression. Then the outward act of expression concretizes, prolongs, and potentiates the internal mental patterns so they continue to condition future intentions.

The external conditioning power of expression works interpersonally. I can direct and focus your attention, for example, by drawing your gaze towards a calming sunset or an exciting nightclub. Alternatively, I could guide you in the practice of compassion or in the deconstruction of the self by way of contemplating the aggregates. My words can incite hatred or action for social justice. Language can bind us together in collective selfishness or shared compassion. Words aim the mind.

This astonishing power to direct and focus attention is what gives the communicative act its potency. Whether we are influencing each other to try a certain food, conveying hatred and fear, or pointing the way to wisdom, communication involves a transmission of meaning from mind to mind. This transmission is often crude because words are not the things or experiences they point to. Each person brings to the elements of language different meanings, emotions, and memories. The conveyed meaning cannot be exact; there are countless unfixable gaps in our descriptions, metaphors, and similes. Despite such capriciousness, attention is still focused and directed, intention still transmitted and received.

In order for the power of language to manifest, spoken or written words must be heard. Listening is the action of hearing. It is the other half of the karmic loop activated in right speech; it completes the act. A request, idea, or emotion is not only offered, but it is also received. The act of listening draws out the act of speaking; it is speech's usual condition and its completion. Other forms of expression, too, are usually made with the intention that they will be received. Music is offered with the tacit expectation that it will be not only heard, but also listened to. Listening, in turn, shapes the expression: music for a different audience would elicit a different expression from the same musician. Artwork would be seen and looked at; architecture would be encountered and inhabited. In this bi-volitional touching of expression and reception, connection is made, the proclamation has impact.

Both the sensory processes of hearing and the conditioned mental processes of interpretation and understanding are at play here. When an expression is received, it may then become the basis for a reciprocal expression. The speaker and the listener may trade roles: the former listener offers something back. This can happen fully, in the case of a conversation, or in an unequal way, perhaps via applause, critics' reviews, comments posted on a blog. Even silence is a response. Reciprocal communication can escalate, building energy with each interpersonal iteration. This loop of communication can enhance wholesome, as well as unwholesome, inclinations.

While the act of speaking confirms and strengthens the internal intentions from which its impulse sprang, it is listening that enables those intentions to be launched out into the world, beyond our reach or control, where they may reverberate for a long, long time. In public contexts, intentions spread from one to many. Adolf Hitler excelled at focusing hatred. Mohandas Gandhi excelled at conveying the power of nonviolence. Jesus excelled at evoking love and compassion. The Buddha excelled at conveying wisdom. The consequences of their communicative acts are still cascading outward, conditioning the thoughts and circumstances of many.

Just as we can focus another's attention, we can distract each other with idle chatter or gossip. Mass media outlets provide us with ample means to distract ourselves, since the advertisers who fund much of that media have a financial stake in encouraging dissatisfaction, greed, and stimulus-seeking.

The effects of acts of communication merge with the effects of other acts of communication, reverberating in our family, social circles, or society at large, where the stream may be further modified by others' wholesome or unwholesome speech. This, too, is cause and effect—karma.

## THE PROCESS OF COMMUNICATION: ENTRY POINTS FOR PRACTICE

When the Buddha separated out speech as worthy of special attention on the Eightfold Path, he knew he was dealing with something with deep roots. He points out that speech is an outflow of the most primary process of perceiving the world.[51] Humans are a kind of animal, and human language can be considered a subset of animal communication, if a very particular and peculiar subset. In the animal world, most, but not all, communication is rudimentary—a growl, a squawk, a gesture, that says, "Keep away!" or "Approaching danger!" or "This is mine!" So far as we know, most animal communication is instinctive and automatic, not mindful, and the physical, animal roots of such communication still operate in us. Speech sometimes seems to just burst out of us automatically in response to provocation from the environment. Learning to see the origins of this automatic behavior and exert control over it is a necessary aspect of right communication. So too is applying mindfulness and care to receiving, or listening to, speech.

### The Emotional and Mental Genesis of Speech

We usually think of speech as voiced expression, but all speaking begins as an emotional urge. Something is felt to be lacking or to need adjustment. Sometimes the emotional origin of the urge towards language is obvious: anger at an injustice, joy at the arising of love, a chilly draft from an open window, a calculation that more supplies will be needed soon. The statements, "Please pass the salt," "Thanks for visiting today," "The self is a constructed notion," all begin not as language but as wordless feelings or apprehensions. All are spoken based on the energy of a felt motivation. Our entire sensitive being, responding to the complex world, is moved. This urge, motivation, or intention is pre-linguistic.

Called forth by these pre-linguistic intentions, words and constellations of words appear very quickly in the mind. Internal speech (and possibly gestures or other expressive action) ride the emotional urge to the cusp of external expression. Then this speech enters the world, carrying the thought and emotional urge with it.

The nun Dhammadinna, a disciple of the Buddha, gave a moment-by-moment reporting of the latter part of this quick process: "First one applies thought and sustains thought, and subsequently one breaks out into speech; that is why applied thought and sustained thought are the verbal formation."[52]

We don't usually apprehend this sequence. However, the meditating mind can become still enough to witness it. Wherever there are multiple steps to a process, there are multiple points at which we can be mindfully attentive. Impulses to harmful speech can be intercepted at several different stages in their development; similarly, beneficial speech can be recognized and approved at the same early stages, then launched with a clear conscience and a sense of joy.

## The Physical Processes of Speech

Becoming more aware of the physical processes involved in producing speech—both as spoken language and vocal sound—can help with the ability to monitor our speech.

The speech act itself is muscular—based upon tensions, controlled by tensions. We can trace the tension, or energy, from its onset. The thought from which words spring begins in the tension of the emotional urge to speak; it then unfolds in the movements of the body that make up the physical speech act. Muscular tension at the diaphragm, felt in the belly, speeds up exhalation to make a sound louder as more air is pushed out. A higher pitch is the result of more tension in the vocal cords.

These tensions, emotional and physical, are embossed upon the voice stream itself as a living, moving indicator of our bodily processes and mind states. Someone yelling has a very tight abdomen and usually tense facial muscles. Tension can be an indicator of suffering, such as when it is ratcheted up by anger or fear. It can also indicate joy, as the body tenses with glee or delight.

When we become more mindful of the physical nuances of speaking, that mindfulness can follow us into everyday speech. For example, a rise in the pitch of the voice often indicates mental stress, as does a rise in volume. If we are aware of the pitch and volume in our voice, maybe we will be able to notice rises in both and, thus alerted, interrupt an ill-chosen statement, or pause and take a deep breath, or change the course of a conversation. Or we may discover something about our tone of voice—perhaps some harshness we had not noticed.

Attention to the stresses and inflections in the voice can help us become better listeners, too. We learn to listen to the music of the voice, not only the words used. When we are more aware of these nuances in the voices of others, we take in their message more fully and perhaps we can also support them in calming the body-mind. We affect each other in verbal relationship, and so by supporting others' mindfulness and calm, we also support ourselves.

Applying mindfulness to the physical aspects of speech offers further potential: by attending to the body, we are attending to the stresses or urges that give rise to speech, and in this way, we gain a window into our inner lives.[53] We can observe the sometimes delicate somatic manifestations of wanting a discomfort removed, a desire gratified, an emotion expressed, or an idea seriously considered by another. If we quiet the mind, we will be able to observe the steps prior to speech, just as the nun Dhammadinna observed them. Where in the body is stress felt? What does the urge to express, explain, or request feel like?

## INVESTIGATING THE PHYSICAL ASPECTS OF SPEECH

Look around you and speak aloud a few of your observations. Make them simple: "I feel my body sitting" or "I see printed words." Stop reading now and try it. Physically, audibly speak.

As you speak, pay attention to the mouth and tongue. Notice their actions, but notice also their quickness and finely coordinated skill.

Note the delicate but immense change from silence to sound.

Notice your other bodily sensations while speaking. What are your diaphragm and abdominal muscles doing as you exhale and speak?

You might notice the tightening of the vocal folds (cords), which must be tense in order to vibrate, like two blades of grass held next to each other.

Change the pitch of your voice, making it higher and lower. What do you notice?

## Discerning Listening

In conversation, two sensitive beings are touching each other in two ways: physically by way of bare sound, and mentally by way of words. In Buddhist psychology, *contact* refers to the coming together of the "external base" (which is experienced as the object that is sensed), the "internal base" (which is experienced as the sensing organ), and consciousness. Mindfulness internally lets us observe both the flow of impressions made by thoughts and the bodily feelings that arise during listening. Being attentive to the world, we can notice the flow of impacts through the ear door. Then, for example, the sound of a waterfall, the functioning ear, and conscious registration co-arise to create the experience of hearing.

When what is heard is a person speaking, we have a special case of contact. The sound of speech touches the ear. As consciousness arises, words are perceived and recognized, and our conditioned ways of understanding these words are invoked. Meanings are gleaned and assembled, and the mind-to-mind transmission enabled by verbal communication takes place. Feelings may be hurt; lies may be believed. Verbal contact when listened to becomes mental and emotional contact, and it is powerful.

Moreover, when two or more humans are together, the communication is never only verbal. In face-to-face contact, the communication channel includes subtle facial and bodily movements, micro-changes in vocal tone and pacing, and perhaps unseen energetic exchanges. The sensitivity of mutual contact and power of feedback apply also to the mutual process of seeing and sometimes to touching.

In the very act of perceiving these things, the listener affects the speaker—that is, the character of the listening impacts what is actually said. Eager or dismissive listening can shape or limit what is expressed. Then changes in what is spoken further affect the listening, and a feedback loop is formed between speaker and listener. Speaker and listener, sender and receiver, may exchange roles again and again. The listener/receiver may also go on to re-send the message, or send a message about the message, to others. Inaccurate, inattentive listening makes it impossible to respond usefully or to retransmit accurately. A listener's commentary also influences others' reception of the message.

By the application of right effort and right mindfulness, the act of listening can change from one of automatic and recirculating reaction to a practice of sensitivity and discernment. The impact of listening can be positive, negative, or neutral. The intentions of listening may be wholesome or unwholesome. When there is sati—mindfulness—choices open up; we can withdraw attention from the unwholesome and give attention to the wholesome: Is there friendliness here or ill will? Clear understanding or pointless stimulation? Making these discernments of our listening is part of the path factor of right speech. It is another place where "the voice of another and wise attention" may meet, giving rise to wisdom.

## EXPRESSION, UNDERSTANDING, AND THE SENSE OF A SELF

Conditioned processes are operating whenever we filter, interpret, make sense of, and react to what is being expressed. No process is more deeply entrenched than that of positing, defending, and polishing a sense of self. Here are the Buddha's words on the self-making inherent in the perceptual process: "He perceives the heard as the heard. Having perceived the heard as the heard, he conceives [himself as] the heard, he conceives [himself] in the heard, he conceives [himself apart] from the heard, he conceives the heard to be 'mine,' he delights in the heard. Why is that? Because he has not fully understood it, I say."[54]

These same statements are repeated in this sutta about what is seen, what is sensed, and what is cognized. Together, these cover all imaginable modes of communication.

Any input that comes to us in these ways, whether from the natural, physical world or as communication from other beings, tends to be appropriated for the construction and refinement of a sense of self. This is true whether that sense of self arises in agreement or in disagreement with the expression perceived, arises as a self, flowing along immersed in the expression, or arises as a self with mastery over the expression. It is true whether an individual self or an aggregated social self is being described. It is true whether the expression triggers delight or aversion. Along with the sensory input and its interpretation, a sense of self arises, constructed on the basis of some relationship to what is perceived. Listening to you, I feel like "me." Reading this poetry, "my" emotions and images are evoked. Receiving this email, I feel "myself" reading, reacting, and responding. "I" am busy, "I" feel stress, so I read or listen in such a way as to reinforce my personal framework.

The problem is, the more we are absorbed in locating and defining a self in relation to the communication we are receiving, the less attention we have left over to actually receive and understand that communication or to be present with the communicator. As we know, pre-existing associations, pre-judgments, and prejudices are impediments to immediacy and accuracy in listening. So the "self-ing" process is at the root of suffering, isolation, and disregard for others, as well as the conflict between accepted ideas and new ideas. Self-making is habitually supported by how we listen, and looking carefully at the mind while we listen is a way to not only greater skill in communication, but also to untangling suffering's source.

Speaking, too, can host the fabrication of a fixed self-concept: as I speak, I feel like me; as I speak, I place myself into the world. When we speak, the self forms moment by moment around the act of expression; the externalizing of our ideas becomes a projection of the self. That is, my talking is a way I put myself into the world. One feels "I am my words." Criticize my words, and you criticize me. Admire my words, and you admire me—you help me feel happy and secure. Even when the mind's words are not spoken, internal "self-talk" is another major basis for one's construction of self and, hence, a key part of maintaining the conditions for suffering.

Other forms of expression also provide opportunities for a sense of self to be conceived: "This is the artwork I created. I have a certain style, traceable to my background and experiences, and so this style represents me." The selfing process is as much a problem for expression as it is for the reception of another's expression. This is especially clear in the arts. Artists will tell you that too much preoccupation with self can strangle the creative process. The more attention is directed toward defining and maintaining a self, including impressing others with one's personalized creation, the less attention is left over to express something true or fresh, beautiful or moving. The creation process becomes problematic, and the finished work can seem stilted or pompous. Others, accurately sensing the problem, may call the work "self-conscious" or "self-indulgent."

What supports greater immediacy of expression? How close can we get to pure, simple receptivity? We can observe the associations and small reactions around the processes of speaking and listening, expressing and receiving. This observation is a function of mindfulness and a practice of right view. With practice, we can notice and release habitual reactions while they are small, before they have interfered with our understanding or our expression. We begin to listen more cleanly and accurately as we begin to loosen our grip on habitual biases. Such intentional practices focus and purify the mind. Mindful listening and mindful expression can be cultivated intentionally through both formal and informal means. We can engage in supportive practices outside the communicative context, or practice speaking and listening directly, in real-time. Any practice that helps us bring greater mindfulness and wisdom to communication will improve both the quality of our receptivity and of our expression. This is right speech as a path factor.

When expression comes from a place of intimate contact with experience, or from resting in silence, or from a mind surrendered to the flow of awareness, then words, music, and art are simply allowed to emerge. One only connects the moment of experience with the expression. One connects the present moment to the camera shutter, to the tip of the brush, to the strings of the guitar. Can one make art from full presence? There may be grasping and clinging: snapping that perfect photo or making that elegant brush stroke or playing those clever notes; there may be the desire for it to be beautiful or "right." We may yearn to make something of lasting value, to stretch the moment of beauty and give it to others. Such grasping will impede pure contact. Yet, a moment later, grasping may be released, and the moment of expression is both a fulfilling act and an act rooted in wisdom and generosity. How direct, clear, and unattached can our expression be?

Through reflective practice, the selfing process usually triggered by communication can be engaged at a deep level. Here, the prospect of improving our communications with better expression and better understanding recedes, and we confront the problem of self-reification directly. Is it possible to set down the burden of fabricating and maintaining an illusory self? What would it be like to know the world and to experience sensory input without turning it into an occasion to polish up a personality? What would it be like to engage in communication with others without hijacking the experience to consolidate our own sense of self?

## EXPLORING SELFLESS EXPRESSION

Select a form of creative expression familiar to you. You needn't be highly proficient, but it is also fine if you are a professional. Set aside at least half an hour where no product is expected, where there is no one to perform for, nothing to be accomplished.

Place yourself in front of an unformed work—at the canvas, the piano, the loom. Notice how it feels to sit where you are, in relation to this means of expression. What is the relationship like with the blank page, the unplanted soil? Is there fear, eagerness, tenderness, awkwardness? When you consider striking a key or placing pen to paper, where does this "voice" come from? Is the body-mind saying something? Does that voice, that impulse, reach out through muscles to an action: a choice of color, a written word?

Stand tenderly at the cusp of inaction and action, aware and vulnerable. Explore loosening up the gateway between action and stillness—paint big, pound a chord, grab a fistful of clay—then drop back to stillness, noticing how awareness vibrates. Between delicacy and boldness, find the continuity of awareness—the place where noise does not interrupt silence, where action does not interrupt stillness. Is a moment of selfless expression possible? Is there the action of "speech" outside of desire? How does it feel to engage this way and to ask these questions?

## MODERATION, LIMITATION, AND SILENCE

As we have seen, the Buddha said that he simply would not speak the untrue, incorrect, and unbeneficial, and he would pay careful attention to the timing of speech that might be unwelcome and disagreeable. This process of discernment suggests an economy of speech—and the Buddha often modeled silence as a skillful response to inquiries and other invitations to engagement.

Even when we are communicating about wholesome topics, moderation is important. In a discourse in which the Buddha reviews principles for Ananda to present to new monks, he includes this advice: "Come, friends, do not talk much, put limits on your speech."[55]

In our unreserved culture, this is a radical suggestion. Without the intention to moderate ourselves, the ease with which humans move from thought into speech can lead to over-stimulation and harmful speech. A memorable Zen saying succinctly captures this problem: "Open mouth, already a mistake."

Traditional meditation retreats are conducted in silence for a reason: to help the mind to settle. Such a vacation from words includes refraining from reading or writing. Quiet environments nurture ease, tranquility, and silence in the mind. Silence is the language of tranquility and concentration, the null product of a calm mind. In the deepest calm of fully absorbed meditation, of the second jhāna and beyond, internal speech ceases entirely.[56]

Silence is the ground from which speech emerges. It is also the reference point for all our listening. Silence invisibly distinguishes one thought from another, demarcates the sentences in speech and the rhythms in music. It is an aspect of right speech to recognize the limitations of speech, to know when and how to let go of both external and internal speech. When speaking and silence coexist, we intuitively recognize this as a manifestation of freedom.

## A SUTTA-BASED EXPLORATION OF WRONG SPEECH AND RIGHT SPEECH

Having investigated so many facets of right communication, we now have sufficient background to approach the core of the traditional teachings on right speech and skillful listening and to appreciate their importance and the breadth of understanding upon which they rest. The discourses give some specific advice. How we understand and practice this guidance remains an open-ended inquiry; the whole-life path hides underneath the simple surfaces.

## Wrong Speech: The Interpersonal Feedback Loop Gone Awry

The Buddha's simplest framing of right speech refers to avoiding wrong speech: "What, bhikkhus, is right speech? Abstinence from false speech, abstinence from divisive speech, abstinence from harsh speech, abstinence from idle chatter: this is called right speech."[57] Seeing clearly the wrongness of wrong speech is a practice of right view, and this is a necessary support for right speech.

Since all of us have engaged in all of these forms of wrong speech, we can look at each of them and stay as experience-near as possible. These are teachings we don't want to keep at arm's length.

### False Speech

Can you get in touch with what it is like to lie or mislead? Can you recall how it feels? What are the motivations for false speech? Generally speaking, lying originates in the belief that there is something we must get or keep or avoid, at any and all costs—a dangerous attachment. False speech leads us into other wrong actions, too. The Buddha told his young son Rāhula, and repeated many times in his teaching, "When one is not ashamed to tell a deliberate lie, there is no evil, I say, that one would not do."[58]

One reason lying is such a potent force is that we identify with our assertions and with what we are protecting. My money, my job, my dignity are on the line. Underneath each of these is "my" life. Find my lie, and you find me—and that me is bad, unsafe, vulnerable. So I will do anything I can to avoid detection.

"There is no evil, I say, that one would not do"—this is a strong statement about the unwholesome and corrosive effects of lying. Perhaps you are familiar with the web it sets out. When we tell a falsehood—in spoken language, with a doctored photo, or in any other medium—we confuse the mind. We have to keep track of where we have lied and how; we cannot simply report what we know. Lies lead to cover-ups and other unskillful behavior. Instantly, lying creates a distance between others and ourselves. There is our interior scheming, there is a gap, and other people are "out there," a living threat. The self we have built tenses up. Lies are most convincing when we (sort of) believe them, but this is playing with fire in terms of our own ability to discern the truth. We lose simplicity. Right view and right intention become less accessible. We cannot trust ourselves; we find little peace.

You may have a good handle on avoiding outright lying, but false communication is not limited to the direct depiction of an untruth in any medium. Lying by omission is one of the most common forms of deceits, especially in the marketplace. Also, remaining silent can discredit another's true report, leave someone feeling unsupported or betrayed, which, in a court of law, could have life or death consequences.[59] Not speaking the truth perpetuates and increases the tangle of the world.

As participants in multiple, nested human systems, our deceits and acceptance of other people's deceits can be cancerous. The recipients of our lies may stop trusting us, even when we tell the truth. Or if they believe us, they may come to distrust all others or to distrust themselves and their own experience. Witnessing our lies, others may feel that lying is necessary to protect their interests too. And hearing but not speaking out about the lies of others—be they our friends, our colleagues, our journalists, our politicians, our business leaders, our leaders in any realm—we may feel compelled to protect ourselves by silence and deceit. Dishonesty and mistrust thus become contagious, infecting a family, a community, or larger group. When false speech becomes pandemic, our minds are easily polluted, and everyone faces a complex, unreliable, and confusing world.

### Divisive Speech

Like false speech, words we believe to be true, but that are divisive, always have a self-serving purpose. We can value our relationships and still fall into identification and the divisions it creates. Perhaps, like me, you feel closely aligned with a wisdom tradition. Are there, therefore, insiders and outsiders? People who got it right and those who are misled and confused? Have you ever spoken in such a way that contributes to divisions among people, perhaps without recognizing the effects of your words?

Divisive speech can also be intentional and malicious. It may undermine another's reputation, arouse suspicion about a group or family member, or contribute to polarizing views on social issues. Racial hatred, class competition and distrust, and divisions associated with sexual orientation inflame the mind. Activated by anger, identity protection, and fear, epithets that are designed to separate groups from each other, and distance ourselves from those not like us, push us towards in-kind divisive responses. Segmented or secretive decision-making by subgroups in a community is also divisive. Divisive speech is a favorite of politicians and is frequently delivered by the media to excite their readers or viewers. There are some highly paid professionals who specialize in this kind of wrong speech.

Divisive speech is sometimes simply an expression of ill will—a mean desire to mess up others' happiness or stability. Other times there may be ulterior motives—an expectation that there is something to be gained by causing dissent. I suspect most of us have felt the motivations behind the saying, "The friend of my enemy is my enemy; the enemy of my friend is my enemy." Words are slung in service of our warfare. Whatever petty gain there may be, the price of divisive speech is enormous. Sometimes, divisive words spring from the preverbal emotional stew, defending and attacking happening before we even know it. In any case, we will have harmed the network of relationships around us.

Negative feedback loops can spread through a society like brushfire. Divisive speech can radiate outward through hate groups and even churches and governments, as social structures are formed that are extensions of our internal mental formations. The fabric of a society can sustain divisive thought with further divisive speech, laws, and institutions. These, in turn, reflect back to condition us;

each individual heart is turned towards enmity by news media, educational systems, and laws. This is entanglement. This is being bound, fettered. This is our petty and even tragic warfare. This is suffering at all layers of the human system. Such is the power of divisive speech.

## Harsh Speech

Do you ever swear? Yell at someone in frustration or anger? How does it feel? Can you connect with the bodily tensions associated with the act of yelling or screaming? Can you recall the mental anguish of the racing, hurting mind as an emotional outburst blossoms as harsh speech? This kind of speech includes rough expression that drags the mind across the gravel of crudeness and ugliness. Harsh speech hurts. It hurts us and those around us. It is a sophisticated version of an animal's grunt or howl. Harsh speech can amplify hatred as it transmits it from one person to another.

Defining harsh speech is not as simple as making a vocabulary list or setting up a decibel meter near our mouths. Different cultures and languages have built-in expectations around freedom of emotional expression and directness of statements. The use of vivid or startling imagery may be a valid artistic choice. Obscenity may be used in a friendly way.

The harshness of a communication is assessed first by how it feels to us mentally and physically. Harshness is emotionally and physically noisy, and our finer capacities of speaking and listening get lost in or suppressed by the din.

Harshness must also be assessed by its outcomes, both between people and inside the mind. Unintended disrespect may be a result, or we may present to others as crude, stupid, or mean. As part of the karmic net, harsh speech may embarrass or silence those whom it targets—even if the speaker is (or claims to be) unconscious of any such intention. People may avoid us if we use harsh speech, or they may be provoked to anger, agitation, or harsh responses.

In some groups and subcultures, stereotyping or ridiculing humor—often along gender, sexual, ethnic, or racial lines—is used unreflectively, almost unconsciously. Insulting communication, adopted as a joke, may become habitual, reinforcing conditioning. Such "humor," just like profanity, yelling, and coarse images, callous the mind, desensitizing it to experience, disabling the nuanced use of language, and fostering agitation. Harsh speech makes stillness more difficult to access and fine distinctions harder to see; unquiet, we cannot discern what is wholesome. We have polluted the outside and the inside.

### Idle Chatter

Idle chatter is speech that offers no benefit but passes precious time and fills up the silence. In our world, idle chatter includes the idle engagement in social media. We know that speech comes out of an emotional urge of some sort. What is the urge behind idle speech? Are we trying to escape from a feeling of emptiness that is revealed in silence? Are we seeking to affirm the self that is temporarily weakened by the absence of anger or lust?

Idle chatter is entertaining; in its bland, time-filling way, it feels superficially good. Try imagining the Buddha's list of conversation topics unsuitable for male monastics as the section headings of your favorite website:

> (T)alk about kings, thieves, and ministers of state; talk about armies, perils, and wars; talk about food, drink, garments, and beds; talk about garlands and scents; talk about relatives, vehicles, villages, towns, cities, and countries; talk about women and talk about heroes; street talk and talk by the well; talk about the departed; miscellaneous talk; speculation about the world and the sea; talk about becoming this or that.[60]

Neither monastics nor lay people need to avoid these subjects absolutely. Accurate knowledge in some of these areas may be necessary to guide right action and right livelihood. Sometimes, social responsibility calls us to be informed about things that may seem rough or unnecessary but that sustain injustice. And talk on such topics can be a skillful way to signal concern, friendliness, and goodwill—sometimes the only way available. Entertainment, politics, and sports are social glue. But it is sobering to consider their potential to waste time and dissipate attention. Can we tell the difference between purposeful and idle engagement with these topics?

Idle expression and aimless media involvement spring from habit and from a sense of disempowerment or purposelessness—a sense encouraged and exploited by the market economy. Conversations that follow society's rivulets of trivia are fed by a media river that is sustained by advertisements and inculcations of consumerist values. When indulged, these activities reinforce distractibility and restlessness. We are sensitive beings, and whenever intentions of greed, ill will, and cruelty are expressed—by spoken or printed word, brushstroke or pixel, gesture or silence—the act of expression, engaged even idly, strengthens those intentions in the mind.

Speaking is a social act, so idle chatter impacts not only us, but also others. What if someone is listening deeply to you, their minds moving with your every word, while you chatter away pointlessly? To waste our time in idle chatter is usually to waste the time of the listener as well. And a focus on unessential things keeps conversations from going deeper. Such communications launch complex chains of consequences into the interpersonal and social contexts—some returning to affect our lives, others extending outwards to merge with the consequences of other actions. We find ourselves inhabiting a social world that is shallow, pointless. The here-and-now quality of the path to untangling is blurred, along with everything else.

PRACTICE
## CONTEMPLATING OUR CONVERSATIONS

Get together with a trusted friend to contemplate the kinds of conversations, including emails, you've engaged in the past week. Speak and listen to each other, guiding your exploration with whatever Dhamma framework feels most poignant right now: greed/hatred/delusion, divisive/harsh/idle speech, speaking and listening productive of the hindrances of lust/anger/laziness/agitation and worry/doubt.

You could also review your week's conversations through a lens of love, generosity, perseverance, truth, and compassion, or according to whether it leads to dispassion or passion, modesty or self-aggrandizement, to being burdensome or unburdensome.

Some balance of humor and horror, bemusement and concern, will serve you. When you've done this review, reflect together on the quality of your practice of right speech.

---

## Right Speech: Wholesome and Constructive Communication

Wise expression is not just about avoiding unwise expression. With mindfulness and effort, guided by right view, we can engage in communication that is truly right—communication that cultivates what is good and helps ourselves and others along the path towards freedom. Fortunately, the Buddha gave some explicit guidance about right speech:

> Mendicants, speech that has five factors is well spoken, not poorly spoken. It's blameless and is not criticized by sensible people.
> What five? It is speech that is timely, true, gentle, beneficial, and spoken in *true friendliness*.

### Timely Speech

In these five qualities of speech, the Buddha encouraged us to give attention to not only what we say and how we say it, but also to when we speak. Have you ever said what you felt was the right thing, but said it at the wrong time? Apparently, this is an old and well-known problem. The Buddha once described all the permutations of speech that is true or untrue, correct or incorrect, beneficial or unbeneficial, and welcome and agreeable or unwelcome and disagreeable. He said that he would not, under any circumstances, utter untrue, incorrect, or unbeneficial speech. But when he uttered true, correct, and beneficial speech, whether it was unwelcome and disagreeable or welcome and agreeable, the timing of that speech would be essential.[61]

Good timing is about how a communication will be received. Unfavorable feedback needs careful timing and delivery, but the same is true of praise. Words of praise that might support their recipient on one occasion might, on a different occasion, encourage self-inflation. We cannot know or control how our words will be received, but when we pay attention and do our best, our guesses improve in accuracy. Timing also affects the mind, possibly giving us the interval needed to skillfully aim our intentions, and thus the words, with care.

Timely speech sees the opportunity in a situation. That opportunity may be the "teachable moment" when the other is receptive, or it may be a chance to deepen conversation, turning from superficial "worldly" things to topics that support the arising of right view.

## True Speech

Truth gives us stable ground upon which to stand. The mind can rest in ease, drawing on mindfulness to speak rather than scheming and squirming. This is "telling the seen as it is seen; telling the heard as it is heard; telling the sensed as it is sensed; telling the cognized as it is cognized."[62]

This truth is necessarily subjective: it is what we have seen, heard, and thought; it is the truth of things *as we experienced them*. We can try to say how things are "out there in the real world that everyone experiences the same way," but the mind always makes sense of the world through perception and the lens of conditioning born of prior experiences. Something closer to seeing and saying things as they actually are becomes possible with mindfulness. With present-moment attention to the world, we will see more clearly what is around us. If mindfulness continues even as we are speaking, the movement from initial mental impulse into language will lead to a more accurate foundation for our subjective response. To speak this subjective truth, we must know it, and the only way to know the subjective truth is by mindful introspection. Inevitably, what we speak will be understood differently by the other, interpreted through the filter of their different background. But the subjective truth is the best we have to offer, and offering it is an act of generosity.

## Gentle Speech

Smooth and respectful, gentle speech is about more than a pleasant aesthetic experience for the listener. Now that we know silence is the birthplace of all speech, we see that gentleness in the voice and mannerisms hovers closer to this quiet ground. The speaker's body reflects the gentleness in being relaxed. The message, regardless of the words spoken, conveys safety, adaptability, and peacefulness.

The actual auditory qualities that define "gentle" will vary with culture and ethnicity: some cultures are generally more animated, others reserved. This teaching invites us to speak gently in ways appropriate to the social context: we are sensitive to the perspectives, backgrounds, and needs of the people we are addressing. We also remain attentive to our own authenticity; our speech is not theater, but a moment of true human contact. Even now, I am trying to speak to you with speech that is gentle enough that I can say what is not always easy to hear but that you will still be drawn to understand. Such speech invites us to attend to the meaning rather than being preoccupied with protecting ourselves. This is especially important when the point is new, challenging, or prophetic. Hard words about a perceived injustice may provoke violent response rather than wholesome change. If there is a difficult or unwelcome point to make, gentle speech does not make it more difficult to hear by expressing it harshly. On the other hand, words spoken in a kindly way help make a difficult message easier to receive. The impact on our mind, as well as on the mind of our listener, will correspond with these qualities.

## Purposeful or Beneficial Speech

This kind of speech stands in contrast to both idle chatter and divisive speech. It brings us to the heart of wholesome engagement with each other. Talk should support shedding rather than accumulating, modesty rather than self-aggrandizement, being unfettered rather than fettered. Purposeful, deliberate speech helps the mind focus on good intentions. It aims the karmic potency of our communication towards the wholesome. It increases ease and concentration. It helps the mind release attachments.

Beneficial speech is also harmonious, unifying, reconciling—benefiting groups and relationships, as well as individuals. It is healing and liberative for society. Words well used have power. Through our speaking and listening with local friends and associates, we can establish relationships that are awake to the distress of the social groups in which we participate. Our families and work groups, our Dharma and church groups, our social and environmental action groups, can be influenced by our individual and collective speech. The power of language radiates out through word-of-mouth and public media, so society as a whole is impacted by the voices of these groups. When there is harm intended, as with speech that is divisive and harsh, that harm is amplified. When the speech is beneficial, its wholesome effects move through the social system.

There are challenges here, though. Whether it is shared by big groups addressing big problems and seeking big effects, or individuals seeking harmony in their relationships, even well-intended speech can bump up against the limits of our wisdom. For example, sometimes it is necessary to address a problem having to do with another's behavior. The Buddha proposed a high standard: that we refrain from criticizing others until we have attained impeccability of heart, character, and learning.[63] (Jesus's version was, "Let the one who is without sin cast the first stone.") We may choose not to criticize at all, but to begin a dialogue that seeks solutions.

We cannot be certain that our speech will prove useful to the other. Beneficial speech is a deceptively deep and challenging practice that calls for interpersonal sensitivity and organizational intelligence, sometimes of a very high order. How will certain words impact the minds of listeners? What are the listeners' life circumstances, capacities for understanding, and current receptivity? Which words will express truth with enough sensitivity to be heard? It is daunting to even consider the difficulty of these questions about beneficial speech. We cannot know the right answers. However, we can pause, consider our choices, direct the mind carefully, and speak as skillfully and sensitively as we are able. We cannot know, but we can offer our best. Wisdom, compassion, and attunement grow from such attempts; beneficial expression becomes more frequent. This is the practice, the learning process, of right speech.

Beneficial speech has a broader sense, too. What shall we talk about when we do speak? What topics are beneficial by supporting the healthy development of the mind? The Buddha gave this guidance: "When you talk, bhikkhus, you should talk about: 'This is suffering'; you should talk about: 'this is the origin of suffering'; you should talk about: 'this is the cessation of suffering'; you should talk about: 'this is the way leading to the cessation of suffering.'"[64]

These are, of course, the Four Noble Truths. The Buddha here prescribes discussing them with concrete specificity and in relation to life as actually lived. In actual life, suffering includes the large patterns of suffering born of unjust and unkind social structures. The first Noble Truth, together with right speech, is saying, "Look at, turn towards and name this suffering when you speak." There is benefit in naming the suffering within you, in your relationships, and in society. We are also invited to name the cessation of such suffering, which will include not only individual reflection, but also collective reflection and wise action.

In a whole-life, always-on path, purposeful or beneficial speech is a tall order. Contemplations of such truths as suffering, hunger, release, and the Path also include subtle practice in Insight Dialogue, where the rising and vanishing of interpersonal contact draws us close to the root of grasping and its release. This is speech as a practice of right view. But the Buddha's advice on right speech is not restricted to any formal interpersonal practice: He says, in effect,

"This is what your talk should be about—all the time, not just in special practice sessions." This is a stiff challenge!

In another discourse, the Buddha suggested ten topics for conversation:

(T)he talk in which a monk engages should befit an austere life and be helpful to mental clarity; that is to say, it should be talk on fewness of wishes, on contentment, on solitude, on seclusion, on application of energy, on virtue, concentration, wisdom, liberation, and on the knowledge and vision of liberation. If a monk finds opportunities for such talk easily and without difficulty, this is the third thing that makes the immature mind mature for liberation.[65]

Notice the extent of this claim. These topics are not merely harmless or tending to create harmony. They are reminiscent of the discernment criterion recommended for right view and our ongoing assessment of the whole-life path. The same list of topics appears in another sutta, where the Buddha said, "If . . . you were to engage in discussion on any of these ten topics, your splendor might surpass even the splendor of the sun and moon, as powerful and mighty as they are."[66] Something important happens within and among people who discuss such things. The impact of a careful choice of topics, too, is the working of the interpersonal and social feedback loops and one aspect of the working of karma.

The social benefits of purposeful speech can extend far beyond our immediate circles. Even as the Buddha extols speaking about contentment and relinquishment, he is also advising us to speak about virtue and liberation. He advises us to say things as they actually are; in this world of relative truths of pain and injustice, the Buddha is calling us to nothing less than prophetic speech. This presents a challenge. We are being called to speak aloud what we believe to be true and useful—even though what we have to say may upset others. Can we express our insightful and compassionate response to this hurting world in a clear statement of a difficult truth? Most people can recall situations in which there was an opportunity to speak a difficult truth to a friend or co-worker. What about speaking the truth to someone in power, or to a wide audience, where responses may be unpredictable? This is not an easy thing to do. At the same time, can we express the kindness of our motivation *and* skillfully time our message? Can we discern when there is benefit and when not? Answering these questions are all aspects of the practice of purposeful or beneficial speech.

## SKILLFUL LISTENING: ATTUNED, COMPASSIONATE, TOLERANT

Just as speaking the truth is not always easy, sometimes it is also not easy to hear the truth. How we listen and how we respond to what is difficult to hear is an important practice of right speech. It becomes more difficult, and maturity becomes more necessary, when what we hear is untrue or spoken with hatred, harshness, and divisiveness. Vicious verbal attacks are part of this life. This is wise listening as the mirror image of wise speech.

In a key discourse, the Simile of the Saw, that is famous in Buddhist countries for its fundamental moral guidance and strong similes, the Buddha offers guidance that reflects the reciprocity of speaking and listening practice.[67] He says, in short, don't speak in these unskillful ways, and if someone speaks to you in these ways, here is how you should respond:

> There are, monks, these five ways of speaking in which others when speaking to you might speak: At a right time or at a wrong time; according to fact or not according to fact; gently or harshly; on what is connected with the goal or on what is not connected with the goal; with a mind of friendliness or full of hatred. . . . Herein, monks, you should train yourselves thus:
>
> "Neither will our minds become perverted nor will we utter an evil speech, but kindly and compassionate will we dwell, with a mind of friendliness, void of hatred; and we will dwell having suffused that person with a mind of friendliness; and, beginning

with him, we will dwell having suffused the whole world
with a mind of friendliness that is far-reaching, widespread,
immeasurable, without enmity, without malevolence."
This is how you must train yourselves, monks.

This teaching on listening urges us to dwell in kindness, without hatred. It is a teaching on listening with a mind of friendliness towards not only the speaker, but also spread far and wide. With this instruction, each relational contact points to our capacity for a boundless mind. The teaching does not stop there. It concludes, "[A]s low-down thieves might carve one limb from limb with a double-handled saw, yet even then whoever sets his mind at enmity, he, for this reason, is not a doer of my teaching."

This call to nonviolence, to tolerance, is redolent of the work of Desmond Tutu, Martin Luther King Jr., and other modern visionaries who linked the development of the mind to the liberation of a people. Whether the challenges and slights are large or small, whether they emerge in our personal relationships or society at large, hearing these threats and insults is a call to tolerance, a reminder of our capacity for boundless compassion. Again we notice that right communication is linked with right action in this whole-life path.

PRACTICE
## SAMMĀ VĀCĀ AND THE GOLDEN RULE

Speech spoken with a mind of true friendliness, mettā, is also right speech. The shorthand guidance for harmonious speech, as for all the ethical factors of the path, is the so-called golden rule: do (and speak) to others in the same way you want them to do (and speak) to you.

The Buddha's advice suggests two subtle types of empathy: internal and external. The first is to know one's own mind well enough to discern what would upset oneself and to formulate an act of speech based upon that knowledge. The second is to reflect on what one knows of another's different mind state, circumstances, and conditioning and to project how one's speech might be pleasing or displeasing to that other based upon these things. Will these words harm myself, others, or both? Will they bring benefit?[68]

You are invited to commit to just one day of practice where every time you speak, you pause to consider how the words you are about to say would impact you and how they would impact the person you're about to speak them to. Just one day, but every utterance. Afterwards, reflect on this experience with a spiritual friend.

## RIGHT SPEECH REINFORCES RIGHT VIEW AND RIGHT INTENTION

When speech is timely, true, gentle, helpful, and spoken with a mind of mettā, it has a powerful effect on the mind of the speaker. The choice to speak in a certain way and the act of speaking in that way both reinforce the mind states from which they arise. As we try to gauge the timing of our speech, the sensitivity necessary for well-timed speech is trained and developed. The care necessary to speak the truth sharpens our ability to discern the truth as well as the ability to put it into words. Gentle speech focuses the speaker's mind on gentleness. Purposeful and beneficial speech engages the mind actively with what is important in life. And speech spoken in friendliness reinforces friendliness, making it broader, more durable—an active, in-life engagement of the path of awakening.

Speaking in these ways has powerful effects on the listener, too. Such speech is agreeable. Because mirroring is an innate human behavior, listeners will tend to reflect back the qualities with which they are addressed. Just as it is possible to create a vicious circle in which unwholesome tendencies are mutually reinforced, it is also possible to create a virtuous cycle in which wholesome behaviors are mutually reinforced. Truth and gentleness, sensitivity to others' changing capacities, a sincere desire for their good, and the willingness to speak up when helpful can contribute to the good of a family or organization or society. These acts establish a virtuous cycle, propelling those who are part of it into increasingly skillful and wholesome modes of communication.

## 〜 REFLECTION

Like walking, speech is a complex, dynamic process that can easily become automatic, but need not. It can be at once spontaneous and fully aware. This is also true for other forms of communication. As we have seen, it is necessary to bring mindfulness into our communication in order to avoid wrong speech—that is, expression that harms others and harms ourselves. But the very act of bringing mindfulness reframes communication as a subject or field for meditative practice. Speech itself, along with other forms of communication, can be the locus of interpersonal practice and wider social engagement.

Sound spiritual teaching, when rightly offered and rightly received, is perhaps the height of generous communication as a formal interpersonal practice. In response to one of the Buddha's teachings, Vangisa spoke these words:

> Truth indeed, is deathless speech—
> this is the ancient Dharma.
> On truth, its study and practice both,
> they say are the Peaceful firm.
> Whatever words the Buddha speaks,
> Nirvāṇa's safety to attain,
> bringing dukkha to an end,
> such words they are the worthiest.[69]

In some spiritual traditions, one seeks to "understand the mind of the master." This implies an uncommon quality of communication. The Buddha was so well established in calm and insight that he lived in the full fluidity of the moment. The wisdom of his words was simply a reflection of this enlightened perspective. He did not have to figure things out; he simply saw things clearly and gave language to what he saw. His words reverberate to this day.

Verbal expression is a crucial part of both understanding and the transmission of understanding. This principle is reflected in the Buddha's teaching: "There are two conditions for the arising of right view: the voice of another and wise attention." Whenever we speak and express wisely, whenever we listen and attend wisely, we nurture in ourselves and in others the capacity to see things as they actually are. We also participate in forming, then and there, here and now, a culture of compassion. The enormous power of wise expression radiates out to form and hold together the wise and just society. This is the natural outcome of such communication. We begin in a small way, by learning to speak with kindness, human to human, as best we can.

CHAPTER 7

~

# RIGHT ACTION

## *Sammā Kammanta*

T he path factor of right action offers us a simple but exquisite challenge. It encompasses every action we take and invites us to ask, does a particular action lead to an increase in the wholesome and a decrease in the unwholesome? Does this action lead to the welfare of myself, others, or both? In speaking of the welfare of others at the same time he spoke of one's own welfare, the Buddha was clearly aiming this path factor at both personal liberation and human flourishing. So it also invites us to ask whether right action applies only to our personal path or must extend to our relationships and to our social influence and impact.

The Buddha chose to give a lean definition of human decency to laypeople and a far more elaborate set of rules to the monks and nuns. This choice makes a lot of sense. We laypeople have such complex lives, dealing as we do with sex, money, power, and the intricate projects dreamed up by our culture. Nonharming—specifically, not killing, stealing, or engaging unwisely with sex and intoxicants—sets a baseline. From there, it's up to us to discern for ourselves how to abstain from these harms in various domains of our lives. It's also up to us to address this urgent question: how do the principles of right action and nonharming require us to respond when we see others harmed by our society? Because, as we'll see, individual, interpersonal, and social action and effect are inextricably connected.

## UNDERSTANDING RIGHT ACTION

The defining principle of right action, and of sīla generally, is the evaluation of actions in terms of their clearly visible effects. It is not about applying some arbitrary moralism. The ethical question is always, do the effects of this action work towards the full spectrum of my wellbeing and that of others, or against it? Many effects are obvious, while others are subtle; some are evident immediately, while others take time to mature.

Actions are relevant to individual suffering because actions condition the mind, and they condition the world that conditions the mind. Actions of all kinds condition the mind by means of the intentions they realize and the mind states they reinforce. This direct conditioning happens with every action of mind and body. Drinking a couple of beers with friends, swatting an insect, making provocative gestures—even little actions bear fruit. All thoughts, images, and emotions bring up associated thoughts, images, and emotions, and numerous internal body-mind feedback loops are set in motion. With repetition, these little actions build neuronal pathways in our brains and trigger biochemical shifts in our bodies. These physical changes, in turn, form a substrate that reinforces our default way of being in the world.

Right action is relevant to interpersonal and social suffering because human systems are held in place and motivated by concrete actions as well as the mental tendencies that underlie how we relate to one another. Actions become part of feedback loops involving other people, society in general, and the physics and biology of the natural world around us. Their consequences then come back to us as external circumstances, which condition the mind indirectly.

The breadth of this teaching is suggested by the etymology of the word for action: *kammanta*. *Kammanta* comes from the same root as *kamma*, or karma; the simplest and probably oldest meaning of kamma is "action." Actions, especially those involving full and informed consent, create results in the mind and in the world: *kamma vipāka*, the fruits of karma.

We cannot distance ourselves from our actions and their fruits. "I am the owner of my actions, heir of my actions, actions are the womb (from which I have sprung)," says the Buddha. "Actions are my relations, actions are my protection. Whatever actions I do, good or bad, of these I shall become the heir."[70]

---

PRACTICE
### LIFE IS ACTIONS MADE VISIBLE

Get together with a trusted friend and set aside a couple of hours to reflect on the most notable features of your life, such as important relationships, key accomplishments and disappointments, professional landmarks, where and how you have lived, things you have made, and memorable experiences of pleasure and of helping others.

Begin with one of you speaking for ten minutes while the other listens. Talk about whatever notable features arise in your awareness. Then consider, how does this particular action live in your life, in your heart, now? Can you recall the action itself as a bodily experience? Do those patterns still feel alive for you, and do they manifest in similar actions in your life now?

After you have each shared for ten minutes, open your practice to fluid interaction, each of you speaking as moved. What other actions do you recall? How do they live now in your life?

As you share more recollections, do the separate actions merge into patterns of character, of lifestyle, of present involvements? In what ways does the tone of your life reflect the sum of your actions?

Close your reflection with at least five minutes of silence. Then express whatever gratitude you may feel for your partner in this exploration.

---

## Right Action as Abstaining

In one of its aspects, right action is a matter of avoiding wrong action. "And what is right action?" asks the Buddha. "Abstaining from killing, abstaining from stealing, abstaining from sexual misconduct. This is called right action."[71] This teaching lists three of the five basic precepts the Buddha gave to all laypeople. In addition, the fifth precept, to avoid using alcohol or drugs that cause heedlessness, points to a broader approach to right action: actions that prevent wrong actions and support right actions can themselves be seen as right action. These actions include choosing to avoid doing anything that induces heedlessness in us (including, but not limited to, indulging in intoxicating substances) and choosing to do things that increase mindfulness and goodwill.

There are good reasons that the classical definition of right action is rooted in the negative definition of abstaining from harm. Lust and the desire for sensual pleasures easily push humans toward harm. The self's hunger to exist and grow manifests in biases, a thirst for power, and utter selfishness. Killing, stealing, lying, and sexual misconduct all stem from minds obsessed with selfish concerns.

When our friendships and our culture normalize and support these urges, the power of our aggregated action often creates big harm. Driven by these urges, humans have created societies focused on amassing power and wealth. They have developed the capacity to destroy themselves, decimate the planet, and make everyday life miserable for many while a very few enjoy vast privileges. They have empowered dictatorships, exacerbated naturally emergent tribal divisions, and, by supporting enormous corporate entities, facilitated transnational coordination that has led to much harm.

When we recognize the enormous pressures created by greed and hatred writ large, we understand why right action of nonharming, when practiced on not only a personal level but also relational and societal levels, is important. It counteracts the behaviors that lead to unbridled individual and social greed, hatred, and delusion.

## Right Action in Relation to Other Path Factors

All of the path factors dealing with morality—right speech, action, and livelihood—are actions in a broad sense. All are performed bodily, all involve the mind's assent as part of their definition, and all produce powerful consequences in the mind. All of them also involve other people, and all have worldly consequences.

The Buddha's holistic understanding of right action includes the inner actions of thought, the movement into speech, and the actions of the body. He spoke often about actions of body, speech, and mind. These three elements of the ethical path are the very definition of sīla; they are interwoven to sustain a life that is caring, just, and nonclinging.

From a whole-life perspective, then, right action is very broad. All of life is patterns of action covered by right action.

As a *practice,* right action is imbued with right view, right effort, and right mindfulness. Right view discerns whether or not an action is ethical and beneficial. Right effort infuses our actions with perseverance and energy to prevent the unwholesome ones and realize the wholesome. Right mindfulness is continually aware of present actions and assesses them in regard to the path, making conscious determination possible.[72] Right action matures as these three components strengthen. As a result, our actions are not ignorant, ineffectual, and automatic.

The other path factors are involved, too. The path factor of right intention lays the foundation for skillful action; we train the mind, and it becomes naturally inclined towards nonharm and compassion.

By way of right samādhi, the mind sees itself ever more clearly and so is able to continually refine its definition of right action.

PRACTICE
**MORAL REFLECTION**

Each of us acts from ignorance in countless ways: Obsessed with our own agendas, we fail to care for a loved one who needs us. Blinded by greed, we take something that does not belong to us or take more than our fair share. We manipulate another with our sexuality, perhaps habitually. We lose ourselves in drink or overwork.

In a private reflection, you can allow memories of unskillful actions to arise, and you can encounter any pain associated with them. The actions may be recent or quite old, and seeing the memories may be emotionally difficult. Cultivate compassion as you encounter your memories, knowing that all harmful actions are rooted in that moment's delusion and in patterns of ignorance. And know that this very practice is part of setting a new course.

Moral conscience about the past and concern for the future—*hiri* and *ottappa*—are classical guardians of right action.[73] If there is any remorse (hiri), let it in; the pain of remorse has a purpose. It teaches us and burns the lesson into our bodies.

If there is a motivation to actively shift from the pattern of ignorance that formed the conditions for your unskillful action, you might resolve to recognize this tendency in the future and so avoid acting on it (ottappa). Envision what it might be like to act differently: how it would feel in the body, what you would be thinking, what kinds of results might manifest. Try to be clear but kind as you resolve to abandon this facet of ignorance and act from clear understanding and human care.

## Right Action as the Core of Virtue

Right action is the core of virtue, and the Buddha referred to virtue as playing the same role as the earth for anyone who wanted to move a heavy object: you can't do it without the foundation; you need somewhere to stand.[74] The perfection of virtue is essential to human decency and communal harmony, and it's a necessary foundation for awakening. In one teaching, the Buddha describes the cause-and-effect relationships between virtue and gladness, between gladness and joy, and connecting onwards to serenity, happiness, and concentration. Seeing clearly and release naturally follow from this causal flow.[75]

We can experience this dynamic here and now. Each moral choice, each harmless relational contact, each moment of abstaining from acts born of selfishness and hatred, enhances our contentment, frees us from fetters, and inclines the mind towards release.

## INDIVIDUAL AND SOCIAL ACTION AND RESULT

Committing to not doing harm naturally leads us to a challenging question: is abstaining from actions that bring harm enough, or do we also need to proactively engage in actions that benefit ourselves and others? After all, if right action covers only nonharming by killing, stealing, sexual misconduct, and intoxicants, then the larger problems of our social circles and society are left uncared for.

These questions are part of an even larger question: is the goal of the Noble Eightfold Path exclusively individual awakening, or is cultivating human flourishing also a goal? And if it includes human flourishing, does this include social responsibility?

These questions have been at the heart of the stereotyped differences between Theravada and Mahayana Buddhisms, the arahat ideal of individual awakening in this life and the *bodhisattva* ideal of forestalling awakening to compassionately liberate all beings. This illusion of division creates unnecessary conflicts in our own hearts. The teachings on right action bring us to the core of this issue.

In chapter 2, one of the six tenets I offered for this whole-life vision is that it is founded on early Buddhist teachings—not Theravada orthodoxy, but the teachings found in the early discourses and to some extent the vinaya, the text containing the rules and conventions for monastics. In those teachings, it is clear that the Buddha lived and taught with a concern for both awakening and human flourishing. He urged both laypeople and monastics to care about and act for the benefit of each other and all beings. The Buddha also was explicit about the value of caring for others. He extolled those who care for themselves, and he extolled those who care for others. But he emphasized that "[t]he person practicing both for his own welfare and for the welfare of others is the foremost, the best, the preeminent, the supreme, and the finest."[76]

The Dhamma only occasionally addresses questions of social and economic justice for laypeople; however, monks and nuns enjoyed a monastic code that leveled racism and classism, although not sexism, and prescribed a life of economic justice, environmental responsibility, and peace. While later schools of Buddhism found ways to bridge awakening and social engagement, the process of integration resulted in some distance from the early discourses. Additionally, the Buddhist religions, early and later, accumulated layers of cultural forms that are not native to people outside their root cultures.

So engaging in a whole-life path that is closely related to both the early teachings and the language of the modern West—that brings a Dhamma perspective to social engagement—continues to be a living opportunity. Contemporary society, with its democratic forms and complex mix of ethnicities, presents challenges that were only obliquely addressed in the Buddha's discourses. Some of these issues press in on us daily. Whether or not we think about politics, we are reaping the fruits of political intentions and actions. Whether or not we consider our race or ethnicity to be important to our identity, we participate in a system where it is important to our function—our privileges, limitations, and perspective. Whether or not we consider our sex or sexuality important aspects of our lives, we contribute to and reap from a social web in which sexuality is an active force. Whether or not our individual intentions create specific socioeconomic structures, we are perpetuating those structures by participating in them. Unconscious participation is ignorance in action. Harm or good may come.

So if we sincerely want to apply the practice of right action in the context of a whole-life path, we can't ignore the question of whether it calls us to actively work towards social, economic, and environmental justice. Does our engagement with the whole-life path call us to care for others and act on that care? If so, how wide do these circles of care extend? How do our actions of care for the world develop the mind and the heart, and in what ways could they unhelpfully create entanglement? A holistic vision of right action must encompass this wide inquiry.

Because the path does not unfold in a vacuum—the human body-mind is intrinsically relational, and we live our lives in utter interdependence with others—all action is action done with or affecting other people, even when we are alone. This means that all action is morally laden, whether we recognize this or not. In this complex human system, ignorance of some injustices is understood as unavoidable. Sustained ignorance in the face of evidence, however, is avoidable, and addressing our blindness is part of the path of refining right action.

## PERSONAL RELATIONSHIPS: THE KEY TO BRIDGING INDIVIDUAL AND SOCIAL PERSPECTIVES OF RIGHT ACTION

Because morality is intrinsically relational, it stands to reason that our relationships with specific people, not only society as a whole, are crucial to bridging the individual and social perspectives of right action. The individual and society are mediated by specific relationships; individual action and social action are mediated by interpersonal action. It follows that peace in relationships is a crucial link between individual and social peace.

From this understanding, it follows that our relationships connect moral action with liberation. Given that action is central to the moral life and that morality is central to the whole-life path, our specific relationships must be fulcrums for maintaining the integrity of the path. This perspective is not new; it is part of all Buddhist practice.

Interpersonal meditation practices, such as Insight Dialogue, and the intrinsic relational perspective that develops from them, can support our approach to this aspect of right action. When we develop mindfulness and concentration in relationship, we experience the refined aspects of the Dhamma and understand them in relational terms. In other words, genuine insight arises in the dynamic circumstances of interpersonal contact. As we mature in this understanding, we experience individual and social liberation, intuitively and forcefully, as a continuum. We experience the unity in the diversity of wisdom and compassion, an insight that shifts our perspective and hones our heart.

Each relationship we experience arises from where we stand in the bigger picture of our relatedness. That relatedness is the ground from which we act, no less and no more than is each individual thought. Each relationship is the holder of harm and good, no less and no more than the social structures that bind us. Each moment of relational contact can blossom into greed, hatred, or delusion, creating separation and harm, or it can blossom in generosity, kindness, and clear understanding, yielding skill, compassion, and freedom, internally and externally.

Recognizing the powerful role that relationships play in our wide path of awakening can be disturbing. It means that even when I am engaged mindfully in social justice work, if my personal relationships are inharmonious, the good I aspire to will always be a step out of my reach. Likewise, even though I am engaged in silent meditation, or other individually construed aspects of mental development, I cannot neglect my relational development, because it too is an important part of the maturation process. The separation I may have counted on, my safe but fragile notion of developing an individual self, is no longer sustainable. Being present to the crumbling anguish of the world comes as part of the package of a life of awareness, inquiry, and care.

However, it can also be inspiring to recognize the awakening power of specific relationships. When our individual awareness flags in the ragged work of a raging world, caring relationships can help us remember and nurture mindfulness and spiritual investigation. When we realize, yet again, that the work of equity will never be fully accomplished, our brothers and sisters in action can keep us from despair. Plus, kind and wise relationships are often the key to understanding the suffering of others and the untangling power of love.

And we cannot forget that worldly power increases when we act together. Our social nature is a force that aims our individual actions towards collective results. Often enough, people act collectively for harm. Yet collective actions that stem from personal urges can also be positively aimed, and being conscious of their potency is empowering. The intentions behind those actions aggregate into social results, which are then impressed on not only our neural-hormonal systems, but also our relational patterns, societies, and cultures: hungry people are fed, systems of justice are improved. Conscious relations can be a force for unwinding the results of unconscious relations. With wise view and compassion as its guides, right action is what makes this unwinding actually happen.

PRACTICE

## HOW RELATIONSHIP CAN INSPIRE RIGHT ACTION ON THE SOCIAL SCALE

The COVID-19 pandemic of 2020 provided a global demonstration of depths and heights of greed and generosity. Internet scams and price gouging were visible alongside neighborly care and selfless service. All at once, personal and community relationships rang out loudly against the sudden quiet of quarantine. The preciousness of our common humanity could, at least temporarily, outshine isolation and discord. Internationally, medical workers, delivery people, public employees, and others risked their own wellbeing to serve others. More intimately, families and work groups, though isolated to prevent the spread of disease, vibrated with care and often stepped forward in service of others. In a sense, everyone became both a social activist and a recipient of selfless giving.

If you are involved in a social cause, do your friendships and a common sense of purpose play a key role in that cause? How could you bring mindfulness and a Dhamma perspective to a group where human relatedness is so vividly alive? Perhaps you can invite a healthy reflection on your own and your friends' inner lives. For example, you could consider where your sense of group identity is creating wholesome relationship and where is it creating hatred or entanglement. Or you could consider how your work together can remain grounded in persistence and modesty and not be affected by laziness or self-aggrandizement. How does compassion thrive within a group?

## MULTIDIRECTIONAL CONDITIONING AND ITS EFFECT ON RIGHT ACTION

In the *Satipaṭṭhāna Sutta*, the discourse on cultivating mindfulness, the oft-repeated refrain refers to being alert and aware of experience internally, externally, and both internally and externally. Actions are mental activities made concrete. So we take this same approach to understanding suffering: noticing it internally, externally, and both. In order to see how suffering manifests both internally and externally, we need to trace action from its internal source (mind) out into the world.

Intentions are the internal, mental bed of action. But momentary intentions do not manifest in a vacuum. They are conditioned by how we see the world, each thought emerging at the tip of all prior mental experience.

Thoughts also emerge in response to specific circumstances. For example, I am more likely to think about giving when I encounter a person or group who needs something. I am more likely to steal when something is left for me to easily take. I am more likely to act violently when I perceive a threat. The mind's impulses are then translated into bodily action—giving, stealing, taking violent action.

The intentions that generate actions are also influenced by our relationships, culture, and social practices, all of which condition the mind. In part, this conditioning is simple: we are likely to join our friends in wholesome or harmful activities because of any number of factors, including enjoyment, peer pressure, and modeling. One of the most famous quotes of the Buddha about spiritual friendship names exactly this dynamic. The Buddha's cousin and attendant rhapsodizes, "This is half of the holy life, lord: admirable friendship, admirable companionship, admirable camaraderie." The Buddha responds:

> Don't say that, Ananda. Don't say that. Admirable friendship,
> admirable companionship, admirable camaraderie is actually
> the whole of the holy life. When a monk has admirable people
> as friends, companions, and comrades, he can be expected to
> develop and pursue the noble eightfold path.[77]

This is a very specific statement. Admirable friends and community support will have a profoundly healthy effect on your path.

In similar ways, we are influenced by the values of our culture. If the culture respects moral exemplars like Mother Theresa, we are likely to adhere to the same values of caring for others. Conversely, in cultures where mistreatment of others is the norm—as it often has been in regard to women, ethnic minorities, and people of different sexual orientations—we are far more likely to blindly follow this pattern in our own behaviors. Actions flow from internal and external conditions.

PRACTICE
## UNCOVERING IMPLICIT BIAS

All of us carry unconscious or subtle stereotypes about groups of people. This is one form of *anusaya,* or latent tendencies. When we speak and act from these biases, we can unknowingly harm others, ourselves, or both.

Perhaps the quickest way to reliably identify your implicit biases is to take an implicit bias test. There are many good ones freely available online; you can locate them with a web search. They will help you unearth biases related to skin color, gender, sexuality, obesity, specific ethnicities, and people with physical or mental disabilities.

The tests themselves do not take a lot of time. I recommend taking several of them, asking several friends to do the same, and then meeting to explore the results. What biases surfaced? Do the results seem accurate to you? Do your friends have similar or different biases? What actions or practices might you undertake to retrain your mind?

This entire exploration will be most effective if you and your friends hold a conscious commitment to compassion for each other.

## HOW ACTION FLOWS THROUGH INDIVIDUALS, RELATIONSHIPS, GROUPS, AND SOCIETY

The natural law of cause and effect functions at each level of the human system—individual, interpersonal, and social—and creates a flow of action between these levels. To better understand how both intention and action (activities of body, speech, and mind) flow through them, we first need to look at how the mind constructs its experience of the world.

The Buddha's teachings on dependent origination, *paṭiccasamuppāda*, are key to understanding the subtle workings of the mind. They say that the essence of cause and effect is this:

> When this is, that is.
> From the arising of this comes the arising of that.
> When this isn't, that isn't.
> From the cessation of this comes the cessation of that.[78]

Our everyday actions flow from intentions that are conditioned by volitional formations, or saṅkhāra. Saṅkhāra are formed of all prior volitional contacts and include memory, emotion, knowledge, character, and more. From the teaming bed of volitional formations, forged in ignorance, consciousness arises and vanishes in each moment. The Buddha's teaching on this is saṅkhāra paccaya viññāṇa: consciousness arises dependent upon all prior formations, or constructions. That is, consciousness is dependent upon, not independent of, each moment's aggregated volitional conditioning. Therefore, in each moment, our individual experience of the world arises and vanishes depending on these present-constructing processes. The kernel of personal identification—all our relationships, all our biases, all our love—are already here.

This seed of consciousness provides the conditions for the arising of the experience of body-mind, and this experience elaborates out through the senses to a self that is fully enfleshed in each moment.[79] Actions stem from this self-in-a-body. And this body-mind is relational inside and out. The experience of a self is formed in relationship, and its actions manifest in relationship. Two people (two aggregated formations that each feel like a self) meet and affect each other internally while simultaneously joining together to manifest shared outward action. The relationship, like the individual, is a locus of action.

The ever-spinning, impermanent aggregation we call a rela-tionship rises and vanishes with contact. From this vortex, the individuals and the relationship follow their sensations and hungers. As each relationship blossoms from the individuals involved, and it interacts with other individuals, the resulting aggregation forms a group. As a group forms, a dynamic group volition also forms—that is, groups are loci of action. Groups also then aggregate. For example, coalitions of groups join together to protect the environment, companies band together form trade associations, or political parties engage together to operate a gov-ernment. Or large organizations act as umbrellas for subgroups: individual churches are under the wing of a master church, for instance, and work groups and divisions function as parts of large business entities. Such groups emerge as forces that drive the aggregated society's constructs. This dynamic is simply the natural law of cause and effect at work.

At all levels of this interwoven, vibrating human system, physi-cal actions are the results of mental activity. At the individual level, when thoughts of harm are present, I am likely to act harmfully. When they are not present, I will not. Mental activity also radiates out through relationships as speech and action. When I am with unethical friends, I am more likely to act unethically. When I am not with them, the likelihood of harm diminishes. The mental activity of groups also radiates out by way of speech and action. When I am in the thrall of my political group's blindness, I am likely to act from ignorance, thus expanding my group's actions into society at large and perpetuating systemic injustice. Conversely, when my society is awakened to the value of compassion, it is more likely that I will awaken with it. And when I am awakening, it is more likely those around me will also awaken. The natural law of cause and effect is always at work, whether we know it or not. Moreover, this causality is multidirectional across levels of the human system.

In the bottom-up view of causality, the smaller system of the indi-vidual human mind is the condition for individual action. Two or more individuals form the condition for the arising of relationship, which acts with shared volitions. Relationships, in turn, are the building blocks of a larger aggregated "we," a group (such as a family, a work group, a social group) that is also a locus of action. Society emerges from many individuals, relationships, and groups.

Top-down causality is also operating. Society's function is society's action. The social structures and values condition—but do not determine—the actions that each group takes. For example, a society in which human life is devalued will be inclined towards cruelty in its institutions, such as systems of justice and access to medical care. Subgroups in such a culture are more likely to compete fiercely for limited resources, creating in-groups and out-groups. This competition will fuel hatred and suspicion among specific members of the population, and individual vigilance, protection, and animosity will proliferate. All of these top-down dynamics are functioning whether or not an individual is physically present with others because the relational conditioning resonates across the gaps in contact. Consider a person walking down the road, alone, thinking angrily about an immigrant that recently moved into his neighborhood. Wholesome and unwholesome actions arise from all levels of this conditioned system. Relationships that are rooted in kindness and generosity will condition development in individuals of those and other wholesome qualities. Relational impacts also extend upwards, affecting social groups and society as a whole. In this way, specific relationships radiate downwards and upwards.

This is the intersection of kamma and conditioning. It functions at the largest social level and at the finest level of each moment of consciousness. Not knowing the full spectrum of cause and effect is a key aspect of ignorance. Ignorance is maintained by delusion, the fog of dullness, preoccupation, and indifference that characterizes a life devoid of mindfulness, inquiry, and moral reflection. Conversely, understanding the presence and function of these levels can help us understand the connection between the individual path and the development of society as a whole. At issue is nothing less than individual and social karma and its structural fruits.

Just as we saw three nested time scales of intention—momentary, episodic, and over-arching—we can see multiple nested scales of relation that are relevant to right action. Moment by moment, individual mental activity generates the intentions that motivate action. Actions take place in specific human relationships; the intentions of greed, hatred, and delusion, or of generosity, love, and discernment continually play out as action in the unfurling stories of our lives. All of this action contributes to and is simultaneously influenced by the overarching intentions carried powerfully by our social groups and society at large.

Our own minds, our relationships, and our society are purified by right actions that reverse harmful mental and worldly structures. Harmful social patterns emerged from aggregated individual and relational patterns, and they will be disentangled at all the levels at which they were constructed. Passive and conscious acquiescence to unjust social customs generates wrong action. We participate in how society operates, so we are called to compassionate response. Just as unwholesome social constructions emerge from group, relationship, and individual volitions, these constructions can be unwound by wholesome volitions and actions.

In short, each of us is called to steward the mind. Together, we are called to steward relationships. In most actions, we will also be called to steward harmonious groups as, altogether, we steward society. We are all participants in and contributors to a world molded by politics, sexuality, and economic and environmental forces. We help form it, and it forms us. No one is exempt; internal constructions and external constructions interact in accordance with the natural law of cause and effect. Each of us will be drawn to participate at different levels of this dynamic human system according to our conditioning and circumstances. The common value is engagement with the totality of the Dhamma as a living influence. That is, right view, effort, and mindfulness are the beacons.

What does the multidirectional causality that flows among individuals, relationships, groups, and society at large mean for the whole-life path? It means we must release a narrow view of the path and an either-or mindset about the focal work of freedom. The aim of the path is not one of these domains; it is all of them. The trend of the path *is* the liberation of the individual mind that comes with the cessation of hunger and ignorance. It *is* the manifesting of love, compassion, joy, and equanimity in each moment of relational contact. It *is* the harmonious groups, beloved community, and social liberation that take the form of fluid systems of care that naturally manifest as structural equity. To engage in a whole-life path is to be called to a moral life that goes beyond our individual behavior to include moral action in relationships, groups, and social structures.

This understanding of the path was modeled in the monastic *sangha*, which was a de facto vision of a wholesome society. Early monastic life had its imperfections, but even as there was an underlying emphasis on each individual's awakening, there was also a keen understanding that it was necessary to care for specific relationships and the monastic society as a whole. Personal responsibility and group needs were essential values of the sangha; mental training and social function were not separate.

## BEING TOUCHED BY THE WORLD
### A PERSONAL STORY

Lately, tears come often. I am a citizen of the wealthiest and most powerful country on the planet. I am a white, heterosexual, cisgendered male. I have been able-bodied and financially privileged. In my family of origin I was the favored son. All of the conditions for blindness and arrogance were here, and for a long time I did not know how insulated I was by the privilege I was born into.

Even as Buddhist practice wore away at the citadel of self and gave me the tools for seeing the mind weave its murky magic, the sense of self-importance, of self-reliance or isolation, hung on like old sinew. Mindfulness was useful, but compassion came slowly in the atmosphere set by an individualist meditation practice and view of the Dhamma.

But life and practice have worked away at me. More than forty-five years of marriage revealed layer after layer of the self's underbelly. Fatherhood sensitized me: I raised three sons and lost an infant daughter to a sudden death. I nearly lost an adult son to cancer. Severe chronic disease ravaged the family. Aging sandpapered my crust; cancer, a second lethal diagnosis that I now live with, and extreme bodily contingencies pierced deep into the flesh. This pummeling was key to opening my heart to the hurt of the world.

Relational meditation practice was an inflection point. Insight Dialogue opened my heart and drove the Dhamma ever deeper. Over these past twenty years, a relational perspective on the Dhamma dissolved what I now realize were socially constructed limitations of an individualist view. My view changed to reflect life's relational truths, and this, together with the pains I'd experienced, began to saturate my heart with compassion and reveal more clearly my habits of arrogance. This was natural law at work. Wisdom expanded to encompass my relatedness, and to be fully in relation is to be fully in compassion.

I was continuing traditional, individual meditation and immersive Dhamma study, and I was teaching Insight Dialogue. Meeting others in vulnerability, time and again I encountered the pain born of trauma and lovelessness. I began to see that all of this pain was present not just "out there," but also in my own body-mind. My heart was unguarded; the acid bath of suffering was burning my own skin. The whole-life path and the actions within it were evolving more than I knew.

Now I find myself caring not only about *people* who are suffering, but also about *peoples* who are suffering. Writing this chapter has forced me to wrestle with that care even as it became clearer in my own life. I've had to pierce and then release some of the limitations I've carried about the nature of the path. Right action looks different when inner and outer hurt scorch the same exquisitely sensitive membrane.

## INNOVATION AND INITIATIVE
## WHEN PURSUING RIGHT ACTION

A whole-life understanding of right action rests on the maturation of right view. But the world of human affairs is complex, and discerning what is wholesome and unwholesome, distinguishing Dhamma from non-Dhamma, often requires a nuanced view. How do we integrate the wholesome conservatism of the Dhamma with the clear need for innovation and initiative when engaging with social suffering, as well as personal and interpersonal suffering?

We might begin by remembering the historically innovative nature of the Buddha's teachings and subsequent Buddhist practices. The Buddha modeled a way of engaging the human experience that transcended formulae; the Dhamma that has come down to us is the gift of the resultant insight and creativity. It was an innovation, and it evolved over many years.

We also remember that the Buddha counseled not being attached to views, including views of the Dhamma: "They shouldn't get entrenched in any teachings they know / Whether their own or that of others."[80] This attachment is taught to be unskillful and leading only to disputes. The Buddha himself modeled this flexibility as he crafted the *pāṭimokkha,* the monastic code. Each rule for the monks and nuns was created in response to specific circumstances, and if any rule was found to not serve the community, it was released. So the tradition has deep roots in adaptability.

Buddhist tradition—from ancient times to the present—has offered a wealth of wholesome patterns of action. These range from the full rigor of the monastic life, with its hundreds of precepts, through the five or eight precepts often used by laypeople. Yet even the most conservative construal of right action is bigger than the precepts. Classical Buddhist teachings emphasize avoiding harm, and yet even the abstemious frame of the layperson's five precepts holds a message of creative action. The precept to abstain from killing points to actions that support life. Not stealing points to actions that support protection and respect for all people's land and resources. Abstaining from inappropriate sexual behaviors points to actions that mitigate abuse and give dignity and respect to all, regardless of sex or sexual orientation. Not lying links to proactively speaking the truth. And avoiding intoxicants keys into wider strategies of sane self-care, which we can see in the actions of groups formed to help people cope with substance abuse and addiction.

Right action has always involved innovation. The call to not harm, prevent harm, and act for benefit requires more than formulaic engagement; it requires creative responses to emerging circumstances. Today there are Buddhist groups organized for social justice and planetary care, for hunger relief and medical assistance, women's empowerment and education. Buddhist thought and practice has been integrated into hybrid programs for communication in prisons, substance abuse recovery, and racial diversity and inclusion. There are many Buddhist groups in Asian countries acting for social and economic justice. For each of these, the precepts remain basically the same, but the modes of living by them vary greatly. Many of these newer Buddhist forms are now agreed upon and accepted in their host societies: Sri Lankan monks educating children, Buddhist orphanages in Thailand, merit-making activities of wealthy Burmese, universities associated with Taiwanese Buddhist churches or teachers, Tibetan cultural preservation within Buddhist monasteries, and so much more. Each of these innovations was once brand new. Some innovations may have fit with existing social norms and pressures; others undoubtedly seemed part of a fringe effort of a Buddhist subculture. But in the long run, the outcomes of such efforts are evaluated by ethical standards: Does it lead to the good of many? Does it lead to a lessening of suffering?

The breadth of suffering, particularly the role of relational habits and social and systemic structures that sustain harm and injustice, call us not just to react but also to be innovative. It calls us to be proactive—to take the initiative, to discern the unspoken voices of pain, and to begin what has not yet begun. Initiating action in service to the Dhamma means being guided by reflection on relinquishment, effacement, and dispassion. In this traditional view, the compassion that motivates action is understood to be balanced by equanimity and so can be trusted to sustain the intentions of the Dhamma.

Innovative actions and taking the initiative will be continually evaluated to see whether they lead to dispassion, to nonentanglement, and to an arousal of energy that is balanced by contentment, as well as whether or not they are burdensome. Given that action for relational nonharm and social equity will at times call for intense engagement, strong stands in the face of ensconced power structures, and the marshaling of deep care for those hurt by blatantly immoral actions, we do not make the mistake of assuming it is necessary to micromanage our mind states to maintain quietude. Rather, we understand that high levels of creativity, with the long view of personal and social wellbeing, will help us realize these values.

PRACTICE

## TAKE THE INITIATIVE ON ONE SPECIFIC PRECEPT

Gather a group of people who share your interest in the Buddhist path and feel called to altruistic response to a social need. Begin by contemplating the five precepts and focusing in on the one you feel called to now: not killing, stealing, abusing sex and sexuality, lying, or using intoxicants. Together, create a positive approach to the precept that would engage you and serve your community.

As you consider where you could proactively effect change, you might first focus on ideas that could be implemented within, say, one to three months. Make regular check-ins a part of your group process to ensure that each person's individual practice of meditation and reflection is supported, that the relational health of the group is nourished by shared contemplations, and that the whole group process is an object of respect and reflection.

Reflect before, during, and after your work together. How do all the path factors show up in your work together? Is right action being supported by right mindfulness? Is it supported by right intention—momentary and episodic? How does it feel to be engaged in a creative group process? Do you feel effective? Do you feel aligned with the whole life path?

Although you can do this practice alone, spiritual friendship will give additional support to your efforts, provide more avenues for joy to arise, and in all likelihood, make the actions you take more effective.

## RIGHT ACTION MUST BE FLEXIBLE AND FITTING

The path factor of right action does not demand specific moral action. Instead, both inner and outer circumstances, including where we are on the path, call for creative responses. Given the enormous array of needs, where do we feel most called to contribute right now? Where can we contribute most effectively? What level of engagement will our worldly circumstances, such as our health, families, and finances, support? And what is being called for now in our inner life?

Perhaps our morality falls on the side of restraint, and our path inclines towards quietude and reflection. Or perhaps our action in response to a hurting world may be to apply ourselves fully to cultivating inner peace. Or the path may call us to take action in a dynamic way, and we find that now is the time for forthright action and proclamatory speech. Or taking action may fall towards preventing harm or towards doing good. As we will see in the path factor of right effort, cultivating the wholesome and abandoning the unwholesome are reciprocal, mutually supported, and equally valued aspects of the Noble Eightfold Path.

In discerning what actions to take, each of us will be influenced by our friendships, social groups, and society and its media streams. Discerning the "truth" to be spoken, the action to be taken, calls each individual or group to a process of reflection. This act of discernment is itself part of the practice of right action. If we take as an example the proactive side of not killing—that is, protecting life—our engagement is likely to be influenced by the ways in which lives are threatened; the social norms that we may or may not choose to abide by; our internal inspiration, motivation, and availability; our level of influence and privilege; our education and interpretation of the scope of this ethical guidance; and countless other variables. From this creative, intuitive, and sometimes rational deliberation will issue the right action to take in order to not kill and to protect life.

Rightness, in the sense of the path, maintains a bottom line of abstaining from harm. This bottom line abides whether or not we're engaged in activist movements. The whole-life understanding of right action can unfold within or beyond the bounds of law. It can be noisy or quiet, passionate or rational. From the outside, it can look like living a life dedicated to meditative development, and/or to loving relationships, and/or to explicit social and environmental activism.

Dismantling systems that cause harm, and supporting systems that conduce to goodness, is right action *when the effort is combined with right view, effort, and mindfulness.* This reversal of wrong actions and fruits is right action. In the language of the path, this reversal includes right efforts to prevent the arising of the unwholesome—in this case, harm to oneself and others—and to abandon existing harm. The corresponding right efforts to develop, maintain, and increase the wholesome—actions and structures that support kindness and compassion—are also right action. We see here the harmonizing of internal (personal) and external (worldly) right efforts by way of intentional action. Even volitional nonaction is a form of action.

All right action is assessed as skillful not only when it is beneficial, but also when it is taken at the right time and done with a mind of true friendliness, as the Buddha noted regarding wise speech.[81] If we engage in actions that are outwardly nonharming or beneficial, but do so with a mind of hatred or acquisitiveness, the results will reveal this checkered motivation.

Wise or right action, in this broadest sense, can be judged in terms of outcomes. It would be unskillful to try to make it a matter of rules or precepts. For example, the form your compassionate action might take must fit the circumstances, as well as your resources and abilities. Specific positive precepts would imply transgression if you were not doing enough, not kind enough, or not generous enough. Specific positive precepts could limit good actions, which can and sometimes should manifest in creative ways, adapting to changing circumstances and needs—sometimes producing unprecedented forms of good and wholesome action.

In sum, there is no Buddhist menu that states what social, environmental, or other issues we must act upon or what our actions should look like. Each individual is called to this work in his, her, or their own way. Taking right action is the wholesome work that will further purify underlying tendencies of each heart, each relationship, each group, and society at large. This is action to heal. We are called to a creative, flexible, individual approach to action born of the increased awareness and sensitivity of the heart. These actions, too, are part of nature.

---

PRACTICE
### THE ACTION OF NONACTION

Not acting can be volitional. It can have wholesome or unwholesome results. Get together with a friend to consider the impact—wholesome and unwholesome—of different forms of nonaction. Here are three starting points for the conversation.

**Nonaction where action is called for:** When have you refrained from acting for the benefit of others even though you were aware that your nonaction could have negative results? That is, when have you mentally approved of not acting beneficially despite a clear opportunity, and call, to do so? For example, when has purposely not acting contributed to the continuation of harm? When have you chosen not to speak out about cruel or criminal activity? Or when have you acquiesced to predatory behaviors or racial slurs? Whatever form your nonaction took, does it still call to you now, or would you prefer to behave differently?

**Nonaction for nonharm:** When have you intentionally refrained from some action because you believed it would harm yourself, others, or both? Go beyond the obvious implementation of the precepts regarding killing, stealing, and so forth. For example, have you ever refused to participate in an organization that was perpetuating racial or class divisions? Have you ever resigned from a group because they have exhibited disregard for disabled or sexually differenced people? Does this form of nonaction still call to you now?

**Nonaction as resistance:** When have you actively resisted harmful social or legal norms? Have you refused to pay taxes that were going to purchase armaments or build unjust prisons? Taken a stance as a conscientious objector to the military? Does this form of nonaction still call to you now?

---

## ～ REFLECTION

Wholesome actions will have worldly results, but they will also yield results in our own hearts. Wrong actions create the conditions for suffering, while right actions create the conditions for release. Because of an action, certain habits of thought, emotion, and behavior are formed, while other habits are weakened. Whenever we act motivated by hatred or by kindness, by greed or by letting go, the brain is changed as a result. "Whatever we determine, whatever we intend to do, and whatever we are occupied with: this is the base for consciousness to be maintained on."[82]

In reviewing our motivations, we need to be guided by right view, particularly a strong sense of whether certain actions will be wholesome or unwholesome. Where do these forms of action lead? Do they lead to dispassion, modesty, and contentment? Do they lead to being unfettered, to shedding rather than accumulating, to aroused persistence, and to being unburdensome? This Dhamma guidance points us towards a life of simplicity and letting go. It lets us distinguish between what is the Buddha's path and what is not. Its direction runs radically counter to modern values of accumulating, making, and getting. But notice that it does not specify details. Because this teaching is stated in general terms, we can readily apply it to many specific aspects of our lives. It works for decisions about mostly personal actions and for actions undertaken with friends or groups. Because its criteria are general and because they focus on outcomes in the mind, this teaching works equally well for the circumstances we share with the Buddha's life in Iron Age India and for circumstances of media hyper-connectivity in the high-tech workplace.

We have seen that this so-called individual mind is itself intrinsically relational, and that skillful, ethical action expresses this relationality in the concrete world. Morality is always established in a community of social relationships. Solitary asceticism is part of but clearly not the only direction of the Buddhist path. Nibbāna is not a void to be experienced in departure from the world. Rather, it points to a mind unfettered by ignorant grasping and egoistic desire, and in such a mind worldly contacts do not catalyze self-obsession. The dual trances of victimhood and power, with all of their delusions and indignities, cannot take hold. Ethical action on behalf of all is the function of the mind freed, and its purpose is the ending of suffering. Early Chan Buddhists knew this well and offered this reflection: how does your enlightenment function? An early Buddhist text, the Digha Nikāya, puts it this way: "Wisdom is purified by morality, and morality is purified by wisdom . . . and the combination of morality and wisdom is called the highest thing in the world."[83]

A moral life, together with the cultivation of right view, effort, and mindfulness, sensitizes us. It diminishes habitual actions that bring harm to self and others. It interrupts ignorant acquiescence to injustice that sustains the self. Each awakened person's level of activism will be influenced by personal inclination responding to what the widened mind understands. Waking up to what you are participating in is part of the path. Each of us will engage differently; the form and intensity of our creative, proactive action will vary according to our circumstances and calling. Material progress and its recent flowering of technological progress follow the same old natural laws of cause and effect. Our navigation of these currents of wholesome and unwholesome, alone and with others, is the work of the whole-life path. The process transforms our view; intentions change, speech, action, and livelihood emerge from this transformed view, and the ongoing refinement process is the work of right effort, mindfulness, and calm concentration.

# CHAPTER 8

~

# RIGHT LIVELIHOOD

## *Sammā Ājīva*

T he fact that you're reading these words says something about our relationship in an economy. First, you probably know where your next meal is coming from; otherwise, you'd be out scrounging for it instead of reading this book. Your ability to read indicates you participate in a culture that not only values education, but could also afford to educate you. And these words would not be here if I had not had sufficient support to take the time necessary to write this book.

More intimately, you and I are in a resources relationship through this book. You purchased it or perhaps borrowed it from someone who did. Some of the condensed energy of your money was paid to the bookseller and publisher, and a fraction of it eventually passed along through me to the Insight Dialogue community. Thus, you and I have had a brief vibration together in our little node in a huge economic system. This is a system of work, resource exchange, and relationships, and how they impress themselves on our character and society is the path factor of right livelihood.

*Right livelihood:* the words point to something broad—to whatever sustains life. Because livelihood touches the ubiquitous, sensitive nerves of comfort and survival, it is primal. With the practice of right livelihood we face the everyday roots of stress. There is greed: when is what I have enough? Hatred: Who stands in the way of my comfort? Who threatens my ability to live as I choose to? And there is delusion: Are my lifestyle choices genuinely harmless? Am I living generously and responsibly within the local and global human systems? There is also bountiful giving, as families, friends, and communities support each other to meet their bodily needs. Both the hurting and the helping are powerfully amplified by the hive-like intensity of collective and global focus on acquisition and survival. Both broad and deep, right livelihood is a path factor with heft.

## RIGHT LIVELIHOOD AS A PATH FACTOR

In Pali, *right livelihood* is called *sammā ājīva*. *Sammā*, conventionally translated as "right," also means "working together." The long *ā* prefix in *ājīva* means "to" or "towards" in the sense of a purpose or goal, and *jīva* means "life." So *ājīva* means "that which is for the purpose of life," that which supports life. Right livelihood means that which supports life in a way that is skillful and wholesome—a way that works together with the other factors towards the mind's untangling, interpersonal goodwill, and societal harmony.

We might, on hearing "right livelihood," imagine that it means choosing a job that does not do direct harm. And certainly, non-harming is the first and most essential value and practice of right livelihood. We might also think it involves participating in a vocation that does not stress us too much. This too is important. Given the amount of time many people in the affluent world spend at a single job—for many, more than ten hours a day—the character of that job puts a very strong stamp on consciousness. This stamp is crafted by repeated actions, ways of relating to people, directing the mind towards certain goals, and marshaling the power of the mind and emotions to attain those goals. Livelihood that demands wrong speech or wrong actions is simply wrong livelihood. It brings harm to self and others. It leads neither to dispassion nor to contentment. We had better be careful about the impression our work life leaves on our mind.

Throughout the workday, the mind is shaped by countless thoughts directed along lines that are, to a large extent, determined by the profession itself. Other thoughts are shaped in the workplace by interactions with coworkers. Some of these thoughts incline the heart towards release; some keep us trapped in selfishness, cruelty, and ignorance. If our work is harmful, we are in a double bind. If we become preoccupied by the harmful aspects of our work, the mind is negatively conditioned. But if we numb ourselves to those harmful aspects, we become alienated and unable to see or discern anything clearly.

This fierce power to condition the mind is a key to why livelihood is a separate factor of the Eightfold Path. Livelihood is narrower than action and, like speech, is a subset of action. But the dynamics by which livelihood pervades all of life and engages the mind makes it an extremely potent mutation of action—whether right or wrong, relationally beneficial or harmful, conducive to liberation or obstructing it.

Because the support of life is involved, livelihood can raise difficult issues that sometimes exert strong pressures towards ignorance and delusion. When the necessities of life—food, clothing, shelter, medicine—depend upon our means of livelihood, we may feel trapped, forced to live a certain way and do certain things that we would not otherwise chose to do. Also, we may feel on edge, concerned about whether our flow of basic needs is secure. This sense of risk may extend to those who depend upon us. A disruption of the economic status quo might jeopardize access to health care for a spouse or funding for our children's education, for example. It might throw our food and housing into jeopardy.

At the same time, the character of our means of livelihood subtly pervades all other facets of our lives. If a job requires dishonesty, the perfume of that dishonesty is not wholly absent when we are on vacation from the job. That vacation—the money for plane tickets, hotel, or meals—came from that livelihood. Lying on the beach in the sun, being a tourist in a new country—all are consequences of our means of livelihood. And we know this, if only at the edges of awareness. We may keep this knowledge at bay with activity, but if livelihood is wrong, it will trouble our sleep and trouble our meditation.

When livelihood is right, on the other hand, we may sense a spaciousness and ease of mind. When our livelihood forms a pattern of beneficial actions, this pattern pervades our life. Whatever we do becomes, subtly, an assent to continuing with this way of living. Whether we are working at something we believe in deeply or just something harmless, there is a lightness of mind about what we earn, and that lightness spills over into our feelings as we use our money and resources. The mind settles; gratitude and generosity come easily.

At the simplest level, earning and spending exist in reciprocal relationship to each other: what we spend becomes someone else's profit or wage; what we earn is generally what another pays for our labor or for the use of some resource we control. Thus, right livelihood is a concern for consumers and producers, employers and employees—and for business owners and investors as well. The tightness of the linkage between earning and spending, and among different income-producing entities, varies greatly with the size and structure of the economy. The ways that rightness of livelihood manifests changes along with these variables.

PRACTICE

**EMPLOYMENT AND CHARACTER DEVELOPMENT**

Gather a group of friends or colleagues interested in the question of right livelihood. Invite each person present to reflect out loud about two sets of qualities developed in their work life: (1) skills and knowledge and (2) personal characteristics.

The first set of qualities might include knowledge of the specific tasks, markets, materials, rules, and so on of their employer, but it could also include knowledge of how customers find happiness, how the business entity is impacting the local economy, what the product development cycles are like, how markets are segmented, and so on.

The second set of qualities might include interpersonal sensitivity one has developed due to the team structure or decision-making practices; leadership abilities; care for one's colleagues; humility in the face of a fast-changing technology or marketplace; patience; or a refined sense of social equity in a diverse work setting.

As each person speaks and listens mindfully, see if there are meaningful patterns, shared difficulties, and shared benefits. Then allow each person to consider whether there are any points of leverage that would move their work situation away from the unwholesome and towards the wholesome.

## AVOIDING WRONG LIVELIHOOD

As with right speech and right action, many of the teachings on right livelihood are very brief. The most basic teaching is that right livelihood is abandoning or abstaining from wrong livelihood. "And what, bhikkhus, is right livelihood? Here a noble disciple, having abandoned a wrong mode of livelihood, earns his living by a right livelihood: this is called right livelihood."[84]

We get a few more specifics when it comes to wrong livelihood: "And what, bhikkhus, is wrong livelihood? Scheming, talking, hinting, belittling, pursuing gain with gain: this is wrong livelihood."[85] Another translation lists the specifics as "trickery, cajolery, insinuating, dissembling, rapacity for gain upon gain."[86] The exact meanings of these terms are not agreed upon, but deception is clearly involved in several of them. Livelihood that involves wrong communication is wrong livelihood.

We can test a form of livelihood against the other two sīla factors, right speech and right action. Dishonesty, the spreading of ill will, and greed all tend to increase disquiet in the mind, disquiet in relationships, and disquiet in society. The interpersonal feedback loops activated by speech and by bodily action operate in our work lives. When these feedback loops involve economic factors—when wrong speech or wrong action become how we gain our living—their problematic effects are amplified. The economic aspect hooks deeply into our personal lives, but also spreads widely—globally, in our time—as a potent combination for good or ill.

In another teaching, the Buddha gave clear advice on specific occupations to be avoided: "A lay follower should not engage in five types of business. Which five? Business in weapons, business in living beings [or, *in human beings*], business in meat, business in intoxicants, and business in poison."[87] What all these businesses have in common is very clear: to engage in them is to engage in harm.

Business in weapons, business in meat, and business in poisons all support killing, making their profit from killing or the possibility of killing. "Business in human beings" would mean slave trade and prostitution; the broader reading, "business in living beings," could refer to the raising or sale of animals for meat, for recreation, or for work under possibly harsh conditions beyond the control of the seller.

Not engaging in the "business in intoxicants" echoes the precept to abstain from intoxicants that cloud the mind and impair judgment, but here refers to work that enables others to use them. It is true that someone could engage in any of these businesses—as an investor, business owner, administrator, or employee—without personally engaging in any of the actions that make intoxicants a problem or personally breaking any of the precepts. However, these businesses contribute directly and indirectly, again through complex feedback loops, to interpersonal and societal problems, increasing disruption and disquiet in society. Those involved in these businesses, and everyone else in the vicinity, must live in the social world that they help create—a coarser, more violent, more dangerous world.

Today, we may not make weapons or intoxicants, but we could own a stock fund that holds shares of weapons manufacturers or chemical companies with irresponsible environmental policies. We could do business with banks that loan money to such companies. We may work for a large, multinational corporation with far-removed divisions or suppliers that produce harmful products or that exploit workers or the environment. We may work for a company, city, or union whose pension fund is invested in "wrong livelihood" companies. Exploitive conditions in the mining of diamonds and gold may mean that our retirement account investing in derivative businesses causes us to indirectly support, if not directly engage in, wrong livelihood. Resources are exchanged. There is inequity—some people benefit, some are harmed. Unjust systems are sustained. Given the layered complexities of today's economy, seeing all of the consequences of the actions we perform as part of our livelihood is nearly impossible. So how are we to understand the path factor of right livelihood?

PRACTICE

### REFLECTING ON OUR SOURCES OF INCOME

On your own or with a trusted friend, prepare a list of where your income comes from. In addition to employment income, be sure to include income from nonobvious sources, such as retirement and pension funds, bank interest, and government subsidies. Are any of these sources linked to killing, stealing, pollution, abuse, intoxicants, or other harming enterprises?

It might not be possible to participate in the economy of a developed nation without indirectly supporting exploitive policies—for example, by how your tax dollars are spent or what wrongs are committed by those who trade the currency of your nation. But you can turn in the direction of waking up to how things are. Consider how you can develop your understanding of this system to diminish your ignorance and minimize the harm caused by your personal financial choices.

If this reflection is disturbing, make this an explicit practice of mindfulness of the first noble truth: thoroughly open the awareness to the experience of bodily and mental distress. Let the teaching in fully.

## PROACTIVE RIGHT LIVELIHOOD

Not doing harm is essential to the practice of right livelihood, but this path factor, like right action, also calls us to consider our livelihoods as opportunities to proactively contribute to others' wellbeing. For some of us, such as health workers, first responders, social workers, and professional activists for social or environmental justice, the service aspect of our work is clear. For others, the social benefits of our work may not be so clear-cut, and an intentional inquiry will serve us well. Where in our professional lives are we contributing to something other than wealth creation? Perhaps specific improvements in safety, equity, mental wellbeing, and other wholesome qualities come from our work. There are farmers who care responsibly for the land, sanitation workers who keep public spaces clean and in working order, librarians who help people access information resources, and politicians who seek to address citizens' concerns. Shopkeepers support our comfort and wellbeing; restaurant workers bring us food and often benevolence. As we look around with this lens of where people's professions provide benefit to others, we find benevolence and compassion hidden in plain sight. Nurturing these wholesome aspects of our work lives is a practice of proactive right livelihood.

Taking proactive right livelihood a step further, we can search for opportunities to forge new links between our income and our values. Motivated by generosity, compassion, or justice, countless people, from union organizers to advocates for equity in education or the criminal justice system, have followed their hearts into activism and found or made jobs in their chosen field. These jobs enable them to earn a living while continuing their good works. There are always new opportunities for people to engage in entrepreneurial activities with social, public health, or environmental benefit.

And whether or not we feel called or able to directly take up the proactive aspect of livelihood, it is possible to support others who are forging new ways of socially responsible livelihoods. Your influence can be amplified by offering financial support to other individuals or organizations focused on enabling others to engage in wholesome, contributory, and personally sustaining professional activities.

## REFLECTING ON PROACTIVE RIGHT LIVELIHOOD

Gather a group of friends—it would be excellent if you can do this practice with work colleagues—to reflect together on the intrinsically wholesome aspects of your livelihoods. Set aside at least two hours for this process, so there can be plenty of time for everyone to contribute, for silences between speakers, and for closing reflection.

Here are some questions to guide your inquiry. How does the work we, or each of us, do contribute to the wellbeing of specific people? How does it contribute to society as a whole? Does this work foster safety or comfort? Does it contribute to social harmony, equity, or environmental protection? Does this work I or we do nourish in us, or in others, wholesome mind states and values? What values? How are they strengthened? How can what is good in this work be protected, sustained, and increased?

After your time together of listening deeply and speaking authentically, close by taking time to reflect on what the practice has unearthed and perhaps how it has touched you.

## LIVELIHOOD AND HAPPINESS

The Buddha's teachings on right livelihood point to intimate aspects of character and values. How we live can incline our lives and our influence on others towards happiness. On one occasion the Buddha was asked by a lay follower what leads to happiness in this and future lives. He replied by citing four conditions: (1) persistent effort, (2) watchfulness, (3) good friendship, and (4) balanced livelihood.[88] Although not framed explicitly in terms of "right" (sammā) livelihood but as conditions for happiness, three of these four conditions are concerned with livelihood or its fruits. The first effort or initiative includes the skill, exertion, and discernment involved in one's job—a wholesome application of necessary and right effort: "There is the case where a lay person, by whatever occupation he makes his living—whether by farming or trading or cattle tending or archery or as a king's man or by any other craft—is clever and untiring at it, endowed with discrimination in its techniques, enough to arrange and carry it out. This is called being consummate in initiative."[89]

Once again we notice that work conditions and orients the mind. A farmer or court official, a customer-service representative or an accountant—each necessarily hones certain abilities and sensitivities on the job and neglects others. Thus, one's choice of work is also a decision about developing skills, exertion, and discernment. (Other talents and sensitivities can be developed away from the job, of course; part of right livelihood involves discernment about what one needs to stay balanced.)

After persistent effort, the Buddha mentioned watchfulness. This refers to "watching" the fruits of persistent effort—taking the actions necessary so that those fruits, your earnings, are not seized by kings, stolen by thieves, burnt by fire, carried away by flood water, or removed by ill-disposed heirs.[90] In this sense, our livelihood includes nurturing and protecting what has been earned. We can bring in here the Buddha's guidance towards shedding not accumulating and towards contentment not discontent. The more elaborate our homes, the more numerous or complex our possessions, the more we will need to do to protect them. Consider the spectrum of door locks, bank account passwords, gated communities, personal bodyguards, police forces, and private or national armies. The greater the disparities of wealth, the more ubiquitous and extreme the measures for protecting wealth. Internal and external toxicity feed each other. If we harm others or foster fearful or hateful mind states, personally or collectively, we are engaged in wrong actions that emerge directly from our wrong livelihood. As a practice, right livelihood will include not only watchfulness, but also sensitivity to the causes and effects of how we live.

Next, the Buddha spoke of good friendships supporting happiness. But this was not random advice; this was guidance to support good friendships as they relate to one's livelihood and resources. Our values—the resources we feel we need to live a good life, what behavior is criticized or laudable in how we live—are strongly influenced by our social context. Surrounded by friends with little regard for natural resources, we will be more likely to pollute air, waste water, and squander silence. If our friendships and social circles favor modesty and disfavor self-aggrandizement, we will be more likely to act in line with these values in what we own, how we raise our children, how we dress, and how we keep our homes and vehicles. In short, our personal friendships can support wholesome and unwholesome living. Likewise, collective and international friendships can nurture values of kindness and compassion beyond our personal economic nest.

The Buddha went on to speak of "balanced livelihood" as a condition of a happy, worldly life. He elaborates on this aspect in another discourse: "Just as the goldsmith, or an apprentice of his, knows, on holding up a balance, that by so much it has dipped down, by so much it has tilted up; even so a householder, knowing his income and expenses leads a balanced life, neither extravagant nor miserly, knowing that thus his income will stand in excess of his expenses, but not his expenses in excess of his income."[91]

This is not a simple rule against indebtedness. New businesses often quite properly go into debt; educational debt for ourselves or for our children may be appropriate. City, state, and national debt are the natural result of a complex economy. At issue is balancing the costs against the benefits and how this balance impacts our minds and, in aggregate, our culture. Will the outcome support a mind of contentment, modesty, and freedom from entanglement? When we include in this question our role in global economies and national debt, or in colonial exploitation of natural resources, the issue can seem overwhelmingly complex, even impersonal. Can we find the right place for personal responsibility? Can we recognize our participation in a debt-enabled economic system and let each action as a consumer be conscious and caring? As in other things, right view is needed in discerning a balanced and appropriate way of living.

In a world economy with gross disparities in economic resources and power, the practices of right livelihood challenge us to deeply question need and extravagance. "Balanced" living is aimed at preventing harm and cultivating harmony both internally and externally. Internally, excesses of wealth can easily inflate one's sense of self-importance and disconnect one from people outside one's economic class. At the same time, excess spending leads one to depend on outside stimulations and comforts for happiness, while fostering waste and greed. Externally, the concentration of wealth leads to the establishment and support of unjust social and political structures. These not only sustain inequity but also carry forward patterns of greed and hatred. The individual, relational, and social patterns incline towards collective and individual suffering of mind and body. This entire picture is sustained by ignorance, and sundering that ignorance connects the path factors of right livelihood and right view.

In teaching a path in which no aspect of our lives is left out, the Buddha's advice to kings and artisans, to monastics and laypeople, bridged a just social vision and guidance for individual behavior. His teachings on resource management included recognizing four causes for the destruction of wealth—debauchery, drunkenness, gambling, and association with evildoers—and four causes for the increase of wealth: abstaining from debauchery, from drunkenness, and from gambling, and associating with good people.[92] He gave similar advice to the young man Sigālaka: "And what six ways of squandering wealth are to be avoided? Young man, heedlessness caused by intoxication, roaming the streets at inappropriate times, habitual partying, compulsive gambling, bad companionship, and laziness are the six ways of squandering wealth."[93]

This simple, basic advice is still relevant today. Reckless spending and living beyond one's means cause stress and encourage greedy and irresponsible mind states. It is essential to note the root motivation for wealth accumulation: sensory lust and self-aggrandizement, the two mental intoxicants (or taints, āsava) that, together with ignorance, are the deepest roots of suffering. Squandering wealth and excessive gathering are both toxic obsessions. These actions may harm others or pollute our environment, but for sure they pollute our minds. Attention to the resources flowing into and out of our lives, a mundane employment of right mindfulness, can serve as an entry point for wisdom and virtue. The way we support our life and the life we support form a mutually reinforcing loop.

Especially where social and economic conditions are in a high state of flux, right view is necessary for discerning right livelihood—and right view involves the ability to see clearly what leads to what. "Right view comes first. . . . One understands wrong livelihood as wrong livelihood and right livelihood as right livelihood: this is one's right view."[94] When we see that certain kinds of livelihood, or certain things that we do in our jobs or with the resources at our disposal, are leading to suffering rather than to the end of suffering, that is right view. Then it is time to do something about it. Right mindfulness and right effort are required here: "One makes an effort to abandon wrong livelihood and to enter upon right livelihood: this is one's right effort. Mindfully one abandons wrong livelihood, mindfully one enters upon and dwells in right livelihood: this is one's right mindfulness. Thus these three states run and circle around right livelihood, that is, right view, right effort, and right mindfulness."[95]

Together, right view, right mindfulness, and right effort enliven our attempts at right livelihood—and all the other path factors.

## BEYOND NONHARMING WORK: LIVELIHOOD AS THE EXCHANGE OF REQUISITES AND RESOURCES

Livelihood includes the entire circulation of value into and out of our lives, including the circulation of resources.

Money is a symbol, a proxy, a token for our time, energy, and thought. As such, it is a tangible medium by which energy is exchanged among individuals, groups, businesses, and nations. From this perspective, corporations or other business collectives are aggregators of human energy. The products of this energy are actual, tangible products—food, lodging, clothing, medicine, and myriad gratifications and delights—that satisfy human's basic urges for survival and pleasure, safety and comfort. So this path factor invites us to explore not only how we earn and spend money, but also how we engage resources—how our resources are expended towards what we eat, how we dress, and where and how we live.

However enormous and abstract it may be, the economy is a relational system. The value of a check, a credit card, or even a coin is based not on the value of paper, plastic, or metal, but on complex human agreements. The purchases we make, the gifts we give, the items we discard all impact the web of life around us—the social web and the ecological web. These chains of consequences impact the lives of others—some of whom we know, many of whom we will never meet—in very basic ways.

For these reasons, our look at livelihood includes how the goods and services that support life circulate among people, both locally and in society as a whole. It encompasses a variety of economic interactions with the world—the support of our families, the social and environmental impact of our investments, the employment practices of stores where we shop, how we pay the babysitter, the charities and causes we give to. This picture also includes the movement of resources between nations and across social strata. As we'll see, the impact of right livelihood is both intimate and extensive.

We do not expect easy answers; in fact, there are more questions than answers. The whole-life path means engaging the questions with sincerity and living in response to what we discover as we do so.

## Learning from the Monastics

The Buddha saw that the actions we perform for our livelihood and the circulation of resources strongly condition the mind, and he saw them as important to forming a harmonious and just society. He considered getting them right to be one of the eight main parts of his prescription for the cessation of suffering.

The Buddha's most fully developed thinking on right livelihood had to do with the monastic life. Guidelines were developed, one at a time, to address specific situations, including problems and abuses; these guidelines continued to evolve long after the Buddha's time. The monastic life was simple but very proscribed, held in the arms of the Pātimokkha: 227 rules for monks and 311 for nuns. These rules were accompanied in the vinaya by explanations and stories about the situations that prompted their formulation.

Although the Buddha gave careful thought to right livelihood for laypeople, his day-to-day life guidance for them was much less specific. We have to comb the discourses for stories or specific instructions given to a parent, ruler, or businessperson. And we are left to navigate more or less on our own the complexities of money, credit, possessions, dwellings, the use of skills and talents, and a diversity of economic relationships. Recognizing that conditions have changed greatly for everyone, and understanding that the Buddha's guidance for monastics requires some interpretation to make sense in the context of a lay life, let us consider the life of the early Buddhist monks and nuns to see if we can find some guidance for a way of kindness and unbinding.

Perhaps the first and simplest thing we can gain is a reality check about what we need for a decent life. Here were people who had chosen to relinquish everything that might encumber their spiritual development. They possessed virtually nothing, including secure sources for their most basic needs, yet they were not living a pinched or debased existence. On the contrary, they were clearly actualizing their highest potential; King Pasenadi described them as "smiling and cheerful, sincerely joyful, plainly delighting, their faculties fresh, living at ease, unruffled, subsisting on what others give, abiding with mind [as aloof] as a wild deer's."[96] The Buddha also counseled the *bhikkhunī* Gotamī to shed rather than accumulate.

Pondering these aspects of monastic life, we can realize that people can get along without almost everything they think they "need." We can see that the dynamics of self-concept, grasping, and suffering are powerful in relation to both money and marks of status (money's symbolic equivalents). Money tends to stimulate greed so that it is difficult to have a sense of "enough." Research indicates that even among multimillionaires, people tend to think they will have enough when they own a sum considerably in excess of their current holdings. This fresh perspective can help us develop gratitude for what we have. It can help us remember that losing some of what we have is not the end of the world. Fears of unemployment or setback lighten when our perspective broadens in this way.

The monastic lifestyle may seem incredibly far from our own, but the urges the monastics faced were human, ubiquitous, and very recognizable. Even the renunciate life could tempt one to hoard, drop hints, or falsify appearances in order to get better almsfood or robes, or to brag or belittle others in the hope of influencing donors.[97]

A key aspect of "livelihood" appears in the terms by which monks and nuns obtained the barest necessities of life, defined as the "four requisites": food, robes, shelter, and medicine. Even these needs were to be met by monastics in a humble, austere way: by accepting "any old scraps of food," tattered robes, a simple hut, and any medicine.[98] These rules were about being free from attachments, so adhering to them was mental training. They were also aimed at making the monastic community easy to support, so they had a practical, social function, which they maintain to this day. Taken together, the requisites help establish a sense of living the Dhamma while eating, sleeping, going about in robes, and even while being ill.

## Contemplating the
## Four Requisites

Although the monastic rules regarding the four requisites are highly detailed, we may take guidance from the principles underlying them and use the four requisites as a framework for examining how these basic needs move through our very different contemporary lives. They are earthy reminders of the path as we eat, sleep, and live. After all, our intentions for freedom from greed, hatred, and delusion, and for the cessation of suffering, are the same as our ordained friends. While focusing on requisites may seem simple, looking deeply at each raises new questions for us.

### Food

After air to breathe and water to drink, food is the most basic bodily necessity. We need food pretty much every day; we might fast for a while, but the effects of doing so are quickly evident. For a monk or nun, the alms round was the source of food and a daily reminder to both monastics and lay supporters that they were interdependent.

Our relation to food is also one of interdependence. Those of us who support a family are involved in giving food as part of that support, and this gift generally extends to the preparation and sharing of that food. The circulation of food right there in the household can be an occasion for delighting in generosity and gratitude.

We can look at how we support others with food, either regularly or occasionally. Maybe we invite friends or relatives to a meal. Maybe we contribute time and labor to help run a soup kitchen or send a check to a relief organization. Maybe someone we know lost a job, and we brought over a sack of groceries. Or maybe, in a period of unemployment, we ourselves used unemployment benefits or food stamps to purchase groceries, or we visited a food pantry. All of these are part of the circulation of value in society, tangible reminders of human interdependence. That interdependence has a powerful conditioning effect on the mind, in its particular details and in its broad scale.

Food is frequently a feature of social interaction. We invite friends over for a meal or offer tea to someone who drops by; we share a meal at a restaurant or go out for coffee. These social forms are usually reciprocal, which means they tend to be stratified economically and support the construction of identities around those economic stratifications. The Buddha sought to create a monastic subculture based on radical equality. His monastic order sought to ignore social and economic differences, along with the caste structure that was gaining strength in society in his time. In our lay lives, our practice of right livelihood can include attuning to inequities that surround us. What are the relational and social results of radical equity? What practices are suggested here? Perhaps we can practice both giving and receiving hospitality in ways that cross economic stratifications. We can reflect on whom we join for a meal. Is there diversity there? What influence might this diversity (or lack of it) have on how we construct our identity?

The restaurant setting alone raises some interesting issues about inequity. The hospitality industry is heavily dependent on foreign nationals, many working without documentation for less than minimum wage, who enjoy none of the protections of law. To order a meal, to take the order and serve the meal, to have no recourse if an employer refuses to pay, or to be aware of these conditions at the edges of our Sunday brunch—these circumstances condition the minds of everyone involved, helping to form and reinforce identities. Many more interdependences and potential inequities are involved in the supply chain that brings our food to us: the labor and resources spent in its growing and harvesting, transporting, and merchandising.

The money we pay at the restaurant or at the grocery store moves out and away, supporting and sustaining people and other businesses. This raises questions about what we choose to eat and about how we obtain it. If we purchase meat, clearly we are paying someone, somewhere, to kill an animal. Included in the picture is the quality of the animal's life before its slaughter. Also included are the resources of the land or the grain used in production of that meat and the contribution animal farming makes to climate change. We can carry this same kind of inquiry into fruits and vegetables.

When we ask who harvested the strawberries or the asparagus, we are compelled to also ask what wages they received for their labor. Did they receive health care? What about their children? Who is making a profit from their work? A food company could be involved in "business in human beings" by way of what is virtually indentured servitude of native peoples on the enormous monoculture farms that have taken over indigenous land in developing economies: banana, coffee, cocoa, or pineapple plantations that have supplanted traditional subsistence agriculture. Also, how or where the food is grown has an ethical aspect. We might wonder whether chemicals that degrade the ecosystem played a large role in fertilizing, protecting, or processing our food.

The circumstances in which we acquire and consume food involve us in complex networks of relationships. These chains of cause and effect are partly within our control and partly outside it. If we have a sketchy awareness of these things but don't feel very connected to them, it is easy to feel that purchasing food products from any source is acceptable. Making different choices may not be simple or easy, but we do have choices. Our path of right livelihood includes asking how we can avoid doing harm in this interconnected world. The fair trade and local foods movements are partial responses to these questions, but the continued questioning is part of our practice of sīla. This reflection is mind training; it is a growth out of ignorance. Acting on what we learn is integral to right livelihood.

The first step is awareness: to assess the impact that food, and the interdependence it represents, has on our minds and the roles greed and aversion play in our decision-making about it. We must eat; only some of us are positioned to grow our own food. Perhaps part of my practice will be to pause before eating to consider the sources of this food, to think of those who lack enough to eat. I may choose to abstain from certain foods for reasons of equity or environmental sustainability. Perhaps I will endeavor to eat mindfully, respectfully, and sustain a sense of inquiry as to how food is part of my path. Then maybe decisions and actions will issue from this mindfulness.

Educating ourselves to the impact of our food choices is one part of awakening to our place in a global network of life and taking charge of its influences on the mind. With greater awareness, our minds will gradually incline towards wisdom, and wisdom will increasingly guide our choices. The path comes alive with every meal.

PRACTICE
## A REFLECTIVE MEAL

Invite friends to a meal that will be a shared, mutually guided reflection practice engaging two elements: mindfulness and contemplation. If possible, have each person coming bring a dish to share with everyone. If possible, invite a diversity of food stuffs, ingredients, cooking styles; keep it interesting.

When the meal has been set out and everyone is seated, begin with some silent time. Have a predetermined guide invite mindfulness of the sitting body, of the senses of smell and hearing, and of mental activity. When the guide signals for the group to emerge from silence, she can also invite everyone to let the awareness expand to notice the group as a whole and the collective aspect of sharing the meal.

While eating, each person is invited to reflect on the specific dish they are eating, speaking aloud as they see fit. What ingredients are there, and where do they come from? What, if anything, do they know about the ecological or economic aspects of those ingredients? What do they know about the sources and impacts of the cutlery or the plates and cups? What does this meal reflect in the way of economic privilege and equity?

## Clothing

We can make do without new clothing much longer than we can manage without food, but clothing is necessary. It is as embedded in human interdependency as food. The monastic codes contain many rules about how robe cloth is obtained and from whom and about the making and care of robes because these interactions proved to have significant effects on the community and on the minds of its members.

We can ask how resources are involved in clothing ourselves and others. Clearly, we expend money, skill, or time to clothe ourselves and others. The picture includes where we purchase our clothes, whether they are new or used, whether we make our own clothing, and whether we give clothing as gifts. Within this are also questions about the level of expense of the clothing and who is included in the circles of care when we provide clothing for others.

Other questions center around caring for our clothing, like whether we have many garments that require the expense and chemical use involved in dry cleaning, and what we do with garments when we are done with them. Do we wear them until they are in shreds? Discard them while they are still serviceable? Pass them along to others or to resale shops? These choices, too, shape awareness and compassion more than we may realize.

We can examine clothing in terms of what our purchases fund. Clothing manufacture is part of a global economy, and where our clothes come from has an impact. Perhaps child labor was involved, or laborers working in unsafe conditions for a subsistence wage. Or maybe our clothing comes through a fair trade channel. Perhaps we shop for clothing at second-hand stores. Do we know who profits from the clothing we purchase, or from the long chain of wholesalers, distributers, and retailers? Perhaps synthetic fibers in the clothing were made with care for the environment; perhaps they have a petroleum base that produces excessive waste. Perhaps our shirts are made of cotton, which requires pesticides and often intensive irrigation. Can we say that synthetics or cotton is the better moral choice? All of these issues point to dukkha—there are no simple answers—and to ways we participate in economic cycles of justice and injustice, creating help or harm for others. This participation is usually without either full ignorance or full knowledge, a condition that can incline the mind towards carelessness and delusion or, with intentional practice of right livelihood, incline the mind towards awareness and compassion.

A more intimate reflection on the requisite of clothing is to consider what we really need. We can examine our own wardrobe in terms of quantity. Monks were limited to three robes: one for the lower body, one for the upper, and an over-wrap for warmth. Such austerity might introduce discomfort or complexity into our lives, but how much clothing, how many pairs of shoes, do we really need? Perhaps with less we could free our time and resources for other endeavors. It stands to reason that this would also free the mind from identification with our appearance and the roles it supports.

Many of our clothing "needs" have to do with expectations at work and in other contexts, not just with the practicalities of warmth and protection. A few jobs require a formal uniform, but most jobs—and indeed most roles in life—require some degree of "dressing the part." How we dress situates us in terms of wealth and social status, influencing not only who may hire or promote us, but also who may consider us as a potential friend, or sell us their puppy, or treat us with respect.

Clothing is involved in expressing our individuality, too—and thus in identity-formation and identity-maintenance. The urge to express the self manifests as lust for clothing and its affordances. Actions stemming from this urge, too, involve complex and interlocking feedback loops. The "vocabulary" of fashion in which we make our expressive statements—be they flamboyant or subtle, assertive or retiring—is an ever-changing dialect deeply involved in the economy. The designers, sweatshops, trade agreements, transportation companies, and retail stores that are part of the clothing supply chain are also, in varying ways, the shapers of our sense of style and taste. There is big money to be made in continually manipulating our sense of what clothing "reads" as stylish, sexy, or businesslike or even as simple, modest, or casual. Have you heard the phrase, "casual chic"?

Our actions in fulfilling our need for clothing affects others. They also affect our minds. Our path of right livelihood compels us to inquire whether the way clothing cycles into and out of our lives contributes to a mind of shedding or to one of accumulating, to a sense of lightness or of burden. Reflection on questions like these is more than preparation; it is part of the practice of right livelihood, much as reflection before speaking is intrinsic to the practice of right speech. There are no fixed answers that work for everyone; living into these questions is part of our path of wise living. It is an engagement with right intention and right view. As the path ripens, we may feel as we put on our clothing that we are intimately wearing our path.

PRACTICE
## CLOTHING INVENTORY AND INVESTIGATION

Go to wherever you keep your clothing: the closets, drawers, shelves, and heaps. First, just mindfully look at what is there. Try to refrain from self-judgment, positive or negative. Just notice what is there and how it feels to be seeing it right now.

Mindfully reach out and pick up one item of clothing. What do you know about what it is made of, where it comes from, whether it the product of a factory or a craftsperson? What sense of self is associated with these pants or this coat? What image do you wish to project? How does this item fit with your professional or social life? Do you like this piece, or do you not like it? Or do you perhaps feel neutral about it?

Mindfully setting down the item, move to another item and engage in more or less the same inquiry. And again. And again. As you repeat this process, begin to also inquire how many pants or socks or shoes you have, and why you might have that many. Does a small number of shoes reflect economic limitations? Does a large number reflect wealth or wishing to project different identities in different circumstances?

Close by reflecting on the Dhamma guidance that points to modesty rather than self-aggrandizement, shedding rather than accumulating. Investigate with clarity and kindness.

## Shelter

Monastics were entitled to seek shelter and to ask for it. Yet an empty hut, the roots of a tree, or an old shed were considered adequate, even preferable, shelter. Although we are laypeople who do not aspire to homelessness, we can nevertheless step back and ask some big questions about the requisite of shelter.

We can ask about the impact our housing has on us and on others who use it. One reflection of the mind and an influencing factor is whether our home is overly large, with much space that goes unused. Likewise, our home may be cramped in ways that limit hospitality we would otherwise wish to give. If our home is difficult to keep clean, it may demand an excessive portion of our time. If it is expensive, our home may siphon off too much of our income that we might do well to spend on other things. In general, a home can serve the physical and social needs of everyone living in it, or it can interfere with our lives. In Dhamma terms, we are asking, is this home burdensome or unburdensome?

Reflecting on our shelter's impact on natural resources can be revealing. Living in nature may bring a feeling of harmony and ease, but placing that house in nature may upset a natural habitat. Living in a home that takes a great deal of energy to heat or cool impacts not only the environment, but also the mind. If we are building or renovating, our choices of materials have an impact. What patterns of resource consumption does this home commit us to? These issues may not be clear-cut. A decision to install an air conditioner could bring ease and support one's meditation, for example, and yet still consume resources irresponsibly, hurting the environment and killing beings, and even disturbing our meditation because of it. We have to ask, what is the proper balance?

We can ask about the societal impact of our shelter. I think of the homes I saw in Korea, especially those jammed together in Seoul, where modest use of materials and space yielded adequate comfort for millions rather than opulence for a few and scarcity for many. Maybe the environmental or human impact of a housing choice makes us uneasy. Would it be sustainable for everybody to live the way I live? Luxury is not necessarily wrong; it is a matter of cause and effect, in the mind and in the world. It is said that luxury comes as a guest and stays as a host. This is mental attachment, and it has an impact. Ownership grants certain powers: how does this influence the mind and those around us? If I own rental property, what are my responsibilities to my tenants? If I am a renter, am I justified in abusing a property? And for those of us privileged with shelter, our path of compassion compels us to think about, care about, and act on behalf of people who are homeless.

Right livelihood calls us to find balance internally and socially. What supports letting go? What supports mindfulness and tranquility? Am I fettered by my home or unfettered? Over time, our shelters become our lay monasteries.

PRACTICE

## REFLECTING ON DOMESTIC SPACE

You are invited to reflect on the size of your home, a practice that is best done with everyone you live with—partners, children, roommates.

Consider each room: how much use it gets, what role it plays in the life of the household, and how essential it is in relation to the other rooms. You might walk from room to room as you reflect together, sitting first in the kitchen, say, and then moving to a living room, then bedroom, and so on. Are there any rooms in the house that get very little use? Are they burdensome—for example, hard to heat or time consuming to clean? Does having this room bring feelings of joy or security or pride? If your home is small and plain, do you feel a sense of lack, of wanting more? How do you feel when friends or relatives visit? If your home is large or opulent, are there times when you are embarrassed when people of lesser means visit? (If it applies to you, extend the reflection to include guest houses or second homes: Are these spaces well used? Do they incline towards shedding rather than accumulating?) Overall, does this home reflect your values?

## Medicine

Monks and nuns were also supported with medicine, the fourth requisite. Keeping the body healthy and strong was always part of the Buddhist tradition. The Buddha spoke of good health as a necessary condition for the hard work of awakening. An infected scrape or an abscessed tooth left untreated can lead to death. Disease also drains bodily energy, distracts the mind with pain, and can lead to clouded thinking. So medicine was considered a requisite, even for those who had nothing.

Modern medicine is more comprehensive than what was available in the Buddha's day, yet our anxiety about it is probably much higher. Knowing that advanced treatment options are available raises the question of whether they are accessible to us and, if so, at what cost. Profit motives and dazzling technology are in delicate counterpoint with our impulse to deny the inevitability of aging, sickness, and death. In this modern system, and within the confines of what is possible with our income and the insurance plans available to us, we must decide what risks to take. Employer-linked insurance may help tie us to a job that has become confining or overtly unethical. If we are an employer, we have choices to make about what health care options are available to our employees. If the government health care system is inadequate, what are our options? Do wealthy people have options that poor people lack? What is safe? What is fair? These questions are part of the path factor of right livelihood.

Today we have access to powerful medications, both over the counter and by prescription. These, too, raise basic questions. Our choices may be guided by wisdom, or they may be guided by a fear of pain or by a grasping at comfort. Sometimes, seeking suppression of symptoms is the truly wise choice; sometimes it is rooted more in fear than deep need. And such fear or desire is easily manipulated by profit-oriented drug advertising, which reveals how we live in an economy that presses forward certain values not out of altruism but for personal and corporate gain. I have been troubled by whether or not my expensive cancer treatment is equitable. If it is not, do I forego it? Modern medicine lands us in some very complex interpersonal and societal feedback loops involving the circulation of both value and information, and these feedback loops always affect the mind. Considering these feedback loops is part of the practice of right livelihood.

Closer to the situations the Buddha's early followers faced, our options for handling relatively minor sicknesses have economic implications, particularly in the case of a pandemic. We may risk our employment if we stay home from work when we are sick. If we are self-employed or working on contract, we may not be able to afford to lose a day's progress towards a deadline. Yet we may risk our health—and the possibility of continued work—if we do not allow the body the time to heal. These problems compound when others depend on our income. Although there are contemporary nuances, these are ancient, universal dilemmas. Their consequences involve not only economics but also chronic anxiety, conflicted loyalties, and the construction of identity, making them yet another arena for inequity and compassionate action. The requisite of medicine invites not only care for others, but also the joy of living the path in sickness as well as in health.

## Other Needful or Useful Matters

We might add transportation to a modern list of requisites. In the Buddha's day, monks and nuns walked and so, for the most part, did his lay followers. Even so, transportation was mentioned in various lists on things to be given.[99]

In modern societies, transportation is deeply embedded in the web of economic exchanges. Our path of right livelihood includes an inquiry into what resources were used to make a personal vehicle; what percentage of our work goes toward owning, maintaining, and insuring it; and how much commuting time our jobs or our recreation costs us. We can consider the vehicle's fuel or electricity and its source and the environmental harm the vehicle does. We might even look at how our commuting fosters the demand to devote space and concrete to roads. We can also turn these questions towards wholesome solutions. Perhaps there are alternatives that will better protect the common good—such as not driving to the country every weekend, reducing trips to the store, or walking and biking more often. I might choose to live in a place or in a way that does not require a lot of driving. I can question my use of air travel—how quickly do I need to be in the next place? Do I really need to take this trip? My current answers to these questions will reveal something about how I am constructing myself and the world.

Computers and other communications devices might be named as another necessity of modern life. We can ask basic questions about how they are embedded in the network of exchange. Where did a device come from, where was it designed and made, what are we supporting when we purchase it? What happens to it when we no longer want it? Do we pass it along to someone to whom it could be of use? Is it recycled? Or does it go to a landfill to release toxic chemicals into the groundwater, or to a developing country where precious components are "cooked out" under health-destroying conditions?

As a final consideration, reflect on the guidance the Buddha gave the nuns and monks about protecting the natural environment. For the simple lives of itinerant beggars, the instructions were rudimentary, but the intention was clear: don't foul the water, don't tramp on the fields or even go into them at certain times of the year, responsibly handle the wastes you produce, and accept only what you need, storing and owning almost nothing. In our multilayered economy, our complex city sewer systems, our participation in activities that foul the air and water all ensure that there will never be a shortage of difficult questions to challenge us and awaken us from entitlement and complacency.

PRACTICE

**ASKING CHALLENGING TRANSPORTATION QUESTIONS**

The carbon footprint of air travel is enormous. It is perhaps the most inefficient mode of travel, the most deleterious to the environment per mile traveled. You are invited to reflect on what you do when you have good reasons to travel that are in conflict with the environmental impact of that travel. Your mother is on the other side of the country; do you fly to see her? She is unwell; do you then fly to see her? There are no meditation retreats in your area; do you fly or drive a long ways to attend a retreat? You teach meditation, or you are a leader in actions for social justice; do you accept invitations to do this work if they require air travel? When do you say yes, and when do you say no? How far do you drive to a rally in support of environmental causes?

## What We Can Do

The enviro-socio-economic questions raised by the practice of right livelihood are potentially overwhelming. The practice of right livelihood does not aim to resolve all ambiguities arising from the requisites of food, clothing, shelter, and medicine or from other necessities and consumables. Rather, we seek to discern and address whatever disturbs the mind here and now and the impact of our actions that disturb the social web we are a part of. For a whole-life, always-on path, we continue to reflect on the basic values that define the Dhamma: Is how I live leading to entanglement and discontent in the present, or towards disentanglement and contentment? Towards shedding or accumulating? How do I live in ways that are increasingly unburdensome? Just as right action inevitably leads us to creative proactivity, so right livelihood leads us to a day-by-day creative inquiry into how we earn and use resources. This inquiry includes considering our participation in local and global economies.

Right livelihood is a practice of stewarding the mind and stewarding the world. Following this practice leads to increasingly refined attention and away from continued obliviousness and denial. No hard line is drawn between our own discontent and the suffering of others. We recognize how we are burdensome to both ourselves and others. As we follow this path factor, we will uncover more and more subtle forces that are disturbing the mind. Because the well-developed mind is aware internally, externally, and both, and because we are so intricately interrelated in this complex human system, refinement and freedom are not selfish pursuits. There is efficacy to attending to the intimate things in our lives—our jobs, our food, our clothing. Focusing our efforts on the things that are currently disrupting the mind wakes us up in the here and now of our lives. This focus can keep us from getting overwhelmed and paralyzed by the enormous issues associated with money and resources. We are taking on incredibly big issues one single bite at a time and always choosing the bite that is clouding or freeing this mind, right here, right now. In the long term, our personal liberative choices will also lead towards economic, environmental, and social justice.

## GIVING (DĀNA)

The goodness towards which we aim our practice of right livelihood is related to the movement of resources. Giving (*dāna*) is perhaps the most effective, uplifting, and healing practice associated with this movement. As we saw in chapter three, the Buddha taught that giving is the first step on the path to unbinding, preceding even the Four Noble Truths and the Noble Eightfold Path. Certainly the Buddha did not imply that taking up the Path means one stops giving. Giving is an ongoing, intrinsic part of the Path. Giving is perhaps the preeminent activity that leads to dispassion, not to passion; to being unfettered, not to being fettered; to shedding, not to accumulating; to modesty, not to self-aggrandizement; to contentment, not to discontent; and to being unburdensome, not to being burdensome. The very act of giving is simultaneously a kind and helpful deed, an enactment of the Path, and evidence that the intentions of the Path are bearing fruit.

Giving is a workable part of the whole-life path; it is something we can *do*. Most fundamental are giving requisites, giving safety, and giving Dhamma. Requisites provide survival and adequate comfort; we give them where they are needed and where we can. Giving safety is the work of sīla; we behave ethically and so give others security. And giving Dhamma is the highest gift; we offer what we can, directly or by supporting our teachers.

Giving is a practice that challenges us even as it opens our hearts. In the context of right livelihood, giving is a flow of resources in a particular direction: from oneself to others. But like all actions, the flow is more than one way.

Giving is a relational act. For the act to be performed, there must be the giver and the recipient, both of whom benefit from the act. The giver needs the receiver in order to experience the joy, selflessness, and mental refinement brought about by the act of giving. The receiver needs the giver to benefit from the material support and to enjoy the warmth and humility of being supported. The Buddha designed this mutual dependence into the monastic rules:

> Monks, householders are very helpful to you, as they provide you with the requisites of robes, almsfood, lodgings, and medicine. And you, monks, are very helpful to householders, as you teach them the Dhamma . . . as you expound the holy life both in its particulars and in its essence . . . In this way the holy life is lived in mutual dependence, for the purpose of crossing over the flood, for making a right end to suffering and stress.[100]

In this teaching, mutual support is explicitly tied to making an end of suffering. Receiving gifts, the monastics were enjoined to question whether they were worthy of these gifts—that is, whether they were living the holy life with full commitment.[101] Like all actions, giving begins in the mind, but it is more than the felt sense of generosity. The entire body-mind is involved in this process, from discerning the need and the ability to contribute to deciding to offer what one can to carrying out the physical act of giving and finally to reflecting on and living with the results of this action. At each phase we are called beyond self-centered habit. As we give, we are eradicating stinginess, smallness of heart. Giving is, by definition, letting go of something, presumably something of value. So it is a concrete way to practice nonclinging. Giving can run contrary to short-term personal desires and, in doing so, is a practice of nongreed. It is also a practice of nonhatred, the essential condition for love; opening the hand opens the heart.

## LIVING THE VALUES OF DĀNA
### A PERSONAL REFLECTION

At this point, I have been teaching meditation and Dhamma for forty years. Always, I have offered the teachings freely, just as they were offered freely to me by my teachers. Twenty years ago, Insight Dialogue become so compelling that I stopped virtually all my other income-producing activities in order to give all my time to teaching, studying, and writing it. Thus, after many years of giving to my teachers freely, as much as my time and means allowed, I slipped quietly but fully into a receiver's role in the economy of dāna.

Over time, I began teaching more widely and receiving enough money to significantly contribute to my own welfare and that of my wife. With this shift came classical, wholesome, necessary, and sometimes uncomfortable questions: Was I living in such a way as to honor the intentions of those who gave money to me? Was I living into the values of the Dhamma—modesty, shedding, being unfettered? It was hard for me to freely accept offerings for my teachings and then use it to pay what felt like a lot for services I needed—plumbing, accounting, auto repair. But the challenge was made greater when paying for anything that seemed luxurious: a meal at a restaurant, a new piece of furniture, someone to help repair the house when I could have done it.

I recall telling a friend how I returned from a long teaching trip with enough money to purchase a nice gift for my wife's art studio. He warned, "Don't let the meditators know that."

I was thrown. What is okay, what is right—sammā—in this weird calculus of a layperson living on money freely offered in response to my sharing Dhamma? Was using that money for gifts to others okay? Vacations? Something other than secondhand clothing? Anyone visiting me would know I was not living in any old hut, eating any old scraps of food, and wearing any old rags. What a great challenge!

A phrase from the suttas, "worthy of gifts . . . worthy of offerings," comes to mind.[102] When I reflect on my use of resources, I have this proxy of community support. When I feel drawn to wasting time or spending money unwisely, my community is in this reflection with me. This idea could be seen as a judgmental, moralistic super-ego, but this is not how I experience it. I accept my own humanity, my imperfections, and the fact that there will be ambiguities at this hybrid intersection of laity and dāna. So I can benefit from the reflection on worthiness with gratitude, as well as humility. I make no claim to getting it right; I only do my best.

There are plenty of hidden gifts. When I have generously offered teachings—to long-term students or people I've never met—and dāna is not offered, there is mostly equanimity, but I also get to watch the interplay of my frustrated wanting and sometimes even aversion. When I am offered cash at a teaching, I have had the great joy of earmarking much of it for gifts to others—a destitute mother in New Mexico, a friend I can take to dinner, or, best of all, teachers I study with. The feeling of being in the ancient flow of Dhamma freely offered is precious.

## Giving's Effect on the Mind

Cultivating the mind by giving is essential to the whole-life path. The Buddha said, "Bhikkhus, if beings knew, as I know, the result of giving and sharing, they would not eat without having given . . . Even if it were their last morsel, their last mouthful, they would not eat without having shared it, if there were someone to share it with."[103]

Elsewhere, the Buddha makes it clear that he is not referring primarily to the material benefits of giving, like better rebirths or being well liked:

> Having given this, not seeking his own profit, not with a mind attached (to the reward), not seeking to store up for himself, nor (with the thought), "I'll enjoy this after death,"— nor with the thought, "Giving is good," — nor with the thought, "This was given in the past, done in the past, by my father and grandfather. It would not be right for me to let this old family custom be discontinued," . . . nor with the thought, "I am well-off. These are not well-off. It would not be right for me (to not give when I am able)," . . . nor with the thought, "Just as there were the great sacrifices of the sages of the past" . . . nor with the thought, "When this gift of mine is given, it makes the mind serene. Gratification and joy arise,"
>
> — but (one gives) with the thought, "This is an ornament for the mind, a support for the mind" — on the break-up of the body, after death, he reappears in the company of Brahma's Retinue. Then, having exhausted that action, that power, that status, that sovereignty, he is a non-returner. He does not come back to this world.[104]

One gives to beautify the mind. Yes, there is joy in giving, and this is lovely and refreshing, but even such joy is understood as impermanent. The deeper value is the refinement of the mind, the release of self-centered habits, engendering a nongrasping heart of inclusion and care. Giving is a practice, and by engaging this practice, the mind is formed in wholesome ways—ways that lead to unbinding.

Another important message embedded in this teaching is that how you give matters. One gives not out of custom or social or even moral obligation. One gives not with a stingy mind, not in a miserly way, but respectfully, mindfully: "(W)hether a gift is coarse or refined, if it is given attentively, respectfully, with one's own hand, not as if throwing it away, with the view that something will come of it."[105]

The effect of this kind of giving provides rewards in that moment, but also forms the basis for further refining the mind, enabling the practice described in this discourse:

> There is the case where you recollect your own generosity: "It is a gain, a great gain for me, that—among people overcome with the stain of possessiveness—I live at home, my awareness cleansed of the stain of possessiveness, freely generous, openhanded, delighting in being magnanimous, responsive to requests, delighting in the distribution of alms." At any time when a disciple of the noble ones is recollecting generosity, his mind is not overcome with passion, not overcome with aversion, not overcome with delusion. His mind heads straight, based on generosity. And when the mind is headed straight, the disciple of the noble ones gains a sense of the goal, gains a sense of the Dhamma, gains joy connected with the Dhamma. In one who is joyful, rapture arises. In one who is rapturous, the body grows calm. One whose body is calmed experiences ease. In one at ease, the mind becomes concentrated.
>
> Of one who does this it is said: "Among those who are out of tune, the disciple of the noble ones dwells in tune; among those who are malicious, he dwells without malice; having attained the stream of Dhamma, he develops the recollection of generosity."[106]

In addition to understanding the hand-to-hand, interpersonal face of giving, we also understand giving as a social act. We are participating with the recipients in the movement of goodwill and resources within a whole social system. An individual giver's heart opens, and he benefits in mutuality, unselfishness, and joy. The individual receiver also experiences the relatedness and joy of an open heart. But the act of giving did not begin with the giver, and it does not end with him, either. We have resources because we have been recipients. We are sharing resources that we have received from others, whether as rewards for hard work or good fortune or as gifts from others. Giving calls us to be like farmers who regard the apples from their orchards as a gift from nature that they are simply passing along—to widen the mind to encompass the fecund system we are part of. This is right livelihood as a living flow.

As we participate in an economic system by way of giving, we are changing the system. When we see another suffering from lack of food, water, medicine, or lodging, and we are moved to give money or other support, we are directly addressing the imbalances in our economy, in addition to helping *this* person. How does it feel to directly help diminish someone's suffering and to swim against the stream of a self-oriented culture? Do we want to contribute to the shared effort to free beings from suffering—hunger and homelessness, as well as ignorance, here and now and in the future? If we are part of a community that has a strong ethic of giving and engages in collective acts of generosity, we have the added benefit of sharing the joy we experience. Community strengthens as givers and receivers share a vision and enact that vision. When building a community of care, giving material support makes that caring visibly real.

Not all of the effects of giving are tangible. An individual is transformed as the personal volition to give becomes a way of living. Specific relationships are crucial for giving to move from individual to social action. The warmth of relationship nourishes healthy and happy couples, families, and work groups. The community is transformed as the group volition to give grows strong. Wholesome intentions are broadcast. Whole cultures that highly value generosity, like the potlatch culture of the Native American tribes of the Pacific Northwest, reflect this value at the level of institutions, families, and individual relationships.

And there is the giving and receiving of Dhamma, named throughout the discourses as the highest gift. Here, we are stepping into a river that has been flowing for 2,500 years. We received the teachings because our teachers were supported by others. When we support our teachers with the requisites, we are giving access to the Dhamma to all whom are reached by this teacher—or institution—from this point forward. The energy of giving flows onward. Do we want to be the ones who, by neglect, dry up this river? Or do we want to participate in this opportunity of abundance? Giving Dhamma, by offering the teachings or supporting those who offer, is a sweet and satisfying practice of right livelihood.

PRACTICE

## PARTICIPATING IN A GIFT ECONOMY OF DHAMMA

It would be good if you could do this practice with one or more friends who share an interest in the Buddha's teachings. Contemplate together from whom you first received Dhamma teachings—meditation instructions, talks, or guidance. If these teachings were not offered in person, who was the author of the book, website, or recorded talk? Was it freely given, or was there a cost beyond the price of the book?

If there was a fee for the teachings, set this example aside and think of other places you have received the teachings where they were freely given. Then trace this thread back. In each case, consider where this teacher received their training. Do you know? Was it freely given? In all likelihood, especially if you have received teachings from monastics or teachers who have studied with monastics, you will not have to look far to locate teachings that have been freely given far, far back. We, and our teachers, are part of a gift economy, with the most valued gift of Dhamma being freely offered, sometimes by the proxy of money, then passed along likewise to others.

Take the time to recollect. Then share with your practice partners how it felt to receive teachings that are so meaningful, so beautiful. How would you value them? Does money work as a measuring tool here, and if so, how much would you pay for them? If money does not provide a good measure, can you launch your heart into that space defined by the word *priceless*?

Now, follow that sense of "priceless" back in time: your teachers, their teachers, their teachers—all the way back to the earliest nuns, monks, and laymen and laywomen and to the Buddha, who received and offered teachings and support that enabled you to receive the Dhamma.

Finally, turn your imagining heart to the future: how will you keep this flow going and freely support the teachings, as well as the people and institutions that sustain them?

---

## ∼ REFLECTION

Right livelihood is sīla in its economic mode. The ways we enter the complex circulation of value in society determines who gets the most basic necessities of life and who has luxury, who is free and who is enslaved, who gets medical treatment and who is left to die. We can think of morality as a refinement of the mind and moral action as the expression of that mind that directly impacts others. We all wield these powerful forces whenever we receive a paycheck, go to the grocery store, volunteer for a cause, support our young children, or help a neighbor in need. Our credit card statement is a moral document.

As one of the sīla path factors, right livelihood is quintessentially interpersonal and social. Our acts influence others and shape us even as we imagine, choose, and enact them. The results of those actions come back to us from others in ways that further shape us. At all scales, our economic participation in society patterns the mind by means of interpersonal and societal feedback loops. In turn, we act in accordance with the mind's patterning—and launch fresh actions of all kinds into the world. Society as a whole comes to reflect our collective vocational, lifestyle, and resource choices; a system is built that sustains individual patterns at the global level.

The path factor of right livelihood proclaims that we can behave in wholesome and beneficial ways within this inescapable circulation of value, that we can wield these karmic forces in ways that lead to social harmony and to liberation.

Perhaps more than any other path factor, the practice of right livelihood unfolds in the earthiness of the physical lives of our bodies. Eating becomes chewing and swallowing liberating teachings. Donning our clothing becomes wrapping ourselves in the warmth and protection of the Dhamma. Our homes become refuges that reflect our values and aspirations. Medicine, and more fully, the endless cycles we live of illness and healing, can be experienced as intimate, living aspects of a sacred life. When the teachings on livelihood are let in fully, their here-and-now quality infuses each living moment.

Right livelihood follows right speech and right action as the last of the three virtue elements of the path. These three interrelate and work together to establish a powerful basis for cultivating the next three factors of the path: right effort, right mindfulness, and right samādhi. The mind freed from the agitation and selfishness inherent in wrongdoing is malleable, calm, and stable. It easily dwells in friendliness and compassion. We are now ready to work directly with letting go of harmful psychological patterns. We are ready to wake up to the details of moment-to-moment experience, and, if so motivated, experience the deepest forms of calm abiding and insight. The next three path factors involve the development of these qualities of the heart and mind, qualities that transform and further refine our view and whole life patterns. How we live is intimately connected with freeing the heart. This is the whole-life path in service of harmony and release.

~

# CHAPTER 9

# RIGHT EFFORT

## *Sammā Vāyāma*

R eading these words takes time and energy, especially attentional energy; you are sticking with it, right to the end of this sentence. Writing and editing these words has taken time and energy too. So as you are reading these words now, our efforts are meeting. We have here, as noted in the discussion of right view, wise attention meeting the voice of another. And sensing into the energy behind wise attention, we can discern the effort component of present-moment experience. The intentional directing of my mind is connecting, via these words, with the intentional directing of your mind, but the energy, the continuity, is, right now, moment by moment, where our right efforts meet.

The path factor of right effort is about developing this energy and our capacity for applying it. A whole-life path is guided by right view, but activated by right effort—*actively* diminishing what leads to your suffering and that of others and *actively* increasing what leads to your and others' wellbeing. Right effort is the energy driving the entire wholesome cycle of interest, discovery, practices, and life changes that enact what we have discovered, as well as the richness of understanding and amplification of internal **effort** that comes with spiritual friendships and community. It is vitality directed in service of ease, compassion, and awakening.

## RIGHT EFFORT AS A PATH FACTOR

Right effort runs through all of the other path factors and through the whole inquiry into how the Noble Eightfold Path can be fully and deeply lived. With right view and right intention, we lay the foundation for wisdom, sensing that freedom is possible and beginning to orient our lives around that possibility. With right speech, right action, and right livelihood, we build street-level wisdom and clean up our act so that we can live harmoniously with others and begin to calm down. Then with right effort, like the remaining two path factors of mindfulness and concentration, we deal with the direct training of the mind.

Translators of the early texts variously employ words such as *focus, exertion, perseverance,* and *diligence* to describe right effort; each points to a facet of *sammā vāyāma,* which is built around the root word *yam,* "to strive or reach."

The classical definition of right effort involves the four wholesome efforts, or four exertions, as they are applied to mental states: preventing and abandoning unwholesome states and cultivating and maintaining wholesome states.[107] While the Buddha's words may seem a bit dry to modern readers, I offer them here so you can gain a sense of their elemental nature.

> And what, bhikkhus, is right effort? Here, bhikkhus, (1) a bhikkhu generates desire for the nonarising of unarisen evil unwholesome states; he makes an effort, arouses energy, applies his mind, and strives. (2) He generates desire for the abandoning of arisen evil unwholesome states. . . . (3) He generates desire for the arising of unarisen wholesome states. . . . (4) He generates desire for the maintenance of arisen wholesome states, for their nondecay, increase, expansion, and fulfillment by development; he makes an effort, arouses energy, applies his mind, and strives. This is called right effort.[108]

We will look at the four efforts in detail later in this chapter. Our focus right now is a sense of activity and energy that are essential if the Path is to be more than just theoretical: "(S)he makes an effort, arouses energy, applies his (her) mind, and strives." Right effort energizes all of the path factors and helps us bridge the gap between aspiring to and actually living this challenging path of relinquishment and care. This universal quality of energizing makes right effort a key path factor in all circumstances.

It takes effort to go against the stream of personal habit—a stream sustained internally by patterns of the body-mind and externally by patterns of relationships and social structure. The Buddha's famous teaching about going against the stream was referring specifically to the stream of sensual indulgence and bad deeds.[109] But right effort is aimed at the entire stream, including ending unwholesome deeds and uplifting and purifying the mind, from which all actions blossom. Here is a summary of the human predicament and how right effort synergizes with right view and right mindfulness:

- Our personal and social norm is ignorance[110]
  and thus utter inattention to ubiquitous
  suffering, its roots, and its possible ending.

- Right view recognizes the stream of
  ignorance, collective and individual.

- Right mindfulness constantly reawakens us out of
  the stream of identification and mindlessness.

- Marshaling these forces of right view and right mindfulness,
  right effort is the energy of swimming towards the
  wholesome and away from unwholesome. It puts wisdom
  and awareness to work and gives them strength, even
  against the grim inflexibility of habit and the personal and
  social streams of continuing mindlessness and blindness.

Right effort rises to the level of a path factor because it is the only way aspiration can become transformation, and because employing the energy necessary to go from one to the other is no small thing. The Buddha told his followers to throw themselves into this work as if the situation were an emergency:

If, by . . . examination a bhikkhu knows: "I am often given to longing, given to ill will, overcome by dullness and drowsiness, restless, plagued by doubt, angry, defiled in mind, agitated in body, lazy, and unconcentrated," he should put forth extraordinary desire, effort, zeal, enthusiasm, indefatigability, mindfulness, and clear comprehension to abandon those same bad unwholesome qualities.

Just as one whose clothes or head had caught fire would put forth extraordinary desire, effort, zeal, enthusiasm, indefatigability, mindfulness, and clear comprehension to extinguish (the fire on) his clothes and head.[111]

The Buddha's call to apply "extraordinary desire, effort, zeal, enthusiasm, [and] indefatigability" is at odds with some of the meditation advice heard today—advice that says there is nothing to do, or that our minds are okay just as they are, or that we should not meddle or tamper with our experience. This sort of advice may be wise in certain contexts, but it is often taken outside those contexts to mean that effort is unnecessary and even wrong. Yet the fact that right effort is a factor of the Buddha's Noble Eightfold Path demands that effort be taken seriously.

PRACTICE
**EXAMINING THE FELT EXPERIENCE OF ENERGY**

*Viriya*, or energy, is a crucial component of right effort. The Buddha named viriya as one of the seven factors of awakening and described it as twofold: energy of the body and of the mind.[112] Like other mental qualities, energy grows when we pay attention to it. Even just noticing the felt experience of vitality—for example, in the spring of your step or in the moment of mental alertness that follows an exciting thought—feeds that vitality. The energy of attention melds with and amplifies the vitality, while mindfulness sustains and reveals detail in the experience.

Here are a few questions to help you become more aware of the application of effort, energy, and exertion in your particular life. Try this practice in three modes: first, sit quietly, alone, and ask these questions; then do the same with a practice partner; and then do the same with a small group of people.

First, consider energy in the body—maybe as qi, a fine vibration, or just as feeling good. What is that energy like? How do you use it? How might you condition the body to raise the background level of vitality? How does being or meditating with another person affect your energy level? What do you do when the energy in the body feels congested, bound up? What do you do when you are tired or ill and don't feel much energy in the body? At such times, can you look more closely for subtle cues that the energy is present—for example, in the breath or sensations in the hands?

Next, consider energy in the mind—maybe as excitement or glee, maybe as a mind free from distraction, vital and engaged. What is that energy like? Does it change as you pay attention to it? How do you use it? What do you do when you don't feel much energy in the mind, as with sleepiness or depression? Can you bring attention to the subtle energy of awareness itself—maybe to the act of shifting attention to different thoughts or objects? What happens to mental energy when you engage with another person? Does their alertness impact you? How does attentional, relational energy change over time?

Finally, consider exertion and strong effort in your life. Where in your life do you make a strong effort to get things done? Where in your life do you go with the flow, with only small course corrections from time to time? Where do you collapse, withdraw, or get lazy? Which relationships arouse vigor and engagement? Which drain you? How do you decide which relationships to nourish and what strategies to engage with your internal ebb and flow?

After you have done this practice alone, with a friend, and with a small group, reflect on how energy manifests differently in these three practice modes.

## RIGHT EFFORT IS
## BALANCED EFFORT

As we have seen, right effort applies to each of the path factors and enlivens the entire Path. Not every attempt at applying effort is helpful, however.

The culture around us provides massively unskillful ideas about effort: *Work hard to earn enough money, then make yourself happy by purchasing and consuming far more than you need. Force yourself into a religious mold and concoct a purely good person; hide and repress what is broken while judging others for their brokenness.* These social constructs present greed, lust, and hatred as the primary motivations for effort, and anxiety and desire as its typical modes of working. We see exertion propelled by an insecure "self," spinning ever more layers of identity. In the media we see agitated people, real and fictional, applying themselves beyond healthy limits and becoming increasingly stressed and burnt out, even when the goal is good. When we apply effort in these ways, we are like a woodpecker who pecked a huge hole in my friend's house. My friend put a coffee can lid across the hole, but the bird kept pecking the same place, ramming his head against the metal rather than moving over a couple of inches. It's not just the quality of our effort that matters, but also how and where we apply it.

Long ago I was on a retreat in a mountain cabin with my teacher Achan Sobin. I worked really hard at my meditation

during this time. I meditated constantly. I tried. I pushed. I perse-
vered. I applied energy. I was intensely diligent. But I was like that
woodpecker cranking against the coffee-can lid. The kind of effort
I applied was painful. My mind was greedy for experience and
accomplishment; my fruit was mostly tension and dissatisfaction.
The shards of concentration produced by such unskillful practice
were fragile, lacking the joy and tranquility that are the basis of
good samādhi. In retrospect, it became clear that I was functioning without a balanced sense of effort. I did not understand how
crucial joy and ease are to right effort. Sometimes, right effort is
like the more strenuous effort required to turn the soil and plant
our gardens; other times it is like the steady gentle application of
the sun's heat as it slowly penetrates the soil and warms the seeds.
Discerning which type is needed for a given endeavor is part of the
practice of right effort.

The Buddha makes it clear that directing effort to alter one's
mental and emotional habits is sometimes essential to progress and
can lead to benefit and pleasure.[113] Yet unwise efforts, like my practice in the mountains thirty years ago, lie behind many people's
fear of and resistance to the application of energy, exertion, or zeal.
If we are going to take more than a hands-off approach, we must
come to an understanding of right effort that is wholesome and
helpful. For a whole-life path, this effort must be sustainable, a
way of being that we can live with every dull or shiny day. Such an
understanding will also recognize the joy associated with a heartful commitment to seeing things as they actually are. This is an
effort that allows us to apply ourselves with confidence.

To be "right," effort must be wisely directed—with the help of
right view—and must support the conditions for liberation. Right
effort inclines towards nonclinging; it leads to freedom from con-
stricting patterns and views and to the development of awakening
factors such as energy, joy, tranquility, and concentration. It is effort
towards unbinding, disentangling. It moves towards dispassion, not
passion, towards contentment, not discontent. Sometimes this effort
takes hard work, perseverance, and gritty application. Sometimes,

it is born of a gentle, persistent turn towards calming down. Effort that is right has the power to lead us toward ever greater altruism and love just as much as toward greater relinquishment.

PRACTICE

## THE EXPERIENCE OF EXTRAORDINARY EFFORT

This is a two-part practice. First, alone or with a trusted friend, reflect on where or when you have applied a great deal of effort to make a wholesome change or maybe to just keep your life from going off the rails. Maybe it was during a time of crisis, like a pandemic or a natural or personal disaster. Maybe it was during a traumatic event in which you were brought face to face with unseen emotional patterns. Maybe it was when you were facing a threat to bodily survival or health. Maybe it was when you were cultivating new levels of meditative development.

What did this time of intense effort feel like in the body? What kinds of things did you think about? What kinds of moods or mind states did you experience? On reflection, do you see benefit having come from this effort?

Next, look at your life for an area you are inspired to bring an extraordinary level of energy to. It might be connected with a meditative development that you now feel ready for. It might be a relationship or type of community participation that you believe to be wholesome. Whatever area you identify, establish your resolve and then *take action*. Step out of your comfort zone; extend your sense of capacity. As you do so, regularly give attention to balance, to the wholesome qualities at the core of your effort, and to the quality of effort itself: what is it like to engage the body-mind fully?

If you reach a clear endpoint for this effort, you are invited to investigate whether the bare capacity to apply yourself has grown.

## RIGHT EFFORT, TRANSFORMATION OF THE MIND, AND PSYCHOTHERAPY ON THE WHOLE-LIFE PATH

One of the Buddha's great insights was that the tightest coils of the mind are wound by grasping at sensations, self, and the constructing process of the body-mind, and that they can be unwound by steadily working with the causes of that grasping and by forming new inclinations of release. Consider the Buddha's description of his own process, which he here offers as a practice for all of us: "Here a bhikkhu, gone to the forest or to the root of a tree or to an empty hut, considers thus: 'Is there any obsession unabandoned in myself that might so obsess my mind that I cannot know or see things as they actually are?'"[114]

*Anything* that obsesses the mind to the point of altering how we see the world—the effort to abandon the unwholesome is *that* broad, encompassing our obsessions, biases, tangles, urges, hatreds, and fears. And the effort to cultivate the wholesome can encompass anything and everything that orients us towards individual, relational, and social freedom. Such fundamental transformation presupposes that the mind is plastic on a very deep level—as neuroscience now shows it to be. Right effort is the industrial powerhouse of this transformation of the mind. For some, right effort might include engaging in contemporary psychotherapy.

With the following exploration, it is not my intention to critique theories and methods that might fall under the rubric of contemporary psychotherapy. I will, however, show how a whole-life path can include, as appropriate to each individual, the benefits of psychotherapy.

### Psychotherapy and the Release of Painful Mental Patterns

Some years ago, following a death in my family, I was experiencing intense difficulty. I was forced to confront my own confusion and needs, as well as cope with the unskillful actions of others. I could feel the tensions in the body; I observed the mind as it latched onto painful memories and associated confusions. Intense awareness of the body allowed me to confront a whole complex of karmic knots.

Along with the deep release supported by meditation and awareness throughout the day, I deepened my understanding via therapy. Supported by the care and perceptiveness of another, I was able to see my mind more clearly. With another, I could see and accept—and ultimately release or abandon—what I could not alone. I came to understand that the letting go that happened in meditation and the letting go that happened in psychotherapy supported each other in the effort to clear the body-mind of the self's specific snarls and of the ignorance that keeps the whole system going.

Psychotherapy can be framed as an interpersonal practice of releasing painful mental patterns. The psychotherapeutic relationship can support right efforts to abandon the unwholesome, which is one way of naming the therapy client's sources of pain, and cultivate the wholesome—that is, healthy mental patterns. Sometimes we can see with others what we cannot see alone. And someone who is skilled in guiding us to understand our own hearts can accelerate and refine the process of relinquishment and cultivation.

On the Buddhist path, the recognition of suffering sparks a search for what will reduce it. "And what is the result of suffering?" the Buddha asks. "It's when someone who is overcome and overwhelmed by suffering sorrows and pines and cries, beating their breast and falling into confusion. Or else, overcome by that suffering, they begin an external search, wondering: 'Who knows one or two phrases to stop this suffering?' The result of suffering is either confusion or a search, I say."[115] Buddhism and contemporary psychotherapy are both part of this search: they share the goal of reducing suffering. However, psychotherapy does not always share the same understanding of suffering and its causes, and its understandings of what releases suffering is only partially aligned with the Buddhist understanding. The key to skillfully integrating the therapeutic approach into a whole-life path is right view.

## Right View Harmonizes Psychotherapy with the Whole-Life Path

The optimal way of incorporating psychotherapy into a whole-life Buddhist path is to find a psychotherapist who is familiar with the Dhamma. Such a therapist would appreciate essential aspects of the wisdom framework, and *this understanding would be reflected in the therapeutic relationship and therapy process*. Then both the client and therapist would approach the therapeutic process and relationship through the lens of right view.

I consider three teachings of early Buddhist psychology to be indispensable aspects of a psychotherapy that is coherent with the whole-life path:

- The self is fluxing and constructed.
- Release from the reflexive force of the self's urges is possible.
- The path is a whole-life thing, replete with lifestyle and morality.

### The Fluxing and Constructed Nature of Self

This is a key component of right view. A psychotherapist working from a whole-life path perspective will have explored this territory in their own life, and it will be the basic context of the therapeutic process and its goals. While the contingent nature of the self may not be explicitly stated, the therapeutic process can be understood as the task of helping the client come to see the fluxing and constructed nature of any given painful construct. This might be a place where intrinsic Buddhist psychology is transformed from theory into practice.

The kind of suffering that is the working territory of contemporary psychology fits into a single Buddhist term: *saṅkhāra*. This term is frequently translated as "constructions," but also as "volitional formations," "fabrications," and "concoctions." Key to understanding the scope and purpose of right effort is seeing how saṅkhāras, as both mental constructions and the constructing process itself, fit in with the arising and the cessation of suffering,[116] of self,[117] and of the world of experience.[118] Right effort, then, in light of the Four Noble Truths, includes but is not limited to abandoning and cultivating some of the specific constructs named by contemporary psychology. For example, self-image, the future, memories, and patterns of relationship are all saṅkhāras, constructed in each moment based on prior constructing processes. The psychology and Path named by the Buddha says that direct apprehension—via meditation, in-life mindfulness, and reflection on the structure and function of the body-mind—of these constructing processes gets to the root of how we perceive and thus live in the world. Such insight points to a liberation that includes yet transcends a reshuffling of the constructing processes. So in this light, the therapist is helping the client to apprehend these constructing processes as they unfold.

There are two key teachings that help guide this therapeutic process of dispassionately observing the constructing process. The five aggregates, or *khaṇḍha*, offer a structural view, and dependent origination, or paṭiccasamuppāda, offers a process view. Taken together, they frame and may help guide the psychotherapeutic process in a way that is harmonious with a whole-life path.

In this liberative vision the working domain of right effort is the elemental body-mind, which places (1) saṅkhāra—including all of our psychological fabrications—as co-arising and vanishing with the subjective appearance of (2) bodily form, (3) feelings, (4) perceptions, and the cognizing process of (5) consciousness. These five aggregates (khaṇḍha) are usually clung to as fixed and real, and a self is imputed to them in such a way as to help us get by in the world. Unfortunately, we don't stop at getting by. The clinging of and to these five heaps is expanded into a complicated self-construct that is born and reborn in each moment and that needs continual feeding and protecting. This self emerges as a nexus of sensory, psychological, and relational preferences and contorted views of the world that can be fabulously out of alignment with actuality. Once clung to and "self-ized," this fluxing process seems to actually exist. The process of forming this experience of "I exist" is described in the Buddha's teachings on dependent origination, paṭiccasamuppāda. In this teaching, too, we see the central role of saṅkhāra, constructions and constructing processes, and thus the key role of right effort in disentangling the body-mind.

In the blind process of self-construction,[119] each moment of cognition is conditioned by a lifetime of accumulated mental registrations.[120] Based on these implicit, conditioned mental processes—we cannot see the construction process actually happening except in the most extraordinary moments of meditative insight—the experience of body-mind emerges as acutely sensitive to its environment.[121] This sensitivity itself—to light, sound, and by extension, people, words, and social structures—is the basis for pleasant and unpleasant contacts[122] that arouse deeply rooted urges for pleasure, self-survival, and withdrawal.[123] These urges propel the system to push and pull at these contacts[124] in an effort to get pleasure and secure the self. This grasping makes the apparent "me" at the center of all this churning seem ever more real and fuels the experience of "I exist."[125] The knot of self is nothing other than the stress generated by the flailing of this tangle. It is fabricated out of empty processes of body-mind, and it is this self that suffers.[126] This is the foundation of a liberative psychotherapy that is in alignment with the whole-life path.

### The Possibility of Release

A second key element of right view regarding psychotherapy and the whole-life path is the possibility of release from cycles of self-inflicted limitation and pain. Freedom, from the perspective of dependent origination, involves a flip: with the cessation of any link in this process, the links around it no longer have the conditions for their arising. They cease. The hungers, the tangles, the stressful grasping that is essential to the survival of this anguished "me" just vanish. By seeing through the magic show[127] with meditative insight, as supported by an ethical life, by other qualities laid out in the teachings, and by wisdom-based psychotherapy, we no longer believe in and reflexively act upon its excitements. Some of the personality patterns based on faulty premises of a self and a poorly constructed worldview dissolve. Established patterns that remain may be activated by contact with the world, but lacking the habitual grasping that sustains them and propels them into further thought and action, they die away. Not taken up, the upsurges naturally fade. Gradual release is easy to understand; completely breaking out of the trance of becoming is challenging.

Neither the therapist nor client need to be utterly convinced that such elemental release is possible. What matters is that we are open to this possibility and willing to investigate it for ourselves. Even just the possibility that such freedom is possible sets a direction towards modesty rather than self-aggrandizement, towards shedding rather than accumulating, towards a release of preferences, and towards contentment. Also, keeping the mind open to this type of release keeps a door open for therapy to go beyond the baseline of ordinary suffering. A more refined happiness is humanly possible, and the right effort applied in psychotherapy can contribute to its realization.

### This Whole Life Is the Path

The third understanding essential to an integrated sense of psychotherapy and the vision of the path offered here is that our whole life, not just therapy or meditation sessions, are part of the process. The quality and consistency of effort required will be optimally served by a whole-life commitment. An approach to mental culture where "nothing is left out" is optimal but not required. Each of us works as we can, and reduction or improvement is also valued. A client may not be ready for whole-life commitment, but the therapist working from the perspective of a whole-life path understands the value of a wide-spectrum process that continues outside the therapy office.

In particular, the therapist sees a life inclined towards ethics as one of the aims of the therapeutic process. The psychotherapists' well-developed professional code of ethics is a good foundation, but ethics are also important as a basis for a whole-life path.

These are the three elemental understandings basic to a therapist functioning with a perspective that is compatible with and supportive of a whole-life path. This is psychotherapy driven by the energy of right effort and guided by wise understanding, or right view.

## Confronting the Double Bypass

A key benefit of integrating Buddhist and contemporary approaches to freeing the mind is that it demands that we recognize and confront the double bypass—spiritual and psychological—that can lead to distance from the work of untangling.

Psychology points clearly to the deeply rooted tangles of behavior and personality, and its practice involves direct engagement with those tangles. The Dhamma points clearly to the potential for seeing the constructed nature of the tangle and to complete unbinding from the forces that perpetuate it. Both perspectives have value; both are named by the Four Noble Truths; each generates its own form of resistance. A whole-life path that integrates therapy and the Dhamma must clearly address both perspectives and forms of resistance.

Spiritual bypassing refers to hiding from suffering and retreating into transcendence, often with the help of meditation, in order to avoid facing painful personality patterns. It might take the form of a narrow Buddhist view that regards naming and looking squarely at patterns such as trauma, problematic attachments, and social anxiety (a strong suit of contemporary psychotherapy) as a pointless, endless process of getting lost in illusions of the personality. It might take the form of meditation engaged as a means of placating or escaping our anger, loneliness, and fear, rather than seeing things as they actually are.

There is also what I call a psychological bypass. This is the stance that dismisses the possibility of awakening and adheres to the consensual ultimacy of the personality. In this view, the best a human can hope for in this life is a workable arrangement of personality and circumstances. Any talk of freedom from the urges of the self is delusory, wishful thinking, not scientifically tenable. The Buddha's vision of freedom is even viewed as life-denying: great sensations, angst, and titanic wrestling matches of the personality are the stuff and purpose of this life. In the psychological bypass, not-self or freedom offer only visions of grayness and apathy.

Both the spiritual bypass and the psychological bypass are motivated by fear and ignorance. The spiritual bypass fears the pain of the world. The psychological bypass fears the pain of losing the world. The release born of dispassion arouses a fear of losing or appearing to devalue all that the constructing mind holds sacred: my pleasures, my art, my family, my joy in nature, my body. Above all, the fear is of losing my precious personality—my self.

The ignorance of the spiritual bypass is that dysfunctional personality patterns are operating unseen; there is a tacit belief that they can be escaped by a narcotic denial. The ignorance of the psychological bypass is simply not knowing that freedom from the trance of self-absorption is possible and refusing to do the work necessary to free oneself from that trance; there is a tacit fear of facing psychological issues and releasing sensory and other attachments, and this fear enables the blind tyranny of the personality to continue. In both forms of bypass, suffering is sustained and awakening is impeded. The spiritual bypass shrinks from the fullness of the first and second Noble Truths: suffering and its origins. The psychological bypass shrinks from the fullness of the third Noble Truth: the possibility that this suffering process can cease.

Skillfully integrating psychotherapy into the whole-life path precludes these two bypasses. It enables us to look squarely at the dysfunctional patterns of the personality and respect the value of reorienting them as part of a path aimed towards happiness and release. At the same time, we accept the challenge and opportunity of the unfettered mind. In addition to a workable refashioning, we understand that a life of nongrasping is a human possibility.

## THE FOUR RIGHT EFFORTS

In the Buddha's radical perspective, the heart of classical right effort can be summarized as "out with the bad, in with the good."

"The bad" refers to those actions that bring harm to oneself and/or others and to those mental qualities that keep us from calming down and seeing clearly. The first two of the wise efforts, preventing and abandoning, address these unwholesome states: we can prevent their arising if we catch them in time, or we can abandon them after they have arisen.

The other side of right effort focuses on encouraging "the good," or beneficial mental qualities. The remaining two efforts, cultivating and maintaining, are about these states: we can evoke them when they are not present, and we can develop and strengthen them when they are.

## What Is Abandoned and What Is Cultivated?

The right efforts to prevent and abandon point to how we can translate into action the Buddha's extensive teachings on unwholesome qualities. In the same way, the right efforts to cultivate and maintain show we can put into action his teachings on wholesome qualities. I'll name the main teachings and invite you to follow your interest to the source discourses. Here is where we see the second tenet of the whole-life path come alive: right effort sustains the ongoing contemplations that turn all teachings into practices.

Just as the range of mental distress is vast, so is the range of mental tendencies that sustain it. The classical core of what is to be abandoned as the mind matures are the five hindrances: sensory desire, ill will, laziness and sleepiness, restlessness and worry, and doubt. In day-to-day mental activity, the unwholesome roots of each thought are identified as greed, aversion, and delusion—the so-called defilements, or kilesa.

One of the most ubiquitous teachings on unwholesome qualities of mind is the one about the intoxicants, or taints (āsava). The liberated mind is perhaps most often named as that which is "taint free." This is the mutually supportive tripod of sensory intoxication, self-making intoxication, and ignorance.

Perhaps the simplest tendency of the body-mind to be abandoned with right effort is clinging, upādāna. Clinging to each of the aggregates of form, sensation, perception, constructions, and consciousness; clinging to hunger, conceit, and views.

There is much more that could be named here, but I'll close this summary by bringing in the Effacement Sutta (*Sallekhasutta*), which names forty-four qualities to be relinquished and forty-four corresponding qualities that, when cultivated, lead to this relinquishment.[128]

What is important here is the range encompassed by abandoning the unwholesome. In one coherent teaching we find everything from the most subtle distortions of view to the very human, everyday derangements of resentment, contempt, envy, fraud, and arrogance. Clearly, the path of freedom from self-obsession and pain is as pragmatic and subtle as it is wide.

The classical core of what is to be cultivated are the seven factors of awakening: mindfulness, investigation, energy, joy, tranquility, concentration, and equanimity. More obviously amenable to day-to-day mental development are the wholesome roots of nongreed, nonhatred, and nondelusion. Directly opposed to the unwholesome roots of greed, hatred, and delusion, these roots imply positive qualities of generosity (nongreed), love (nonhatred), and wisdom (nondelusion).

Another core construct of wholesome qualities are the five faculties: confidence or faith, energy, mindfulness, samādhi, and wisdom. Cultivating the brahmavihāras—the illimitable qualities of true friendliness, compassion, sympathetic joy, and equanimity—is another classical aspect of Buddhist mental culture. To this we could add the wholesome qualities like patience, generosity, and determination that are named in Buddhism as the *paramita*, or perfections.

For the wide view of cultivation, I return to the Effacement Sutta because the teaching is so valuable to developing relatedness and social decency. For example, "A person given to cruelty has noncruelty to lead him upwards." And so it is with all the reciprocal practices of wholesome and unwholesome qualities.

I'll close this brief review of cultivating the wholesome by reminding us of the eight Dhamma touch points we've been referring to: dispassion, being unfettered, shedding, modesty, contentment, seclusion, aroused persistence, and being unburdensome.

Aiming our lives in this way sets up a continuous encouragement of wholesome qualities.

## The Four Right Efforts in Depth

Now we can begin to see how preventing, abandoning, cultivating, and maintaining fit together in a whole-life path, and the role of the discourses in providing guidance for this path.

### The Effort of Preventing

Preventing unwholesome states from arising includes making ethical choices, but the first effort goes beneath these choices to address thoughts and mind states. Prevention begins simply, with our lifestyle. If we know we are tempted by something, we can stay away from it. If harsh speech or recreational drugs are weaknesses of ours, we can avoid those who engage in them. We stay away from such situations and people even if those situations are not inherently unethical. What counts is the effect a situation or relationship has on us. If television commercials or alluring websites provoke acquisitiveness, avoid them. If a certain snack food predictably leads to uncontrolled eating, don't keep a supply of it in the cupboard. If a person elicits cruelty from you, avoid him or her. All of these are gross forms of the effort to prevent.

The first effort also has a micro level: a moment-by-moment guarding of the senses, including the mind. At this micro level, mindfulness monitors all the senses so closely that one is aware that one has been triggered towards an unwholesome mind state before it has fully bloomed. The Buddha described this practice as one of the most difficult but important aspects of right effort required to end suffering.[129]

When I first came upon this teaching, I couldn't understand why the Buddha said that, of the four efforts, prevention took the most energy. I had put tremendous energy into the second effort—abandoning unskillful states—in my daily life, in therapy, and in meditation. What could be more difficult than that? But as I observed the workings of my own mind, the vigilance and subtlety of this prevention process gradually became clear to me. In the canyon-river-rushing moment of sensed experience, the effort of preventing the rise of the unwholesome unfolds in a flash. Monitoring the mind calls for vigilance and patience, for determined right effort.

However, the subtle genesis of an unwholesome state is not something that only the highly trained and proficient can notice. Most people will have instinctively noticed the small gap before the arising of mental and emotional phenomena. This gap between the trigger and the arising of mental reaction is observable even in children. A young child who has fallen and hurt herself will often take a few seconds before crying. The moment after falling presents a deluge of sensory and mental input: sensations of pain, spatial disorientation, and surprise. Fear and maybe anger may come a heartbeat later. How upset the child becomes may depend on who is around. If a parent who typically has become upset and solicitous at every little scratch is present, the child's reaction may be different than if she were on the playground with a teacher who has responded more moderately.

Adults can observe the fluid, malleable moment of arising in formal practice and in daily life. When we become able to observe the gap before a reaction is fixed, we can turn a friendly and compassionate curiosity towards the mechanisms by which we are triggered. Someone insults me. A feeling of hurt, then an angry thought, spring up. I'm paying attention. I let go. In practice, the mind becomes steadier, better able to do the fine-grained work of interrupting its momentum—preventing—right there in the gap.

And we can see how friendships inclined towards kindness, compassion, and nongreed will diminish the flow of unwholesome thoughts; in wholesome company such states are simply less likely to emerge and so won't need to be dealt with. Engaging in such friendships is structural prevention, and it is very effective.

PRACTICE

**PREVENTION IN FORMAL MEDITATION**

In a single meditation session, for a week of meditations, or in an extended retreat, set an intention to notice and release clinging before it takes hold. The content and subtlety of the clinging you apprehend will be directly correlated with the degree of tranquility and concentration you develop. If you meditate using a primary object, let that primary object be simple, like the breath or the sitting body. If you practice with an open-ended awareness, watch carefully for clinging to wandering thoughts that might arise before you realize you're caught.

Begin your meditation by noticing the body and inviting it to calm down. Then gently notice whether there are sensations, thoughts, or states to which the mind holds. Is there an interesting idea or image? A pleasant or unpleasant sensation? It is usually the case that if one particular contact seems to endure rather than rise and pass quickly away, some degree of clinging is happening. Releasing or relaxing the clinging before it ripens into a full-blown thought or sensation is our practice. Take your time. Be curious rather than pushy or judgmental. What is the experience of clinging? Of release?

---

### The Effort of Abandoning

Usually we become aware of unwholesome thoughts after they have arisen—often long after they have moved in and set up shop in the mall of our personality. Now what?

If we miss the opportunities to either avoid triggers or to head off a reaction before it unfolds, we can still deal with it using the second effort—the effort of letting go, of abandoning already arisen unwholesome thoughts and mind states.

Letting go begins with not pursuing, but also includes releasing as soon as we notice. There is a burst of judgment or conceit; rather than let it run its automatic course, can we change direction? We do this over and over again: on the cushion or in traffic or talking with a difficult person. The thought not pursued fades, shrinks, dies for lack of fuel. It does not (usually) need to be crushed; it just needs to not be fed.

Sometimes letting go is painstaking work that takes years. Sometimes purification does not come easily, but is a long, difficult, often repetitive process. Deeply seated confusions and karmic knots come up over and over again, perhaps with little sign of change or weakening. In addition to making use of the gap before the reaction, psychotherapy, practices of self-acceptance, and some methods shared by the Buddha can perhaps help. Because the heart, *citta*, is reforming, friendships rooted in loving honesty can also support this work. Relationship—the listening stillness and loving presence of another—can be a powerful force in freeing us to abandon ancient patterns of constriction.

Holding, and therefore release, always involves the body, not just the mind. Therefore, body practices are, like mental culture, important to abandoning. Mindfulness and acceptance interrupt the production of stress hormones and can help us endure the effects of those already released. Conversely, when we relax muscle tensions, the body memory of stress patterns clears out. Often, deep patterns are not accessible to either will or intellect. Deep breathing, vigorous exercise, or laughter may be the best place to begin. Meditation can calm the bodily formation at a deep level, enabling release far below the level of conscious awareness.

Abandoning can be a long-term process, but it can also sometimes be quick—and, perhaps surprisingly, joyful. I recall a moment of release following a long period of painful reactions to how I was working on a long-term task with a group of friends. After prolonged intensive meditation retreat, I was simply walking outside when a weight seemed to slide off my body. The words arose, "I'm done." It was a clear shift. The repeated waves of mindfulness and tranquility in formal meditation had undermined the foundations of my castle of pain. Also, I had repeatedly, diligently, engaged in inquiry into present-moment experience, with both simple mindfulness and with the guidance of the Dhamma, especially dependent origination. At the same time, the mind had been softened by an abiding attitude of kindness towards myself and others, and this helped release the patterns of mental grasping. Then in the lightest swell of a mental touch, the castle dissolved into the current. The lightness, and above all the dropping of attachment, endured. There was residue, for sure, but the quick release was also true.

Happy states in general tend to steady the mind; those that accompany a clean disconnect from an unwholesome reaction can steady the mind quite strongly. This arising of joy is exceptionally beneficial, because it orients the mind-body system towards further letting go. It helps us understand on a very deep level that letting go is okay, and this understanding eases all future work of preventing and abandoning. The happiness of letting go also has a clarity that is interpersonally contagious. We visibly manifest for others the benefits of the path.

## The Effort of Cultivating

The third effort is aimed at the arising of wholesome qualities that have not yet arisen. This can seem almost like trying to create something from nothing. Yet these wholesome qualities are not entirely absent from most human minds; most are part of our neurological heritage and our relational and social milieu. We can have moments of appreciation in the midst of the deepest depression; our feet can still remain stable on the floor as intense anxiety flows through us; moments of kindness visit even people who are generally mean. It may be that we have learned to ignore a wholesome quality and to settle quickly into patterns of discord. In the third effort, we take this first step of attending to unaccustomed and sometimes faint or flickering resonances of beautiful qualities.

Like the first effort of preventing, the third effort can be very difficult. Both involve subverting familiar habits in favor of something elusive and unproven. This can feel incredibly uncomfortable. For example, we may find that noticing anger is scary and then find it even scarier to touch a moment when the familiar angry self is not present. Who am I other than my anger? Am I safe when I'm not angry? While cultivating generosity, we may touch deep feelings of lack and insecurity. Cultivating confidence, we may confront patterns of self-doubt or media messages that we are inadequate. This is why effort is necessary; we are going against the stream.

Intentionally noticing fleeting wholesome qualities is a starting point; the effort to cultivate the wholesome finds its homeland in bringing to mind and nourishing skillful qualities. *Conviction, energy, sustained application, diligence,* and *endeavor* all describe full engagement with the wholesome. We give ourselves over as fully as we can to nurturing mindfulness and samādhi, true friendliness and patience. We return again and again to some facet of goodness, applying the mind in each and every moment to the nonflagging of compassion, equanimity, or generosity. When conditions are suitable, we might devote our precious free time to attending special retreats, untiringly cultivating an uncommon degree of tranquility and making space for exceptional equanimity.

Meditation retreats provide excellent opportunities for this third effort of cultivation. I'd been meditating for a few years with occasional guidance from my teacher Anagarika Dhammadinna, and I felt inspired by the benefits of greater mindfulness, by a clearer perspective on my life, and by just an inkling of how the Buddha's teachings can be observed in a grounded and daily way. I had no idea, though, what I was getting into with my first two-week meditation retreat.

The first few days were easy, even delightful, in their peacefulness and occasional discovery. Then came the physical pain of sitting. Then came the mental pain of agitation; my mind just would not shut up, and I expected that it should and would. Then came the judgments of others, then the judgments of self, then the realization that I was only halfway through this thing. When bliss struck, I thought it was great. *Wow, I've really done something!* But then it passed, and no matter what I did, it would not come back. Whipsawed, I kept at it. I sat through the pain, the bliss, and the utterly mundane tour of my mental concoctions. I sat through the self's gyrations.

I did not have the words for it, but I was intensively cultivating perseverance, an aspect of right effort, and along with it, right mindfulness. Right view was emerging directly from experience, but cracking old viewpoints of self and path didn't come easily. The utter lightness and delight and the bright sense of life possibility that I felt after the retreat closed were direct results of this intense effort to cultivate wholesome qualities.

The first and third efforts require presence, patience, and unwavering attention. The Buddha, rather than trying to minimize these challenges, acknowledged them bluntly: these two efforts can, at times, be as difficult as meeting intense pain—and require as much focused energy.[130] But establishing new wholesome qualities is possible and not always so difficult. With even a little history of success, we gain confidence.

PRACTICE

## NOTICING WHOLESOME STATES IN THE BODY

Noticing how wholesome states manifest in the body is a good way to cultivate them. Give attention to the bodily feelings associated with some particular quality. Begin by focusing on one quality—for example, friendliness, mindfulness, or contentment. Look for how you experience this quality here and now. Don't get thrown off by clichés about how you *should* experience it. Friendliness may or may not be felt in the heart area; courage may manifest in the neck, not just the belly. Dwell intimately with the felt experience. In addition to a bodily locale, look for felt qualities, such as a sweetness and simplicity in kindness, a brightness in mindfulness, or a lightness in renunciation.

Sustain this attention; be curious. Inquire, without words, into any connections you experience between mind and body states. Let the body-mind relax, or slide, into the experience.

Simple, sustained attention to these manifestations in the body allows the quality to resonate. The body's nervous and hormonal systems become familiar with the quality, grow comfortable with it. When the quality disappears, perhaps we can evoke it again, or simply let it be gone. The body memory supports the neural and hormonal memory, increasing the likelihood that the wholesome qualities will arise and strengthening them when they do.

---

### The Effort of Maintaining

In the suttas, the description of the fourth effort is somewhat richer than those of the other three. This effort is exercised "for the sake of the maintenance, nonconfusion, increase, plenitude, development, and culmination of the wholesome that has arisen."[131] These reasons are partly synonymous, emphasizing the importance of the fourth effort, and partly different in nuance, presenting different aspects of the effort itself.

Once we have learned to dependably evoke a wholesome quality, an interesting range of practices become possible. Experiencing the quality—which was always an innate capacity—has become a trained ability. We are no longer searching for the quality; now we can work with it. This effort is easier than the third effort and often quite enjoyable. Now we can maintain the wholesome mind state steadily for a while. We can see if it has become polluted and purify it if needed. We can check its boundaries, let it go and bring it back up again, and increase its scope or intensity. There is a facility and naturalness in maintaining these skillful qualities.

The Buddha's chief disciple, Sariputta, describes the facility born of a fully mature fourth effort:

A bhikkhu wields mastery over his mind, he does not let the mind wield mastery over him. In the morning he abides in whatever abiding or attainment he wants to abide in during the morning; at midday he abides in whatever abiding or attainment he wants to abide in at midday; in the evening he abides in whatever abiding or attainment he wants to abide in during the evening. Suppose a king or a king's minister had a chest full of variously colored garments. In the morning he could put on whatever

pair of garments he wanted to put on in the morning; at midday
he could put on whatever pair of garments he wanted to put
on at midday; in the evening he could put on whatever pair of
garments he wanted to put on in the evening. So too, a bhikkhu
wields mastery over his mind.[132]

Work with the factors of awakening, the brahmavihāras, and
other good qualities can take on a new dimension once we have
learned to find them easily in the body-mind. These qualities tend
to build on themselves and on each other. They thrive on attention.
Their "maintenance, nonconfusion, increase, plenitude, development, and culmination" is largely a matter of learning to work with
positive feedback loops. As we attend to the quality, it grows stronger. With practice, we become more skilled at not getting in our own
way; we allow the feedback loop to work. We learn to make finer
distinctions between these qualities.

As skill in developing these states grows, the mind becomes
steadier and able to see more clearly. This level of familiarity, carried forward into extended meditation retreat, can provide the
basis for extraordinary development of mettā, compassion, and
other qualities. Practicing calming the mind, investigating the
wholesome quality, and directly giving attention to what has
already arisen of mettā (or mindfulness, samādhi, and so on), we
can rely on our recognition of that quality at times when the mind
wanders or gets confused. The inspiration to persevere is buoyed
by confidence, a clear sense of direction, and prior direct experience of wholesome results.

This fourth effort to maintain is powerfully supported by our
spiritual friendships—and made difficult by unwise social contacts. If our development is genuine, it will manifest in our social
encounters, where every day kindness, mindfulness, and generosity have a wide field in which to exercise. In addition to setting
in motion a natural, social feedback loop, we can intentionally
develop our friendships to foster the right effort to maintain what
is good. We can also engage in formal interpersonal practices like

Insight Dialogue that intentionally foster wholesome qualities and spiritual friendship. In life and in practice, honesty breeds honesty, and so we choose honest friends. It is the same with generosity, kindness, and patience. Likewise, meditative qualities such as mindfulness, energy, and tranquility all benefit from the support of others, in formal practice and in our families and at work. In formal interpersonal meditation, this power of mutual enrichment is amplified. Mindful people remind us to be mindful just by showing up. And our mindfulness likewise reminds others. Maintenance becomes easy, joyful, and a natural effort.

This effort to maintain and further develop wholesome qualities is the *raison d'être* of spiritual community. It is well recognized that people gathered together with the explicit intention of living wisely provide good conditions for dealing with unskillful behaviors. But sustaining and refining wholesome qualities is a community's crown jewel. In a well-functioning intentional community and in skillful formal interpersonal meditation, there are copious wholesome feedback loops of compassion and of moral integrity and harmlessness. Generosity that may have only flickered in an individual private life rises up brightly when received with gratitude and naturally reciprocated. Joy that may have been shared with a single friend can be sustained and grow as it spreads through a larger group. The visible results of shared hard work and diligence, applied to tasks that no one person could accomplish, bring confidence and further commitment. The momentum of the whole carries each individual in the direction of the group's shared values. This is the power of social norms aimed by wisdom.

The norms of society at large, though, are often a drag on the maintenance of wholesome qualities. The fourth effort moves against the stream of our culture of acquisition and selfishness. The work of maintenance is necessary because, untended, wholesome qualities can become eroded or polluted. Old habits push towards the status quo. Family and friends may offer the same old stimuli and may become upset if we do not make the expected responses. Large segments of the economy are devoted to inciting and amplifying greed or hatred. Also, as our practice deepens, hidden knots of lust, aversion, and confusion come to the surface, potentially overwhelming the good qualities we have developed. This is why we give energy to maintaining these qualities; this is one reason good friendships are essential and why fully understanding right effort is important. Maintenance and development stabilizes the gains of the first three efforts, as the path we walk on is made wider and firmer by our perseverance and skill.

PRACTICE
## EXPERIENCING THE QUALITIES OF THE EFFORT TO MAINTAIN THE WHOLESOME

Whether in formal, silent practice, during intentional practice with friends, or simply woven into your everyday activities, give specific attention to each of the qualities named by the Buddha as part of the fourth effort: "maintenance, nonconfusion, increase, plenitude, development, and culmination of the wholesome that has arisen."

Begin by taking a specific wholesome quality and seeing where this is already manifest in your life. Reflect on how you value mindfulness or honesty, for example, or wise sexual boundaries, or how you take it as a given that you try to not harm living beings. Reflecting on your life, notice how this is "maintained" naturally through your everyday behaviors and intentionally through specific efforts.

Then consider "nonconfusion." How have the chosen quality and its practice become clearer to you? Is the process of reflecting on them making them sharper?

Then go on to "increase": where have you been making the effort to increase the honesty or nonharming? How is the effort to increase aided by giving attention to it?

"Plenitude" invites a reflection on the abundance, the ubiquity of this quality in your life, how it may lie hidden in your thoughts and emotions and suffuse your social encounters. Can you, at times, sense an abundance of patience (with a client or friend) or kindness (with a child or partner)?

Then consider "development" of this quality. How is it being further stabilized, or made more widely effective, in your life at home, at work, or in your friendships?

And finally, what do you see of "culmination" regarding this wholesome quality? Where is it excellent, bright, spotless, stable, effective? How do you see that culmination affecting your mind or impacting your life with others?

## The Interrelationship of Abandoning Unwholesome States and Cultivating Wholesome States

We have looked at the four efforts individually, but in practice they are profoundly interrelated. In particular, a basic dynamic is at work in the second and third efforts: abandoning the unwholesome and cultivating the wholesome are reciprocal. We can work with this dynamic directly, and the initial results are immediate. When agitation is abandoned, calm is present; when calm is cultivated, agitation is abandoned. When anger is abandoned, kindness—or at least nonanger—is present; when friendliness is cultivated, anger is abandoned. The Effacement Sutta provides a good example of this dynamic. The Buddha offered specific guidance along just these lines, but seeing this dynamic for yourself can be inspiring.

For formal meditation practice we could explore this seesaw dynamic with, say, agitation and tranquility. When you intentionally calm the body, does the physical agitation diminish? Does the mind follow and become more serene? Conversely, when you bring up energy, does laziness dissipate? But it might be more instructive here to experience how an everyday unwholesome quality is affected by the evocation of a wholesome quality. How might envy, for example, change when the light of altruistic joy is shined on it?

## DIMINISHING ENVY BY CULTIVATING ALTRUISTIC JOY

The classical antidote to envy is joy at another's happiness or good fortune, *mudita*. Bring to mind someone towards whom you feel envious. They may have professional attainments that you wish you had, or possessions, respect, or family harmony that you long for. Note the experience of envy. Do you begrudge them their good fortune? Is there anger? Is there judgment: "They don't deserve that; I do." Is there greed, wanting, a feeling of lack? How does all of this feel in the body? Comfortable or uncomfortable? Is the mind tense or relaxed? Clearly, there is no contentment.

Holding this person in mind, reflect on their humanity. Like you, they are vulnerable to loss. They, too, live in the cauldron of an insecure life. Like you, they long for ease, happiness, and pleasure. Rather than focus on the material or professional gain, however, sense beneath it to whatever relaxation, ease, and contentment they might be experiencing. With these good things in their lives, can you empathically sense their pleasure, keen interest, or maybe joy? Allow yourself to appreciate these pleasures. Appreciate the rarity of ease and how it can enable a softening of the heart. Do you wish for them this softening, this relaxation? Can you appreciate the goodwill and generosity that might accompany good fortune? When you locate this appreciative joy, attend to it, nourish it. Perhaps call forth the thought, "May their joy last long."

Now gently check in on the prior experience of envy. Has it diminished? Did an increase in the wholesome bring about a decrease in the unwholesome?

## THE FOUR BASES OF POWER

Fully developing wholesome qualities will sometimes demand extraordinary effort. The Buddha's teaching on the *iddhipāda*, or bases of spiritual power, describes four forms such exceptional effort can take: desire (*chanda*), energy (*viriya*), heartful commitment (*citta*), and investigation (*vīmaṃsā*). *Iddhi* means power or potency, while *pāda* means base or basis (literally, "foot"). The iddhi referred to in the discourses are supernatural powers derived from exceptional levels of samādhi, but the qualities that were considered necessary for developing them—the bases of these iddhis, the iddhipāda—are mental states that synergize with and drive samādhi beyond the gravitational pull of mental habits.

The Buddha considered the development of these bases to be important for liberation, quite apart from any special powers they may lead to. He said, "[T]hose who have neglected the four bases for spiritual power have neglected the noble path leading to the complete destruction of suffering."[133] The mental qualities that make up the iddhipāda are our primary concern here because of their synergy with right effort. Some development of these is necessary to achieving any goal in life, not just superpowers. Each is fostered by our own dedication and by the strength generated by alliances with dedicated meditation partners.

Chanda, wholesome desire or zeal, is desire specifically directed towards spiritual attainment. Without desire, there will be no effort at all. The strong desire to cultivate samādhi, in particular, can be tricky. Desire can bring the necessary perseverance, as you are motivated by the longing for peace and understanding. Yet without the balance of wisdom and equanimity, chanda can get out of hand as spiritual greed centered around a sense of self: *I* will attain samādhi. *I* will become spiritually accomplished. Zeal is effectively amplified and sustained in relational practice, but "*we* will attain" is as corrupt a notion as "*I* will attain." When properly balanced with wisdom, which includes a keen eye for spiritual materialism and self-inflation, chanda motivates and energizes spiritual engagement. Tension in the body-mind is a good indicator, for me, of whether my zeal is greedy or wise. With greed comes clinging, and with clinging comes tension. If I feel the tension of desire, usually in my solar plexus, I know my chanda is entangled with grasping.

Viriya, energy or perseverance, is the second base of extraordinary effort. Bodily energy and mental energy provide the fuel for the path of awakening. As perseverance, viriya is that quality that does not get discouraged but that keeps going when things are difficult or boring, or when there are setbacks or pain. With viriya, we do not shrink from challenge but rise to meet it. In relational practices, a partner's drop in energy may be countered by the sustained energy of the others with whom they are meditating. It also often happens that when two or more are meditating together, a spark arises between them that, alone, would not have been available. Likewise, energy already arisen can increase very quickly between two or more meditators, as attention, interest, and discovery are reflected in the between. But sometimes samādhi develops unnaturally quickly and leads to uncontained energy. This can happen in individual or interpersonal practice. The mind can become more powerful than we are able to handle, and visions, lights, and delusions may follow. Likewise, when there is more viriya than the body can handle, shaking, spontaneous jerks, sweating, and other symptoms may indicate that the body is trying to self-regulate. High levels of energy can be dangerous in meditation and need to be approached with care; integration in the entire body-mind is essential. Conversely, doubt or depression derail viriya. Like uncontrolled excitement, doubt, lust, and other unskillful qualities can direct energy toward agitation, away from samādhi. Energy is an effective part of our meditation practice, but it must be balanced by patience and serenity. When viriya is strong and balanced, my mind usually feels clear and alert, body awareness is strong, and sustained practice comes easily. The energy is often associated with pleasant bodily sensations and a steady, bright mind.

*Citta* can mean mind or heart. It is the third base of power, and I understand it as heart, or full-hearted commitment. We are moved and inspired by the Path. The mind is absorbed with the Path, fully intended towards ease, towards unbinding. This full mental and emotional commitment builds and sustains the motivation to practice and a singleness of mind within practice. These can be excellent conditions for the arising of samādhi, as well as for mindfulness, investigation, and, with skill, tranquility. Devotion can be a strong source of the energy of citta. My teacher Venerable Punnaji Mahathero noted that religion is marked by the emotional commitment to a view and a path. This commitment can go wrong, or it can be crucially helpful. Religious emotion supports the basis for power of citta, heartfulness. Meditating with a likewise committed spiritual friend, heartful engagement comes naturally. When I'm inspired by the Buddha's example or awed by the Dhamma, and especially as a teacher when I am moved by compassion for dedicated followers of the Dhamma, citta grows strong. Hard-headed rationalism or materialistic aims put out this fire of citta, and an immature inflation of our aspirations or our personal importance sets it out of kilter. Humility and steadiness, together with right view, keep heartfulness on the rails.

Vīmaṃsā, the fourth base, is careful investigation, examination, or discernment. The strength of investigation itself becomes a source of power in practice. The ardor of inquiry brings a brightness of mind, stability, and a continued flow of energetic commitment. We understand the benefits of the path and clearly perceive the endless suffering that is born of ignorance. We apprehend the value of spiritual strength, of energy and application. This cognitive and intuitive bodily understanding—wisdom—aims and informs the other bases. It sees beyond mundane pleasures, sees through to the higher happiness of peace. In interpersonal practice, mundane interest can grow into vīmaṃsā. Insights and challenges are reflected and shared; the Dhamma is recalled, and perspectives from outside our own conditioning are made available via speaking and listening. I experience vīmaṃsā as a natural result of *dhammavicaya*, the awakening factor of investigation of phenomena. Mindfulness is strong; I am guided by understanding yet not lost in thought. Both dullness and shallowness of contemplation, where we distractedly bounce off a presenting experience, oppose vīmaṃsā. Meanwhile, the agitation that comes with a greed for knowledge needs the balancing quality of vulnerability to the unarticulated whispers of the body-mind.

Without these four energizing qualities, the iddhipāda, our path and efforts may be drained, weak, and unreliable. These are all natural qualities, however, and innate to everyone. And they can all be cultivated, sometimes to a very high degree. A wise balance of individual and interpersonal practice helps. Simply realizing that zeal and energy, devotion and examination, have a place on the spiritual path can be a big step forward.

PRACTICE
## WORKING WITH THE IDDHIPĀDA

You can become more familiar with the four bases of spiritual power by trying each one out in a focused experiment. You can also assess your current practice using the iddhipāda as a framework. For the latter, you might recollect a time of strong commitment to some aspect of the path (such as samādhi, the classic aim of these powers) or, better yet, engage this inquiry when you find yourself in the presently unfolding experience of strong practice, alone or with others. What is the source of motivation; what is driving the experience forward? Spiritual desire? Energy as such? Heartful commitment? Investigation?

You could experiment with each of the powers, but only if there is a genuine core of each quality upon which you can draw. At a specific silent meditation session, begin with chanda: look for, contemplate, fully experience, without reserve, spiritual desire. Do you truly seek the peace of relinquishment, the open heart of love, the brilliance of the unified mind? Find and nurture any seed of "Yes!" and guide that energy towards your meditation. If you're contemplating the aggregates, let the longing bring you closer to and more intimately confronted by the mystery of perception or the evanescence of consciousness. If you are meditating by observing the breath, let this longing be the source of steadiness and perseverance unlike any you've experienced before—a steadiness aimed towards a serene and gathered mind.

You can do this same practice using energy, full-hearted commitment, and investigation into your source of power, your motivation. Also, explore this same inquiry while meditating with another likewise committed person. Speak what you notice of spiritual desire; listen deeply to their expressions of it. Does it take on nuance? Does it grow? What of the energy, heartful commitment, and investigation as you practice together? Observe carefully how these qualities are affected by or being reflected between you.

## REVISITING BALANCE

Amidst all this talk of strongly applying the mind, it is good to remember and refine our understanding of the need for balance. The Buddha was well aware of the element of balance and built it into the teachings on the iddhipāda. In the *Vibhaṅgasutta* he advises that the helpful application of these qualities is "neither too slack nor too tense; . . . neither constrictive internally nor distracted externally."[134] A monk, Venerable Sona, once practiced walking meditation until the soles of his feet were split and bleeding. He became discouraged about the possibility of progress on the path, thinking, "I am one of the Blessed One's most energetic disciples, yet my mind has not been liberated from the *intoxicants* by nonclinging," and wondered if he should return to lay life.[135]

The Buddha appeared and asked if, before Sona became a monk, he had been skilled at playing the vina (a stringed instrument). When Sona answered yes, the Buddha asked if a vina could be in tune and playable with its strings too taut or too loose. It couldn't. Hence, the Buddha advised, "[I]f energy is aroused too forcefully this leads to restlessness, and if energy is too lax this leads to laziness. Therefore, Sona, resolve on a balance of energy, achieve evenness of the spiritual faculties, and take up the object there."[136]

Notice that the balance here is not between effort and no effort, between effort and taking it easy, but a balance between effort that is too strenuous for a given task and effort that it too lax for that task. Real balance is about the skillful modulation of effort to support maximal maturation.

Given the complexity of the mind, it's not surprising that even balance is multifaceted. In addition to arousal and calm, the Buddha spoke of balance in terms of the five spiritual faculties: faith balances with wisdom, and energy with samādhi, while mindfulness assesses and helps steer the process. Faith and wisdom yield different qualities of effort. Faith, or confidence, is more related to chanda and citta, or desire and heartful commitment, while wisdom is more closely linked to vīmaṃsā, or careful investigation. From a practical standpoint, when you encounter strong pain or imminent death, when you encounter depths of self-hatred or patterns of trauma, you may be able to call on past experience, on a clear understanding of your emotional or physical challenges, and on an understanding of the universality of impermanence. These are all in the direction of the wisdom faculty. But there will be times when you encounter things you don't understand, that you can't see through to a clear outcome. At such times, the faith faculty will be there to support you: *All beings experience pain, all must die, all encounter inner darkness. I am not alone in this. It is all changing and out of my control. And even when there is pain, there needn't be mental suffering.* This is an effort of yielding the heart, not of grabbing the bull by the horns. It is a way of faith, quietude, and inner friendliness.

Balancing the spiritual faculties of energy and samādhi is similar to the balance that the Buddha pointed to in his advice to Sona: neither too slack nor too loose. But there is more to it than that. The actual qualities of mental and bodily energy are needed simultaneously with the qualities that comprise samādhi. Vitality and alertness are to be brought together with serenity and gatheredness of mind. So the effort in both formal meditation practice and embedded in our lives is one of attending to alertness and calm. We learn how they can co-exist and support each other rather than thinking that more of one means there must be less of the other. For example, if you are at retreat and perched at the edge of insight, could being less alert so you can be steadier in the face of a dissolving self support a breakthrough understanding? No. The alertness (energy) needs to co-arise with mental steadiness (samādhi), so the mind remains steady and awake while the fabricated world falls apart. At certain crucial moments in the growth of a relationship or at the edge of psychotherapeutic insight, mindfulness guides us to skillfully sustain energy and concentration, faith and wisdom, so clear knowing can arise. Likewise, acceptance and zeal, humility and confidence, do not cancel out one another: the key is balance. All of this understanding of balance is included in our understanding of right effort.

## THE POWER—AND NECESSITY— OF RELATIONSHIP IN DEVELOPING ENERGY AND PERSEVERANCE

In the path factor of right effort we see perhaps the clearest indication as to why spiritual friendship was deemed by the Buddha to be central to the path. Spiritual friendship does far more than make the path of awakening sweeter and more pleasant; it is a crucial factor in cultivating energy and perseverance. Whether our focus is on the four efforts or on the four bases of power, our basic relational nature will work with or against the effort of untangling the heart. Two or more people together support wholesome qualities by modeling them to each other and mutually reminding each other of their value. With others, we can find encouragement, appreciative joy, and the power of wholesome social norms. Others also help us to abandon the unwholesome. Other people help bring to the surface otherwise hidden unwholesome tendencies: I cannot see alone what I see when I am with you. Meanwhile, you provide the acceptance and safety I need to be present with and release harmful patterns like self-hatred, bias, fear, and doubt.

In formal practices we see how meditating together amplifies and refines qualities like mindfulness and energy. From this, enthusiasm and confidence increase, and we see right effort blossom from the shared spiritual life. When we ignore or even go against our intrinsic relatedness, we are drained by dwelling longer than necessary in the barrenness that is an inevitable factor on everyone's path. We all must cross the desert. Doing so without the sustenance of compassionate encounter, with teachers, co-meditators, or community, is at the very least unnecessarily difficult. It may be impossible. It certainly was not the Buddha's vision of the spiritual life, which was lived in sangha. Meanwhile, solely individual practices can foster the illusion of self-reliance that can build up notions of a powerful—or broken—personal self. Just as individual practices are essential for developing wholesome effort, interpersonal practices and a relationally lived life are essential for a sustained, powerful path.

Here we are harnessing the power of relatedness in service of the right effort for awakening. Our path includes strong and explicit practices of mindfulness and samādhi, and these practices are both individual and relational. In explicit practice, the relational power of right effort becomes obvious; it is clearly experienced and known. In such practice, we are sensitized to human relatedness and begin to notice throughout our lives the countless moments of mutual influence towards the wholesome. And when we notice the accumulation of emotional debris from our mindless and lust-driven encounters with others, we feel the burden of it more acutely because we have experienced free and living spiritual friendship. We know the difference. Simply, we turn away from the unwholesome: out with the bad. We have smelled the fragrance of release, and this is where our hearts turn, in all of our contacts with others: in with the good.

## 〜 REFLECTION

We seldom know the results of each effort we make. Sometimes we just become aware that something has shifted along the way and that life has become better because of it.

> When . . . a carpenter or a carpenter's apprentice looks at the handle of his adze, he sees the impressions of his fingers and his thumb, but he does not know: "So much of the adze handle has

been worn away today, so much yesterday, so much earlier." But when it has been worn away, the knowledge occurs to him. . . . So too . . . when a bhikkhu dwells devoted to development, even though no such knowledge occurs to him: "So much of my taints has been worn away today, so much yesterday, so much earlier," yet when they are worn away, the knowledge occurs to him that they have been worn away.[137]

This wearing away may present itself as a mitigated narcissism or penetrative release of self-concept. Anger may now be better controlled or sundered from its very foundations. Unbinding has many fragrances; all are redolent of release. This is good in the beginning, good in the middle, and good in the end.

This perspective, which is part of right view, makes right effort possible. All that arises is known to pass away. Pain and pleasure, joy and sorrow, are not lasting; they are not "me" but dependent upon conditions. There is nothing to cling to and no one to cling. Strong but balanced effort more naturally arises when this is the orientation of the mind. Right view infuses energetic application with unselfishness and the taste of release, of relinquishment. With the safety of this knowledge—even a glimmer of it—we can apply ourselves fully. Right effort is applied to morality, so safety is created for ourselves and others. Right effort is applied collectively for social and ecological justice. Right effort is applied to developing mindfulness and samādhi, so we can see clearly. Right effort is applied to wisdom, which leads to compassion and release. Right effort also sustains acceptance of the messiness of being human. The results are simple. When the mind is grasping, we see the grasping as deluded habit, as greed based upon wrong view. We let it go, as we are able to in that moment, and accept what remains. And when the mind is in harmony with wise view, when it is not grasping, then the strength of commitment is trustworthy. Effort is natural. Now the always-on nature of the whole-life path is not an idea; it is clearly how things are. Nothing left out.

# CHAPTER 10

# RIGHT MINDFULNESS

## *Sammā Sati*

s you read these words, what are you aware of? Words forming in the mind? Is there discomfort somewhere in the body, whispering in the background? Do the sounds in your environment momentarily intercede? What is it like to have a book asking you all these questions?

And how do you know the answers to any of the questions I'm asking? Does awareness turn towards the mind, the body, the sense of hearing, and know what is going on? Is this just a matter of shifting attention, or is there more to it than that?

Sati is recollected awareness. Insomuch as awareness is essential to the monitoring of the body-mind, sati is essential to the entire Eightfold Path. As awareness of our thoughts and actions, sati is the basis of wise choices and so foundational to morality. Put another way, if we are not aware of our thoughts and actions, they will spring only from habit. The mind just rolls on according to its conditioning. This may produce wholesome or unwholesome results. Without sati there is only a stream of reactions to circumstances; with sati there is choice. Sati is the inflection point of freedom.

When we examine sati as a factor of the Path, we are not exploring any or every form of mindfulness, but right mindfulness specifically. Mindfulness may be applied to worldly benefits, but the path factor of sati has specific functions. It enables an ethical life, it guides the path as a whole—including all the path factors—and it is a key mental quality for the arising of liberating insight. To the extent possible, you might make reading about sati a practice of sati.

## INITIAL DEFINITIONS OF SATI

A key aspect of the practice of sati is the integrated awareness of an object and knowing you are aware. In practice, this layered but unified awareness is intentionally sustained even as different objects, like distractions, present themselves. The mind is brought back to the object of choice, such as the form of the sitting body, the movement of the breath, or awareness itself; there is a knowing that the mind was distracted and is now back with the object.

Sati is also recollecting a framework through which we observe present-moment experience. Frameworks form a kind of overlay on experience regardless of what is being observed. I could be taking a walk outside and could directly observe the object—the body walking. But I could also observe the impermanent aspect of that experience; the functioning of various sense doors, such as touching the ground or seeing; or the functioning of perception, such as colors and objects being recognized. Any or all of these observations could occur while I'm walking; all are enfolded within the experience of walking. Sati is remembering to notice the framework—such as impermanence—that guides each of these observations. It is holding in mind the object, including an object that is a mental framework for noticing a more concrete object.

Even in this gentle mindfulness of impermanence and of an open field of awareness, we find a specific invitation to recollect, to dwell with, some object or quality. The recollective nature of sati is not a random construal. The word *sati* is etymologically related to Pali words for memory. Sati facilitates the formation of memories (one is present as events unfold) and their recall (one can turn the attention inward and become aware of prior impressions). Sati is remembering in a way similar to what's meant when we say, "Remember, Grandpa is hard of hearing." It indicates not calling on stored memory, but maintaining—remembering to sustain—awareness of that fact. Sati remembers the Buddha's teachings, keeps them in mind, providing a basis for understanding. It is a natural capacity of the human mind that can be cultivated and refined.

PRACTICE

## WALKING WITH AND WITHOUT A FRAMEWORK

Take a walk alone, setting the intention to explore mindfulness in two ways: as guided by a gentle framework of impermanence (anicca) and as an open awareness that has no specific object or framework. It will be helpful if you can walk in a place without too many potential demands on your attention, such as traffic lights or people you know.

As you begin walking, attend to those aspects of experience that are obviously changing: the moving body, sounds, trees in the wind, or vehicles going by. Rather than focus on the objects, key in on the never-the-same quality. When this quality is clear to you, let go of the attentional effort and rest or flow with the sense of change—the change of mind, of world.

If you're so moved, explore a shift to open awareness. You could launch this part by looking around, including looking up and defocusing the eyes to attune to any sense of breadth of field. While you're walking, let awareness fill this field. There is the sense that awareness is the field, that the field is awareness. It may be as if the body is walking through the aware field. Anytime you get locked into a stream of thought, look around to re-establish the perception of space, then mindfulness of the space, and then release even that to just walk in and as the field.

As you close your walk, reflect on the quality of mindfulness cultivated then and there.

## Misconceptions About Sati

I mostly use the Pali word *sati* in this chapter because the word *mindfulness* has developed an unhelpfully large range of meanings, including some that can be misleading. The recent popularization of mindfulness has introduced many people to some aspects of meditation and, indirectly, to Buddhist thought. While this popularization has been helpful in many ways, we need to carefully consider the definition of *sati* from the standpoint of the Buddha's teachings on the human situation: does this sati lead to dispassion, not to passion, to being unfettered, not to being fettered, and so on?

One misconception of sati is that it equates to nonjudgmental present-moment awareness. The word *awareness* here points in the right direction, but awareness that is devoid of intention can be easily carried away, like a bubble in a stream. It can also lead to avoiding unwanted emotions as we follow the distractions that the mind invents in the face of difficulty. Meanwhile, *nonjudgmental* can imply amoral, and because we are speaking about *right* mindfulness, the ethical element is essential. Some thoughts that arise are unskillful, harmful; knowing this—judging the thoughts as unskillful—is critical to the right effort to abandon the unwholesome. Note that judging the thoughts is not the same as judging oneself.

In the discourses, the Pali term *sampajañña* is nearly always coupled with the word sati, and the context and purpose of sati is carried in the term *sampajañña*. *Sati-sampajañña* allows us to attend to an object, with a sense of method, and an overall purpose. For example, sati allows us to balance noticing the form of the body (object) and maintain a continuity of noticing without interfering (method or attitude), while not losing touch with our desire to train the mind towards nonclinging (purpose). In formal meditation, these nested frames of intention or purpose, method, and object can be quite explicit. As we develop continuity of practice in all activities, these layers may be operating unseen, the implicit qualities of a skillful mind. Sati-sampajañña is sometimes mistaken for bare attention (manasikāra). Bare attention can be very useful. However, it is not the same thing as sati; it is a subset or facet of sati.

Understood here as *right* mindfulness, sati is an intrinsically wholesome, broad, and flexible quality of mind. As a native attribute, sati can and does arise spontaneously. It can be cultivated formally in settings like retreats and meditation practice and informally in daily life. One of my teachers, Venerable Punnaji, defined sati as the introversion of attention: the mind looking inward at itself, both at what is going on in the mind and at sati itself, the act of observation. With a little difference in how sati is developed, it can be the doorway to liberating insight or to deepening calm. It is the foundation of all embedded life practice.

Sati is essential for both solitary and interpersonal formal meditation practice. It allows us to balance relating externally to another person and being aware of our internal responses—while not losing touch with agendas (the topic of conversation, kindness) or overall purpose (compassion, perhaps, or both persons' movement towards unbinding). In informal practice, awareness of these objects may be tacit or intermittent. Still, sati underlies the qualities we recognize as poise, self-possession, and presence. People with a great deal of sati will be relatively unflappable because they do not lose track of their larger purposes; reactivity cannot gain a foothold, so they are able to choose their manner of engagement.

Sati can even be present while we are experiencing a hindrance like aversion. It can observe the aversion for what it is in real time, without attaching to the object or spinning off into aversion for the aversion.[138] When we bring sati to accompany a reactive state, sati's nonreactive character tends to downregulate and de-automate the reactivity. Sati can also invoke right effort when more active intervention is necessary, and it can call on right view to help make that judgment. Applied to desirable qualities, such as gratitude, sati can increase them. As the Buddha notes, we become what we give attention to.[139] Sati helps us see deeply into the truth of our experience with its complex web of causality—sometimes seeing right to its core and giving rise to insight, the understanding that brings freedom.

PRACTICE

## MINDFULNESS OF THE UNSKILLFUL MIND

The next time you feel distracted, petty, aversive, or complaining, try taking several short, mindful pauses to become aware of the unfolding, automatic nature of the mental activity. Stop whatever you are doing, turn the attention inward, and watch the show. Can there be awareness even as there is this sloppy or unpleasant quality of mental activity? How does the body feel as these thoughts and mind states churn within? Don't try to hold this sati for too long. Give the mind some rein to bathe in its suffering, but pause after a couple of minutes. Are you *trying* to think these thoughts, to have these emotions, or are they happening automatically? Does being mindful affect the experience?

## RIGHT MINDFULNESS AS A PATH FACTOR

Sammā sati shares the goals of the Eightfold Path: liberation and human flourishing that is rooted in the eradication of ignorance and the sundering of hunger individually, relationally, and socially. It takes its orientation from right view and right intention. We practice sati in order to release what is unwholesome. Seeing clearly the impermanent, un*sati*sfactory, and selfless nature of phenomena is inherently liberating. Sati also recognizes the wholesome when it is already present. So sati supports common human decency and deep untangling.

Sati also monitors all of the path factors, allowing balance and development. Awareness of present moment experience is essential for a path of awakening to even be possible, and this elemental masterstroke is found in the teachings on right mindfulness.

As we have seen, the goal and intention of a practice—its why—shape both means and outcome. Sati can have mundane goals. For example, an instruction from the Buddha about mindfulness helped King Pasenadi change his habit of overeating; as a result, his health improved.[140] Sati can also free up the cognitive field and help someone to experience the present moment with immediacy, which in turn enhances creativity, organization, performance, and appreciation. Sati also enriches compassion, enhances social ease and skill, and inclines the mind towards kindness and generosity. The practical applications of mindfulness are boundless; it would be skillful to integrate the wisdom aspect with these efforts to improve the personality and physical wellbeing.

Sati aimed at mundane welfare, while wholesome, is only indirectly a factor of the Path. The goal of stress reduction—often repeated in connection with meditation and mindfulness—is a good example of an important, mundane goal. If our aim is something like improving performance at work or in a sport, that is probably most of what we will get from our practice. Yet by helping release everyday suffering, a limited goal like this can free energy and focus, allowing some insight into the suffering system. So the Path goal of personal, relational, and social unbinding can develop from the simple seed of wishing for less stress or better sleep. Also, the worldly goal can be a doorway to wisdom-based practices and study, and even a base upon which we can piggyback the liberative intentions of mindfulness. Bringing right view together with right mindfulness is the basis of this shift.

Many of the Buddha's teachings on the formal development of mindfulness are found in the Satipaṭṭhāna Sutta. This discourse, which has several parallels in the early Buddhist texts, forms the basis of vipassanā meditation practice, which in turn forms many Westerners' understanding of mindfulness and of Buddhism as a whole. A number of excellent resources on sati unpack the Satipaṭṭhāna Sutta; I won't try to duplicate that work, although I will touch on it lightly later in this chapter. Our focus here is sati in the context of the entire Eightfold Path. The other factors of the path need sati's help to function, and sati needs their support to be efficacious and sustained.

---

PRACTICE

**ENCOURAGING SATI IN OTHERS**

The benefit of developing sati is so profound that the Buddha urged us to use any interpersonal influence we have to encourage and support others in their development of sati: "Those for whom you have compassion and who think you should be heeded—whether friends or colleagues, relatives or kinsmen—these you should exhort, settle, and establish in the development of the four establishments of mindfulness."[141]

For those who teach in a formal way, for example in elementary school, university, or via social work, this is a clear directive to include the development of sati in the content of their teaching. For those who do not teach, it points to the interpersonal practice and support of sati in all contexts. Take a moment to consider whom you might support in cultivating mindfulness. How would you do so humbly and respectfully?

---

## Sati and Sīla

Sati's contribution to ethical behavior is especially vital. At a very basic level, when sati is strong—when we are really paying attention to how we live—we naturally recoil from unwholesome behavior. Unwise or unkind behavior just feels bad; anger hurts; mean thoughts are painful. When I am mindful, it is obvious to me that rough speech and cruelty are unwholesome. Obviously unwholesome actions—like obviously rotting foods—just do not seem tempting!

Just as sīla depends upon sati, sati depends upon sīla. The ethical factors of right speech, right action, and right livelihood, along with right view, can be considered prerequisites for the meditative development of right sati. In the absence of sīla, sati lacks an important condition. Immoral actions generate inner noise; an immoral life is inherently filled with tension. When the mind feels regrets and worries, consciously or unconsciously, it does not settle; it cannot or will not see clearly. Obsessed with self, it cannot see or appreciate others. Mindfulness is the basis for wise relationships, for cutting through the mind's tendencies towards isolation and selfishness. Present moment awareness of self, other, and both naturally incline the heart towards generosity and care.

Sati also acts as a guard or monitor. It watches the sense doors for input that might provoke us to unwholesome behavior; it watches the mind's responses for arising or currently present mind states that might lead us to unwholesome behavior or that are unwholesome themselves. Sati lets us know when we are about to go down some not-so-good road. If we have been unaware or overburdened and the present moment has slipped past us, sati lets us know. Without sati's support, we can be overwhelmed. The Buddha offered a gruesome simile about the effect of leaving the mind unguarded: a cat hastily swallowed a mouse whole, and that mouse ate away at the cat's innards, bringing suffering and death. Similarly a celibate monastic who, with unguarded mind, goes into town and sees people scantily clad, may find that lust invades the mind and overpowers it.[142] Any of us, encountering something we desire or detest with an unguarded mind may find our composure eaten away from the inside and our self-control ruined. Sati helps us cope with intense reactions to sensory input. And life is, inescapably, sensory input.

For example, a barbed reply might seem *so* appropriate and *so* deserved in the moment, but with sati, we can remember our care for the other person, or remember how such responses have affected us in the past, or remember our commitment to practicing kindness. When sati is strong, we are able to see momentary attractions in a larger context: the context of our values, of how we want to live, and of cause and effect. And sati lets us see the moment in the context of consciousness itself; aware that we are aware, we are able to choose. The capacity for choice is the foundation of ethical action.

Right effort also needs sati's help. Clear seeing, and the ability to recall what we are doing with awareness and why, are essential in diminishing the unwholesome and cultivating the wholesome. Without clear awareness and understanding—sati's collaboration with right view—we cannot know where or how to direct effort. Sati is also an essential support for right samādhi. The nun Dhammadinna explained: "Unification of mind, friend Visakha, is samādhi; the four foundations of mindfulness are the basis of concentration."[143]

When sati is strong, reactivity naturally calms down. The body-mind calms down. When there is sati, we tend not to follow agitating influences and so are less likely to be swept away by the excitement of lust or anger into unethical behavior. Calmly present with our feelings of ambiguity or pain, we no longer need to block them out or distract ourselves from them. We are no longer driven to the distractions and excitements we formerly used to shield ourselves from difficult truths. As a result, we are less likely to get caught up in identity-making, shading the truth, and proliferations of all kinds. Sati's calming effect can manifest as the ability to relax, to focus clearly on work or relationship, or to gather the mind in deep and undistracted concentration.

PRACTICE

**BRINGING SATI TO UNETHICAL BEHAVIOR**

I'm going to offer a highly distasteful practice. Maybe you won't want to do it; maybe you can't do it. But try. Next time you find yourself doing something unethical, right then and there call up sati-sampajañña—mindfulness with clarity and purpose. Perhaps you are gossiping or stretching the truth. Perhaps you are misstating something on an expense report or tax form. Perhaps you are scheming toward sexual engagement with someone who is in a committed relationship. What do you notice in the body? What intentions are present? Does the moment of sati contrast with the prior moments of habitual delusion? Can you even sustain sati and still do this thing?

## FIVE QUESTIONS OF SATI

When I teach, I often refer to five questions to define sati. In fact, the action of asking each question actually creates sati. These questions are:

*Why* am I cultivating awareness?
*What* am I aware of?
*How* am I cultivating awareness?
*Where* am I aware?
*When* am I aware?

Taken together, these questions allow us to better understand sati's power and many dimensions. I will first offer a brief practice that invites you to touch all five questions and see how each resonates in experience. Then we will look at each question in more depth, linking them to the discourses, to our lived experience, and to the purpose of the whole-life path. We will see that a quality of awareness that has no definitions, no boundaries, or even any objects naturally evolves across all of these domains.

PRACTICE
**FIVE QUESTIONS OF SATI**

Arrange a time for undisturbed reflective practice. You can do this practice either alone or with one or more spiritual friends.

Alone, you will enjoy the freedom to move at your own pace and drink deeply of silence. With spiritual friends, you will enjoy the steadiness of energy and investigation, as well as the wider perspectives made possible in shared inquiry. Either way, let your practice be marked by patience and interest.

Present each question to the mind, and then pause. Let the alert silence do its work. Ask, then stop. Stop thinking, stop inquiring. Just let the tip of awareness rest on the tip of the moment. Don't seek a definitive answer, but dwell with the effect of the question. Does the mind become more awake in the present moment?

**Why am I cultivating awareness?** You could begin with calling to mind purposes you are familiar with, like peacefulness, clear thinking, or mitigating suffering. Beyond the thoughts, though, what do you sense as the direction of the heart?

**What am I aware of?** What do you notice first when you observe what you are mostly paying attention to? Thinking that is a flow of words? A bodily sensation? Sounds in the environment? How does the mind shift when there is an objective noticing of what is being attended to?

**How am I cultivating awareness?** Notice your current capacity to investigate the qualities that are sustaining the mindfulness. Is there ardency, steadiness, and clarity? Are you noticing internal or external experience? Or the rising and vanishing of the objects that form "what" you are aware of?

**Where am I aware?** Is there a "here" in this silence? Is the body "here"? Is body one thing and awareness another? Where is here?

**When am I aware?** Is there something called "now"? Try for just a moment to be mindful in the past or the future. It is not possible. What is the experience of a never-ending now?

Any one of the queries in this five-question practice can be engaged as a formal or informal practice, anytime, anywhere. You are encouraged to experiment with them as you cultivate sati individually and interpersonally, embedded in life and in formal practice. As your practice evolves, continue to ask big-picture questions: "Do my 'what' and 'how' fit my 'why'? Am I practicing in a way that will have the effect I seek? Is my mindfulness practice harmonious with my life?"

## Why Am I Cultivating Awareness?

As noted earlier, we are not exploring all mindfulness, but right mindfulness. Inherent in *right, sammā,* is a sense of the whole Eightfold Path, a sense of purpose. This is elicited in the Buddha's use of the compound *sati-sampajañña,* usually translated as "mindfulness and clear comprehension" or "clear awareness." (The roots of the term *sampajañña* are *pajānāti,* "to know," and *saŋ,* "together" or "thoroughly.") We return to the architecture of the Path: everything rests on the trio of right view, effort, and mindfulness. We make the effort to notice why we are cultivating awareness because right view is intrinsic to mindfulness that is right, sammā.

The purpose of our practice establishes its direction, its boundaries, and its potential. Our purpose always determines our practice, including what we do, how we do it, when and where we do it. Maybe the goal is to lose weight; maybe it is to become more productive at work by getting a handle on stress; maybe it is to be of finer service to others; maybe it is liberation from the pain of samsara. Any of these motivations, when recollected, involves some sati. Any of them might be an occasion for developing sati further. The path factor of right mindfulness speaks of a purpose in line with the path goal of kind release.

In traditional Buddhist settings, meditation sessions begin with taking the three refuges: Buddha, Dhamma, and Sangha. Some teachers also recommend beginning by recollecting your teachers and perhaps even their teachers. These are practices of right inten-tion, and both of these recollections are setting up the why of sati.

We might also consider the eight criteria of Dhamma that we reference for the whole-life path, including, for example, whether our practice is aimed at being fettered or unfettered, at modesty or self-aggrandizement, at shedding or accumulating, at persistence or laziness. Like the other reflections, however, the aim is always to go beyond mundane thinking. Let the words—*modesty, shedding*—launch the heart into direct experience, wordless and intimate.

The question of why will ultimately lead the mind beyond concepts. The question is not answerable in any ultimate sense. The *experience* of why is an intuition, the harvest of a lifetime of open inquiry.

PRACTICE
**ASKING WHY, TOGETHER**

Take some time with a spiritual friend to explore why mindfulness matters to you. Your practice may be energetic and quick or slow and reflective; either will be helpful. But for this practice to support your more subtle silent meditation, I recommend a slower pace, one threaded throughout with patient pauses. Do the Buddha's teachings feel relevant and alive in those pauses? Or if not, do the more modern teachings on mindfulness inspire you and invite you to dive deeper into a sense of purpose? How does developing mindfulness fit in with your sense of life's direction and value? Listen deeply and speak the truth.

## What Am I Aware of?

What am I aware of? is a question as large as life itself. Two power-ful categories of appropriate objects of mindfulness are offered in the Pali discourses. First, for vipassanā meditation, we have the four foundations of mindfulness, which also offer a useful framework for everyday embedded practice. The second category is the whole of the Buddha's teachings as practices. Observing present-moment experience through the lens of the Dhamma provides an enormous and fruitful field for formal and informal practices of sammā sati. In this category we find the brahmavihāras of true friendliness and compassion also specifically included within the practice of sati.

### The First Sati Category: The Four Foundations of Mindfulness

The Satipaṭṭhāna Sutta and its equivalents are the root teaching on developing sati.[144] In this discourse, the Buddha names four groups of meditation objects of varying levels of subtlety, ranging from apparently physical objects, such as the body, to the subtle mental qualities of rapture and equanimity.[145] The four traditional groups provide a solid basis for understanding formal meditation, particularly vipassanā practice. They provide skillful handles for examining experience, combining breadth with enough focus to help us not get lost. They narrow the range of attention from everything at once to something more manageable, and give us something specific, in some cases even tangible, as an anchor for awareness.

These four groups—body, feelings, mind, and dhamma frameworks—are often referred to as the "foundations" of mindfulness. The commentaries say that the word *satipaṭṭhāna* derives from a later word, *paṭṭhāna*, "foundation" or "cause." An alternate derivation is from *upaṭṭhāna*, literally "placing near," "attending," or "being present." To say "foundations of mindfulness" is to cast the topics or themes given in the sutta as the objects of awareness: *sati focuses on the body; that is how sati is developed.* To talk about the presence, attention, or adjacency of sati is to put the emphasis on the activity: *sati is stationed near the body, present and attentive; that is how sati is developed.* Thus, we can speak of sati as the adjacency of attention. This second construal is also more open to the goal of sati. After all, the ultimate goal is not just to develop sati but also to open the possibility of liberating insight.

By placing sati next to one of these familiar objects—body or breath, feelings, mind states, hindrances, enlightenment factors, and the rest—we come to see certain things. We catch glimpses and finally a clear vision of how suffering arises; how it, and we, are without fixed essence; and how everything is impermanent. The objects or themes of contemplation function like lenses through which we can look at something else.

**Body.** The starting point for most meditators is also the most reliable point of return at any stage of development, for formal and informal, personal and interpersonal practice: the body. Its immediateness, its tangible felt quality, makes it a workable starting point for setting up awareness.

The Satipaṭṭhāna Sutta offers a variety of formal, individual practices involving the body. One can contemplate the position of the body under four broad postures (sitting, standing, walking, lying) or the body's activities (such as walking, reaching, speaking, or defecating). The activity of breathing can be contemplated on its own. The body can be contemplated in terms of its constituent elements (using the ancient schema of earth, air, fire, and water, or a modern schema) or its specific parts (using a traditional list or in another way). The body can be contemplated in comparison to the stages of breakdown of a corpse. In the Pali *Kāyagatāsatisutta,* mindful attention to the somatic bliss of the four jhānas is presented as another body-based approach to developing sati.[146]

---

PRACTICE
## MINDFULNESS OF BODY

A movement discipline such as yoga, t'ai chi, or qigong—or even simple, unstructured stretching—can be a vehicle for developing sati if we bring sati to them. Inquire: what happens when you make a special effort to bring an intimate awareness to each and every element of the movement? Also experiment with attending to the body with awareness during everyday activities—maybe the physical sensations of driving a car, riding a bicycle, working at the computer, taking a shower, cooking a meal. You could also practice with specific bodily actions, like bending or reaching, to bring sati into everyday life. Try doing one of these activities or actions at least once with meticulous attention and a sense of purpose.

**Feelings.** The Satipaṭṭhāna Sutta also offers practices attending to feelings (vedanā)—that very basic level of sense impression that is simply pleasant, unpleasant, or neither. The sutta also distinguishes between "worldly" and "unworldly" versions of these feelings. Because feelings arise early in our experience of a thing, noticing them explicitly can make us less likely to spin off into proliferation. As a formal, personal meditation practice, the feelings framework combines very well with walking and lying meditation. We can also notice responses of pleasant, unpleasant, or neither during the day. From fleeting pleasure during the day's first sip of coffee to annoyance at a stiff neck or uncomfortable chair, mindfulness can ride along with any experience so long as we don't get lost in identification and fuse with it. Refined sati can help us recognize the power vedanā wields in our lives and help free us from the automatic reactions to pleasant and unpleasant contacts.

I was years into the process of writing this book when repeated illness and bodily weakness culminated in a diagnosis of multiple myeloma, an incurable cancer. The onset of experimental chemotherapy resulted in acute renal failure, which nearly killed me, then another form of chemotherapy was followed by a stem cell transplant. I spent months lying down or sitting in a reclined position, resulting in muscle wasting. The attendant miseries were intense. Muscle pains, bone pains, nausea, profound weakness, and mental debility were not exceptional events; they were the norm.

Throughout this time, the mind was carefully observing all aspects of experience, from the approach of death in the hospital bed to the fog of chemo-brain. When it came to the most persistent pains, I would turn to present-moment sensations and inquire into the feeling tone. The mind found which sensation was most prominent, like a muscle cramp or nausea, and attention would naturally rest with that object. This practice did not take discipline—only interest. The tacit question was, "What is this experience?"—that is, what is the *actual* experience, not my reaction of aversion or despair? Where in the body am I experiencing the nausea? Noting the feeling in the solar plexus, for example, I would then ask what this unpleasantness is really like. Did it have a location? Was it stable or moving? And above all, what was the immediate, pre-conceptual experience of unpleasantness—a kind of vibration of the mind rather than a construction of some problem with the body?

I could take this same approach with the reactions to pain. Mindfulness of feelings revealed that depression had a feeling tone, including unpleasant states of body and mind, and attending to this vedanā nearly always lifted me out of identification and proliferation with the reactions. Unpleasantness was just what it was; it did not proliferate, and it ceased to be scary. And at its best, the phenomena were interesting and might even, for a moment, become quite neutral.

This quality of practice was not always possible. Sometimes I was just miserable and wanted only to moan or complain. Sometimes the body's reaction to pain was beyond my conscious control. But by way of practice, mindfulness of feelings was nearly always an effective way to cope with extreme states of body and mind. And knowing I was aware was the only refuge I knew that worked across the full spectrum of these experiences.

PRACTICE
## MINDFULNESS OF FEELINGS

You are invited to practice *vedanānupassanā*, mindfulness of feelings, in two forms: while silently sitting in meditation and while socially engaged.

First, sitting silently, observe any bodily sensations that are present. Give attention to whichever touches are most prominent. Settling on one sensation, attune to the preverbal, direct felt sense of that touch. Is it unpleasant? If so, rather than push it away by diverting attention elsewhere, get interested. What exactly *is* this experience of unpleasant? Don't label it as pain or fall into other habitual reactions. If it is pleasant, what is the nature of the pleasantness? Rather than fuse with and delight in the feeling, get intimate with just the feeling tone as such, a kind of vibration of the mind rather than a material phenomenon. And if your practice is well settled, you might also look for neutral sensations; there are always countless ones awaiting your attention.

As a second form of practice, remain alert—mindful—to the felt responses that arise as you encounter different people. When pleasant sensations arise, does the mind remain aware or just fall into identification with the pleasurable situation? And when a social encounter is uncomfortable or stressful, can sati simply know this aspect of experience?

**Mind.** Just as feelings are more mercurial than this body, citta—states of the mind or heart—are also subtler, quicker. The third group of practices offered in the Satipaṭṭhāna Sutta refers to knowing the current condition of one's mind according to a list of eight characteristics—lustful, angry, deluded, distracted, great, unsurpassable, unified, liberated—and their eight opposites. These sixteen possibilities are simply, factually known. It can be helpful to label them, but often there are no words for a mood or mind state. The state can simply be experienced with an attitude of "It's like this right now." Noticing mind states can be especially helpful for waking up amid the countless nuances of relational meditation. In formal practice, noticing mind can be an extraordinarily subtle practice, but in daily life we can just note our present mood and whether or not it fits with the Buddhist template of mind states. Simply noticing without identification can be a useful practice of sati.

## MINDFULNESS OF MIND STATES

This is a two-phase practice. First, sit quietly and observe the present mind state. It can help to look for a specific quality, like whether the mind is foggy or clear, agitated or calm; this will help you to discern that aspect of experience with enough precision to locate it in the second phase of practice. After there is familiarity with the mind's mood or quality, see whether you notice the presence or absence of that particular quality while doing simple actions, like dish washing or food shopping. Gradually, enlarge your vocabulary of the heart ("heart" is another translation of *citta*) and use this frame of reference anytime in your daily life.

**Dhamma frameworks.** The final group of practices from the Satipaṭṭhāna Sutta is, like those of the body, a broad group. Under the heading *dhammānupassanā*—mindfulness of the frameworks of specific aspects of phenomenal experience—there are multiple lists. The classic core, across early and later collections of the discourses in Pali, Chinese, and Sanskrit, are the five hindrances and the seven factors of awakening. In the next category we will look at the other frameworks for sati, such as the five aggregates of clinging and the Four Noble Truths, when we consider the Buddha's teachings on Buddhadhamma as a foundation for mindfulness. For now, we'll stay focused on this classical core.

Meditating using the framework of the hindrances and the factors of awakening, we notice whether each one is present or absent, plus the conditions that can lead to its arising. In the case of the hindrances, we are also aware of how each can be removed and prevented. In the case of the factors of awakening, we are also aware of how each can be developed and perfected.

The treatment of the unwholesome mind states and the hindrances shows something of the essence of sati. Such unwholesome states of mind could be candidates for the much more active treatments that are part of right effort, such as replacement with wholesome qualities or restraint. And they should be if there is a danger of inappropriate action or if a hindrance is so obsessing the mind that it is interfering with sati. But when sati is able to observe a hindrance, doing so is a skillful option. Sati allows us to be present, calmly, with obstacles such as lust, sleepiness, and doubt. Its calm presence can lower their energy level and sometimes completely dissolve them. Joining sati with investigation, we learn what they are, how they arose, what they are about. Over time and coupled with insight, this kind of attention can dissolve the roots of harmful tendencies—something that repeatedly driving them away cannot do. The hindrances also provide a workable platform for dhammānupassanā, mindfulness of dhammas, in everyday life. Can we wake up to anger and what happens when we do so? What about lust or doubt?

Likewise, we can cultivate the factors of awakening anytime, anywhere, including in formal vipassanā practice. There are seven factors of awakening, but the operating principle behind dhammānupassanā, this fourth foundation of mindfulness, is the same for each: giving attention to a factor will cause it to grow and stabilize. Such practice can be undertaken internally and individually or by employing the power of interpersonal practice to sustain attention on this "what" aspect of mindfulness.

Mindfulness of energy, for example, will first draw out the qualities of energy—of body, of mind—as we discern the energetic component of present-moment experience. Noticing the energy is itself an energizing experience; it is interesting, enlivening. As we continue to attend to the energy, it continues to naturally increase, eventually reaching a point where intentionally holding it as a framework of awareness is no longer necessary; the energy is self-sustaining. This same dynamic holds true for all of the factors of awakening: investigation grows when we investigate; rapture increases when it is attended to; likewise with tranquility, concentration, and equanimity. Even mindfulness itself increases when we are mindful of it.

## MINDFULNESS OF A SINGLE HINDRANCE AND SINGLE FACTOR OF AWAKENING

This practice can be done with a friend or on your own. Choose a single hindrance to observe. I recommend beginning with an easy one, like laziness. Speak out the experience of it: what is the listless, uninspired mind like? How is this felt in the body? Does it change as you notice it? And so on.

After a time, shift to a single factor of awakening. Again, a simple factor such as investigation of states is a good place to begin. What is it like, in the very moment you are speaking and relating with another, to turn attention inward? Is the inner landscape complex or simple? Easy to observe or obscure? Notice that investigation is happening as you do this. How does investigating impact the state of mind being investigated? Is the mind stable? Impermanent?

After you have done both steps, take time to reflect with your friend on the mindfulness engaged during this practice.

## The Second Sati Category: The Buddha's Teachings as Practices

Reflecting on specific aspects of experience was a central practice in early Buddhist teachings. Calling the Dhamma to mind and holding it in mind was framed as a practice of mindfulness, forming the ultimate melding of right view and right mindfulness: sustaining a wise view. Here is one of many teachings where this type of reflection is so named:

Dwelling thus withdrawn (in body and mind), one recollects that Dhamma and thinks it over. Whenever, bhikkhus, a bhikkhu dwelling thus withdrawn recollects that Dhamma and thinks it over, on that occasion the bhikkhu develops the enlightenment factor of mindfulness; on that occasion the enlightenment factor of mindfulness is aroused by the bhikkhu; on that occasion the enlightenment factor of mindfulness comes to fulfillment by development in the bhikkhu.[147]

This same discourse connects such directed thought with the other factors of awakening such as investigation of states or of energy. This understanding of sati sometimes surprises people who think of mindfulness as restricted to present-moment awareness of whatever one is doing, but advice like this runs through the discourses. Such thinking is not a matter of random intellect, however, but of directing the mind in such a way that it brings the mind into the moment with awareness. We are observing present-moment experience while giving special attention to the frame of reference. In this way, awareness is being cultivated at the same time that the wisdom of the teachings is saturating the mind's constructing processes. As the constructing and re-constructing become integrated into our life perspective, they enable the "sure heart's release."[148]

The discourses' teachings on the structure and function of the mind and teachings on the human dilemma are offered as reflections for both formal practice and for engaging with throughout our lives. Present-moment reflection, taken to heart, is how the teachings transform from concept to experience. This is how all Dhamma teachings become practices. Good examples of this are found in the connected discourses on the aggregates, or khandha. In one discourse after another, the Buddha offers different angles by which one can reflect on present-moment experience using the framework of form, feelings, perceptions, constructions, and consciousness. One observes their rising and passing away, their not-yours nature, their fragility, and how they are made into an abode and a preoccupation. They are construed as a must for destroying suffering; as a measure of awakening; as the source of gratification, danger, and escape; and as the arising of aging and death.[149] In all of this the point is practice: anytime, anywhere, you can look into your own experience and use this framework to see for yourself. Doing so, remembering to bring this teaching into the moment, is a practice of right mindfulness.

Another refined object of mindfulness is mettā and the other brahmavihāras. Once again we are drawn beyond a narrow interpretation of what sati is and how it is cultivated. Among his teachings on the factors of awakening, the Buddha offers this guidance on the "liberation of the mind by mettā." The liberation by compassion, joy, and relational equanimity is included in this teaching: "Here, bhikkhus, a bhikkhu develops the factor of awakening of mindfulness (likewise the other six factors of awakening) accompanied by mettā, based upon seclusion, dispassion, and cessation, maturing in release."[150]

A subtle practice is being described in this discourse. Mindfulness, as well as each of the other factors of awakening, is cultivated with mettā as the primary reference point. So present-moment experience is observed, and the qualities of friendliness, spaciousness, and other aspects of mettā are given priority. These are done under circumstances of seclusion from sensory delight, and we know by reference that sustained and diligent practice—based upon cessation and maturing in release—is being pointed to. Its development leads to refined dwellings wherein one can perceive "the repulsive in the unrepulsive . . . the unrepulsive in the repulsive"[151] and other sophisticated perceptual permutations. But even such refined teachings fit within the whole life tenet of "all teachings can be experienced here and now." Some taste of this teaching is available to us. What matters here is our understanding of the breadth of formal objects of sati, and mettā is one of those objects. With this understanding, our formal mindfulness practices, as well as the practices embedded in our daily lives, can benefit from a wide array of wholesome approaches.

~

All of the foundations within these two categories for the what of sati, even the concrete foundations of body and the strongest Dhamma foundations, can become so refined as to essentially vanish. When attended to steadily and skillfully, the body may first be experienced as insubstantial and then as not existent at all. Feelings become increasingly subtle as pleasure and pain subside. Mind states and dhammas lose their form in the alert stillness of ripened sati. Mettā settles into "the beautiful as its culmination." Again we find ourselves placed at the crest of suchness.

The what of sati is multifaceted, just as our lives are multifaceted. It is important to find the right approach for our circumstances, for our mind states, and for the kind guidance we enjoy from our spiritual friends.

## How Am I Cultivating Awareness?

The Satipaṭṭhāna Sutta powerfully addresses how to skillfully cultivate sati: "And what . . . is right mindfulness? . . . [A] bhikkhu dwells contemplating the body in the body, ardent [ātāpī], clearly comprehending [sampajañña], mindful, having removed covetousness and displeasure in regard to the world . . . This is called right mindfulness."[152]

This dense teaching is a kind of mindfulness boilerplate: it is applied to each of the four foundations and also appears when sati is described elsewhere as part of the Noble Eightfold Path. In addition to being found in the Satipaṭṭhāna Sutta and Mahāsatipaṭṭhāna Sutta, it shows up in many of the shorter instructions in the collection called the Satipaṭṭhānasamyutta.[153] Clearly, it was a description important to the early Buddhist communities.

### Ardent, Clearly Comprehending

Three adjectives characterize the mindful meditator—ardent, clearly comprehending, and mindful. Understanding and internalizing these terms, feeling what they point to, will contribute to our sense of how to cultivate sati in our lives and our formal practice.

Ātāpī, the word translated here as "ardent," can also mean diligent or active. It points towards a mind that is energetic—a lively awareness. Ātāpī was originally applied to ascetic practice and so implied zealous, even strenuous practice. It also describes a mind laser focused on its goal, not drifting aimlessly. *Ātāpī*'s range of meanings indicate that right intention and right effort are relevant to this path factor.

In formal practice, being ardent or diligent means sustaining continuous sati, as far as possible, and bringing enough energy to practice that sati is bright and clear. In asking how we are recollecting right now, we can check whether there is bodily and mental energy that would indicate ardency. In informal practice, it is more often a matter of returning to sati, gently but clearly, over and over again, each time we remember. In interpersonal practice, this recollection naturally includes being aware of others, as well as of one's own mind. Awareness of both self and other generates its own ardency due to native relational sensitivity and the mutually influencing quality of reflected mindfulness. When the interpersonal practice is explicit and mutual, this natural reminding builds a positive feedback loop of diligence.

### Setting Aside Greed

The meditator is also described as "having removed covetousness and displeasure in regard to the world." Sati does not arise when we are fully identified with or lost in greed or in dejection. Nor does it arise when we are preoccupied with politics or personal affairs. The release of these things may require considerable right effort. Right sati can start when we have loosened our hold on constricted reactions even a little. A moment's partial freedom can allow a little sati, which in turn supports more letting go, leading to increased sati. When allied with right view, mindfulness naturally leads away from attachment and aversion. Another name for this quality is equanimity; sati and equanimity are natural partners.

Setting aside greed and displeasure with respect to the world, far from being applicable only to formal, silent mediation, is never more needed than when we're actually in the world, dealing with the world's stuff. It is one thing to work with this option on retreat, sheltered from most of the stresses of the world. It is another to actually ride it in the rough-and-tumble of daily life—in the midst of political turmoil, economic distress, and pandemics, for example.

Can we be fully in the world and still not swamped by our reactions to its seductions and demands? When we are, sati is readily established. And sati is the key to remembering this possibility. Eventually, it becomes a natural inclination of the heart.

Another aspect of greed involves the desire for elevated states or even for mindfulness. Likewise, we can be greedy for the sweetness of mindfully seeing our co-meditator and being seen by them. Such greed can easily infect the interpersonal practice of right mindfulness. We can easily confuse wholesome zeal with grasping at pleasant states or lovely relational moments. This grasping usually leads to forcing experience in order to sustain what we like. Patience and accurate observation are called for: What is actually present right now? What will lead to contentment, not to discontent? This is how we practice: contemplating each thing simply and directly, as free as possible from conceptual overlays, without getting lost in reactions, proliferations, or identification.

PRACTICE
**SETTING ASIDE GREED FOR EXPERIENCE**

The next time you engage in formal practice—individual or interpersonal—give special attention to whether or not there is a lust for some new or special experience. It can be subtle; after all, we are apparently doing something as we meditate, and so we want a result. Where does zeal for Dhamma—*dhammachanda*—become just chanda, desire for pleasantness or outcomes? Can you touch a quality of practice that is free from grasping and still fully engaged?

## Internally, Externally, and Both

Another part of the Satipaṭṭhāna Sutta's refrain is striking in its simplicity: contemplating the body as a body or feeling as feeling—each thing in itself. No proliferation, no conceptualization. This bareness is amplified as the refrain is repeated in full many times and is the basis for a few important practice directives. Here is the first of them: "In this way he abides contemplating the body as a body internally, or he abides contemplating the body as a body externally, or he abides contemplating the body as a body both internally and externally."[154]

The Abhidhamma and commentaries, and many later Buddhist schools, interpret "internally" as referring to one personally and "externally" as referring to other people. Some contemporary teachers have developed other interpretations, but this seems to be the meaning in the suttas and for a long time afterwards. Externally, one can see and hear others and reflect on what one has observed. But, with the exception of Insight Dialogue, there are few vipassanā practices that provide guidance on meditating with others.

Detailed guidance for the internal-external-both aspect of "How am I practicing mindfulness right now?" can be found in my book *Insight Dialogue*, under the guideline "Open." To support our whole-life practice of sati, I'll describe a spatial approach to this vipassanā instruction, as well as what we can call a perceptual frame approach.

Mindfulness established internally and externally can be understood as attending to a spatial quality in our practice. In this framing, internal mindfulness can be established most easily in the body. As we practice traditional vipassanā, it is often experienced as a sense of "in here,"—in this body, embodiment, and locality. Mindfulness established externally, in this way of speaking, is attending to the other with the constructed sense of them being "out there." So there is a sense of me and you, and mindfulness can move easily and intentionally between the two.

In Insight Dialogue or out in the world, the spatial dimension can be practiced with agility. With mindfulness established *both* internally and externally, we soften the focus of attention—and it can help if we relax visual focus—and encompass self and other in the same moment of mindfulness. This practice can be undertaken in nature, with trees and sky supporting external mindfulness. In company or in nature, a sense of "both" can become very stable and, with practice, can include attending to different aspects of the relational experience:

the space between, the sense of wholeness, and, as relaxed concentration increases, a dissolving of the construction of separation. We can dwell in the wide-open awareness of the illimitables—mettā, compassion, altruistic joy, and relational equanimity—where the other person or people you are meditating with are not objects of focal attention but are simply known in the large field of awareness.

Internal mindfulness also means "from the inside," or subjective awareness. This approach to practice works with the constructed perceptual frame of self and other. Whether we are aware of our own body or something outside ourselves, we attune to the "internal sense base" of seeing or hearing. There is attending to contact at the eye door and also the experience of feeling and of perceiving qualities and forms. This takes some training, but it is a powerfully deconceptive practice. In this understanding, mindfulness established "externally," or from the outside, would guide us to attune to the objective base, external base, or phenomenal experience of that thing. Mindfulness that includes both the inside and outside perspective is a nondual practice that is cultivated via a delicate dance of the mind, where we move between attending alternately to the *process* of sensation-perception and the *object* of perception. Becoming familiar with each enables a relaxing of both, where awareness and object, which had been experienced as self and other, are gently unified.

It should be noted that in both this subjective-objective and the "in here, out there" ways of practice, there is not a fusion of self and other in respect to losing our sense of balanced awareness. On the contrary, mindfulness is stable and bright, and the paradox of not-self-in-relation is accepted without mental confusion or stress.

These two lenses on mindfulness established internally, externally, and both arrive at the same experiential result. In here, me, subjective experience, and out there, you, objective experience, are fluid constructions. This is one of the conventions the mind establishes for practical purposes. It places the I in the world and in relation to others. We find that with well-established sammā sati, these conventions are released, and we touch the suchness of the awareness-world experience.

## INTERNAL AND EXTERNAL *ĀNĀPĀNASATI* WITH ANOTHER PERSON

Arrange to meditate with another person. It will be helpful if one or both of you are familiar with Insight Dialogue practice, but you can do this practice without that background.[155]

Sit facing each other, but with the eyes closed. Take fifteen minutes or so for each of you to calm the body-mind internally. A good foundation to use for mindfulness is the form of the whole sitting body.

At an agreed time, initiated by one of the two of you speaking, slowly open the eyes and notice there is a person in your visual field. Move your attention between mindfulness of your own sitting body (internally) and their body (externally). As you notice the differences, you may speak of them, or you may choose to remain silent. Relaxing the focal quality of awareness, see whether each of you can zoom out to a wider field that includes awareness of self and other simultaneously. What is this both quality of mindfulness like?

Focus your attention internally once more, closing the eyes. Attend specifically to the rise and fall of the breath. Let sati stabilize. Then, as before, open the eyes, but stay with the *internal* mindfulness of breathing (your own breath). Then shift to noticing your co-meditator's breath, visible in the movement of their body or face.[156] As before, shift between noting the breath internally and externally. Then widen the field of awareness to notice the breath both internally and externally.

Close your practice with respectful gratitude. You may choose to reflect on the experience with your co-meditator.

### Rising, Vanishing, and Both

The Buddha continues the instructions on this more subtle *how* of mindfulness: "Or else he abides contemplating in the body its nature of arising, or he abides contemplating in the body its nature of vanishing, or he abides contemplating in the body its nature of both arising and vanishing."[157]

Whatever the gross object—breath, feelings, thoughts, another person's speech, or even the relationship itself—we can attend to the rising edge of experience, the vanishing edge, or both. Attuning to each of these facets has a different quality.

Attending to the rising edge leads to a sense of "this exists." We are riding a wave into shore, perched on the edge of the surfboard. The world is coming into being new and fresh each moment. There is no prediction; the illusion of control is abandoned. Anticipation is never resolved. The mind is alert. There is nothing to hold on to.

Attending to the vanishing leads to a sense that nothing seems to exist, that all is dissolving. It's like being carried out to sea on a receding wave; our feet don't touch the bottom, and there is no ground. Moment by moment, there is nowhere to land. The grasping hand of attentiveness holds nothing; the liquid shadows hold no form.

Attending to both the rising and vanishing, we are perched on the tip of the moment. There is no past or future. Mindfulness can't register what it experiences in the office of the self; there is no one at the desk. There is not even the opportunity to notice that no two moments are alike; the comparing mind has vanished.

Time and again the Buddha names the apprehension of rising and vanishing as a definitive liberating insight.[158] Even a glimpse of the rising and vanishing of the world conditions the root release of grasping; the trance is broken.[159] We see that attending to rise and fall, too, is arbitrary; there is only flux.

～

Simply asking, "How am I practicing mindfulness right now?" launches us into sammā sati. Mindfulness does not depend upon the answer, only upon the awareness generated by the inquiry. Internal and external, rising and vanishing, and all the rest are powerful frameworks for investigating present-moment experience. Just asking the question *how* and letting the mind rest suspended in the moment of inquiry awakens the brightness and receptivity of awareness.

## Where Am I Aware?

Our sense of place is constructed. It is impermanent, fluid, co-varying with body-mind in each moment. Even so, *where* is a useful question for establishing our mindfulness practice. This question of where is simple and grounded. In turning the mind to the experience of here, we can enjoy the embodiment.[160] The mind is given the opportunity to instantly release its proliferations and land in the moment regardless of what we are doing or whom we are with.

It is true that this same question of *where* jettisons us into the living paradox of here-not here, of being-not-being, of thingness and no-thingness. We may even end up there by surprise, and when this happens, it is not uncommon to contract in unfamiliarity and fear. Knowing that this shift is possible will protect you; this is not just sati, but also sati-sampajañña, where we have a sense of what we're doing and why. So we release clinging, release method, and relax. Enjoy the embodiment and relax into it. As we relax, any contraction is likely to soften. Continue the kind investigation: Is the body one thing and awareness another? Is this here?

This is intimacy with experience. Between awareness and what you are aware of there is distinction but no distance. If you are aware of your hand, is it nearby? Separate from awareness? United with it? Is there any distance between a thought and awareness of the thought? Can you locate here? Could mind be anywhere else? How close is here? Is here the body? Is here awareness? *Where* am I recollecting?

PRACTICE
**MINDFUL OF WHERE IN NATURE**

Alone or with a friend, go to a place of natural beauty where you can rest quietly and undisturbed. After settling the body-mind, notice where the body is. Does awareness feel intimate with the body? Then let the awareness relax and grow wide, taking in the trees, sky, or waters: Is this place here? Is awareness one thing and this place another? Am I a part of it? Separate from it? How close, how intimate can this mind and this place be?

## When Am I Aware?

We know *when* to be a construct, but like *where*, it can be a profoundly useful one. In any moment we ask, "When am I aware?" the answer will always be, "Now." Can the mind ever not be in now? Try that—try being in the past or the future? Is now findable; can the mind hold it? But that is the exquisite beauty of asking the question, and in not finding an answer, we arrive at the suchness of experience. *When* am I recollecting?

PRACTICE
**THE SACRED ERRANDS**

Sometime when you are off doing errands—shopping, banking, anything—make the commitment to ask yourself, "When am I being aware?" Is it now? Is the mind knowing this experience in the future or past? Does this most mundane experience transform when the rising and falling of now is continually known?

## Tathatā: As Such

The Buddha completes the instructions on mindfulness of subtle objects with an instruction that takes us beyond gross object and beyond process: "Or else mindfulness that 'there is a body' is simply established in him to the extent necessary for bare knowledge and mindfulness. And he abides independent, not clinging to anything in the world."[161]

With each guiding question—why, what, how, where, and when—we arrive at experience per se, where there are no answers, no definitions. This is the liberative nature of right mindfulness. We may begin with the practical, even essential aspect of awareness of mind and world; doing so helps us maintain and navigate the Path on a day-to-day basis. But as the heart settles, the clinging that sustains the constructing processes of the self begins to let go. In this tender and often painful life, this release is priceless. This experience, even when temporary, is a reference point available to all of us, and even just thinking about it and considering it as a possibility is a step in the direction of release. How much more precious is the actual experience?

In this instruction, the object—body, breath, or other person—is incidental. The framework is known, but the real object is awareness itself. This yields to the subtlest but most basic, accessible practice, the dropping of any framework or even any sense of practice. The practice of sati involves learning to recognize awareness, learning to experience attention being given to the ongoing action of noticing, and stabilizing this noticing. Once stable, practice is released. This is nonmeditation meditation, a practiceless practice.

When sati is established by remembering awareness rather than by remembering a specific object, sati is flexible, supple, able to move with experience. We can be doing anything, and, in the moment when awareness itself is remembered, sati is established. We can have what we most seek, but as my teacher Anagarika Dhammadinna said, "You must ask." This is why studying the Dhamma can be a manifestation of sammā sati even though we are not remembering a specific object like the breath or bodily posture. A person studying the Dhamma is practicing sammā sati because sati's purpose (liberation) and method (reflexive attention) are encoded in the object of attention (a sutta or a dhamma talk, perhaps, or the Dhamma as present in an Insight Dialogue contemplation). Sammā sati is also like this when we recollect the practices of compassion and joy.

Working with objects is indispensable for guiding our path of effacement and release, and it can remain useful into the most advanced stages of meditation. Objects serve as training wheels in formal meditation, where conditions can be somewhat controlled. They train us to meet, with sati, the rushing impermanence of the rest of life. Because they are clear and definite, these frameworks can also be pulled in to help stabilize a less structured meditation that is losing clarity. But remembering the frameworks named in the four foundations is a practice, a technique for cultivating; it is not the life of sati. The mind makes that mistake, taking the remembering of the objects as the manifesting of sati itself. The conceiving mind conceives of itself as so smart, so important. But it, too, is empty. When sati is well cultivated, it is natural. This, then, is the native and ongoing sensing of awareness itself.

## ADJACENCY: DWELLING WITH RATHER THAN FALLING IN

As we cultivate mindfulness, we quickly realize that, whatever our efforts and intentions, the mind will continue to fabricate all kinds of thoughts and moods; sensations will continue to snag us. Life and mind are like that—dynamic. Sati is being awake in life and intimate with actuality, yet *maintaining a reference point in awareness*. This perspective, which I call *adjacency*, is helpful for both traditional, silent, formal meditation and relational, interactive meditation. There is a sense of awareness and of an object of awareness and an intimate relationship between the two.

In our usual experience, when something touches the mind or the body, a reaction emerges based on natural bodily responses, prior history, and prior constructs. The sequence by which these elements form the reaction is described as *dependent origination:* From contact comes a sense impression that may be pleasant or unpleasant. That impression arouses an urge in the body-mind—for more pleasure, for stability, for safety, and the like. The energy of that urge causes a gripping that can manifest as moving towards or as trying to get away; either way, it's a falling in. The mind has taken up residence in the reaction. With the gripping there is also a moment of becoming. In this slip into identification, this forgetting, adjacency vanishes. In the act of identifying with its sensations, perceptions, and reactions, awareness fuses with the object. We virtually leave the object behind and spin off into pure reaction: the samsaric life.

The remembering, sati, is noticing the functioning of awareness. That is, awareness is a landing place for awareness. Adjacency means that awareness is known *along with* the object. Our landing place could be the body or sensations; it could be just remembering the awareness.

In some meditative training, we learn to cut off any reaction as soon as it is noticed and return to an object—the body, the breath, and so forth. At times, this lesson is skillful and appropriate for taming the heart. But there are also times when, in that moment of noticing, the reaction and awareness coexist. We can wake up and dwell with what is happening—the reaction—without cutting it off. We return to mindfulness in a way that allows us to know the reaction as it continues to unfold. In such moments, sati is adjacent to the reaction—familiar or intimate with the reaction. This is neither cutting off the reaction nor falling into it. This dwelling with is a condition of intimacy with experience. It is a domain of insight and release.

In adjacency, we know that this thought, with this kind of feeling tone, is arising and passing away. We are familiar with the valence, with the charges and forces operating between the act of knowing and that which is known. Delicately and curiously, we experience the urges to cling or grab or push away. We experience them with some objectivity—as forces of nature rather than needs of a self. These are the forces that induce the body-mind to fall in, to become identified and lost in the reaction. But for now we are not falling in; we are observing. As adjacency ripens, knowing can unfold. Any perceived gap vanishes. Experiences may dissolve into experiencing.

During this experience of dissolution, people can have difficult emotions. Fear of other. Fear of disembodiment. Disorientation that can come as grasping relaxes. If we are about to be overwhelmed by a reaction, it can be safer to withdraw from the experience of the dissolving self, perhaps by lightening up on the sati or maybe shifting attention to mundane thoughts or sensations. Easing back from this experience can be a skillful exercise; our minds are sensitive and we should be gentle as our awareness practices gain strength. Intimacy with experience and with our own reactions is not always comfortable.

Withdrawing from intimacy, however, has its drawbacks. In interpersonal practice, cutting off reactions may result in distancing us not only from our own internal responses, but also from the person we are meditating with. Cutting off the intimacy of sati results in a more internal and solitary focus, even while practicing with another person. Shared practice can become awkward if we don't approach ourselves and others with compassion. There is no rush; there is nothing to get. Awareness, not me and not you, does the work, and awareness is infinitely patient.

With adjacency, we have a sense of knowing awareness. In the same way that we rest alongside our own thoughts and reactions as they rise and fall, we can rest in the presence of another human being. When sati is stabilized by samādhi, there is no effective difference.

---

PRACTICE
**A TASTE OF ADJACENCY**

---

Sit quietly. Give the body-mind a few minutes to calm down, perhaps by bringing attention to the felt form of the sitting body, or noticing where there are tensions in the body and inviting release. Or perhaps you settle easily with the breath.

After you've calmed, pay attention to the thinking mind. Just notice that thinking is happening. At some point, invite a noticing of awareness. Do not try to stop or get away from the thought or associated feelings. Can you notice both awareness and the ongoing flow of thinking? A question like, "Who is doing this thinking?" can help (but only if you do not try to answer it). How do mindfulness and thinking stand in relation to each other? Are they close to each other? Distant? Engage this sense of adjacency, of *both* awareness and thinking, with curiosity.

You could also try this practice with other sensations, like hearing or bodily sensations. Or do this practice while meditating with another, noticing the awareness even as the sense of self, other, and relationship hover in that knowing field.

## WHAT IS THE EXPERIENCE OF SATI LIKE?

I have noticed certain qualities that manifest when sati is established in formal meditation, as well as informal practice. Whether I am teaching personal or interpersonal meditation, or simply seeking to cultivate mindfulness in my daily life, I sometimes attune to these qualities to check whether the practice is on track.

I present these six qualities here in the form of an exercise, a way of checking your mindfulness at any time, in formal or informal practice, alone or with others. Whereas the five questions of sati can help you drop into the direct experience of mindfulness, this set of qualities of sati is descriptive. You can use it in any way you see fit.

**Awareness of awareness.** This is the foundation. Do you notice right now that awareness is operating? How does that feel? What is the mind-state of knowing you know?

**Continuity.** This is the necessary condition for the ripening of sati. Are there breaks in the flow of mindfulness, like thoughts or visual distractions? Does the mind lose itself as the person you are with shares a thought or a story? Or does the mind get hooked by memories and such? What is the felt experience of smooth and steady sati?

Does the presence of another remind you of or distract you from this continuity of awareness? If you are alone, is the mind sneaking out for self-made entertainment breaks?

**Nonidentification.** This is the natural result of awareness being the primary object. The mind does not cling to phenomena that could become the self, nor does it have the resources in that moment to fabricate and sustain the sense of self. The classic identifications of *I, me,* and *mine*[162]—are they popping up now in relation to what you see, hear, and above all, feel and think? Does the personality build itself up as you are with other people, or release its grip in the light of awareness or compassion? When the sense of self does get strong, can it be readily dropped as you re-enter the flow of experience?

**Intimacy.** Intimacy with whatever is being experienced naturally results from the clearing of thought and emotion. Do sensations, thoughts, and the presence of other people feel immediate, bright? Do they feel distant, disembodied? Do physical movements feel smooth and whole, co-fluid with awareness? Is life close by, in touch? Does it change as you observe?

**Naturalness.** This quality of mind is experienced as inherently natural. There is the sense of remembering what is already here rather than fabricating a mind state. Are there times when the awareness is flowing naturally, aware of itself without artifice or directed effort? How do you experience the energy of these times? If you are engaged with others, what is the quality of relationship as this naturalness manifests? Reading now, is awareness part of nature?

**Receptivity.** The mind is receptive; whatever is experienced is met without grasping or resistance. Do you feel balanced, open to the world? Is there smoothness of receptivity, of nonresistance, or is the mind defended, recoiling, and hard? What is the felt experience of this receptive awareness? Can receptivity be nurtured, as when one listens to hear a faraway bird?

## CHECKING THE QUALITIES OF SATI

The six qualities of sati can be used to reflect on and refine any of your practices of mindfulness, formal or informal, individual or relational. I suggest bringing them up at the close of a series of meditations, whether you're on retreat, practicing silently at home over the course of a week, or participating in a quarterly check-in for your Insight Dialogue group. See whether asking about these qualities inspires the practice.

During this meditation session, inquire whether each of these qualities is present:

- Awareness of awareness
- Continuity
- Nonidentification
- Intimacy
- Naturalness
- Receptivity

## CULTIVATING MINDFULNESS TOGETHER

While any of the path factors can be cultivated with other people, the relational practice of mindfulness merits special attention. When two or more are gathered with the intention to cultivate sati, a powerful synergy takes place. Each person becomes a mindfulness mirror. Their awareness in the present moment reflects back to the other that mindfulness is operating and that it is important, and this reflection strengthens their awareness. This awareness then reflects that spark of presence back to them, which reminds and strengthens their mindfulness, and so on. It is a candle in a house of mirrors. In such a container, the qualities associated with sati, such as continuity, nonidentification, and intimacy, swell and begin to saturate our lived experience. Human social sensitivity amplifies this saturation, serving to increase the energy and naturalness of the mindfulness. The receptivity to other people fosters receptivity to the totality of experience. Sati grows in this wholesome cycle. This is intrinsic relationality in service of awakening.

Understanding mindfulness must include understanding its roots in human relatedness, its impact on our lives with others, and the features of intentional interpersonal practice. As infants, the development of a sense of a self-center that is the locus of awareness, a sense that "I am aware," is made possible by being seen by others, particularly others who are experienced as safe and stable. Being seen by others is internalized as self-awareness and forms the foundation for mindfulness, for awareness of the experiencing body-mind. So it should come as no surprise that when the external observer is made concrete in the form of a meditation partner, as happens in formal interpersonal practices like Insight Dialogue, one's experience of mindfulness can be greatly amplified. It was never solely internal or individual to begin with. This spark of reflected awareness can then easily be picked up by the co-meditators and at times may even be experienced as having a tangible quality to it. That is, one may experience sati strongly in both body and mind states.

At the same time, recognizing and attuning to the relational aspects of sati will reveal the relational aspects of our internal thought processes. These thoughts arise from a life conditioned by countless relational contacts, and they are arising in the context of this moment of relational contact. The apparent "I" who is thinking is not an isolated unit, and its thoughts are not displaced from this interpersonal context. This understanding provides a helpful handle for coming to know the constructed nature of the discursive mind. Even our inner dialogue, our word-based thoughts, are relational because language is a relational, social phenomenon; we learn to speak to ourselves by learning to speak with others. Both the language we use and the internal ways we present problems and views are derived from and continue to reflect relational experience.

It follows that mindfulness internally, no less than mindfulness of and with others, is as intrinsically relational as it is individual, and its power to liberate the mind from unskillful patterns will operate both privately and socially. Practicing alone, we are always in relation; practicing in relation, we are always alone.

The individual, and each individual in relationship, is not an isolated unit. Each rises and falls every day in the sea of our wider culture. Maintaining mindfulness throughout our lives, not just on the meditation cushion, is an essential part of the whole-life path. Ethics relies on this living sati, and so does wise understanding. In wakeful contact with others, we come to see lust or anger that may remain latent when we are practicing mindfulness in physical isolation. Our biases, blind spots, and well-practiced cover-ups begin to reveal themselves when sati that has been formally practiced with others is released into the world of tussle, operation, and bump. We see again how right mindfulness conditions the arising of wisdom. Ignorance of systemic bias is not wise; knowing it is. Ignorance of latent social fear and greed is not wise; knowing it is. We do not need to "get rid" of these things; with love, we allow mindfulness and wisdom to do their work, which will always lean towards release.

The Buddha clearly understood the power of human relationality and did not limit his definition of mindfulness of the teachings to individual practices of reflection. He explained that the mindfulness factor of awakening is present when we are hearing the Dhamma from others and when we are teaching the Dhamma.[163] He also referred to, three foundations, satipaṭṭhāna, all associated with the teaching relationship.[164] They involve three situations in which a teacher—apparently the Buddha himself—teaches groups of students. In the first, none of them listen or apply themselves; in the second, some listen and apply themselves, while others do not; in the third, all the students listen and apply themselves. In each case, although his satisfaction differs, the Buddha maintains equanimity and sati, and he declares this awareness to be a satipaṭṭhāna: a foundation for mindfulness. So the balanced mind state *while in relationship* is taken as a foundation for sati. Thus, the idea of a foundation for the practice of sati is not exhausted by the four topic categories of the Satipaṭṭhāna Sutta. These three additional satipaṭṭhānas show both sati and the idea of a frame for sati as extended to interpersonal practice by the Buddha himself.

For this reason, a whole-life path will encompass mindfulness practices that are engaged with others, those taken up individually, and those that can unfold supported by society as a whole. Alone, we can engage the refined details of the inner life, particularly the existential confrontation enabled by experiencing the rising and vanishing of phenomena, especially when sati and samādhi become balanced and strong. It is also true that rising and vanishing presents itself with much subtlety in the between of co-meditation. The paradox of stability and groundlessness can be known and sustained. Also, although awareness of socially engaged behaviors can be engaged socially, mutually, or unilaterally, in all cases it is engaged most effectively with other people. Turning mindfulness towards itself can be engaged individually, but may at times be particularly effective in the cauldron of formal interpersonal practice, where steadiness of sati is sustained by a mutual effort that has been relaxed by love and compassion. Recognizing the constructed nature of the self is possible in formal, personal practice, and this very insight gains traction as mindfulness is brought to bear at the forge on which the self is cudgeled into existence: in relationship with others. Clearly, a wide path towards effacement, relinquishment, and wisdom will be rooted in this broad understanding of the development of sati.

## ⌒ REFLECTION

Sati is so simple, so elemental, that it is hard to define. It is awareness—just awareness—yet it is awareness nondiscursively aware of itself, aware of a context, aware of an underlying purpose.

Sati as the Buddha taught it—sammā sati—supports letting go of the basic hungers that give birth to the grasping mind. It is essential to anyone who wants to cultivate a nonclinging mind that is inherently compassionate and kind. Reflective awareness of itself is crucial to any society that intends to mature in compassion. The knowing quality of sati makes possible the whole-life path.

There are many possible ways to cultivate sati—with a gross object like the breath or body, with a subtle object like rising and vanishing of phenomena, with awareness of mettā, with awareness of present-moment relatedness, with awareness of awareness. To know what is most fitting for us at any given moment, we need to see what works in our direct experience. Usually, simple, concrete practices, like silent mindfulness of the body, are good places to begin. When we know what sati feels like, it can be helpful to include other people in our practice. Interpersonal practices will give sati portability in our lives and flexibility with how the body-mind actually behaves. Also, interpersonal practice tends to be where sati is most helpful for diminishing harm and increasing joy for ourselves and others. Communal practices, unfolding in a culture of awakening, will support the individual and interpersonal practices while setting the conditions for a just and humane society. The support of spiritual friends and teachers, the gift of occasional retreat practice, and continued exploration of mindfulness in life will all work together to help us cultivate familiarity and skill with mindfulness. Sammā sati is a practice that truly infuses the entire path, from the first steps to the dying process we will all confront.

Developing sati is essential for any person or culture that wants to nurture qualities like true friendliness, compassion, and appreciative joy, because such qualities depend on the mind getting over its self-obsession, at least partially and temporarily. Whenever it does, we get more freedom here and now. The classical role of sati in enabling insight into impermanence, suffering, and not-self comes from a ripening of the very awareness we can experience while reaching for the kitchen faucet. While sammā sati is oriented towards freedom from stress and confusion in relation to the world, all sati tends to bring a lessening of suffering. Even when the purpose is limited, the result tends to be a little taste of awakening, and the fineness of that taste can lead to a deepening of purpose. Mindfulness illuminates the purpose latent in every moment, here and now.

⌢

# CHAPTER 11

# RIGHT SAMĀDHI

## *Sammā Samādhi*

t is natural for the mind to pay attention to interesting things. As you read these words, perhaps you want to know what I'll say next. So the mind stays put—word after word, sentence after sentence. What qualities of mind do you notice in this sustained attention? Is the mind relaxed or agitated? Is it gathered in this one place or dispersed here and there? Is being gathered experienced as pleasant, unpleasant, or neutral right now?

It is also natural for the mind to jump from thing to thing when stimulations appear via the sense doors. Maybe as you are reading the phone rings, an email arrives, a bird flies by, or a friend comes in. Or maybe the mind fabricates a thought that is more compelling than what I'm saying right now. The mind goes out to this new object, grabs on for a bit, absorbs any pleasure it offers, and then moves back to this book or on to the next stimulus.

Steadiness of mind matters when it comes to the Noble Eightfold Path. Sammā samādhi, usually referred to as right concentration, is the eighth and last path factor. This placement is no accident;

it is the most refined path factor, the most contrary to the entice-ments and excitements that are the natural result of our sensitive perceptual systems and social restlessness. And now that the human mind's tendencies are amplified by technology, unifying the mind is a point of rebellion, an uncompromising reference point of balance and strength. It is a key catalyst for the deepening of all the path factors and the arising of insight. Samādhi is essential to unbinding.

## RIGHT SAMĀDHI AS A PATH FACTOR

Samādhi can only be properly understood through experience; how-ever, descriptive teachings can support the experience by guiding the mind. The Pali term for this path factor, *sammā samādhi*, denotes a mind that is calm and centered. The word *samādhi* derives from *sam-á-dhá*, meaning "to collect" or "to bring together," which sug-gests the unification of the mind. The word *samādhi* is also almost interchangeable with the Pali word *samatha*, which comes from a different root: *sam*, meaning "to become calm or serene." The aspect of calmness or tranquility is critical to a full and broadly effective understanding of *samādhi*. So we see that *samādhi* has two key ele-ments: the mind is gathered, whether one-pointed or spacious, and the body-mind is calm.[165]

The English word *concentration* is a frequently used but imperfect substitution for the word *samādhi*. *Concentration* does imply that the mind is concentric, or centered around one point; however, many Western cultures associate intensity and often force with the unified or focused mind implied by *concentration*. The element of calm is left out of the everyday usage of this word. For example, someone could be highly focused on a business problem or basketball game, but inwardly agitated. This is why I've left the word untranslated in this book.

In sammā samādhi the mind is relaxed, centered, and happy. There is no struggle, no desire. But the mind is quietly alert, still and stable, in focus but not "focused." That is, when samādhi is ripe, there is no effort, no agent who focuses. The mind settles on one point because of happiness and contentment, not because of restraint or force. In many cases, volitional effort may be necessary to establish samādhi, but once it is established, no volition is necessary. At this point, one is not "doing" anything. Instead a calming of experience, a cessation of reaction has taken place.

Both serenity and one-pointedness can naturally arise, but how much these two qualities are refined is what makes samādhi unique in its developmental requirements and in its effects. Samādhi is the liberative catalyst of the Path, and some degree of unification is essential to unbinding. This is the aim of sammā samādhi; this is what makes it sammā. It leads to dispassion, not to passion. Importantly, this includes dispassion regarding the extraordinary pleasure of *pīti*, or rapture, that often accompanies samādhi. Samādhi also leads to shedding rather than accumulating, to modesty rather than self-aggrandizement. All too often, greed for experiences pollutes the development of samādhi. But as we will see, the mind settles as conditioned by happiness and ease—not due to force and not driven by greed.

## NATURALLY ARISING SAMĀDHI

Most of us have experienced relaxed, immersive engagement while doing something that challenges and interests us. We might become wholly absorbed in an athletic, intellectual, or artistic process—like playing basketball, improvising on a musical instrument, programming a computer, weeding a garden, or writing a book. Full emotional engagement in a task or an urgent situation that has not teetered out of control can also be portals to a relaxed but total unification. Such gathered states of mind are experienced by meditators and by non-meditators alike in the course of everyday life. A contemporary term for this kind of joyful immersion is *flow*. Flow is a form of samādhi.

In many religious traditions, such states are elicited by expressions of devotion, particularly gratitude and praise. At these times, the devotee stands apart from mundane preoccupations and experiences a diminished concern for self, a sense of full involvement and rightness, and a joy that tends to gather momentum on its own.

Another common entry point for mental unification is deeply engaged relationship. When two people are focused on each another or a shared concern, the conditions may be just right for samādhi—full engagement, low stress, adequate novelty, and a sense of emotional ease. People experiencing this kind of friendship are not seeking excitement; contentment is the reward.

Because samādhi can arise as a natural human phenomenon, our task is to learn how to nurture it and, in cooperation with right view, to work wisely with it—in life and in meditation, in solitude and in relationship. Samādhi usually rises to its full, liberative potential gradually and over time. Although samādhi as a path factor includes the most explicitly refined—and even unworldly—practices and experiences, meditators are still uncovering a natural, latent capacity. Samādhi is not monolithic in practice or in result, as evidenced by the breadth of treatment in the discourses and the millennia of meditative and mystical methods across traditions. The Buddha's teachings are clear: special experiences are no more than distractions; relinquishment, effacement, and wisdom are the point; and our practices and applications of samādhi will reflect this understanding.

A gathered mind provides significant worldly benefits, from fostering mental ease to providing skillful ways of dealing with pain. But the relationship of samādhi to wisdom, and its role as a catalyst for insight, are what make sammā samādhi so essential to freeing the mind.

## SAMMĀ SAMĀDHI AS JHĀNA

Samādhi's more rigorous manifestation in Buddhist meditation is a group of eight deep meditative states known as the jhānas. The Buddha sometimes offered a basic description of the first four jhānas as the definition of sammā samādhi, the path factor. This classic description is found many times in the suttas:

And what, bhikkhus, is right *samādhi*?
    Here, bhikkhus, secluded from sensual pleasures, secluded from unwholesome states, a bhikkhu enters and dwells in the first jhāna,

which is accompanied by thought and examination, with rapture and happiness born of seclusion.

With the subsiding of thought and examination, he enters and dwells in the second jhāna, which has internal confidence and unification of mind, is without thought and examination, and has rapture and happiness born of *samādhi.*

With the fading away as well of rapture, he dwells equanimous and, mindful and clearly comprehending, he experiences happiness with the body; he enters and dwells in the third jhāna of which the noble ones declare: "He is equanimous, mindful, one who dwells happily."

With the abandoning of pleasure and pain, and with the previous passing away of joy and displeasure, he enters and dwells in the fourth jhāna, which is neither painful nor pleasant and includes the purification of mindfulness by equanimity.

This is called right *samādhi.* [166]

The jhānas are clearly specialized, refined states of body-mind. Why does a whole-life path need to consider something so rarified? Because this path includes well-developed formal practices, which are unique in their power and liberative impact. The jhānas mark one end of the meditative spectrum of stillness. Understanding and, if possible, experiencing this immersion is basic to understanding all samādhi.

In the jhānas, the mind exhibits the two facets of samādhi to a high degree: it is extremely calm, and it is fully absorbed, or settled on the object. As the description implies, "entering" the first jhāna is a discreet experience. With the immersion, the five hindrances of sensuous desire, ill will, sleepiness and laziness, restlessness and worry, and doubt are temporarily inactive. At the same time, four qualities essential to the jhanic experience are present: thinking (*vitakka*), examining (*vicāra*), rapture (*pīti*), and happiness (*sukha*). As jhāna practice proceeds through its first four levels, the mind settles further, and a progression takes place that my teacher Venerable Punnaji calls a diminishment of experience. Thinking and examining drop away in the second jhāna. In the third jhāna, rapture, with its overtones of excitement, also fades, leaving an extremely calm happiness or pleasure (sukha). In the fourth jhāna, pleasure and pain both fade away, and one experiences equanimity. Sati is present to the extent required to know if there is rapture, pleasure, or equanimity. But the emphasis is on allowing the body-mind to grow extremely tranquil.

The stillness of the fourth jhāna is the basis for experiencing the four formless (arūpa) jhānas. As perceptions of form are transcended, the absorption of the infinity of space arises. Transcending this absorption state, one experiences the infinity of consciousness. The dimension of nothingness (or no-thingness) follows. Finally, one arrives at the experience of neither perception nor nonperception.

These eight jhānas are taught as progressive, each being incomplete and to be transcended in favor of the next, more refined one. The Buddha called the first three jhānas, refined as they are, "perturbable," while the fourth and beyond were "imperturbable."[167]

Jhāna practice generally requires a calm environment and a high level of dedication over a long period of time, from weeks to months, and still we may or may not experience the rapture or profound serenity described in the discourses.[168] Regardless, setting aside time to develop refined samādhi is well worth the effort. The jhānas are refreshing; they bring joy and inspiration for further practices of calm and insight. Likewise, there are pronounced positive impacts on our lives. Deep calm reveals what is uncalm, making us aware of unease, stressful patterns of thought, and fraught relationships that had been hidden beneath a layer of agitation. Now, knowing what ease feels like, we are more likely to be able to spot stress and more inclined to favor ease. We begin habitually inclining towards dispassion, contentment, modesty, and nonentanglement. This is the true, natural beginning of relinquishment.

## SAMĀDHI AS AN AWAKENING FACTOR, A SPIRITUAL FACULTY, AND A SPIRITUAL POWER

Right samādhi integrates with the six other factors of awakening and the four other spiritual faculties and powers.

The seven factors of awakening are qualities that synergize to bring about liberating insight; they also describe the mind that has matured into awakening. Samādhi is one of these seven factors; it rests on the development of pīti (rapture or joy) and sits between tranquility and equanimity. Because samādhi co-arises with all the factors of awakening, it is clear that, even as the mind is unified, it must also be flexible and robust enough to meld with investigation and to be infused with energy. Samādhi must also be balanced with sati such that, together, these two factors lead each other to increasingly subtle understanding of things as they actually are.

In many of the teachings on the five spiritual faculties, skillful practice is also explicitly defined as balancing samādhi with energy. A mature understanding of samādhi encompasses this co-existence of effort and ease, of energy and serenity, of adaptability and one-pointedness.

The five spiritual faculties (*indriya*)—faith/confidence (*saddha*), energy (viriya), mindfulness (sati), samādhi, and wisdom (*paññā*)—can help guide our meditation practice towards the strength and stability required for insight. It is a kind of developmental formula: give attention to these five qualities, balance them, and you will know you're on the right track.

These same five qualities are also grouped together as spiritual powers (*bala*). The message here is different: these five qualities are each powerful, and their synergy is exceptional. Having cultivated them, you are empowered to meet the challenges and enjoy the fruits of meditative development.

PRACTICE
**BALANCING SAMĀDHI WITH ENERGY AND EQUANIMITY**

The Buddha offers this instruction on the integration and balancing of calming and arousing factors:

A monk intent on heightened mind should attend periodically to three themes. He should attend periodically to the theme of *samādhi* . . . to uplifted energy . . . (and to) the theme of equanimity. If (he) were to attend solely to the theme of *samādhi,* it is possible that his mind would tend to laziness. If he were to attend solely to the theme of uplifted energy, it is possible that his mind would tend to restlessness. If he were to attend solely to the theme of equanimity, it is possible that his mind would not be rightly unified for the ending of the *intoxicants.* But when he attends periodically to the theme of *samādhi,* attends periodically to the theme of uplifted energy, attends periodically to the theme of equanimity, his mind is pliant, malleable, luminous, & not brittle. It is rightly centered for the stopping of the *intoxicants.* [169]

You can explore this teaching yourself. Sit quietly, just observing the body-mind in a natural way and allowing ample time for it to calm down. As you do so, occasionally investigate whether the mind is agitated or calm, gathered or scattered. Does it feel grounded, stable? There is no need to force samādhi just bring attention to those component qualities.

After a while, give attention to the quality of energy in both body and mind. Is there a steadiness, perseverance of attention? Is the body awake, the mind alert? Again, no force; just inquire and notice what is present.

Then shift the attention to equanimity. As sensations or thoughts arise, is the mind grasping at them or letting them rise and pass away on their own terms?

Shift among these three observations in a relaxed but consistent way. Notice whether the mind begins to become better able to see present experience clearly.

## THE WORLDLY BENEFITS OF SAMĀDHI

Besides supporting other path factors, fostering wisdom, and strengthening virtue, sammā samādhi has significant benefits in our worldly lives. The interwoven benefits flow from a common source, meditative unification, and are significant aspects of a whole-life path.

First, there are the benefits of the calm aspect of samādhi. Deep calm reveals what is uncalm. Having experienced even brief moments of a still and gathered mind, we more clearly know the noise of the mundane mind.

The human mind is frantic by design. As humans evolved in a world of dangerous and unexpected things, mental alertness was rewarded with survival, and these traits were passed down genetically. This survival-level alertness continues to be reflected in our attentional habits; the mind is constantly scanning the natural and social environment for threats and rewards and reacting as quickly as possible to any new information. Neurotransmitters, stress hormones, and other liquids of vigilance are activated, and as they remain in circulation, they continue to affect our mind states. Thoughts arising out of this agitated state arouse more hormonal secretions. The stress response can also incorporate muscle tension and even changes in the states of our cells. Our vocabulary struggles to keep up with such experiences: the words *anxiety, fear, nervousness, strain, tension, trauma, affliction,* and *restlessness* touch only the surface of the human condition.

If we attend to, observe, foster, and protect even mundane restfulness, we support the conditions for sammā samādhi. As our definitions of restfulness and stillness shift to the new level illuminated by samādhi, we can see noise where before we may have thought we were "pretty relaxed." The heart, the intention, turns in the direction of this stillness, preferring it over the agitated states we once believed were our only option.

Another worldly benefit of sammā samādhi is the simple fact that it is extremely pleasurable. Samādhi is described throughout the discourses as the most reliable way to experience pleasure. Indeed, the pleasure of jhāna is described as the peak of bliss.[170] This is not just any old pleasure, but a very specific type: pleasurable states of body and of mind that are not dependent upon external conditions. The Buddha referred to this type of pleasure as "indeed the path to enlightenment."[171] Sammā samādhi's first supporting conditions, as we saw in the earlier description of the jhānas, are seclusion from sensual pleasures and seclusion from unwholesome states. The pleasure that is developed in this way is "the bliss of renunciation, the bliss of seclusion, the bliss of peace, the bliss of enlightenment."[172]

The pleasurable feelings and mental steadiness of sammā samādhi arise most readily and most clearly in the absence of unwholesome states of mind. The hindrances—sensual desire, aversion, sloth and torpor, restlessness and worry, and doubt—and the calm attentiveness of samādhi are mutually repellent. The pleasure of samādhi also keeps us out of trouble because it is just more enjoyable than the hindrances and immoral action. When we are experiencing it, we are simply not interested in messing up our happiness. It is a refined state, and while we are experiencing it, and for a time afterwards, the gross pleasures are not only unattractive, but also repugnant.

An extension of this effect is that our desire for sensual pleasures is likely to decrease. Sensual pleasures lose their luster as a consequence of seeing them more clearly. When the mind is calm and unified, it becomes apparent that each moment of experience is impermanent, dependent upon changing outer circumstances, and raw and shot through with suffering. Compared to meditative pleasure, sensual pleasure is unreliable and agitating. We come to prefer the pleasure of a gathered mind simply because it feels better. Indeed, the Buddha's own experience was that each successive refinement of pleasure in samādhi formed the basis for further release: "As long as I hadn't entered into and withdrawn from these nine progressive meditative attainments in both forward and reverse order, I didn't announce my supreme perfect awakening."[173]

Unlike many of our sources of sensual pleasure, meditative pleasure is free, nonaddictive, wisdom inducing, and based in moral behavior. It is also independent of outer circumstances and available anytime to anyone who applies themselves.

In the happiness of samādhi, we begin to let go of sensual pleasure. We no longer feel so driven to acquire, to have stimulating experiences, and to attach to other people as sources of entertainment and self-validation. Our energy may be turned towards actions that fit a nonselfish value system.

Having tasted stability, the unified mind comes to naturally value peace, and our attentional resources are freed up for us to care about and give to others. Also, because we have become more sensitive to what agitation looks like, and its suffering nature, when we encounter this agitation in others, we appreciate their pain and are readily moved to ask, "How can I help?" Less reactive and self-obsessed, we respond to others with compassion.

The collectedness we foster in meditation manifests in other contexts, such as our work and play. Having learned to remain relaxed as experiences unfold within the body-mind, we more easily remain relaxed and gathered as we apply the mind to tasks. Patience increases. We can stay with things, see tasks through to their completion, and give all we can as a result of this inner strength. Relationships and groups grounded in samādhi are likewise more harmonious and effective.

Finally, clear thinking becomes more accessible. The mind that has come to enough stillness to see through its own murk can also see more easily through the murk of the world. Life's complexities sometimes demand detailed investigation. Interpersonal dynamics, multi-layered problems, and competing social values are all hallmarks of the engaged life. The still place of samādhi can, with nourishment, be available to us in the midst of complex situations. We may not always know what to do, but because the mind is balanced, we are less likely to rush into premature action and less likely to be swept up by our biases and views. Action issues from the mind, and the clearness born of samādhi is a good source of origin.

---

PRACTICE
**REFLECTING ON STATES OF SAMĀDHI**

Get together with a friend who shares your interest in the calm, unified mind. After taking some silent time to settle the body-mind, present in sequence each of the following reflections:

- What experience of easeful focus have I had while working?

- What experience of easeful focus have I had while playing or engaged in an avocation?

- What experiences have I had of relating to someone where we have become deeply calm?

- What is our experience now of samādhi?

- How does calm pleasure compare to times of individual and relational excitement?

## Samādhi's Effects on the Experience of Pain

One particular worldly benefit of samādhi is that it changes our capacity to respond to pain. Physical pain is part of everyone's life, and having access to samādhi is sometimes the best medicine.

For many people, one of the early gifts of meditation practice is learning to receive pain without reaction. Meditators on retreats often experience pain from prolonged sitting or from the bodily tensions that arise as mental difficulties come to the surface. At first, the pain usually increases as a result of aversion and resistance. We want to stop meditating, get up and walk around, and shift positions. If we have been completely fooled by the pain, we may want to take a pain-relieving pill or see a doctor. As meditation develops, and perhaps as we turn to teachers for guidance, we begin to find the capacity to relax, to receive the pain and allow it to rise and fall as it will. This experience is a classic beginning of samādhi. The mind becomes more still as it attends to the pain, and by consciously shifting from resistance to receptivity, we are learning what it is like to be still. While strong pain can create a strong distraction, it also provides a stable basis for mental attention; the mind is riveted to the compelling unpleasant feeling. When this attention is combined with acceptance, samādhi naturally increases. When the mind is sufficiently unified, even strong pain can be completely sundered. Unpleasant feeling (vedanā) is a mental experience, and it can just end.

Throughout the Buddha's discourses we find instances where meditative absorption, including the jhānas, helped someone cope with severe physical pain. When his jealous cousin Devadatta tried to kill the Buddha by rolling a boulder downhill at him, the boulder missed but a shard broke off and badly cut the Buddha's foot. His sensations were described as "racking, sharp, piercing, harrowing, disagreeable." Nevertheless he simply spread his robe on the ground and lay down on it on his right side, one leg on top of the other, "mindful and clearly comprehending." Various deities visited him and praised his way of meeting the pain. Most spoke of handling the pain with mindfulness and clear understanding—with sati and sampajañña—but the last deva spoke of the liberative and protective effects of samādhi as another source of his ability to endure such pain: "See his samādhi well developed and his mind well liberated—not bent forward and not bent back, and not blocked and checked by forceful suppression! If anyone would think such a one could be violated . . . such a lion of a man . . . what is that due to apart from lack of vision?"[174]

PRACTICE

## BRINGING SAMĀDHI TO PAINFUL BODILY EXPERIENCE

You can directly experience how mental unification benefits the ability to meet pain. While prior meditative experience with well-established samādhi is helpful, it is not necessary. Diligent practice, perhaps motivated by the pain itself, will suffice.

You can begin this practice when you are experiencing a specific pain, or you can use it to quietly attend to the minor discomforts that the body generously provides. If you are practicing with a particular pain, I recommend a steady pain, such as headache, chronic joint pain, or the pain resulting from an earlier injury. Sudden pain is very difficult to deal with; the body's reaction to recoil and tense can be too challenging to remain present with.

Begin by finding a posture that is as comfortable as possible while still maintaining a straight back. As you settle down, bring awareness to the whole body, just noticing its shape and the touch points on the cushion, chair, or bed. Let the attention rest a moment with the felt image of the bodily form.

It is likely that after not too long the mind will naturally gravitate to the area that's in pain. Allow this to happen; pain is functioning as an ally to gather the mind. What do you notice about the mind's response to the unpleasant feeling? Is it drawn in? Is it also repelled, wanting the pain to go away? Be curious about this experience. What is the size, the shape, of the pain? Is it moving or still? Does it have a texture or a rhythm? This inquiry specifically opens intimacy with the sensation. You want to get to know it because in the bareness of experience, the vedanā, the feeling tone, is far more workable than our constructed reactions of "pain," "don't like," and "must get rid of." The pleasant or unpleasant aspect is just phenomena.

Achieving this neutral intimacy is easier said than done, but as you continue your practice of drawing near, of gentle familiarity, the mind is settling. The body-mind's myriad micro-reactions to the felt experience are diminishing. The sensation comes to no longer be held at a distance; the sensation as object of awareness may merge with the awareness itself as a result of the mind becoming calm and gathered, establishing samādhi.

## Otherworldly Benefits

In addition to samādhi's worldly benefits, the early texts spoke of extraordinary powers that could be developed with exceptional samādhi. These powers range from telepathy to walking over water, and emphasizing the ability to know one's own and possibly others' past lives. Although we will not explore these powers here, I suggest letting these teachings challenge you with glimpses of capacities that seem far beyond our mundane lives.

## SAMĀDHI AND WISDOM

The most important benefit of sammā samādhi to the Eightfold Path is that it creates the conditions for seeing deeply into the nature of phenomena and so for letting go. It also opens onto an experience of the dispassion and cessation of nibbāna, cooling. The Buddha often taught that as the result of samādhi, one "sees things as they actually are, [which naturally results in the experience of] disenchantment [which conditions the arising of] dispassion . . . [which naturally leads one to] realize the knowledge and vision of liberation."[175] The Buddha pointed unambiguously to the purpose of samādhi: "Bhikkhus, develop samādhi. A bhikkhu who is experiencing samādhi understands things as they really are."[176]

He continues this particular teaching with a classical analysis, saying that the meditator understands the impermanence of the eye, visible forms, seeing consciousness, contact, and feelings. And so it is for all six senses—the five physical senses and the mind. But we find the same message throughout the discourses: samādhi is the primary catalyst to the most potent liberating insights.

The reasoning behind this teaching is clear, at least to the extent that reason can apply to such subtle regions of human experience. The agitated mind simply does not have the staying power needed for the work of liberation. The always vibrating mind tires easily; the stable mind enjoys enduring and effortless energy. The distracted mind cannot dwell long enough with any phenomenon to know that its nature is impermanent, stressful, empty of self. The stable mind can rest with dynamic, even difficult, phenomena and penetrate to the core of the human experience. I often think of it in terms of signal-to-noise ratio: In a noisy room it is difficult to understand what someone is saying; in a quiet room they can be easily understood. The signal—the person's speech—gets lost in the noise of the crowd. The nature of rising and vanishing, of not-self, of the fabricated nature of the experienced world, is mostly indiscernible in the noise of the agitated mind. With tranquility and samādhi, we see clearly and naturally into the fundamental nature of things. The liberating signal is clearly discerned.

The feverish mind, the normal, untrained mind, is every moment unknowingly weaving the world into existence. This is a finding of contemporary psychological science and cognitive science, and it is a well-tested teaching of the Buddha: ignorance is the condition for the mind's constructions and ongoing process of constructing the world (avijjā paccaya saṅkhāra). To the untrained mind, this understanding seems far too contrary to everyday experience. Clearly, we say, this world exists, and it is out there just as I perceive it to be. When asked whether everything exists or everything does not exist, the Buddha replied, "[F]or one who sees the origin of the world as it really is . . . , there is no [holding to the view] of nonexistence in regard to the world. And for one who sees the cessation of the world as it really is . . . , there is no [holding to the view] of existence in regard to the world."[177]

This is not an idle philosophical question. Beliefs in the solidity of the world, in the self or the "we" that is experiencing the world, and in the qualities and natural laws of that world are the conditions for grasping, self-obsession, and the countless behaviors that bring suffering and harm to ourselves and others. On the other hand, a fixation on emptiness—nothing exists—can lead to nihilism, despair, and even amorality: none of it matters, so grab what you can. Both perspectives are deluded; both yield a life dominated by a fermenting ignorance. But the mind unified can know, beyond concept and beyond doubt, the paradox of is and is not. Such insight, such release, is made possible by samādhi.

From such experiences of deep knowing, life is changed decisively. Existence is known as it is: inherently unstable and thus stressful at the most subtle level. Clearly, there is no abiding self at the core; all is process. This is the basis for relinquishment; in the lived life, we let go. There is greater care for others because we know, deeply and fully, that everyone is in this fundamental human predicament of instability. Generosity comes easily because the self is not holding to and protecting what it feels to be "mine." This is the functioning of wisdom as compassion and generosity. This is the fruition of right view. Clearly, sammā samādhi is an essential ingredient of a whole-life path.

PRACTICE
## CONTEMPLATING THE EASEFUL MIND

In one of my favorite discourses, Ananda asks Sariputta about an experience that was rooted in samādhi. Sariputta gives a beautifully precise description of an experience in which a single insight arose, over and over again, in an utterly still mind.

On one occasion, friend Ananda, I was dwelling right here in Savatthi in the Blind Men's Grove. There I attained to such a state of *samādhi* that I was not percipient of earth in relation to earth; of water in relation to water; of fire in relation to fire; of air in relation to air; of the base of the infinity of space in relation to the base of the infinity of space . . . .

But of what was the Venerable Sariputta percipient on that occasion?

One perception arose and another perception ceased in me: 'The cessation of becoming is nibbana; the cessation of becoming is nibbana.' Just as, when a fire of twigs is burning, one flame arises and another flame ceases, so one perception arose and another perception ceased in me: 'The cessation of becoming is nibbana; the cessation of becoming is nibbana.'

On that occasion, friend, I was percipient: 'The cessation of becoming is nibbana.'[178]

You are invited to pause to consider the stillness and stability of mind Sariputta experienced as his insight into nibbāna unfolded. He describes a mind that continues to be touched by sensory experience—the apparent solidity of material things (earth) and other physical sensations—but that does not hold to them, not even for the fraction of a second required for the perception process to recognize solidity, temperature, and so forth. No conceptualization happens: Sariputta offers his description of this experience to Ananda after the fact. In the moment, it was pure apprehension.

Pause now to reflect on such a mind that is an open field: alert, profoundly stable, sensitive, but not thrown off balance by any phenomena. This is an ease at the fringes of what we can imagine—an ease beyond bliss, even beyond pleasure.

Please do not assume that this is such a refined state that it is not possible in your own life. What is the fragrance of this teaching when you accept the whole-life tenet of finding all teachings in the here and now? What within you knows, feels, or intuits what the experience might be like when the mind is saturated with equanimity, empty and receptive—in this wakeful ease where becoming itself ceases?

## SAMĀDHI AND INSIGHT PRACTICES

Because of its refining effect, samādhi is widely taught as the basis for insight practices—that is, for the pursuit of wisdom by means of formal meditation. You calm the mind by practicing either the jhānas or a lighter degree of calm unification. Then you shift the emphasis to the cultivation of right mindfulness. From there, you might alternate between emphasizing sati and samādhi, or these two qualities naturally balance themselves as practice develops and the mind becomes increasingly refined. With a bit of stillness, you can be stable enough to observe moment-to-moment experience. As you do so, the mind becomes more still. This greater stillness, then, enables you to see more deeply into the unfolding moment. This cycle continues in such a way that sati and samādhi become fully melded.

There is an age-old debate about how highly unified and refined someone's mind needs to be to practice vipassanā. Some people teach that at least the first jhāna is essential for the arising of insight. At the same time, Theravada tradition has it that the second through fourth jhānas actually bring about such stillness of mind that insight does not arise; the mind is nearly inactive, absorbed in bliss or, later, in equanimity. In some lineages, vipassanā meditators are explicitly steered away from jhāna practice.

It is true that all four jhānas can lead to grasping at pleasant experiences. The second jhāna and beyond still the mind so much that it is not inclined to observe the nature of phenomena. But jhāna practice can condition an open-minded stability that supports apprehending the rising and vanishing of phenomena and the nature of subject-object relations. In particular, when jhāna practice is exited and the re-emergence of thoughts, feelings, and self-constructing processes is observed, their impermanent and empty nature is known. Insight naturally arises.

Throughout the discourses we see that tranquility and insight are both necessary; each steadies and facilitates the other. When both are strong, intoxicants are abandoned; this is synonymous with liberation. Tranquility and insight will not always be developed at the same pace, but with skill in practice, even a little of either leads to an increase in the other; both get developed in the end. Ananda summarized the possibilities thus: "A bhikkhu develops insight preceded by serenity . . . [or] develops serenity preceded by insight . . . [or] develops serenity and insight in conjunction . . . [or] a bhikkhu's mind is seized by restlessness about the Dhamma. But there comes an occasion when his mind becomes internally steady, composed, collected, and unified. Then the path is generated in him."[179]

"The path is generated"—again we see the unique power of absorption. The mind drops beneath its own constructing processes; the trance of becoming is dispelled. In a direct and concrete way, we cease to perceive substantiality where there is only flux, pleasure where there is agitation and craving. We apprehend the emptiness of the self-making processes. We may fall again under the mind's alluring trance, but the fog has begun to thin out. The heart begins to let go.

Whatever the nature of our meditation practice, we can trust that giving some priority to sammā samādhi will greatly support our entire path. Right samādhi is an essential element of the path to wisdom, to dispassion and disenchantment. Yet the most refined samādhi is not a prerequisite for wisdom.[180] Obsession with attaining higher jhānas is not helpful. Better to consider how samādhi steadies and purifies the mind. We will be guided by our own experiences of even modest serenity and be inspired by others' descriptions of the experience. If and when you feel called to develop the jhānas, trust in the benefits it will bring to your entire whole-life path.

## Volitional Practice of Sammā Samādhi and the Paradox of Striving

The Buddha certainly taught that strong effort is usually required for stronger or more stable levels of samādhi. An oft-repeated vow he offered is, "Willingly, let only my skin, sinews, and bones remain, and let the flesh and blood dry up in my body, but I will not relax my energy so long as I have not attained what can be attained by intrepid strength, by intrepid energy, by *intrepid* exertion."[181] Such a teaching seems to conflict with the ground of samādhi in tranquility and the teaching that we can only invite and prepare for its manifestation.

It is true that unskillfully forcing the mind tends to yield fabrications of what we *think* samādhi is. Our tense notions create a brittle concentration or, more properly, fixation of mind. The mind is unable to remain balanced in the face of the insights and mind states that come with the concentration itself. Another danger of forcefully focusing attention is that it will yield trance states rather than insight. Yes, there may arise pleasurable states of body-mind, but absorption in that pleasure and distance from lived experience make this kind of practice a dead end.

Yet cultivating sammā samādhi with the support of volitional effort is the focus of classical meditation practice. Most of us have seen images of monks and nuns seated for hours in meditation, retreat halls full of diligent yogis doing what needs to be done, and *sanyasins* engaged in grueling rituals and practices. Such intensive, immersive spiritual rigors are based in the third and fourth right effort: to develop and maintain wholesome qualities. In the modern West we are situated in a culture of doing, and in the attempt to keep the spiritual path free from the agenda of accomplishment, many have largely rejected such striving. It seems to be wrought with building up an adept self, with spiritual materialism and grasping. Most troubling to us, it seems a futile enterprise. How, we wonder, can one attain serenity when the effort of practice is inherently tense?

The Buddha was asked this very question—or rather, a disciple of another teacher asserted that volitional effort cannot result in true letting go because of the attachment and desire it brings. In response, the Buddha offered a simile of a man walking to a park. Using the framework of the four spiritual strivings, or bases for spiritual power (iddhipāda)—desire (chanda), energy (viriya), heartful commitment (citta), and investigation (vīmamsā)—he noted that the man walking to the park must have the desire to go there, but once he arrives, does he still manifest the desire? He must put forward the energy to walk there, but once he is there, must the energy still be engaged? He must set his heart on getting to the park, but when he is there, is his heart still set on getting there? And he must engage the motivation of inquiry to get there, but once there, is that faculty still activated?[182] So clearly, one may engage all of these powers to develop samādhi, especially when one faces an unruly heart, but the strivings are released as the mind becomes unified and serenity comes forward.

As you consider volitional approaches to formal and informal practices, keep in mind this paradox of striving and how you can practice in a skillful way, putting forth strong effort to overcome habitual tendencies while knowing that this more assertive effort will be released as the mind develops. Notice any aversion to or reaction against any teachings that emphasize effort, persistence, and striving, and perhaps open your heart to a new, or very ancient, way of approaching the unification aspect of the path.

## SETTING THE CONDITIONS FOR SAMĀDHI: VIRTUE, PURIFYING THE MIND, AND OTHER FACTORS

How we live contributes to or detracts from the development of sammā samadi. We read repeatedly of people, mostly monastics, who could easily attain jhāna.[183] Sariputta, perhaps the Buddha's most esteemed disciple, describes the masterful bhikkhu as one who "wields mastery over his mind, he does not let the mind wield mastery over him."[184] These people were living in such a way as to condition a relaxed, attentive quality of mind. Virtue and purifying the mind are key. There are other mental factors that contribute as well.

### Virtue and Monitoring Sense Input

Throughout our consideration of the whole-life path, we've seen the relational and social value of virtue. A moral life also directly serves the development of samādhi and thus insight. With virtue, samādhi may arise by natural law. The Buddha explained the simple logic behind putting virtue first:

> For one who is virtuous and endowed with virtue, there is no need for an act of will: "May non-remorse arise in me!" It is a natural law, monks, that non-remorse will arise in one who is virtuous.

> For one free of remorse, there is no need for an act of will: "May gladness arise in me!" It is a natural law that gladness will arise in one who is free from remorse.

For one who is glad at heart, there is no need for an act of will: "May joy arise in me!" It is a natural law that joy will arise in one who is glad at heart.

For one who is joyful, there is no need for an act of will: "May my body be serene!" It is a natural law that the body will be serene for one who is joyful.

For one of serene body, there is no need for an act of will: "May I feel happiness!" It is a natural law that one who is serene will feel happiness.

For one who is happy, there is no need for an act of will: "May my mind be *samādhied!*" It is a natural law for one who is happy that the mind will be *samādhied*.

For one who is *samadhied,* there is no need for an act of will: "May I know and see things as they really are!" It is a natural law for one with a *samādhied* mind to know and see things as they really are.[185]

This cascade of causes and effects begins with virtue; if we want this natural law to work for us, we must attend to sīla.

Guarding the senses is essential to maintaining virtue; without it, virtue itself is unstable. The Buddha put it like this: "If there is no sense control, O monks, then the basis for virtue is destroyed for one who lacks sense control. If there is no virtue, then the basis for right samādhi is destroyed for one who lacks virtue."[186] Though monitoring sense input and avoiding that which generates distraction and agitation may run against our personal habits, and against the norms of the dominant culture of stress, doing so is part of supporting the virtue that conditions calm samādhi. The eyes are touched by an image; the brain grabs onto that image to understand it. Pleasant and unpleasant play across the moment while memories and ideas burst forth with each thing seen, heard, or cognized. All of this activity unfolds mostly by reflex: we don't try to activate the mind this way and, indeed, slowing it down—or even stopping it—is not so easy.

PRACTICE
## GUARDING THE SENSES

Gather a group of like-minded friends for an afternoon (or longer) of individual and interpersonal meditation practice. Begin with silent practice, where each meditator individually investigates what activates the mind. The abiding inquiry is, how do arising thoughts and feelings reflect a life of unguarded senses—social stimulations, intellectual pursuits, chasing sensory pleasures? Don't recoil from your agitation; welcome it as a starting point of authenticity.

Then invite everyone into dyads to explore what has been noticed. It will help if you have the support of Insight Dialogue or a similar calming and focusing practice. Pause often while speaking and listening to drop beneath judgments and preconceptions. Relax the body and calm the mind as your practice settles enough to watch, in the very moment of speaking and listening, the arising and vanishing of habitual agitations. Allow the mind to settle. As it does so, also name the calm aspects of experience.

After a short Insight Dialogue session, maybe half an hour, go back into individual meditation. Invite a simplicity of practice, like awareness of the whole body or the in and out of breath, so you have a reference point for seeing whether the body-mind is settling. Again, you are invited to notice the role of worldly stimulation, but now perhaps you can begin to give attention to what happens when such stimulation is diminished, as you sit alone with eyes closed. What is this process of calming down like? Gradual, quick, pleasant, neutral?

For as much time as you have, alternate between half-hour sessions of individual and interpersonal meditation, reflecting on guarding the senses and virtue as conditioning factors for samādhi. When you have completed your time together, reflect as a whole group on what you have noticed and on any inspiration for life and practice going forward.

## Purifying the Mind

The Buddha used the image of refining gold as a simile for purification. First the gold is washed in a trough to remove earth, sand, and gravel. Then it is washed again to remove finer sand and again to remove black dust. Then it is melted repeatedly, which removes further impurities and makes the gold pliable and able to be worked. He likened the earth, sand, and gravel to bad conduct (immoral action) and the finer sand to sensual thoughts, ill will, and violent thoughts. At this point one's samādhi is not yet entirely peaceful; it is being maintained by suppression of the defilements. But after further washing and after annealing—further purification—meditation, and indeed all of life, becomes much easier. This purification process is central to establishing samādhi; it yields a mind that is strong and adaptable to any task.[187]

Despite seeing the intimate relationship between virtue and samādhi, we may still find that the mind is distracted, jumpy, or lazy. As we work with such a mind, we can appreciate the role of right effort in preparing the mind for the development of samādhi.

The mind-door itself must be carefully watched. We arrange our minds, our friendships, and our circumstances so that distractions do not arise. This is the effort of preventing. A retreat provides an environment of supportive conditions, but even there we will need considerable vigilance to avoid being drawn into our habitual small projects, distractions, and judgments. At home, we may protect our meditation time by unplugging the phone or turning off email, texts, and other notifications. Something as simple as taking care with seating, to be sure the meditation posture is sustainable without pain, will help eliminate distractions. These are simple ways to protect the practice environment.

We also may protect our minds throughout our daily lives. We can give care to what we listen to and read, our internet habits and the media we take in, the pace of our schedule, and our inclinations towards social feeding, including whom we spend time with and the conversations we have. Because other people are arguably the most interesting and stimulating type of sensory input, attending to our social lives is critical. Physical conditions, like adequate exercise, restraint with sugar and caffeine, will also make a difference. In short, our daily habits influence the availability of samādhi. Poor choices contribute to the arising of distractions and unwholesome, unskillful thoughts. Care is needed if we wish to cultivate even the lighter states of sammā samādhi—the experience of flow in combination with some right view—in daily life. It is essential for cultivating deeper samādhi and especially so for beginning to cultivate jhāna, for which the protection of a retreat setting may be necessary.

## Mental Qualities Leading to Samādhi

Along with the dynamics of virtue and purification, the suttas also mention several chains of causally related factors that either culminate in samādhi or have samādhi near their end. If we launch one of these chains and do not interrupt it, we are likely to arrive at some degree of samādhi—much as if we get on the correct bus and stay on it until we reach our destination, we will arrive there.

One such sequence, which appears in many suttas, begins with the absence of the hindrances (seclusion from unwholesome states).[188] When sensual lust, ill will, sleepiness and laziness, restlessness and worry, and doubt are absent, gladness naturally arises; from gladness comes delight; from delight, tranquility; and from tranquility, samādhi.

Consider the similar ways that confidence, happiness, and contentment/gratefulness condition the arising of samādhi. Each can be a starting point.

### Confidence

When one has successfully abandoned defilements of the mind, it is natural to gain great confidence in the Buddha, Dhamma, and Sangha. When gladness arises from such confidence, "rapture is born in him; in one who is rapturous, the body becomes tranquil; one whose body is tranquil feels pleasure; in one who feels pleasure, the mind becomes unified."[189] In more everyday terms, confidence in the teacher and the teachings, like safety in a social setting, allow the body-mind to relax and stabilize. They also allow for full application of effort because the heart is not clouded by perplexity.

Confidence in a teaching is not a popular notion in our culture. Skeptical doubt, rooted in a scientistic attitude, is pervasive—and, ironically, often adopted without examination. The word *faith* can arouse cynicism, especially among people who have been damaged by religious cruelty. But here we see a confidence in the Dhamma that is grounded in the experience of its effectiveness in one's life. Such confidence can bring a yielding of the heart and the ease that comes with it. It can lead naturally to samādhi.

### Happiness

Happiness itself is a wholesome quality. Many of its manifestations are involved in the development of samādhi: the "rapture and happiness born of seclusion."[190] Associated qualities are gladness (*pāmojja*) and delight (*nandi*)—that is, delight specifically in Dhamma, not sensory delight. Bodily pleasure, when it is not too extreme, can give way to tranquility and nondistraction. The tranquility is calmness of body and mind; the nondistraction is gatheredness; while happiness (sukha) is a pleasant mind state that is not dependent upon outer conditions. The pattern of rapture, tranquility, and pleasure preceding samādhi is established throughout the Buddha's teachings; for example: "I say, bhikkhus, that samādhi too has a proximate cause; it does not lack a proximate cause. And what is the proximate cause for samādhi? It should be said: happiness."[191]

Cultivating happiness is an important skill. But note that this is a happiness that is infused with serenity. It is quite different from the happiness of interpersonal excitement or stimulation or of the temporary satiation of a hunger—a tasty meal or sexual encounter, for example.

The strength of the pleasure and elation felt as the elements of samādhi begin to come together can seem overwhelming, even causing a loss of samādhi. This has happened to many people as they approach the jhānas for the first time. In my case, the rapture threw me entirely off balance, and it took me years to surrender to it. It was so stimulating, so exciting, that the mind was swept away in thrill and desire for its continuance.

It is important to know that the bliss is natural. It is just part of the path of development in meditation and can simply be allowed to run its course without interference. When the mind reacts with clinging or fear, mindfulness can help us to understand their temporary nature and to not identify with them. When the power of samādhi leads to the arising of unfamiliar phenomena, it can be helpful, even necessary, to have the guidance of a teacher. In the Buddha's time, as in ours, the mind can be unhinged, but loving care and meditative skill can turn a potential problem into a wholesome breakthrough.

PRACTICE

## WHAT IS KEEPING THE MIND FROM SETTLING?

The Buddha shared how he encountered a host of minor impurities that interfered with his development of samādhi. They included inattention, sloth and torpor, fear, elation, inertia, excess energy, deficiency of energy, longing, perception of diversity, excessive meditation on forms, and doubt. He described each of these as an "imperfection of mind" to be abandoned.[192]

What if during our meditation, or any time we aspired to a settled mind, we held the question: What, if anything, is interfering right now with the steadiness of my mind? Then, examining experience, we consider: Is there inattention? Is there laziness or sleepiness? Is there fear? Elation? Inertia? Is there too much or too little energy? Is there longing? Am I being drawn here and there by a diversity of ideas, emotions, and sensory inputs? Am I fixating too heavily on forms that are seen, heard, or felt? Is there doubt?

Perhaps just asking these questions, these observations, would leave the mind simple, settled. It might be worth a try.

## Contentment/Gratefulness

Cultivating contentment and gratitude are good approaches to quieting and gladdening the mind. These practices are accessible under any circumstances—when the mind is agitated or calm, when things in the world are going well and when they are going badly. In times of difficulty, it is a matter of directing the mind toward whatever is good just now. If you have difficulty with pain, direct the mind to the parts of the body that are not painful right now. If you find little to appreciate, just notice that you have shelter, that you know where your next meal is coming from. If even these things are insecure, you can still be grateful that you know the value of being grateful. In addition to calming the body-mind, contentment and gratefulness are long-term practices that bear long-term fruits.

PRACTICE

### CALMING AND CENTERING THE MIND IN CONTENTMENT

You can think about what you're grateful for as you do household chores, as you walk, before sleep, before a meal or while enjoying a meal. Simply consider all the good in your life, from eyes that can see and ears that can hear to the safety of your home or warmth of your clothing. Other skillful reflections include contentment with people you care for and the beauty of wise teachings that you have access to.

Remember what is good; notice it. As you do so, does the mind become contented? As contentment grows, does the body-mind relax? Is relaxing pleasurable? Pay attention to these things. Also notice any glow of ease that may arise as you circle around and soak into the felt sense of contentment.

This reflection is not a matter of denying the things that are not as you want them to be, of denying the fact of dukkha, but a skill in directing the mind so that it can see what is good in a clear and balanced way.

## SAMĀDHI AND RELATIONSHIP

Throughout our lives we have calmed and been calmed by others—by mother and friend, by therapist, priest, or teacher. Throughout our lives we have been guided by others to stay on track—to follow conversations, play games, complete tasks. We calm each other in love. It is certainly true that we also stimulate each other into distraction and anger, triviality and fear, but our focus here is on the wholesome side of our relational nature. In groups, humans find safety and cohesion. The apparent constancy of the self-in-relationship and of group identity can bring ease and the comforting illusion of continuity. In the company of others, we may or may not seek wisdom, but at least the achingly lonely heart can take a rest.

### How Regular Tranquility and Focus Can Become Sammā Samādhi

By interest in or care for others, our attention can be riveted on them. Thus, the seeds of wise samādhi—serenity and unification of mind—can sprout in our lives with others. By tapping the common roots of calming and gathering the mind, any wholesome relationship can support the conditions for the arising of tranquility and samādhi. Mundane relaxation and focus on tasks are starting benefits, but they are a long way from sammā samādhi. How can a relational encounter be turned from one yielding ordinary calm or focus into an experience of sammā samādhi? The two differentiating features are the quality and intensity of the samādhi.

First, the quality of samādhi is sammā, or right. It is samādhi for the purpose of seeing things as they actually are. The experience may be pleasurable, but this pleasure does not result in clinging; it is the natural pleasure of contentment. Even when there is sweetness, novelty, or safety in the moment of relational contact, there is no clinging or desire to prolong the experience. Nor is there lust for an exciting, interesting exchange.

Second, the intensity or strength of the samādhi is such that it allows attachment to craving, conceit, and views to melt, and the ignorance that they sustain melts at the same time. Weak samādhi will not enable insight. Somewhat steadier samādhi may enable clear seeing, but sometimes it may be destabilized by the power of the insights it enables, effectively cutting them off before they have a chance to fully manifest.

Quality and intensity—right view and right effort—are what ripen the natural calm and focus of wholesome relationships into sammā samādhi. This understanding guides skillful practice.

PRACTICE

## REFLECTING ON THE COMMON ROOTS OF
## CALMING RELATIONSHIP AND SAMMĀ SAMĀDHI

Reflect on the felt sense of calm that comes with the security of a loving relationship. For some, this will be a readily available reflection. For others, there may be a need to dig deep and find moments that were all too rare. This loving relationship could be one that is presently active or one from your past. Few relationships are unambiguously peaceful and secure, but the invitation here is to focus on those times in or those aspects of a certain relationship that brought ease. Take some time to picture the person or the two of you together. Above all, bring attention to how this image of calm security feels in the body. Are there feelings of relaxation, of physical warmth and groundedness? And in the mind, is there calm, a kind of letting down of the vigilance that is carried at so many other times?

Now shift your attention to whether this quality of calmness is manifesting in the body-mind now, as you contemplate. If not, move your attention back to the memory and let that memory stabilize. When you come back again to the present moment, do you notice a smoothing, a soothing, of the body-mind? Does the body relax; does it become more comfortable? Does the thinking process slow down and grow more spacious?

Finally, gently rest your attention on the body as a whole, inviting any ease you have noticed to saturate the body here and now. Let your attention rest with the felt sense, the shape of the sitting form. Just let the mind rest there awhile. Then inquire, is the body-mind stabilized? Does it dwell more or less happily with the meditation object of the body? Is this the genesis of samādhi?

## Sammā Samādhi in Wholesome Group Settings

The Buddha was well aware of the power of relationship for cultivating samādhi and the other factors of awakening: "Bhikkhus, as to external factors, I do not see any other factor that is so helpful for the arising of the seven factors of awakening as this: good friendship. When a bhikkhu has a good friend, it is to be expected that he will develop and cultivate the seven factors of awakening."[193] Interpersonal contact can support the development of samādhi in relational practice. During retreat, for example, samādhi may have its initial conditions nurtured by a riveting yet settling topic of conversation or by group conditions that foster exceptional safety and warmth. When someone becomes agitated during meditation, their partner(s) in practice may provide steadiness. It is as if one meditator borrows the tranquility of the other(s). When one is drawn off topic, the other(s) may bring them back. Mental ballast is being developed in the relational setting.

As atomized individual tranquility begins to manifest as a group experience, each individual's further calming will stabilize the calm of the whole. When participants in a group experience the signs of samādhi, such as somatic bliss or exceptional clarity of sense perceptions, and possibly name them aloud, these experiences may be transmitted, or at least prompted among others, further elevating the group or shared experience of samādhi. If the wisdom element is kept strong—that is, if the intention of practice remains clear, and practitioners don't get swept up in grasping at pleasurable or unusual experiences—the flow of all the factors of awakening is set in motion, and sammā samādhi is on track to enable the fruitfulness of investigation, energy, and joy.

In addition to the way good friendship fosters diligence in practice, how might meditation, like the rest of the holy life, be supported and made excellent by relational practices?

## How Samādhi Can Affect Relationship

Just as relationship can nourish samādhi, samādhi can refine the quality of relational encounters. The unified mind does not wander; as we are with other people, we pay attention to them fully. The unified mind is relaxed; relationally, this translates into dwelling with others undefended, and the undefended mind naturally experiences mettā. In shared moments of samādhi, two or more people come to see clearly not only into the nature of the personal body-mind, but also into the operation of relatedness itself. The living experience of relationship, or what might be called the relational field, becomes the object of awareness. In dynamic mutuality of awareness of and release into flux, mind becomes increasingly bright and calm. Mind, or minds, settle on one point, but that "point" is spacious, not localized. Language naturally drops away as serenity and gatheredness increase, but the possibility of speech remains open. A few words may express or point the mind or transmit experience from one person to another, and then language may again drop away. Pleasant somatic experiences may arise, but when practice is mature, there is no elation or clinging.

The insights that grow from relational samādhi show us the grasping and freedom at work interpersonally and socially. Due to these insights, self views are abandoned: the self that was constructed in relationship is deconstructed, released. Rigidity dwindles, power structures weaken, and energy is freed up for further insight. The individual practitioners are transformed, and the group itself is transformed. It is worth noting that from such relational practice, wholesome worldly action is as natural a result as liberation of the heart.

We see once again the power of spiritual friendship and sangha in the whole-life path. By tapping the roots shared by relationship and samādhi while maintaining the skillful guidance of the Dhamma, the path factor of samādhi can be cultivated, maintained, and increased. Because this samādhi has been developed in part in the dynamic container of relationship, we can expect it to be malleable and naturally available across a wide range of life's conditions, including while we're with others out in the world. The mind settles even while we're actively engaged with others, so the peace naturally endures as we participate in life.

## CLASSICAL METHODS FOR CULTIVATING SAMMĀ SAMĀDHI

Cultivating samādhi begins with settling conditions in the world and in the mind and by nurturing harmony in our relational lives and social milieu. At some point, we move directly into formal practices of sammā samādhi. We'll unpack three primary methods for this: the brahmavihāras; mindfulness, specifically satipaṭṭhāna; and breath meditation (ānāpānasati). I will also highlight a teaching that points to four more methods and results of samādhi practice.

### The Brahmavihāras

Mettā, or true friendliness, is a practice of spacious receptivity of mind. Mettā is the foundation of the other three brahmavihāras (divine abidings): practices of compassion, sympathetic joy, and relational equanimity. Once the mind is spacious and fully rested in nonaversion (*adosa*), a natural friendliness and care arise. Some mettā practices begin by cultivating the experience of spaciousness, using the imagination to extend the heart or mind above, below, and in all directions. In interpersonal practice, imagination is not required: mettā often arises spontaneously as the mind-heart expands to encompass our partners. This expanded mind is imbued with feelings of care, as a mother towards her child, that wishes gladness and safety for all beings.[194]

When mettā is used as a samādhi practice, the mind settles on the spaciousness itself, on people, on the bodily sensations that arise, and even on the words and phrases used for the imagination practice. Pleasant, relaxing feelings associated with friendliness and care often arise. These feelings conduce to happiness that can lead to samādhi while preparing our minds to interact with more care in daily life. Mettā, or core relatedness, ripens naturally into its companion qualities of compassion and sympathetic joy; these latter two are the expansive accessibility to being touched by others who are experiencing pain and joy. Equanimity that maintains this spacious, relational aspect is the fourth brahmavihāra. It evolves from the prior three as suffering and joy, always impermanent, are met in a balanced way.

The settling of the mind that emerges from the intentional cultivation of mettā and its companion qualities forms a bridge between formal samādhi practices and relational meditation. Also, cultivating the brahmavihāras provides an excellent transition from mindfulness-based insight practices to meditations oriented towards the development of samādhi.

## Satipaṭṭhāna: The Four Foundations of Mindfulness

The nun Dhammadina extolled satipaṭṭhāna as a means for developing samādhi: "[T]he four foundations of mindfulness are the basis of samādhi; the four right kinds of striving are the equipment of samādhi; the repetition, development, and cultivation of these same states is the development of samādhi therein."[195]

Many people have experienced this causal link between mindfulness and samādhi. In addition to supporting calm, mindfulness practice—specifically, the practice of steadily attending to a chosen object, most notably one of the four foundations of mindfulness—fosters a focused mind. We touched on this teaching in our investigation of right mindfulness, so here is just a summary relevant to the development of sammā samādhi.

In the Satipaṭṭhāna Sutta (e.g., MN 10), the meditator is advised to maintain awareness on the foundations of the body, feelings, mind states, and dhammas, or present-moment experience through a specific framework. Mindfulness of the body could include mindfulness of the breath, the body's posture, its nonattractive guts, the constituent elements, and the various stages of decay of corpses. Feelings were elementally framed as pleasant, unpleasant, and neither pleasant nor unpleasant, and further as carnal or spiritual. Mind states included those with and without greed, hatred, and delusion; contracted or scattered; expansive or unexpansive; supreme and not; immersed in samādhi and not; and as liberated and unliberated. For mindfulness of dhammas, present-moment experience is observed through the frameworks of the hindrances, factors of awakening, aggregates, sense fields, and Four Noble Truths.

Any one of these foundations can support the development of samādhi when the meditator settles the mind on just that facet of experience. When the meditator sits quietly over a period of time just observing the body's posture, for example, the body-mind will calm down and gather around the object. Further guidance in satipaṭṭhāna is to observe the rising, vanishing, and both of each foundation. As we will see below, this observation, too, can be a strong basis for developing samādhi. The Buddha clearly taught that one who is developing mindfulness in these ways is also developing samādhi. Remaining present with any of these foundations, the mind can become very steady.

## Breath Meditation (Ānāpānasati)

Ānāpānasati is a practice of resting attention with the in and out breaths. Settling the body comfortably, one begins by discerning long in and out breaths. Then one discerns short in and out breaths. Then one breathes experiencing the whole body and next breathes tranquilizing the bodily formation. One then breathes in and out sensitive to rapture and then to pleasure, being sensitive to mental formations and tranquilizing mental formations. One then experiences the mind while breathing, gladdens the mind, steadies the mind in samādhi, and finally releases the mind. As the meditation develops, one breathes in and out while contemplating impermanence, dispassion, cessation, and finally focusing on relinquishment.[196]

Approaching this breathing meditation with a balance of ease and consistency is key to cultivating samādhi. Because the mind and body are intricately interwoven—indeed co-arising and cocreating the felt experience of the present moment—any movement of the mind generates a bodily response, and any tension or release in the body brings a corresponding movement of the mind. So each breath is a display of the totality of that moment's experience: clinging or nonclinging, tranquil or agitated, scattered or stable. The profound simplicity of the object—the breath itself—ensures that any excursions of attention can be clearly known when we remember to notice. The remembering to notice is the sati; the settling in response to returning home to the body-mind during this very breath is the samādhi.

You may note in the *Ānāpānasatisutta* the gradual refinement of the meditation as it progresses from bodily breathing to relinquishment.[197] To support your practice, you can also explore one of ānāpānasati's many sister practices, including counting breaths; focusing progressively on relaxing, then stillness, then vividness; and actual physical breathing techniques drawn from the yogic traditions, some of which can be particularly helpful for calming the body-mind when the habits of tension are raging.

PRACTICE
**READ AND REFLECT**

At some point, the capacity for samādhi grows less dependent on carefully protecting ourselves from distractions—especially external distractions—because the mind just stops reacting to them so strongly. The mind is no longer drawn to its old patterns of clinging, pushing away, and becoming numb. It has become, in some measure, pure, and the purified mind does not grasp.

I offer the following text for contemplation on the experience of samādhi. If you are familiar with the formal practice of Dharma Contemplation (DC), you can find a partner or gather a group to engage those five phases of practice (see the "Resources" for guidance on DC practice). If not, you can just read, re-read, and reflect on—alone or with others—the following text, letting it saturate the body-mind.

With or without formal technique, settle the mind steadily on the text. Relax with each word, each phrase. Pause often and let the words drop away. Allow the images to inspire you towards samādhi. What refinement of the mind is possible as a result of sammā samādhi?

Suppose, bhikkhus, there was a house or a hall with a peaked roof, with windows on the northern, southern, and eastern sides. When the sun rises and a beam of light enters through a window, where would it become established?

On the western wall, venerable sir.

If there were no western wall, where would it become established?

On the earth, venerable sir.

If there were no earth, where would it become established?

On the water, venerable sir.

If there were no water, where would it become established?

It would not become established anywhere, venerable sir.

So, too, bhikkhus, if there is no lust for the nutriment edible food . . . for the nutriment contact . . . for the nutriment mental volition . . . for the nutriment consciousness . . . consciousness does not become established there and come to growth.[198]

For all of us, potential distractions and temptations come to the mind, but, like a ray of light passing through empty space, they can simply pass on by rather than disturbing it. Does this feel possible for you? What is the experience now of the undisturbed mind?

## Four Methods and Four Results

In addition to these three well-known teachings on unifying the mind, the Buddha offered a set of four practices. I've listed them and underlined the results of each so you can easily review this teaching and distinguish the results from the associated practices.

1  In practice, a person "quite secluded from sensual pleasures, secluded from unskillful qualities, enters and remains in the first absorption . . . second absorption . . . third absorption . . . fourth absorption. This is the way of developing immersion further that <u>leads to *pleasant abiding here and now*.</u>"[199]

2  In practice, a person "focuses on the perception of light, concentrating on the perception of day regardless of whether it's night or day. And so, with an open and unenveloped heart, they develop a mind that's full of radiance. This is the way of developing immersion further that <u>leads to gaining knowledge and vision.</u>"[200]

3  In practice, a person "knows feelings as they arise, as they remain, and as they go away. They know perceptions as they arise, as they remain, and as they go away. They know thoughts as they arise, as they remain, and as they go away. This is the way of developing immersion further that <u>leads to mindfulness and awareness.</u>"[201]

4  In practice, a person "meditates observing rise and fall in the five grasping aggregates: 'Such

is form, such the origin of form, such the ending of
form. Such is feeling . . . Such is perception . . . Such
are constructions . . . Such is consciousness, such
the origin of consciousness, such is the ending of
consciousness.' This is the way of developing immersion
further that leads to the ending of _intoxicants._"[202]

I find this teaching noteworthy because it makes clear that
samādhi is not a monolithic quality. Also, the practices of samādhi
are more varied than usually construed. Some of the practices
offered are not widely associated with samādhi. Some of the results
have been associated only with so-called insight practice, but they
are clearly described here as samādhi practices. Just the fact that
the Buddha offered such a spectrum of practices and results may
open up our sense of this path factor. You might explore these
different practices—on your own or, far better, with a competent
teacher—and reflect on what practices best suit you.

## ADDITIONAL APPROACHES
## TO CULTIVATING SAMĀDHI

The formal practices named so far have become the principal
Buddhist samādhi practices. Other practices taught or implied in
the early Buddhist teachings likewise support the development of
serenity and unification of mind. The following additional methods
may contribute to your whole-life path.

### Attend to Twofold: Serenity
### and Unification

Samādhi is one of the factors of awakening, so we can usefully apply
to it the Buddha's teaching on cultivating these factors generally.
The cause-and-effect relationship is simple: when we give attention
to the components of one of the factors, that factor will increase. For
example, the "nutriment" for tranquility (*passaddhi*) is given as tranquility of body and tranquility of mind:

> And what, bhikkhus, is the nutriment for the arising of the unarisen enlightenment factor of tranquility and for the fulfillment by development of the arisen enlightenment factor of tranquility? There are, bhikkhus, tranquility of body, tranquility of mind: frequently giving careful attention to them is the nutriment for the arising of the unarisen enlightenment factor of tranquility and for the fulfillment by development of the arisen enlightenment factor of tranquility.[203]

Because tranquility is a precursor and component of unification, we can enjoy this guidance as we develop the path factor of sammā samādhi. The Buddha applied this same causal relationship to developing samādhi; in this case, the aspects to be attended to are serenity (calm) and nondispersal (unity, collectedness).

I was surprised when I first came across this teaching and immediately tried it in my individual meditation. To my delight, it worked exactly as described. Attending to even a wisp of serenity allowed that serenity to grow deeper, steadier, smoother. Attending to the unity of the mind settled it more. It was helpful to me to give attention to the serenity and the unity separately, and I found samādhi was sustained and deepened as I gently alternated attention between one and the other.

## Cultivating Factors of Awakening as a Group

Another practice of samādhi associated with the factors of awakening rests on the understanding that those factors are causally related states that can be launched with mindfulness and followed to their natural conclusion: mindfulness leads to investigation, which leads to energy, an onward to joy, tranquility, samādhi, and equanimity. Samādhi appears as the sixth factor of those seven, after tranquility and just preceding the quiet pinnacle of equanimity. I have taught this sequential approach to the seven factors of awakening in many Insight Dialogue retreats and found that even relatively new meditators are able to develop significant steadiness and brightness of mind.

When you're following the instructions of sequential development, keep in mind that these factors also can and do arise simultaneously. In this case, the practice is noticing which factors are strong or weak in any given moment, similar to the satipaṭṭhāna foundation of dhammānupassanā, mindfulness of present-moment experience using the framework of the factors of awakening. Samādhi that co-arises in this way is by nature flexible and robust; it can meld with investigation and be infused with energy. Samādhi and sati can also balance each other so that, together, they lead to increasingly subtle understanding of things as they actually are.

## Giving Attention to Wholesome Pleasant Experiences

Practicing with the natural law that bodily and mental ease are conducive to happiness, and that these, in turn, support the mind's unification, is a way to bridge formal and informal, personal and interpersonal, practices of sammā samādhi. The practice of giving gently sustained attention to pleasant experiences is a key element of entering the jhānas. In particular, placing one's full attention on the somatic pleasure that arises with the onset of bliss can quickly lead to an increase in the pleasure itself. The body-mind enjoys the pleasure and can become well established on it. This cycle may cascade into rapture (pīti). The practice of observing joy, ease, or pleasure can be employed in our everyday lives, and it will be supported by clearly understanding the purpose and value of joy and calm. Usually, when the gentle pleasure of a peaceful moment arises, we zone out in that pleasure. But if mindfulness, guided by right view, is turned towards the pleasure and to the peaceful conditions behind it, clinging can be avoided and the ease is likely to increase, grow stronger, and settle the body-mind.

## Sustained Attention to Specific Objects

Practices like attending to awakening factors or wholesome mental pleasure have the distinct benefit of sustaining attention on objects that are pleasant, interesting, and reliably beneficial. Giving sustained attention to a particular object can also foster unification.

There are countless practices like this associated with different sense doors. Practices utilizing visible objects would include *kasiṇa* meditation, or looking at colored disks and, later, the mental impression of such disks. Other visual practices include focused attention on candles, intricate works of art such as *tankhas*, or icons, and statues of revered persons. Practices employing the auditory channel include chanting, reciting a mantra, listening to musical drones or other compositions, and open listening in nature. Mental images, including a variety of internal visualizations ranging from corpses to deities, are joined by mental focus on the recollection of memorized discourses or lists drawn from canonical teachings.

The senses of smell and taste have a few specialized practices of samādhi, such as very slow and mindful eating. The body-sense is a common basis for unifying the mind in walking practices, attending to painful sensations, and maintenance or observation of bodily postures or movements. We recall that connecting all of these practices is our understanding of samādhi as being calm, gathered, and aimed by right view.

## LISTENING TO ONE FADING NOTE
A PERSONAL STORY

In my teens I attended a workshop and one day chanced upon an open hall with a beautiful piano. I descended the stairs that lead to a stage encircled by empty seats; the ample skylights lit the way. I played for a while, and when I was done, I listened as the last note rang towards silence. But I noticed the mind jumped to thinking rather than pure, wordless listening. I played another note and listened, but again the mind went elsewhere while there was still energy in the vibrating string. I decided that before leaving the room I would commit myself to following the sound all the way to silence, free of interruption, free of inner words.

Time and again I struck a note, settled the attention on the note, received the sound, and rested there. Time and again, the mind asserted its purposeless momentum—until it did not. The sound faded, the mind faded, and there was silence.

I looked up. The hall was vast. The light from the skylights had shifted with the afternoon sun. The hall positively rang with silence. The language I might use now to describe the experience was that the luminosity of the room and the luminosity of the mind were co-arising. The experience was profoundly pleasant, deeply peaceful. I had touched the natural samādhi of the mind gathered peacefully around one object.

## Intentional Relaxation

We know that samādhi is supported by relaxation. So it stands to reason that intentionally relaxing the body and/or mind can help us cultivate and maintain right samādhi.

There are countless practices for relaxing the body and mind. Mindfully scanning the body, from head to toes and back again, is one such practice. Tensing and relaxing different body parts is another. Rhythmic exercises, like walking, running or swimming, ground the body and can be aimed towards relaxation. The slow body movements and energetic balancing often associated with t'ai chi, qi gong, and yoga can also be deeply relaxing. Breathing deeply, gradually slowing the breath, and other breath techniques also fit this mold.

These practices can be helpful to our well-being regardless of whether or not we engage them as part of our whole-life path. But if you intend to link these practices to sammā samādhi, you would do well to check in on the view and intention associated with the practice. Is this practice felt, perhaps intuitively, to be a part of the heart's movement towards dispassion, not towards passion (not, "I will get more relaxed so I can dash out and have even more thrilling experiences")? Is there an underlying value of contentment, not discontent (not, "I hate being tense, and I'm going to get rid of this and all unpleasant experiences")? Is there some understanding, perhaps in the background, that the human condition just has these times of stress, of discomfort, of dukkha (perhaps we practice knowing, "This moment's stresses are simply part of the ever-changing human condition")? It is not necessary to think about all these things, but the foundation of your practices of right view, intention, and effort will help these relaxation practices remain well grounded in the whole-life path.

We can also just give some time to relaxing the body as we sit at home. As we do, we can inquire, is the body really at ease in this position? Is the back relaxed, and are the legs at ease? Is the face tense? Making the small adjustments that condition ease will help to relax the body mechanically, but this is also an act of kindness that itself calms the body-mind.

## Relaxation During Worldly Engagement

We can encourage samādhi by intentionally becoming aware of tension as it begins to manifest in the body and then changing or stopping the activities that cause it. We can give ourselves the gift of attending to one thing at a time. If we are doing housework, we can do only that without worrying so much about the problems at work or what we have to do tomorrow. Perhaps we can attend to listening to music or to enjoying a work of art or a view out the window. If we attend to relaxing as we do so, understanding that this is part of our sammā samādhi practice, the mind can be quite happy and contented with these things. As we take walks, nurture our pets, attend to the garden, are we just taking care of a task on our to-do list, or could this task also be a contribution to samādhi? The intention is one of relinquishment, of nonentanglement. Our engagement is not pretentious and not dependent upon outcome. Just setting the mind in this direction is enough.

Intense focus, mental or physical, is most commonly associated with our culture's notion of concentration. As discussed at the beginning of the chapter, there are many activities that invite physical and/or mental absorption—natural samādhi. Focusing on math problems, business tasks such as creating organizational structures or budgets, or games such as chess or golf are examples. A tense mind will tire quickly in these tasks, but if the mind achieves some relaxation, you may work longer and better, with more ease and more enjoyment. Concentration in athletics is one mark of excellence; because of the demand that sports place on the body, relaxation is essential for high performance and low injury. In situations like these, the ease of samādhi yields joy that is energized and aligned with the task at hand. In sports this feeling is sometimes called "being in the zone," but it is found in many endeavors that fully engage the mind. The key to turning these activities into skillful practice is intentionally fostering tranquility at the very same moment that a high degree of focus is noticed.

## Thinking and Samādhi

Each samādhi-development method presented here includes an element of gently directing the mind towards an object: breath, body, relaxation, even the qualities of samādhi itself. This direction runs counter to notions of samādhi practice as an almost formless one-pointedness on a single object to the exclusion of thought. When samādhi ripens into absorption, thought is certainly no longer manifesting. But we see in the teachings that these practices are progressive and that their development includes specific objects. This progression fits well with the mind's natural tendency to seek interest. It means that the mind is engaged enough to guide one's practice.

Thinking can be a viable and workable part of many samādhi practices. In his teachings on the jhānas, the Buddha was explicit about this: initial thought and evaluation (also referred to as "pondering" or "sustained thought," depending on the translation) are present in the first jhāna. Until the second jhāna, samādhi does not indicate the total absence of thought.

In fact, the mind settling on, and becoming saturated with and immersed in, wholesome thought powerfully supports sammā samādhi. Thought can lead beyond thought; language can lead beyond language. Samādhi is both a means and a result of such practice. You may be able to experience this practice by setting the mind on a concise, pithy contemplation over an hour or two. Even discussing, teaching, and learning the Dhamma are named as skillful aspects of this development that can move through inspiration, joy, rapture, pleasure, and tranquility to samādhi.[204]

Even as we recognize that directed thought can be an effective samādhi practice, we are instructed to not dwell too long or intensively on any thought, good or bad, because of its potentially exhausting effects on the body-mind. The Buddha learned this himself through experience: "[W]ith excessive thinking and pondering I might tire my body, and when the body is tired, the mind becomes disturbed, and when the mind is disturbed, it is far from samādhi. So I steadied my mind internally, quieted it, brought it to singleness, and concentrated [unified] it. Why is that? So that my mind should not be disturbed."[205] In other words, in addition to ardent practice that includes thought, just relax. Let the body be serene. Let the settled mind rest naturally. No push—just stability.

PRACTICE

## USING DIRECTED THOUGHT
## TO CULTIVATE SAMĀDHI

This practice can be done alone or with one or more practice partners. It is easier to arrange a time for practice when you are the only person involved; however, the practice itself may more readily gain traction with the support of others.

The Buddha frequently offered a reflection on the basic characteristics of life—impermanence, suffering, and not-self—in the form of questions that point to a causal chain:

What do you think of this, bhikkhus? Is form permanent or impermanent?

Impermanent, venerable sir.

Now, that which is impermanent, is it unsatisfactory or satisfactory?

Unsatisfactory, venerable sir.

Now, that which is impermanent, unsatisfactory, subject to change, is it proper to regard that as: "This is mine, this I am, this is my self"?

Indeed, not that, venerable sir.[206]

This same reflection was offered for the other four aggregates of feeling, perception, constructions (saṅkhāra), and consciousness.

After settling into meditation and relaxing the body, introduce the first question: "Is form permanent or impermanent?" Think about that. All the visible, tangible forms, all the things in the world that appear to the mind as solid and stable, are they permanent?

When this reflection has become clear enough, ask whether or not they are satisfactory. When this reflection has settled, think about whether forms can properly be construed as self, as me or mine. Take your time with each question; let it soak in.

You may chose to remain only with form or any one of the other aggregates, or you may move through all five. Whichever practice helps you remain with, think about, ponder only these central questions will support samādhi.

It may take awhile—maybe even many practice sessions during which you memorize the questions and become familiar with the steadiness of directed thinking—but there will come a time when the mind settles deeply. The questions are then maintained more as a felt presence in the mind; language drops away. At this stage of practice it is perfectly fine to release the questions and let the mind settle, aware of itself and calmly gathered.

## ∼ REFLECTION

The beginning of sammā samādhi is simple: "Here are the roots of trees. Here are empty places. Get down and meditate. Don't be lazy. Don't become one who is later remorseful. This is my instruction to you."[207] And yet a whole-life path can include many practices that support the calming of the body and settling of the mind.

The Buddha spoke about jhāna a great deal, sometimes referring to this totally immersive experience as synonymous with right samādhi. But he also referred to it as just a subset of the larger group of possible forms of samādhi. For each of us there are approaches and different levels of engagement that will be of greatest benefit. Our practice calls for patience, for repeatedly dwelling in these huts of stillness. Our practice is skillful when it reflects the breadth of samādhi and its supporting factors. How peaceful do you need to be? Simply peaceful enough to reflect clearly, to dwell harmoniously with others, and participate wisely in community.

There are lesser forms of samādhi, when the mind is not scattered but also not supremely still. I take it as true that serenity and collectedness, when co-arising to any degree, constitute samādhi. With right view, this becomes sammā samādhi. It may not be highly developed, but it is a start. Such stability of mind unmistakably has a positive effect on all the other path factors. Serenity stabilizes mindfulness; we can better remain present with experience when the mind is even a bit calmer and more focused. Effort will be more clearly directed and kept on track by a mind that enjoys some degree of focus. Right speech, action, and livelihood benefit from the mind's steadiness and calm both because unethical behavior is suppressed when the mind is concentrated, and because the calm mind is more able to recognize the agitation associated with actions like lying, stealing, intoxication, and sexual misconduct. With at least a modicum of unification, we can see our own views more clearly, but we also become more acutely attuned to the world around us. Right view thus is fostered by even modest sammā samādhi.

The greater the samādhi, the more the mind can respond skillfully to its own proliferations and to the circumstances of a changing world. But a quality of samādhi that rises and falls with conditions, internal and external, is enough to make a difference. And the Buddha's teachings leave little doubt that samādhi is the precursor to liberative insight, to seeing things as they actually are, and thus to relinquishment and unbinding.

Sammā samādhi enables deep transformation of the heart. It fosters wholesome relationships and, to the extent that it infuses larger groups, enables sensitivity and smoothness of function. In a culture of noise and show, sammā samādhi challenges our mental habits and addictions to stimulation. If we attend to its cultivation, formally or informally, alone or with others, we will be amply rewarded. Tranquility of body and mind need not be so far away from our everyday experience. Meditative focus engenders insight, but it also elevates everyday mental focus. Even the beginnings of unification of mind are wholesome. Just as the most powerful and refined samādhi increases with diligence, so do its precursors of tranquility and simplicity. Gradually, sammā samādhi seeps into our lives as balance, ease, focus, and equanimity.

Consider what practices of samādhi are fitting for you right now. What works towards that balance of aroused persistence and contentment, of zeal and calm confidence? How can you welcome the calming and focusing power of relationship? These are guides as you craft your whole-life path.

~

# CHAPTER 12

# CRAFTING YOUR WHOLE-LIFE PATH

I hope this book helps you intuitively understand and see that all the factors of the Noble Eightfold Path are already operating in your life. Perhaps you can sense the whole of the Path and recognize that each thought, each purchase, and each human encounter is part of the Path. This is the beauty of a whole-life perspective: it recognizes the breadth of possibilities for each moment.

Based on this whole-life understanding, you are equipped to take the first concrete steps on your unique version of the whole-life path. This chapter will offer additional suggestions for deciding where to begin and some things to keep in mind as you craft and live your whole-life path.

## FINDING A STARTING POINT

There are eight path factors, each so nuanced and rich, and life naturally offers us countless options for engaging each one. You already may be feeling inspired by some of the information or practices in the path factor chapters. Or as you've been reading, you may have been applying ehipassiko, seeing for yourself, by road-testing some of the ideas in these chapters and finding them to be right (sammā), or oriented toward unbinding. If so, you already may have identified a natural starting point—or more than one—for your whole-life path. Tell a friend about them or write them down. At the intersection of calm and action, what will you do next?

If, however, all the possibilities seem a bit overwhelming, the following suggestions may help you determine where to begin.

## Use the Present Moment

The present moment is always an opportunity for inquiry, a chance to change the inertial stream of everyday living. Life is brief. You may live and die busy and distracted, carried by the current of your genetics, family history, and culture. Present-moment inquiry allows you to begin consciously steering through the stream rather than letting it sweep you where it will.

Your first questions might be about how you're currently navigating the waters of your life: Am I living in alignment with my values? Does my life reflect this wisdom perspective that I've now grown into? Or you might ask questions about the waters themselves, using the path scan (chapter 3): What path factors are operating now? Which need attention? Is there one factor I might develop further in this very moment?

Right view, intention, effort, and mindfulness are fundamental to the operation of the mind, so they are always functioning. This means you can, at any moment, inquire into each: What is happening right now in my mind? What is my view now? Am I seeing things as permanent, or do I recognize the changing quality of body-mind? What are my intentions now, the motivation behind the action or relationship I'm engaged in here? How is the quality of my effort, my energy for the path? And is mindfulness present now? What am I aware of right now? Asking what the mind is doing is a mental act that is an explicit, skillful enactment of the path. You can review all of the path factors in a similar way. With a simple inquiry, your whole-life path can spring to life in this instant.

## Link a Path Factor Practice
## with an Everyday Action

Another way of using the present moment is to recruit particular everyday moments or actions into the service of cultivation. Perhaps you could use the moment of awakening. I have found that being aware as I move my body out of bed and set my feet down on the floor—which foot touches first—is a way to relaunch right mindfulness. Perhaps you meditate silently each morning because that is the most naturally quiet and uninterrupted time and because practice in the morning supports calm throughout your day. Mealtimes might serve as opportunities to practice generosity or reflect on compassion. Or each weekend can be a time to recollect your virtues or reflect on the prior week's application of wise effort. In my practice, the time right before sleep is always given over to reading the Buddha's discourses. Whether I read for two minutes or half an hour, it sets the mind in a wholesome direction, reminding me to give priority to the Path. What times of day or week, together with what path elements, fit your needs, your heart? Try something specific, and if that doesn't work, set it aside and try something else.

## Look to Specific Aspects
## of the Dhamma

Giving, morality, and mettā, the Buddha's on-ramp to the Path, which we explored in chapter 3, may be a good starting point for you right now. Reflect on giving you've already been doing—to housemates, children, meditation teachers, social causes—then add a new act of giving. Reflect on the most developed aspects of your morality, like not stealing, and then think of one thing you can do to up your game, like not speaking harshly or falsely. Do the same with the heavenly abode of mettā: where and towards whom do you currently feel warmth and care? Expand this care to include at least one other person or being. Also, explore compassion and altruistic joy. Maybe your next trip to the store, your next phone conversation with your child or parent, or your pet's next visit to the veterinarian could become an opportunity to **grow** your compassion.

You may choose to jump to the fourth preliminary, relinquishment. Find one thing to release in order to simplify your life and free your heart. Maybe you'll let go of a corrosive relationship. Maybe you'll forego a habitual but unnecessary stressor at work. Maybe you'll shed an attitude that drags down your physical health. Maybe you'll give away some possessions. Or maybe you'll drop a bias that you've begun to sense is narrowing **your** vision and shutting your heart. Engage in wholesome countermeasures that will ease the disentangling.

Or jump into the heart of the path and call to mind the intoxicants. Apply them as a life lens. Is ignorance at work to the extent that you don't see how a thirst for pleasure drives the small and large decisions that make up your life? Do you see how the self struggles to find comfort, to feed on experiences that make it grow fat, and that this search for self-stability is stressful and endless? Now reflect on the antidotes, the detox program of relinquishment, effacement, and wisdom that can liberate you from the matrix of blindness and hunger. That liberation is what the whole-life path is for, so it helps to understand what this detox process looks like in our lived lives.[208]

Relinquishment, effacement, and wisdom all operate within us, and in our relationships with others and with our greater society. Relinquishment can mean releasing internal voices of cruelty and doubt. It can also mean letting go of self-centered behaviors in your intimate relationships. And it can mean joining with others to diminish harmful habits of consumption that you know are destroying the ecosystem. Effacement is the erosion of self-centeredness and, indeed, of the view that the self is a stable, important entity that must be pleasured and protected. The work of effacement takes place simultaneously in individual reflection, in selfless care for loved ones and mutual commitments to generosity of spirit, and in the decentering actions of social activism, where the wellbeing of many is elevated in relation to your private needs or desires. And wisdom, the liberating move out of blindness, happens with personal study and life observation; it happens in relationships that awaken you and your partners to a world beyond the confines of your family and cultural conditioning; and it happens as you engage with a community of spiritual friends who will generously surface your narrowness even as you do the same for them. Each detox aspect, in each individual and relational domain, is a place you can practice.

## Choose an Arena of Everyday Life

Intimate relationships will reveal unseen stuck places—places that can easily be overlooked when you are alone in life or alone in meditation. Marriages, close friendships, and harmonious family lives are difficult to maintain because there is always a growing edge, and growth often brings discomfort. But this is also why relationships can be effective starting points for creating a whole-life path: in them we find relinquishment and effacement at work.

You will also import wisdom by bringing the Dhamma teachings directly into your relationships. Practice mindfulness and right effort in your interactions with your significant life partners, whether or not they join you in doing so (although mutual effort is especially powerful). Bring in a seed of wisdom, like reflecting on cause and effect when you are with them; this will give you a reference point outside the conditioned system of emotional reaction and can help loosen the grip of habitual viewpoints and patterns of relational behavior. Where it is fitting, invite them to contemplate with you.

Intimate relationships are also our best opportunities for cultivating the relational factors of awakening—mettā, compassion, joy, and relational equanimity—any of which may be an appealing starting point for building your path. Caring for our children or our elders are not abstract practices of mettā or *karuna* (compassion); they are living enactments of those qualities. The joy we experience when a loved one has a success or recovers from an illness is genuine muditā. Notice this! And whenever we cling and fixate on others, wherever we fail to flow with the inevitable changes inherent in relationship, we will suffer. These moments are the best opportunities to cultivate relational equanimity. Equanimity is often a natural result of a mature and trusting relationship; it is a reliable source of sustained harmony.

Likewise, our work lives are powerful arenas for relinquishment, effacement, and wisdom. Physical work, especially in nature, can be grounding, enlivening, and conducive to consistency of inner work. The challenges of professional relationships, like our personal relationships, will reveal the places we are urging to become something, to be seen as competent, productive, successful. Where these goals overlap with our sense of commitment to excellence, they can be a useful part of a whole-life path. But when the goals of self-making and pleasure—including avoiding pain—become primary, the real work of the path comes in. You can inquire, what view of purpose and happiness is at work? What intentions motivate my actions? My engagement with these people and this organization is following some well-established harmful patterns; how can I amp up the mindfulness, and where can I import wisdom teachings to help unravel the attachments and stress?

The same can be said of our social engagements generally, especially social activism. The places where we are stuck in self-reference, lost in relational reactivity, will become known in the cauldron of service, where the challenges are enormous and progress often slow. However, in addition to offering the same interpersonal friction that operates in our professional and personal lives, activism carries the gift—and challenge—of care for a wider world. When we are confronted by social injustice, by environmental degradation, and by economic inequity, our interpersonal challenges are accompanied by the heartbreak of enormous suffering and the anger at callous perpetrators. Here, too, the Noble Eightfold Path can be put to work. Right view of suffering, cause and effect, and the necessity of sīla become pressingly obvious. Right intention, within yourself and your friends in the work, will call you to ask questions about compassion for all who suffer, oppressors and oppressed. Right speech can raise your standards of what is true, useful, and timely and what it means to speak difficult words with mettā. Right mindfulness, especially if engaged as a communal value, can be explored as a means of bringing emotional regulation and intelligence to the battlefields of justice and care.

Aging, illness, and death are universal teachers and have likely already touched you in some way. And trust me, they're not done with you yet! When you're ill, how might you cultivate right effort to nurture the wholesome faculties of faith, or even energy? As you age, how can mindfulness help you keep breaking the habit patterns associated with time, old plans, and past purposes? How can right samādhi foster ease as the body goes through its inevitable decline? Asking these questions can lead you to a starting point for your whole-life path.

~

Wherever or however you begin, do it now. The greatest gap you will experience is between reading this book and engaging in your first tangible steps of a whole-life path. Jump that gap!

Start with one thing, such as a practice on the meditation cushion. Do that for a month. Then maybe add a practice at work. From there, consider how you can continue to fold in additional practices in a way that allows you to remain joyful and curious and is not overwhelming or burdensome. What inspires you—a path factor, a life problem, a motivating relationship, a social concern? Follow your genuine interest or look for genuine urgency.

You are always at the cusp of greater freedom. Each moment offers a choice: continue in ignorance, or wake up to the heart's greater potential for nonharming, care, and peace.

## OTHER HELPFUL THINGS TO KNOW

As you begin to craft your whole-life path in earnest, allow me to share some additional information you might find valuable.

## The Value of Formal
## Practice and Study

Key to a whole-life path is the understanding that everyday engagements, formal practices, and study work together to bring about the peace and goodness you seek. Contemplating the Dhamma throughout our days brings wisdom into the folds and creases of life. Simple actions, everyday relationships, and thoughts about and engagement with your political, social, and economic world are all illuminated by the ongoing practice of right view.

Formal meditation practices can infuse our daily experience with a honed sense of moment-by-moment awareness. It also provides the unique conditions for the arising of liberating insight. When we see deeply the constructed nature of the selfing process, when we see the stress inherent in so much of what we took to be pleasurable, when boundaries of self and other dissolve into mutuality of awareness, these insights infuse the whole of our lives. Such deep release shades each subsequent moment with serenity and compassion.

At the same time, meditation practice can make the mind malleable and curious, supporting the opportunities for change and release set in motion by our family and working lives. And the open-hearted tolerance called for in everyday encounters fosters the diligence and long view that sustain formal practice. Just as sunshine and earth are both needed to sustain life, meditation and everyday wholesome engagements work together to sustain this whole-life path of release.

Sustained meditation, loving relationships, and full-hearted social engagement share a profoundly wholesome quality: they all provide access to the luminosity of awareness. This luminosity may be experienced privately, with the eyes closed, when the thinking mind releases itself and the limpid nature of awareness quietly stabilizes. In interpersonal meditation or nongrasping intimacy with a beloved other, the heart may find itself fully at rest. Not only are the hungers of the heart stilled, but the mind is also alert and open. The luminosity of the between, with a child or a meditation teacher or a dear friend, slides into selfless stability. And in some moments of social movements, the brightness of mind can be spontaneously amplified and made universal by the energy of compassionate action. Friendliness escapes the bounds of the personal; the light and energy of care show their universal qualities, and the feelings of lack that plague our culture are—just then, for those who are ready—lifted. Such are the fruits of the whole-life path.

## Expect the Terrain to Vary

You can gauge the authenticity of your engagement with the path factors as much by the challenges that arise as by the joy or perceived successes. As right view ripens, you are likely to be confronted by the apparent conflict between spiritual joy and existing habits of self-pleasuring. As right livelihood matures, your domestic relationships may need to negotiate the value shifts that are the hallmark of the Dhamma. These challenges are exactly where the Noble Eightfold Path happens.

Sometimes the whole-life path is clear. A wholesome way through life lays out in front of you obviously and easily, and you have plans to attend retreats, visit with spiritual friends, study, and simplify your life. How does that feel? Don't forget to notice when things are going well.

Sometimes the path is natural, easy. It's a fresh spring day and getting rid of burdensome possessions is exactly what you want to be doing. Maybe you do a path scan and find all the path factors humming along. Or you've passed up an opportunity for a high-profile assignment at work because self-aggrandizing just doesn't fit for you anymore and you'd much rather work quietly at something that feels meaningful. There is no drama, no public reward—just life living itself well.

Sometimes the path feels like work. You wake up and really don't want to meditate; you'd rather just have a cup of coffee, catch up on the news, and then go to work or call a friend. But then you remember the times when you've indulged the desire for excitement or pleasure and ended up feeling empty or ungrounded through the day. Or you recall the times when you have meditated even though you really didn't feel like it and how good it felt when you stood up, just a half hour later. So you do the work; you sit.

Sometimes the path is pleasant. You gather with friends for Insight Dialogue, and the joy of spiritual companionship infuses your evening practice of engaging with the suttas. That night, practicing right view is a joyful process. Or you have had a harmonious and productive meeting about an economic justice initiative and are experiencing the joy of engaged care.

Sometimes the path is unpleasant. Maybe you've decided that speaking truthfully is an essential practice for you right now, and this is calling you to an encounter with a relative that you've put off for a long time. You have reflected on what is true and what is beneficial. You are prepared to speak with a mind of true friendliness, and you have discerned that now is the right time. But still, it's not easy or pleasant. Or perhaps you are three days into meditation retreat and the body is sore, the mind is wild, and you lament that you have four more days ahead of you.

Sometimes there is visible, fast progress. Perhaps in meditation retreat or psychotherapy you have come to the edge of a self-view that has been pulling at you for years—inferiority conceit, superiority conceit, whatever. For some reason, mindfulness clearly sees what could not be seen before; the right effort to abandon the unwholesome unfolds rapidly and visibly, and a heap of burden is released. The step towards freedom is clear.

Sometimes the path appears slow or even to be going backwards. Sure, your mindfulness is improving, but all you are seeing is lust and anger. You do a path scan and can barely discern any path factor at work. The mind feels more like a swamp than a limpid pool. Wisdom is distant. You feel like you work hard and get nowhere. You don't give up, but you don't like it.

With a whole-life orientation, we come to accept the "gradual training, gradual practice, gradual progress" the Buddha spoke about.[209] And as your engagement with the whole-life path goes through natural ups and downs, diligence will carry you through. As the Buddha put it, "[A]ll skillful qualities are rooted in diligence and meet at diligence, and diligence is said to be the best of them."[210]

## Lean in to Your Community

Sometimes you will feel lost and need help. Moments of spiritual loneliness arise, feelings of insufficiency or despair, and sometimes the whole notion of spiritual possibility—of awakening, of goodness, of happiness—seems not only distant, but maybe even impossible. At these times, it is helpful to remember that we don't engage the path in isolation; the practical and spiritual life is necessarily lived in relation with others. And we do not engage the path alone; spiritual friendship is essential to the life of awakening. Not in isolation and not alone—this is not an abstract idea, but a pragmatic assertion. It turns us towards the resources we have: friends, teachers, retreat and social centers, media resources, online and in-person courses, social benefit initiatives, and more.

We need these resources. We need each other. We need good organizations. In addition to our own diligence and clear intention, we need the renewal of mutual reminding. Can you turn towards your spiritual friends or reach out to a learning community, locally or online, for camaraderie or guidance? Perhaps you can also allow your pain all the way in and reflect with compassion on the countless other beings who feel similarly lost. You are not alone in feeling alone.

Relationships are not just a necessary or workable part of the whole-life path, but are also intrinsic to our spiritual maturation. Throughout this book I've suggested spiritual practices that require others who share the intentions of the Noble Eightfold Path. Insight Dialogue, for example, is a formal, interpersonal practice of right view, mindfulness, effort, speech, and samādhi, and the power of relationship can accelerate and amplify the wholesome effects of meditation. But treating all people with respect and acting with compassion are also ways of living the whole-life path. Intentional relational engagement stands respectfully alongside personal efforts to release hunger and penetrate ignorance. On this path, we find benefit in being alone, and we find benefit in being with others.

## Maintaining and Assessing the Path

Once the idealizations and magical thinking that come with newness to the whole-life path—and are part of so much religious reflection—have burned themselves out, what remains is still profound but also deeply normal and wholesome. Trusting this, there can be ease. We trust ourselves to act with generosity and compassion. We trust others. We live with less hunger and more balance. Our behavior may not always be wise or ethical, but doing our best lightens the load of remorse and corrosive doubt. Even with lapses, the mind is well aimed.

From such a perspective, we make the effort to maintain our path, just as we would brush our teeth or clean our homes—as a natural, comfortable, sensible part of our ongoing activities. We begin to find the aliveness of the path as we eat and dress; our clothing becomes our robes. Just as we craft our engagement with particular path factors, we do so with the path as a whole. You could do daily check-ins on the six tenets or eight path factors on your own or weekly check-ins with our spiritual friends. Perhaps you approach your practice methodically—by moving cyclically through the eight factors, one per month, for example. Maybe your approach is ad hoc, intuitive, sensing that *now* is the time to devote more energy to continuity of mindfulness or the reflection on impermanence. The point is to step in, to be born again on the Path in each moment.

As always, we return to the principle of ehipassiko, come and see. Each time you try something new, ask, is it sammā, right, wise? Does it lead to tangling or disentangling? Is it increasing the wholesome and decreasing the unwholesome? And most basic is the long view, the results of the path as a whole: Does suffering increase or diminish? Are your relations with others less or more harmonious? Does your life contribute to a just and humane society?

You can also gauge how the path you're crafting is supporting you by how you meet life's big challenges: death, loss, pandemic, social and economic upheaval, relational catastrophe. At times of such suffering, you may remember that mindfulness of pain produces far less suffering than resistance to it. When there is anger, divorce, suspicion, loneliness or worldly failure, you may recognize that these conditions plead for the balm of right view: this is impersonal, impermanent, and I am not alone in such suffering; it is universal to all sentient beings. When the realities of aging or illness grab you, when you feel overwhelmed by a world on fire, perhaps you can meet the anguish with grace. Perhaps as death approaches, you will greet each moment as a chance to fathom impermanence, and when the time comes, you will mindfully rest with awareness as the candle goes out.

In short, even though things on your path may not be as you would like them to be, equanimity allows you to meet things as they are with grace and act from balance. In this equanimity, there is contentment along the whole-life path.

～

The Noble Eightfold Path leads to individual awakening, relational harmony, and a humane and just society. This is the aim of the Buddha's teachings as depicted in the earliest discourses. Accordingly, engaging individual, relational, and communal practices naturally forms a path in which no moment and no teaching is left out. This is our call to confident engagement: these teachings can be experienced here and now. There is more pain in avoiding this path of wisdom and love than there is in letting it fully into our hearts. There is more joy in engaging this Path fully than in submitting to the harangue of pleasure and pain that we call normal. I encourage you: proclaim your path, reclaim your life.

# TWO KEY SUTTAS

## AN 8.53, *Saṅkhitta Gotamiyovādasutta*, To Gotamī[211]

The Buddha offered this teaching to Mahāpajāpatī Gotamī, the Buddha's stepmother and maternal aunt. In Buddhist tradition, she was the first woman to seek ordination for women. Ordained by the Buddha himself, she became the first bhikkhunī, or Buddhist nun.

In the sutta, the Buddha offers both the negative example, what is *not* the Dhamma, and the mirror image of what constitute the correct teachings. In the quotation below, I have chosen to add line breaks to highlight each pairing of negative and positive qualities.

"As for the qualities of which you may know,
'These qualities lead
to dispassion, not to passion;
to being unfettered, not to being fettered;
to shedding, not to accumulating;
to modesty, not to self-aggrandizement;
to contentment, not to discontent;
to seclusion, not to entanglement;
to aroused persistence, not to laziness;
to being unburdensome, not to being burdensome':
You may categorically hold, 'This is the Dhamma,
this is the Vinaya, this is the Teacher's instruction.'"

## MN 8, *Sallekhasutta*, Effacement[212]

In this discourse, the Buddha is approached by a senior disciple, Maha Cunda (pronounced *Choonda*), who asks, "Now does the abandoning and relinquishing of those views [of self and world] come about in a bhikkhu who is attending only to the beginning of his meditative training?"

The Buddha responds that self view can be addressed by the understanding "[t]his is not mine, this I am not, this is not my self." He goes on to explain that person may evolve high levels of meditative attainment—the jhānas, in particular—and having done so, "He might think thus: 'I am abiding in effacement.' But these attainments are not called 'effacement' in the Noble One's Discipline: these are called 'peaceful abidings' in the Noble One's Discipline." That is, even after high meditative attainments, self view may remain fully in place. He then names the real process of effacement: the erosion of self view and the self-centeredness that comes from it.

It is a teaching of stunning breadth. Its range includes the refined attainments of deliverance, as well as the whole of the Noble Eightfold Path. But the inclusion of decidedly earthy human qualities like insolence, arrogance, laziness, and their opposites puts these qualities of human decency and maturity clearly on par with right mindfulness, concentration, and other more recognizably Buddhist qualities.

The entire list of forty-four qualities is named four times. The first, given below, is how one should practice effacement by cultivating the wholesome opposite of each negative quality. The second lists the same qualities with the purpose of how to incline the mind. The third set is to point out what is "leading upwards." The fourth set names these qualities as a way of extinguishing. Extinguishing self-fixation is one way of naming the purpose of the entire Path.

"Now, Cunda, here effacement should be practised by you:

(1) 'Others will be cruel; we shall not be cruel here': effacement should be practised thus.

(2)    'Others will kill living beings; we shall abstain from killing living beings here' . . .

(3) . . . take what is not given; we shall abstain from taking what is not given . . .

(4) . . . be uncelibate; we shall be celibate . . .

(5) . . . speak falsehood; we shall abstain from false speech . . .

(6) . . . speak maliciously; we shall abstain from malicious speech . . .

(7) . . . speak harshly; we shall abstain from harsh speech . . .

(8) . . . gossip; we shall abstain from gossip . . .

(9) . . . be covetous; we shall be uncovetous . . .

(10) . . . have ill will; we shall be without ill will . . .

(11) . . . be of wrong view; we shall be of right view . . .

(12) . . . be of wrong intention; we shall be of right intention . . .

(13) . . . be of wrong speech; we shall be of right speech . . .

(14) . . . be of wrong action; we shall be of right action . . .

(15) . . . be of wrong livelihood; we shall be of right livelihood . . .

(16) . . . be of wrong effort; we shall be of right effort . . .

(17) . . . be of wrong mindfulness; we shall be of right mindfulness . . .

(18) . . . be of wrong concentration; we shall be of right concentration . . .

(19) . . . be of wrong knowledge; we shall be of right knowledge . . .

(20) . . . be of wrong deliverance; we shall be of right deliverance . . .

(21) . . . be overcome by sloth and torpor; we shall be free from sloth and torpor . . .

(22) . . . be restless; we shall not be restless . . .

(23) . . . be doubters; we shall go beyond doubt . . .

(24) . . . be angry; we shall not be angry . . .

(25) . . . be resentful; we shall not be resentful . . .

(26) . . . be contemptuous; we shall not be contemptuous . . .

(27) . . . be insolent; we shall not be insolent . . .

(28) . . . be envious; we shall not be envious . . .

(29) . . . be avaricious; we shall not be avaricious . . .

(30) . . . be fraudulent; we shall not be fraudulent . . .

(31) . . . be deceitful; we shall not be deceitful . . .

(32) . . . be obstinate; we shall not be obstinate . . .

(33) . . . be arrogant; we shall not be arrogant . . .

(34) . . . be difficult to admonish; we shall be easy to admonish . . .

(35) . . . have bad friends; we shall have good friends . . .

(36) . . . be negligent; we shall be diligent . . .

(37) . . . be faithless; we shall be faithful . . .

(38) . . . be shameless; we shall be shameful . . .

(39) . . . have no fear of wrongdoing; we shall be afraid of wrongdoing . . .

(40) . . . be of little learning; we shall be of great learning . . .

(41) . . . be lazy; we shall be energetic . . .

(42) . . . be unmindful; we shall be established in mindfulness . . .

(43) . . . lack wisdom; we shall possess wisdom . . .

(44) `Others will adhere to their own views, hold on to them tenaciously, and relinquish them with difficulty; we shall not adhere to our own views or hold on to them tenaciously, but shall relinquish them easily': effacement should be practised thus.

# NOTES

1. "*Āsava*," in T. W. Rhys Davids, William Stede, editors, *The Pali Text Society's Pali–English Dictionary* (Chipstead: Pali Text Society, 1921–1925), 115. Available online, as part of the Digital Dictionaries of South Asia, dsalsrv04.uchicago.edu/cgi-bin/app/pali_query.py?page=115.

2. Bodhi and Ñāṇamoli, *The Middle Length Discourses of the Buddha*, 50.

3. This combination of the Buddha's humanness and his liberation is condensed as "Refuge in the Buddha."

4. SN 47.8.2, *Sūdasutta*, The Cook

5. Our primary references are the Pali discourses and comparably early teachings from the Chinese and Sanskrit literature.

6. SN 44.7, *Moggallānasutta*, Moggalana

7. SN 22.86, *Anurādhasutta*, To Anuradha, trans. Thanissaro. Available online at accesstoinsight.org/tipitaka/sn/sn22/sn22.086.than.html.

8. This is refuge in the Dhamma.

9. SN 45.2, *Upaḍḍhasutta*, Half of the Holy Life, and many others.

10. Urgency is captured in the Pali term *saṃvega*; patience or, more accurately, cool confidence, is captured in the term *pasāda*.

11. AN 10.51, *Sacittasutta*, One's Own Mind

12. SN 15:1, *Tiṇakaṭṭhasutta*, Grass and Sticks, trans. Sujato. Available online at suttacentral.net/sn15.1/en/sujato.

13. MN 56, *Upālisutta*, To Upāli

14. AN 8.31, *Paṭhamadānasutta*, Giving (1)

15. This third preliminary is named as mettā based upon the connection between "heavens" and the "divine abidings," or *brahmavihāras*.

16. AN 8.53, *Saṅkhitta Gotamiyovādasutta*, To Gotamī, trans. Thanissaro. Available online at accesstoinsight.org/tipitaka/an/an08/an08.053.than. html. Also available in the appendix. *Vinaya* is the code of conduct for monastics. The Buddha often referred to his teachings as *dhammavinaya*.

17. Giving over one's power to outside authority—what Venerable Punnaji Mahathero refers to as heteronomy (the opposite of autonomy)—is a contemporarily relevant way of naming the fetter normally translated as attachment to "rites and rituals."

18. The full integration of human goodness and liberation is powerfully represented in the Effacement Sutta, the *Sallekhasutta*, MN 8, which is included in the appendix.

19. AN 1.49–50, *Pabhassarasutta*, Luminous, trans. Thanissaro. Available online at accesstoinsight.org/tipitaka/an/an01/an01.049.than.html.

20. MN 64, *Mahāmāluṅkyasutta*, The Longer Discourse With Māluṅkya

21. AN 10.104, *Bījasutta*, The Seed, trans. Thanissaro. Available online at accesstoinsight.org/tipitaka/an/an10/an10.104.than.html.

22. MN 117.15, *Mahācattārīsakasutta*, The Great Forty

23. MN 19, *Dvedhāvitakkasutta*, Two Kinds of Thought

24. MN 9, *Sammādiṭṭhisutta*, The Discourse on Right View

25. MN 9, *Sammādiṭṭhisutta*, The Discourse on Right View

26. AN 5.25, *Anuggahītasutta*, Assisted

27. See Sn 4.5, *Paramaṭṭhakasutta*, On Views, trans. John D. Ireland. Available online at accesstoinsight.org/tipitaka/kn/snp/snp.4.05.irel.html.

28. AN 6.63, *Nibbedhika Sutta*, Penetrative, trans. Sujato. Available online at suttacentral.net/an6.63/en/sujato.

29. SN 56.11, *Dhammacakkappavattanasutta*, Setting in Motion the Wheel of the Dhamma

30. SN 56.11, *Dhammacakkappavattanasutta*, Setting in Motion the Wheel of the Dhamma

31. AN 2.125–126, *Ghosasuttas*, Voice, trans. Thanissaro. Available online at accesstoinsight.org/tipitaka/an/an02/an02.125-126.than.html.

32. SN 45.2, *Upaḍḍhasutta*, Half the Holy Life

33. See AN 8.54, *Dighajanusutta*, Dighajanu

34. SN 5.3, *Kisāgotamīsutta*, With Kisagotami

35. DN 33, *Saṅgītisutta*, The Chanting Together, trans. Walshe

36. AN 1.23–24, *Ekadhammasuttas*, A Single Thing, trans. Thanissaro. Available online at accesstoinsight.org/ tipitaka/an/an01/an01.021-040.than.html.

37. One important reason to nurture diversity in our relationships.

38. MN 141, *Saccavibhaṅgasutta*, The Exposition of the Truths

39. SN 27.7, *Sañcetanāsutta*, Volition

40. MN 117, *Mahācattārīsakasutta*, The Great Forty. The Pali terms in this passage are *takka* and *vitakka* (thinking and thought), *saṅkappa* (intention), *appanā* and *vyappanā* (application and focusing of attention), *abhiniropana* (directing the mind), and *vacīsaṅkhāra* (verbal constructions preceding speech). These are not full synonyms, but serve to highlight aspects of the idea.

41. SN 12.44, *Lokasutta*, The World

42. SN 14.12, *Sanidānasutta*, With a Source

43. AN 6.63, *Nibbedhikasutta*, Penetrative

44. SN 14.12, *Sanidānasutta*, With a Source

45. Ibid.

46. The root of greed (*lobha*) is sometimes named as lust (*rāga*); greed and lust both point to the mind wanting, pulling towards. The root of *dosa* is sometimes translated as "hatred"; aversion and hatred both point to the mind pushing away, rejecting. Taken as a group, the three unwholesome roots are also referred to as the defilements (*kilesa*).

47. See my treatment of the relationship between nongreed and generosity, nonaversion and love, and nondelusion and wisdom in *Insight Dialogue: The Interpersonal Path to Freedom* (Boston: Shambhala, 2007), 60–64.

48. MN 78, *Samaṇamuṇḍikasutta*, Samaṇamuṇḍikaputta

49. MN 113.29, *Sappurisasutta*, The True Man

50. Mv 8.26.1–8, *Kucchivikāra-vatthu*, The Monk with Dysentery, trans. Thanissaro. Available online at accesstoinsight. org/tipitaka/vin/mv/mv.08.26.01-08.than.html.

51. AN 6.63, *Nibbedhikasutta*, Penetrative

52. MN 44, *Cūḷavedallasutta*, The Shorter Series of Questions and Answers

53. Other modes of communication and reception, like writing, music, and gesture, also have subtle physical precursors, and these can be observed with mindfulness as well.

54. MN 1.20, *Mūlapariyayasutta* The Root of All Things

55. AN 5.114, *Andhakavindasutta*, At Andhakavinda, trans. Thannisaro. Available online at accesstoinsight. org/tipitaka/an/an05/an05.114.than.html.

56. SN 21.1, *Kolitasutta*, Kolita

57. SN 45.8, *Magga-vibhaṅgasutta*, Analysis

58. MN 61, *Ambalaṭṭhikarāhulovādasutta*, Advise to Rāhula at Ambalaṭṭhika

59. AN 10.176, *Cundasutta*, Cunda

60. AN 10.69–70, *Kathāvatthuasuttas*, Topics of Discussion

61. MN 58, *Abhayarājakumārasutta*, To Prince Abhaya

62. MN 112, *Chabbisodhanasutta*, The Sixfold Purity

63. AN 10.44, *Kusinārasutta*, Kusinara

64. SN 56.10, *Tiracchānakathāsutta*, Pointless Talk

65. AN 9.3, *Meghiyasutta*, Meghiya, trans. Nyanaponika and Bodhi. Available online at tipitaka.fandom.com/wiki/Meghiya.

66. AN 10.69, *Kathāvatthuasutta*, Topics of Discussion (1)

67. MN 21.11, *Kakacūpamasutta*, The Simile of the Saw

68. SN 55.7, *Veludavareyyasutta*, The People of Bamboo Gate

69. Sn 3.3, *Subhasitasutta*, The Well-Spoken, trans. Khantipalo Mills. Available online at suttacentral.net/snp3.3/en/mills.

70. AN 5.57, *Abhiṇhapaccavekkhitabbaṭhānasutta*, Themes

71. SN 45.8, *Vibhaṅgasutta*, Analysis

72. MN 117, *Mahācattārīsakasutta*, The Great Forty

73. Iti. 42, *Sukkadhammasutta*, The Bright Protectors, trans. Thanissaro. Available online at accesstoinsight.org/ tipitaka/kn/iti/iti.2.028-049.than.html#iti-042.

74. SN 49.3, *Gaṅgā Peyyālavagga*, The River Ganges—Eastward

75. AN 11.2, *Cetanākaraṇīyasutta*, Volition

76. AN 4.95, *Chavālātasutta*, Cremation Brand

77. SN 45.2, *Upaḍḍhasutta*, Half the Holy Life

78. SN 12.1, *Paṭiccasamuppādasutta*, Dependent Origination

79. For more on dependent origination, see the discourses in the *Nidāna Saṃyutta*, SN 12.

80. SN 4.14, *Tuvatakasutta*, The Discourse on Being Quick. In Gil Fronsdal, *The Buddha Before Buddhism: Wisdom from the Early Teachings* (Boulder, CO: Shambhala, 2016), 117.

81. AN 5.198, *Vācāsutta*, Speech

82. SN 12.38, *Cetanāsutta*, Volition

83. DN 4.22, *Soṇadaṇḍasutta*, The Qualities of a True Brahmin

84. SN 45.8, *Magga-vibhaṅgasutta*, Analysis; MN 141, *Saccavibhaṅgasutta*, The Exposition of the Truths

85. MN 117, *Mahācattārīsakasutta*, The Great Forty

86. *Mahā Cattārīsaka Suttaṃ*, Discourse Pertaining to the Great Forty. Translated from the Pali by I. B. Horner, Associate of Newham College, Cambridge. First Published in 1954. Copyright the Pali Text Society.

87. AN 5.177, *Vaṇijjāsutta*, Trades

88. AN 8.54, *Dīghajāṇusutta*, To Dīghajā, trans. Thanissaro. Available online at accesstoinsight.org/tipitaka/an/an08/an08.054.than.html.

89. Ibid.

90. Ibid.

91. Ibid.

92. Ibid.

93. DN 31, *Siṅgālautta* The Buddha's Advice to Sigālaka, trans. Kelly, Sawyer, Yareham. Available online at suttacentral.net/dn31/en/kelly-sawyer-yareham.

94. MN 117, *Mahācattārīsakasutta*, The Great Forty

95. Ibid.

96. MN 89, *Dhammacetiyasutta*, Monuments to the Dhamma

97. SN 4.14, *Tuvatakasutta*, Quickly, trans Thanissaro. Available online at accesstoinsight.org/ati/tipitaka/kn/snp/snp.4.14.than.html.

98. AN 8.30, *Anuruddhamahāvitakkasutta*, Anuruddha

99. AN 7.49, *Dānasutta*, Giving, trans. Thanissaro. Available online at accesstoinsight.org/tipitaka/an/an07/an07.049.than.html. *Patimokkha, nissaggiya* 19, trans. Dhamma Sāmi and Thierry Lambrou. Available online at en.dhammadana.org/sangha/vinaya/227/30np2.htm.

100. Iti 107, *Bahukārasutta*, Very Helpful. trans. Thanissaro. Available online at accesstoinsight.org/tipitaka/kn/iti/iti.4.100-112.than.html#iti-107.

101. AN 3.98, *Tatiyaājānīyasutta*, Thoroughbred (3)

102. AN 10.16, *Āhuneyyasutta*, Worthy of Gifts, and many others.

103. Iti 1.26, *Dānasutta*, Giving, trans. Ireland. Available online at suttacentral.net/iti26/en/Ireland.

104. AN 7.49, *Dānasutta*, Giving, trans. Thanissaro. Available online at accesstoinsight.org/tipitaka/an/an07/an07.049.than.html.

105. AN 9.20, *Velāmasutta*, About Velāma, trans. Thanissaro. Available online at accesstoinsight.org/tipitaka/an/an09/an09.020.than.html.

106. AN 11.12, *Mahanamasutta*, To Mahanama (1), trans. Thanissaro. Available online at accesstoinsight.org/tipitaka/an/an11/an11.012.than.html.

107. See MN 141, *Saccavibhaṅgasutta*, The Exposition of the Truths, and parallels

108. MN 141.29, *Saccavibhaṅgasutta*, The Exposition of the Truths

109. AN 10.51, *Sacittasutta*, One's Own Mind

110. The use of the word *ignorance,* here and throughout this book, refers to *avijjā,* which translates as not (*a*) knowing (*vijjā*). One may know that there is a lot of pain in one's life, for example, but not know about the reflexive mental patterns at the root of much of that pain.

111. AN 10.51, *Sacittasutta*, One's Own Mind

112. SN 46.52 *Pariyāyasutta*, A Method of Exposition

113. See, for example, AN 2.19, *Kusalasutta*, Wholesome

114. MN 48.8, *Kosambiasutta*, The Kosambians

115. AN 6.63, *Nibbedhika Sutta*, Penetrative, trans. Sujato. Available online at suttacentral.net/an6.63/en/sujato.

116. SN 12.65, *Nagarasutta*, The City

117. SN 22.1, *Nakulapitusutta*, Nakulapita

118. AN 4.45, *Rohitassa Sutta*, Rohitassa (1)

119. Ignorance is the condition for the arising of constructions· *avijjā paccaya saṅkhāra.*

120. Constructions are the condition for the arising of consciousness: *saṅkhāra paccaya viññāṇa*.

121. Consciousness is the conditions for the arising of mind-body, which is the condition for the arising of the six sense bases: *viññāṇa pacaya nāma-rūpa, nāma-rūpa pacaya salāyatana*.

122. The six sense bases are the condition for the arising of sensitive contact, which is the condition for the arising of pleasant and unpleasant feelings: *salāyatana paccaya phasso, paccaya vedanā*.

123. Feelings are the condition for the arising of hunger, craving: *vedanā paccaya taṇhā*.

124. Hunger is the condition for the arising of clinging: *taṇhā paccaya upādāna*.

125. Clinging is the condition for becoming (the arising of self), which is the condition for the enfleshed sense of I am this body: *upādāna pacaya bhavo, pacaya jāti*.

126. The birth of self is the condition for the arising of suffering: *jāti pacaya dukkha*.

127. SN 22.95, *Pheṇapiṇḍūpamasutta*, A Lump of Foam

128. MN 8, *Sallekhasutta*, Effacement. (See the appendix.)

129. AN 3.49, *Ātappakaraṇīyasutta*, Ardor

130. Ibid.

131. AN 8.2, *Paññāsutta*, Wisdom

132. MN 32.9, *Mahāgosiṅgasutta*, The Greater Discourse in Gosinga

133. SN 51.2, *Viraddhasutta*, Neglected

134. SN 51.20, *Vibhaṅgasutta*, Analysis

135. AN 6.55, *Sonasutta*, Sona

136. Ibid.

137. SN 22.101, *Vāsijaṭasutta*, The Adze Handle (or The Ship)

138. In the Theravada commentarial tradition, the Abhidhamma states that unwholesome states cannot be present simultaneously with sati; what we experience as simultaneous is actually very quickly changing adjacent states of sati (wholesome) and, say, anger (unwholesome).

139. MN 19, *Dvedhāvitakkasutta*, Two Kinds of Thought

140. SN 3.13, *Doṇapākasutta* A Bucket Measure of Food

141. SN 47.48, *Mittasutta*, Friends

142. SN 20.10, *Biḷārasutta*, The Cat

143. MN 44, *Cūḷavedallasutta*, The Shorter Series of Questions and Answers

144. MN 10, *Satipaṭṭhānasutta*, The Foundations of Mindfulness. SN 45.8m, *Vibhaṅgasutta*, Analysis. DN 22, *Mahāsatipaṭṭhāna*, The Longer Discourse on Mindfulness Meditation, trans. Sujato. Available online at suttacentral.net/dn22/en/sujato.

145. Recent scholarship suggests that the Satipaṭṭhāna Sutta and its equivalents developed into their current form over many years following the Buddha's death. Whatever the origin, this teaching was clearly central to early Buddhist thought and practice. It has been tested by communities of experts, particularly monastics and dedicated lay practitioners, and found to be effective for developing liberating insight.

146. MN 119, *Kāyagatāsatisutta*, Mindfulness of the Body

147. SN 46.3, *Sīlasutta*, Virtue

148. AN 8.64, *Gayāsīsasutta*, Gaya

149. SN 22, *Khandhasaṃyutta*, The Connected Discourses on the Clinging Aggregates

150. SN 46.54, *Mettāsahagatasutta*, Accompanied by Loving Kindness

151. AN 5.144, *Tikaṇḍakīsutta*, At Tikandaki

152. MN 10, *Satipaṭṭhānasutta*, The Foundations of Mindfulness; SN 45.8 *Vibhaṅgasutta*, Analysis, and others

153. SN 47, *Satipaṭṭhānasaṃyutta*, Connected Discourses on Foundations of Mindfulness

154. MN 10, *Satipaṭṭhānasutta*, The Foundations of Mindfulness

155. A guided contemplation recording for this practice is available on the Insight Dialogue Community website: insightdialogue. org/teachings/guided-anapanasati-with-another/.

156. Care should be given in choosing a partner and setting up practice to not add the burden of practicing with someone towards whom you feel, or might come to feel, a sexual attraction. If such attraction arises, you could try giving attention to just the bare physicalness of the body being seen, noticing if the mind detaches from its lust. If this does not work, I suggest you set aside this practice and re-approach it another time, another way, or with another person.

157. MN 10, *Satipaṭṭhānasutta*, The Foundations of Mindfulness

158. AN 8.54, *Dighajanusutta*, Dighajanu

159. SN 12.44, *Lokasutta*, The World

160. Note that you or someone you are meditating with may have something in their background, such as trauma, that makes it difficult or unsafe to attend to the body. Please engage this powerful recollection of *here* with care.

161. MN 10, *Satipaṭṭhānasutta*, The Foundations of Mindfulness

162. SN 22.59, *Anattalakkhaṇasutta*, The Characteristic of Not-Self

163. SN 46.3, *Sīlasutta*, Virtue

164. MN 137, *Saḷāyatanavibhaṅgasutta*, The Exposition of the Sixfold Base

165. SN 48.9, *Paṭhamavibhaṅgasutta*, Analysis (1)

166. SN 45.8, *Vibhaṅgasutta*, Analysis

167. MN 46, *Mahādhammasamādānasutta*, The Great Discourse on Taking Up Practices

168. Perhaps the need for long, unbroken practice is more indicative of the frantic lifestyles most of us maintain today than it is of the human organism's basic capacity.

169. AN 3.102, *Nimittasutta*, Themes, trans. Thanissaro. Available online at suttacentral.net/an3.102/en/thanissaro.

170. MN 14, *Cūḷadukkhakkhandhasutta*, The Shorter Discourse on the Mass of Suffering

171. MN 36, *Mahāsaccakasutta*, The Greater Discourse to Saccaka

172. MN 66, *Laṭukikopamasutta*, The Simile of the Quail

173. AN 9.41, *Tapussasutta*, With the Householder Tapussa, trans. Sujato. Available online at suttacentral.net/an9.41/en/sujato.

174. SN 1.38, *Sakalikasutta*, The Stone Splinter

175. AN 10.2, *Cetanākaraṇīyasutta*, Volition

176. SN 35.99, *Samādhisutta*, Concentration

177. SN 12.15, *Kaccānagotta*, Kaccanagotta

178. AN 10.7, *Sariputtasutta*, Sariputta

179. AN 4.170, *Yuganaddhasutta*, In Conjunction

180. Ibid.

181. SN 12.22, *Dutiyadasabalasutta*, The Ten Powers (2). I have substituted the word *intrepid* for the original translation, *manly*, to make this already challenging teaching more accessible.

182. SN 51.15, *Uṇṇābhabrāhmaṇasutta*, The Brahmin Uṇṇābha

183. See, for example, SN 21.4, *Navasutta*, The Newly Ordained Bhikkhu

184. MN 32, *Mahāgosiṅgasutta*, The Greater Discourse in Gosinga

185. AN 11.2, *Cetanākaraṇīyasutta*, Volition. I've created the construction *samādhied* to stand in for *concentrated*, the translator's original rendering of the Pali term *samādhiyati*, which is the adjectival form of the passive verb *samādhi*.

186. AN 6.50, *Indriyasaṃvarasutta*, Sense Faculties

187. AN 3.101, *Paṃsudhovakasutta*, The Soil Remover

188. See DN 2, *Sāmaññaphalasutta*, The Fruits of the Ascetic Life; MN 39, *Mahāassapurasutta*, The Greater Discourse at Asapura; and others.

189. MN 7, *Vatthasutta*, The Simile of the Cloth

190. MN 39, *Mahāassapurasutta*, The Greater Discourse at Asapura

191. SN 12.23, *Upanisasutta*, Proximate Cause

192. AN 3.100, *Loṇakapallasutta*, A Lump of Salt

193. SN 46.50, *Bāhiraṅgasutta*, External Factor

194. Sn 1.8, *Karaniyamettāsutta*, Loving Kindness

195. MN 44, *Cūḷavedallasutta*, The Shorter Series of Questions and Answers

196. MN 118, *Ānāpānasatisutta*, Mindfulness of Breathing

197. Ibid.

198. SN 12.64, *Atthirāgasutta*, If There Is Lust

199. AN 4.41, *Samādhibhāvanāsutta*, Concentration, trans. Sujato. Available online at suttacentral.net/an4.41/en/sujato. Note: the phrase in italics varies from Sujato's translation.

200. Ibid.

201. Ibid.

202. Ibid.

203. SN 46.2, *Kāyasutta*, The Body

204. AN 5.26, *Vimuttāyatanasutta*, Liberation

205. MN 19, *Dvedhāvitakkasutta*, Two Kinds of Thought. Note: In order to avoid the word *concentration*, I have substituted the word *unified* for *concentrated* in the last phrase of this quote: "So I steadied my mind internally, . . . and *unified* it."

206. SN 22.59, *Anattalakkhaṇasutta*, The Characteristic of Not-self. This same logical sequence, offered as a teaching and as a practice, is found in many other discourses.

207. AN 7.70, *Arakenanusasanisutta*, Araka's Teaching, trans. Andrew Olendski. Available online at accesstoinsight. org/tipitaka/sn/sn47/sn47.010.olen.html.

208. DN 25, *Cakkavatti-Sihanadasutta*, The Lion's Roar on the Turning of the Wheel

209. MN 70.11, *Kīṭāgirisutta*, At Kīṭāgiri

210. AN 10.15, *Appamādasutta*, Heedfulness

211. Trans. Thanissaro. Available online at suttacentral. net/an8.53/en/thanissaro.

212. The quotations in this section are from Bhikkhu Bodhi and Bhikkhu Ñāṇamoli's translation; see "Author's Note."

# RESOURCES

## Additional Support for a Whole-Life Path

For more practice suggestions and support, please visit my website, GregoryKramer.org, and the Insight Dialogue Community website, insightdialogue.org.

## Insight Dialogue Practice

Insight Dialogue is an interpersonal meditation practice that brings together meditative awareness, the wisdom teachings of the Buddha, and humans' natural relatedness. Stemming from the same traditional roots as silent meditation, it also has the same purpose: to help meditators develop mindfulness, compassion, and liberating insight as they investigate present-moment experience.

Six meditation instructions, or guidelines, form the core of Insight Dialogue practice. The guidelines help participants establish the meditative qualities of the mind. The guidelines also help participants sustain these qualities while they reflect on topics that encourage a direct and intimate inquiry into the human experience. In this way, relational contact and meditative qualities of the mind help bring root wisdom teachings into lived experience, here and now. Although Insight Dialogue is grounded in the Buddha's early teachings (the Pali Canon) and the practice of insight meditation, or vipassanā, people of all faiths and backgrounds are welcome and find benefit in the practice.

For more on the practice of Insight Dialogue, please see my book *Insight Dialogue: The Interpersonal Path to Freedom* (Boston: Shambhala, 2007), or visit the website for the Insight Dialogue Community: insightdialogue.org.

## Dharma Contemplation Practice

Dharma Contemplation (*dhamma* in Pali) is a simple contemplative practice that supports our entry into the Buddha's teachings. It can be practiced individually, yet as a group practice it is singularly powerful at revealing layers of meaning in these profound early texts.

The Dharma Contemplation process has similarities with the Christian tradition of Lectio Divina and the layers of knowledge (*paṭisambhidā*) described in the Theravada Buddhist tradition. Participants begin by contemplating a short excerpt of the Buddha's teachings. The practice then unfolds in five distinct phases, during which participants speak the truth and listen deeply. Participants move from engagement with just the words of the text to the emotional resonances it evokes. This is followed by an analytical investigation of the meaning and then an inquiry into the essences embedded in the text. Finally, meditators set the text aside and explore present-moment experience: what truth might I speak now, naturally, having been touched by the Buddha's words? Overall, Dharma Contemplation is more intuitive than reasoned, though the talents of the thinking mind are included.

In Dharma Contemplation the wisdom we are contemplating comes directly from the Buddha via his oral teachings, which have been passed down in the Pali texts for two thousand years. Just as we can experience intimate and elucidating contact with a good friend or teacher—mind to mind, heart to heart—we can do so with the Buddha, experiencing his legacy in a remarkably direct way: human to human, Buddha to Buddha. Dharma Contemplation provides a structure to help us realize this capacity.

For more information about Dharma Contemplation, including my book *Dharma Contemplation: Meditating Together with Wisdom Texts*, practice phases, and sample texts, please visit the Insight Dialogue Community website: insightdialogue.org.

## The Insight Dialogue Community

The Insight Dialogue Community is a sangha, or community of spiritual friends, dedicated to awakening together. Our community extends globally, coming together in relational practice on teacher-led retreats, in online cohorts, in local peer-led groups, and in organizational teams. We warmly welcome all people who want to explore with us the practices of Insight Dialogue and Dharma Contemplation and teachings of relational Dhamma.

The Insight Dialogue Community is registered in the United States as a not-for-profit 501(c)(3) organization. It was formally founded in 2005 to support the teachings and the growing relational community.

To learn more about the Insight Dialogue Community, including our teachers, programs, practice groups, and retreats, please visit us online: insightdialogue.org.

## Sutta Translations

In addition to Bhikkhu Bodhi's translations of the suttas discussed in my author's note, I recommend the following two online sources for accessing early Buddhist texts:

- SuttaCentral (suttacentral.net)
- Access to Insight (accesstoinsight.org)

Both provide comprehensive access and good translations of the root teachings.

# ACKNOWLEDGMENTS

A book that took form over two decades yields many people to acknowledge. I first began to assemble and teach these materials in 1999, in the form of a series entitled "In His Own Words." These talks were offered to the Portland Insight community, and their kind support encouraged me to develop these teachings into their second phase, a relational framing of the Buddha's words from the discourses. The third iteration was presented to the nascent Insight Dialogue Community in 2003 in the form of a program entitled "A Whole Life Path." Once again, a small but global community encouraged further development of the material and the relational and whole-life perspective behind them.

Sometime in the mid-2000s, I thought I had the makings of a useful book. I assembled the texts I'd posted online, the talks that had been transcribed, and copious additional notes, brought some coherence to them, and handed a 400-page rough manuscript to Martha Turner, who had provided such useful input on my *Insight Dialogue* book. She worked mostly alone—while I traveled all over the world teaching Insight Dialogue retreats—to produce a draft manuscript from these materials. I thank her for bringing some initial order to the early text. She also provided two important components: First, she clarified that right livelihood should be rooted in resource exchange. Second, with her background as a scholar of early Christianity, she helped me to coax from the suttas the humanity of the people and culture of the Buddha's time.

The next major revision was undertaken by Erica Pittman, while I was again traveling and teaching. At Erica's insistence, we added ample practice sections, and I am grateful for those additions.

By now, I had been diagnosed with an incurable cancer and feared I'd never get this book done. A couple of years into treatment, I was finally capable of thinking and writing again. At this point, a host of generous, smart, interested people came forward, each in their own way, to support the two-year immersive process of rewriting the entire book and editing it.

Amy Rost, an editor recommended to me by my friend Joseph Goldstein, brought to the work some much-needed trimming, but more importantly a degree of clarity and punch that somehow maintained my own voice. I still don't get how she did that, but the enhanced readability this book may have is largely due to her skill.

Jean Wu supported me throughout this entire writing process in more ways than I could name. In addition to supporting my many teaching and administrative activities, Jean's intelligence and quiet energy allowed me to remain focused on the book. Her purview expanded to managing, with Amy's support, the book publishing process.

People who read different sections of the book and provided feedback include Anita Bermont, Bhikkhu Bodhi, Leigh Brasington, Lori Ebert, Malcolm Frow, Fabio Giommi, Phyllis Hicks, Dave Leggatt, Lucy Leu, Joe Murphy, Holly Nelson-Johnson, Mu Soeng, Donna Strickland, and Jan Surrey. I am grateful for their intelligence and generosity. I want to specifically thank Riët Aarsse and Jill Shepherd for their help checking my sutta references. I am also grateful to the Insight Dialogue Community members and practice groups who gave feedback on the early drafts. These spiritual friends, internationally and online, at retreats and in small groups, took up these teachings, and I appreciate their encouragement.

During the editing, I realized that I had enough additional material to create a second, sister book, offering readers additional practice ideas to support their whole-life path. As of this writing, that "work-book" is being compiled by a generous team that includes Riët Aarsse, Ann Herington, Annette Holba, Tzuming Liao, Laurie Mettam, Sarah Richardson, Rick Steinberg, Ozum Ucok, Susan Wiley, and Jean Wu. I am grateful for their efforts.

# INDEX

unwholesome, abandoning,
221–223, 234
wholesome, cultivating, 232
wholesome, maintaining, 230–234

Rāhula (Buddha's son), 118
rapture, 293, 295, 297, 316–317
receptivity, 283
reflection, 47
reflective learning (cintāmayā), 66
reflexes, 86–89
refuges (Buddha, Dhamma, and
Sangha), 257–258, 316
relation/relationships
abandoning, support for, 226
action flows through, 148–153, 162
conscious relations, 145
groups, 150–151
interpersonal meditation
practices, 144
intimate, 345–346
meditating together, power of,
242–243, 322
morality and, 143, 162
nested scales of, 152
personal relationships, 143–146
right action on social scale, 145–146
right mindfulness and, 253–254,
288
role in awakening, 144–145
samādhi and, 294, 320–324, 340
self, experience of, 149
shared intentions, 89–98
social engagement/actions,
141–146, 346
stewarding, 152–153
wise intentions, 101
relational practices, 5–6, 16–17,
154, 351
compassion, 345
giving (dāna), 195–197
of mindfulness, 284–287
right view, 60–67
speaking and listening, 64–67
relaxation, 334–336
release, 36, 38, 217–218, 280, 344
relinquishment, 37, 157, 344
qualities to be relinquished, 222,
356–358
remorse, 140, 312
renunciation, 31–32, 100–101
bliss of, 300
wisdom and, 71

resistance, 219
resolve, 75
resources
exchange of, 178–194
resource management, 176–177
restlessness, 221, 295, 300
right (sammā), 32, 33
right action (sammā kammanta),
135–163
as abstaining, 138–139, 155–156, 159
Buddha on, 137, 138, 155
causality and, 148–153
conditioning and, 146–148, 161
ethical considerations (sīla),
136–141
as flexible, 155, 158–161
flow through individuals,
relationships, groups, and society,
148–153, 162
individual and social action,
141–146
innovation and initiative in,
155–158
intentions and, 147–149, 152
life as actions made visible
(practice), 137–138
mental activity and, 146–148
moral reflection, 140, 162–163
nonaction, 160–161
path factors and, 139–140, 159
path scan for, 24
purification through, 152
reflection on, 161–163
relationship, and right action on
social scale, 145–146
right livelihood and, 170, 203
right view, effort, and mindfulness
and, 139, 159, 162, 163
skillful actions, assessing,
159–160, 162
social engagement and, 141–146
social perspectives of, 143–146
suffering, actions and, 136, 161
taking initiative on one specific
precept (practice), 157–158
understanding, 136–141
virtue, as core of, 141
wrong actions, reversal of, 159
right concentration, 291–292
See also right samādhi
right effort (sammā vāyāma), 205–244
balanced effort, 210–212, 240–242

definition of, 206
Effacement Sutta and, 222–223
effort of abandoning, 225–227, 234
effort of cultivation, 227–230, 234
effort of maintaining, 230–234
effort of preventing, 223–225
energy (viriya) and, 208–210, 240, 241–243
extraordinary effort, 208, 212, 235–240, 310
four bases of power, 235–240
four right efforts, 220–235
mind, transformation of, 213–220
out with the bad, in with the good, 220–221
as path factor, 206–208
path scan for, 24
psychotherapy and, 213–220
reflection on, 243–244
right action and, 139, 159
right livelihood and, 177
striving, paradox of, 311–312
synergy with right view and right mindfulness, 207
unwise efforts, 210–211
what is abandoned and what is cultivated?, 221–223
wisdom and, 206, 244
wise direction of effort, 211–212
working hard, 210–211
right intention (sammā saṅkappa), 69–101
automatic responses versus conscious direction, 86–89
compassion and, 346
conditioning and, 86–87
conscious direction and, 86–89
definitions of intention, 70–71
directing the mind, 71
episodic intentions, 75–76, 93
facets of intention, 70–72
furthermost refinement of intention, 98–100
karma and intentions, 83–86
mind's inclination, experiencing the first touch of (practice), 76–77
momentary intentions, 73–75, 93
nested intentions, 79–81
overarching intentions, 76–78, 152
path scan for, 23
reflection on, 100–101
removal of intoxicants through, 88

reverse engineering the moment (practice), 80–81
right action and, 139
right speech and, 132–133
right view and, 69–70
shared intention, 89–98
shared intention, three questions, 94–98
shared intention, three time scales, 92–93
three wise intentions, 101
time scales of intention, 79–82, 92–93
volition and, 71, 73
wholesome intention in a team process (practice), 97
wholesome and unwholesome intentions, 81–82, 86–89
wrong intention (practice), 72
right livelihood (sammā ājīva), 165–203
action and, 167
balanced livelihood, 175–176, 189
character development (practice), 168–169
clothing as requisite, 184–187, 203
computers, 192
conditioning of the mind, 167, 174
enough, sense of, 180
environmental protection and, 192
exchange of requisites and resources, 178–194, 203
food as requisite, 181–184, 203
giving and, 194–202
happiness and, 174–177
medicine as requisite, 190–191, 203
monastic life as example, 179–191
money and, 178, 180
needs, 179–191
nonharm and, 170–171, 172
occupations to be avoided, 170
as path factor, 166–168, 203
path scan for, 24
proactive, 172–173
reflection on, 202–203
requisites for, 180–191
resource management, 176–177
right action and, 170, 203
right speech and, 170, 203
right view, right effort, and right mindfulness, 177
shelter as requisite, 188–189, 203

sources of income, reflection on
(practice), 171–172
transportation needs, 191–193
understanding of, 166–168
wealth destruction, causes for,
176–177
wrong livelihood, avoiding,
169–171
right mindfulness (sammā sati),
245–289
adjacency, 259–260, 279–282
ardent, clearly comprehending,
269–270
awareness and, 248
awareness, cultivation of, 269–275
awareness of present moment, 251
awareness, questions on, 248–249,
256–258
balanced mind and, 286–287
body and, 260–261, 271–272
Buddha's teachings as practices,
266–268
calmness with obstacles, 265
cultivating together, 284–287
definitions of sati, 246–247
Dhamma frameworks, 264–266
encouraging sati in others
(practice), 252
ethics and, 252–255, 286
experience of sati, 282–284
feelings and, 261–263, 271–272
five questions of sati/awareness,
255–259
four foundations of, 259–266,
286–287, 325–326
frameworks, 246, 247–248, 259,
264–266
hindrances, treatment of, 264–266
internal or external mindfulness
(or both), 271–274
meditation objects, 259–265
mettā and, 268, 269
mind and, 263–264
mind looking inwards, 249
mindfulness of energy, 265
misconceptions about sati, 248–250
as path factor, 250–255
path scan for, 24–25
purpose, sense of, 257
questions on, 248–249, 256–258,
275–278
reflection on, 287–289

relational practice of, 284–287, 288
right action and, 139, 159
right effort and, 207
right livelihood and, 177
rising, vanishing, and both,
274–275
samādhi and, 308–309
sati, cultivation of, 269–275
sati, term use, 244–247
sati categories, 259–269
sati focus on the body, 259
Satipaṭṭhāna Sutta, 251–252,
259–272, 326
sīla, 252–255, 286
tathatā (as such), 277–278
unskillful mind and (practice), 250
unwholesome, recognizing,
250–251
when am I aware?, 277
where am I aware?, 276
right samādhi (sammā samādhi),
291–340
as awakening factor, 296–298
awakening factors, cultivating as a
group, 331–332
balancing with energy, 297–298
calm/tranquility, 292, 296, 299, 309,
317, 320–322, 340
characteristics of, 292–293
concentration and, 293
conditions for, 312–320
confidence and, 316–317
contentment/gratefulness and,
319–320
cultivating, 324–338
definition/terminology, xi, 292–293
easeful mind, 307–308
in group settings, 322–323
happiness and, 292, 295–296,
300–301, 313, 317–318
insight practices and, 308–312
jhānas and, 294–296, 299–300,
308–310, 339
mental qualities leading to, 316–322
mental unification, 294, 301, 309,
323, 340
mettā and, 324–325
mindfulness and, 325–326
as naturally arising, 293–294
nonvolitional, once established, 293
one-pointedness, 293
otherworldly benefits, 305

# ABOUT THE AUTHOR

Gregory Kramer teaches meditation, writes, and is the founding teacher of the Insight Dialogue Community. He is the author of *Insight Dialogue: The Interpersonal Path to Freedom,* from Shambhala Publications; *Dharma Contemplation: Meditating Together with Wisdom Texts; Seeding the Heart: Practicing Lovingkindness with Children;* and other books and articles. Gregory has practiced meditation since 1974 and studied with esteemed monastics, including Anagarika Dhammadinna, Ven. Balangoda Ananda Maitreya Mahanayaka Thero, Achan Sobin Namto, Ven. Punnaji Mahathero, and others. Since he began teaching meditation worldwide in 1980, he has pioneered online meditation and contemplation practices. His primary focus since 1995 has been developing and sharing a relational understanding of the Dhamma, and Insight Dialogue, an interpersonal form of Buddhist insight meditation, and groups are now active worldwide. He also developed Dharma Contemplation, a text-based contemplation practice.

Gregory holds a PhD in Learning and Change in Human Systems from CIIS. He cofounded Harvest With Heart, a hunger project in the Northeast United States, and Spiritual City Forum, an interfaith dialogue program in Portland, Oregon.

Formerly a composer, NEA Composition Fellow, and founder of the Electronic Art Ensemble, he has made significant contributions to music technology and holds multiple patents in the field. He is recognized as the founding figure of the field of data sonification. He founded the International Conference on Auditory Display (ICAD), published the first book in that field, and edited numerous white papers and journals on the topic. He holds patents in sonification and has lectured internationally in the field.

Gregory lives in Orcas, Washington, and is married and the father of three grown sons and seven grandchildren.

Made in United States
Troutdale, OR
11/28/2023